MW00838053

Going the Distance with Babylon.js

Building extensible, maintainable, and attractive
browser-based interactive applications using JavaScript

Josh Elster

Going the Distance with Babylon.js

Copyright © 2022 Packt Publishing

All rights reserved. No part of this book may be reproduced, stored in a retrieval system, or transmitted in any form or by any means, without the prior written permission of the publisher, except in the case of brief quotations embedded in critical articles or reviews.

Every effort has been made in the preparation of this book to ensure the accuracy of the information presented. However, the information contained in this book is sold without warranty, either express or implied. Neither the author, nor Packt Publishing or its dealers and distributors, will be held liable for any damages caused or alleged to have been caused directly or indirectly by this book.

Packt Publishing has endeavored to provide trademark information about all of the companies and products mentioned in this book by the appropriate use of capitals. However, Packt Publishing cannot guarantee the accuracy of this information.

Group Product Manager: Pavan Ramchandani

Publishing Product Manager: Bhavya Rao

Senior Editor: Sofi Rogers

Senior Content Development Editor: Rakhi Patel

Technical Editor: Joseph Aloocaran

Copy Editor: Safis Editing

Project Coordinator: Manthan Patel

Proofreader: Safis Editing

Indexer: Sejal Dsilva

Production Designer: Alishon Mendonca

Marketing Coordinator: Anamika Singh and Marylou De Mello

First published: August 2022

Production reference: 2140323

Published by Packt Publishing Ltd.

Livery Place

35 Livery Street

Birmingham

B3 2PB, UK.

ISBN 978-1-80107-658-6

www.packt.com

Writing this book would not have been possible without the people that have been important in my life. To my father, for gamely reading each chapter, knowing ahead of time that none of the material is even remotely near his wheelhouse. To my wife, for believing in me even when I didn't and for putting up with me when I'm cranky. To my brothers, for their unwavering encouragement and faith in this project and in life. To Mitch Gitelman, for indulging in a long walk with me on a fine Washington Spring Day. Finally, this book is dedicated to the memory of Adrian Barcus, a.k.a. "Colonel Ransom." Regardless of how long or far you might search, a better person will not be found.

– Josh Elster

Foreword

If at that time you had told me that one day someone would be motivated enough to write an actual book about it, I would have laughed a lot. And still, here we are. When Josh told me that he was on the verge of writing a real book about Babylon.js, I barely believed him.

The book that you have in your very hands right now is the culmination of a fantastic journey where people from around the globe joined and contributed to a common project without expecting anything more than a thank you. That fantastic community helped create hundreds of great projects and convince big names such as Microsoft and Adobe to bet on and contribute to a GitHub project for their 3D-based projects.

I know this is probably a really classic cliché to employ, but I genuinely want to thank Josh for having poured his soul into this book in order to help our community to learn our platform.

I encourage you to use this book as a first step to joining the community and participating in our common effort to build a powerful and easy-to-use 3D engine freely available to all.

David Catuhe,

Creator and leader of the Babylon.js open source project, group engineering manager for the Microsoft Stream web client, technical expert on the WebGL/Javacript/TypeScript web technologies

Contributors

About the author

Josh Elster spends most of his days working as a software engineering lead for a technology start-up and his nights patrolling the Babylon.js forums and working on various side projects. Unlike Bruce Wayne, however, he did not have a traumatic childhood incident involving bats.

From his home in the Windy City of Chicago, Josh likes to spend time outdoors, particularly in his woodshop when the weather indicates, and gaming, making music, or reading when it doesn't. His website is `https://www.liquidelectron.com`. A limited social media user, he can be found on LinkedIn and Twitter.

A huge thanks to everyone who helped me keep going on this journey. Special thanks are owed to my family, for their faith in me and this project. To Jason Carter and Kaustubh Manglukar, who were there at the conception of this book, Raanan Weber, who put up with my incessant questions (until one day he didn't), and to Carolina Herbster Mesquita Jorge, for allowing herself to fill that spot – there's no way that this book would be a worthwhile read without your valuable contributions. To the members of the Babylon.js community – you are the heart and soul of the Babylon.js project. Thank you for being part of and making such an amazing endeavor!

About the reviewers

Reviewers

Jason Carter is humbled by his position and opportunity to lead the incredibly talented Babylon development team at Microsoft, having spent his entire career at the intersection of storytelling and technology. At the start of a career spanning decades, he spent years bringing animated characters and scenes to life at Dreamworks and later Disney Animation. Afterward, he then went on to help make holograms feel real by bringing the HoloLens to life. The latest stage in his career is to ultimately help the world create and share interactive 3D web experiences.

Raanan Weber is the tech lead of the 3D web engine Babylon.js. His first contribution to the framework was back in 2014, and he is not planning to stop any time soon. Among his latest contributions are the WebXR abstraction and the framework's new build system.

Raanan lives with his wife and son in Berlin, Germany. He spends his weekends walking his wonderful dog and playing as much music as possible.

Carolina Herbster Mesquita Jorge is a computer graphics developer based in Brazil. In her free time, she likes to play video games, crochet, and play with her dog, Courage.

Subject matter experts

Erich Loftis

Andrei Stepanov

Technical experts

Gary Hsu

Cedric Guillemet

"Evgeni_Popov"

Justin Murray

Dave Solares

Patrick Ryan

Table of Contents

3

Establishing the Development Workflow 39

4

Creating the Application 59

5

Part 2: Constructing the Game

6

7

8

Building the Driving Game   197

9

Calculating and Displaying Scoring Results   231

10

Improving the Environment with Lighting and Materials 265

Part 3: Going the Distance

11

Scratching the Surface of Shaders 295

14

Extended Topics, Extended

Preface

The world of 3D application and game development is a vast and actively changing landscape. With all the stunning capabilities of modern GPU hardware exposed to the web browser via WebGL, AAA-quality interactive rendering can be achieved by anyone with some knowledge of JavaScript. Babylon.js is just the right tool to use for an effortless experience and a robust application built using WebGL technologies.

Although changes in and the evolution of browser software and hardware standards continue at their own pace and on their own schedules, Babylon.js is a framework that prioritizes maintaining backward compatibility. Code written for BJS 2.0 is highly likely to run with little to no modifications in BJS 5.20, so product managers and stakeholders can use BJS with confidence about the long-term stability of the code.

If Babylon.js is the ticket for WebGL, then this book is your ticket to mastering Babylon.js. Well, you probably won't become a twentieth-level Babylon.js developer by the end of this (let's be real for a moment), but you'll certainly learn the key concepts and techniques that will enable you to progress down that path should you so choose!

All of this is starting to become a kind of bad sales pitch, so let's drop the pretense and talk brass tacks. You want or need to learn about 3D game or app development. As a human being, you also desire entertainment. This book attempts to satisfy both of those needs by avoiding being too boring wherever possible while still delivering the big knowledge bombs. Entertainment and enlightenment, all in one package.

Who this book is for

This book is for artists who avoid coding because they think they're bad at math (give yourself more credit!), game designers whose fingers long to leave the spreadsheet, and developers dreaming of worlds yet to be made. This book is for students who want to learn outside of their classrooms, teachers who want their students to learn inside their classrooms, and parents who want their teenage kids to learn something, anything at all.

What this book covers

Chapter 1, The Space-Truckers Operation Manual, gives an overview of the world of Space-Truckers and 3D development with Babylon.js.

Chapter 2, Ramping up on Babylon.js, gets us started with (or refreshed on) Babylon.js with a simple 3D animated scene.

Chapter 3, Establishing the Development Workflow, puts a solid design-and-build time experience into place to allow rapid future development.

Chapter 4, Creating the Application, involves building a stateful application that will host the game.

Chapter 5, Adding a Cut Scene and Handling Input, takes us through imperatively creating an animated "cut scene" and learning how to handle user input of different types.

Chapter 6, Implementing the Game Mechanics, starts off the construction of the main route planning phase of the game. Here, we will augment the existing physics with orbital mechanics and simulated gravitational forces.

Chapter 7, Processing Route Data, involves adding random encounter tables that correspond to a space biome.

Chapter 8, Building the Driving Game, takes us through dynamically generating a route and allowing players to drive along it.

Chapter 9, Calculating and Displaying Scoring Results, deals with capturing and showing stats on player performance in a reusable dialog with the help of the GUI Editor.

Chapter 10, Improving the Environment with Lighting and Materials, covers how we can improve the look and feel of the game by enhancing key visual elements.

Chapter 11, Scratching the Surface of Shaders, discusses extended analogies explaining shaders and writing shader code that doesn't involve writing any shader code.

Chapter 12, Measuring and Optimizing Performance, explains the heuristics and approaches for testing the runtime performance and the strategies for improvement, along with dynamic runtime optimization with the SceneOptimizer tool.

Chapter 13, Converting the Application to a PWA, explores preparing the application for installation as a **Progressive Web Application** (**PWA**). We then go through publishing this to a major App Store and adding support for offline usage.

Chapter 14, Extended Topics, Extended, looks at AR/VR with WebXR and Babylon Native before a foray into photorealistic raytracing and Babylon.js in a CMS or e-commerce scenario.

To get the most out of this book

You'll want to be at least passingly familiar with JavaScript before engaging with the activities in this book, at least to the point where you are not fazed by looking at code that may initially be unfamiliar. Knowing basic 3D concepts and terms is also helpful. If you are new to Babylon.js, JavaScript, or 3D development, then a fantastic place to start is the Babylon.js start page at `https://doc.babylonjs.com/journey/theFirstStep`.

Software/hardware covered in the book	Operating system requirements
Babylon.js 5.x	Windows, macOS, or Linux
WebPack v5.0	
ECMAScript 2016+	

A web browser with the Mozilla or Chrome rendering engine is recommended, as it has the greatest level of support for various WebGL and WebGPU features. Safari (WebKit) is known to be significantly behind the other engines listed in its support with similar functionality.

If you are using the digital version of this book, we advise you to type the code yourself or access the code from the book's GitHub repository (a link is available in the next section). Doing so will help you avoid any potential errors related to the copying and pasting of code.

The Babylon.js community is the most valuable resource around for getting help with everything related to BJS. As an Open Source project, Babylon.js is kept alive by its' dedicated community of contributors. Who can contribute? Anyone. What can be contributed? Almost anything. Join the BJS community on the official forums at `https://forum.babylonjs.com` *and meet the gang!*

Download the example code files

You can download the example code files for this book from GitHub at `https://github.com/jelster/space-truckers/`. If there's an update to the code, it will be updated in the GitHub repository.

We also have other code bundles from our rich catalog of books and videos available at `https://github.com/PacktPublishing/`. Check them out!

Download the color images

We also provide a PDF file that has color images of the screenshots and diagrams used in this book. You can download it here: `https://packt.link/CGb69`.

Conventions used

There are a number of text conventions used throughout this book.

`Code in text`: Indicates code words in text, database table names, folder names, filenames, file extensions, pathnames, dummy URLs, user input, and Twitter handles. Here is an example: "The `createSpinAnimation` method is called from `createStartScene` to make the `spinAnim` variable available to the rest of the scene's controlling code."

A block of code is set as follows:

```
planets.forEach(p => {
    p.animations.push(spinAnim);
        scene.beginAnimation(p, 0, 60, true, BABYLON.Scalar.
RandomRange(0.1, 3));
});
```

When we wish to draw your attention to a particular part of a code block, the relevant lines or items are set in bold:

```
planets.forEach(p => {
        glowLayer.addExcludedMesh(p);
        p.animations.push(spinAnim);
        scene.beginAnimation(p, 0, 60, true, BABYLON.Scalar.
RandomRange(0.1, 3));
    });
```

Any command-line input or output is written as follows:

```
npx webpack –config webpack.common.js
```

Bold: Indicates a new term, an important word, or words that you see onscreen. For instance, words in menus or dialog boxes appear in **bold**. Here is an example: "Clicking **Run** should now show a nifty-looking starfield in a skybox you can pan around."

> **Tips or important notes**
> Appear like this.

Get in touch

Feedback from our readers is always welcome.

General feedback: If you have questions about any aspect of this book, email us at `customercare@ packtpub.com` and mention the book title in the subject of your message.

Errata: Although we have taken every care to ensure the accuracy of our content, mistakes do happen. If you have found a mistake in this book, we would be grateful if you would report this to us. Please visit `www.packtpub.com/support/errata` and fill in the form.

Piracy: If you come across any illegal copies of our works in any form on the internet, we would be grateful if you would provide us with the location address or website name. Please contact us at `copyright@packt.com` with a link to the material.

If you are interested in becoming an author: If there is a topic that you have expertise in and you are interested in either writing or contributing to a book, please visit `authors.packtpub.com`.

Share Your Thoughts

Once you've read *Going the Distance with Babylon.js*, we'd love to hear your thoughts! Scan the QR code below to go straight to the Amazon review page for this book and share your feedback.

`https://packt.link/r/1801076588`

Your review is important to us and the tech community and will help us make sure we're delivering excellent quality content.

Part 1:
Building the Application

This first part of the book establishes the important foundations that will be leveraged in future chapters. Starting with a survey of Space-Truckers and Babylon.js, we will construct the main pillars of the game's hosting application. Although a basic understanding of Babylon.js is recommended, the main requirement is to have some knowledge of JavaScript or a similar programming language.

This section comprises the following chapters:

- *Chapter 1, The Space-Truckers Operation Manual*
- *Chapter 2, Ramping up on Babylon.js*
- *Chapter 3, Establishing the Development Workflow*
- *Chapter 4, Creating the Application*
- *Chapter 5, Adding a Cut Scene and Handling Input*

1
The Space-Truckers Operation Manual

It's not considered to be a very emotionally evolved stance to judge a book by its cover, but have you seen the cover of this book? If it's something you like, then please, by all means, do judge this book by its cover, you counter-culture influencer, you – carry on reading!

If for some reason you don't like the cover, then bully for you for literally turning over a new page to see what's inside – unlike *some* superficial cretins. We're above that sort of petty judgment, after all.

> **Note**
>
> Sometimes, relevant information will be presented in these Note boxes. Other times, these same boxes will contain completely irrelevant but possibly irreverent information. At all times, or at none (sometimes), should you pay attention to what's in these boxes.

Regardless of whether you're on Team Cover or Team Content, it's clear you're incredibly smart and well mannered for the simple fact that you've started reading this book. We're about to embark on a journey together over the next 14 chapters. This is not the type of journey that you might encounter flipping through channels while you search for something to watch before bedtime. This is a journey across the wide and vast terrain that is the **Babylon.js** ecosystem. It isn't a safari, but it is a sojourn. One thing it is not, however, is an Odyssey. Primarily because you don't have to actually go anywhere, and you get to go back to your regular life whenever you're not reading this book, but perhaps for other reasons too.

> **Important Note**
>
> Like its less-distinguished cousin the Note, Important Note boxes will occasionally make an appearance. Generally, these are used for Things You Might Regret Not Knowing About Before…

We are going to cover a huge amount of ground over the course of our sojourn, our journey, but you won't be traveling unprepared. Our overall objective here is to build a game hosted by and in a generic web application. Over the course of three separate parts, we're going to progressively do three things:

- Create and set up an application and development workflow that gives *Space-Truckers: The Video Game!* a place to live

- Layer on additional functionality to our application (hosting *Space-Truckers: The Video Game!*)

- Zoom out on the level of detail to take on a wide range of enhancements and add to our good knowledge

Each chapter will build on the work established in the previous chapter. It's possible that the code in one chapter will need to be modified in subsequent chapters, and that should be looked at as a reflection of our evolving understanding of how the application needs to be structured to accomplish the goal at hand. Every chapter (save this one) contains links to the game's code in the same context as the chapter's text, in addition to live demos and Playground links specific to the content.

While we are building upon the application, we will also be providing fewer and fewer line-by-line code details in favor of providing extra context and/or information relating to how something works "under the hood." Don't worry, the code and Playground samples are still there to help you find your way! We'll be exploring concepts that in themselves can occupy entire texts longer than this not-very-short book, and we'll be doing so with less room to expand on those same topics. As a result, we will be looking to cover some areas at a high level while others will be discussed to a greater depth.

We're going to start by walking through the game from the standpoint of the player, then we'll move on to look at the underlying game and application design. As a finisher, we wrap this first travel segment up with a tour of the Space-Truckers GitHub repository and other online resources. Let's start with the ending, in classic literary fashion.

> **Note**
>
> For the movie version of this scene, picture a shimmering dissolve with appropriate sound effects as we transition to a different world…

Introducing the World of Space-Truckers

Astronomers recently started receiving a mysterious signal, apparently from outside of our Solar System. Far from being random noise, the signal appears to contain structured data in the form of text, audio, and visual content – an alien transmission! The transmission starts with a basic primer on terminology and math and rapidly works its way up to describing some sort of large plastic disc imprinted with something the message called "multi-media interactive content" that is then connected to a display device and spun around (how ludicrous!) at thousands of RPMs while a laser beam reads grooves burned into the spinning disc. Laser beams. Grooves. Spinning wheels. All ridiculous, but there's no accounting for alien sensibilities, right?

The following is a reconstruction of the content that was recovered from that transmission and burned onto what is now known as the "Dead Sea CD." Due to the nature of its journey through space and time, parts of the transmission were not received, and the data contained was unrecoverable. At the same time, the connected nature of the data resulted in other parts being corrupted. Consequently, many of the images and still frames you are about to view represent data that has been patched back together using the best tools and resources at our disposal.

Talented teams of professional engineers, scientists, and even sociologists have worked long and hard to bring about this reconstructed image of what we believe the people who left us – or sent to us – this record look like:

Figure 1.1 – Best guess at the appearance of the originators of the Space-Truckers transmission

The next section contains the reconstructed text and image content recovered from the transmission. Because the original message was expressed symbolically and not in any human language, the latest GPT-3 text generation AI was trained on the transmission's symbols so that it could then produce the content that follows and format it consistently with the rest of this book.

So, You Wanna be a Space-Trucker?

```
BEGIN TRANSMISSION
```

Figure 1.2 – Reconstruction of the Space-Truckers transmission.
Probably intended as a "day in the life" image

Being a Space-Trucker isn't for the faint of heart, nor is it for the lonely of mind. There are hazards and dangers to be found in spades – but there's also the allure of fortune and fame. Ever since legendary Space-Trucker Winchell Chung's (call sign: Rocket Cat) famous "Grand Tour," every kid across the system has grown up aspiring to emulate him. After using the last of his reaction mass to deliver his cargo, he saved millions of starving children suffering after the Great Space-Potato Famine. Sadly, that selfless act left his Space-Rig adrift with no way home. Chung's Space-Truck was lost as it drifted off into the Darkness Beyond the Sun. His last transmission, garbled as it was, contained a single recoverable fragment of text:

"The cold, hard equations care not for starvation or famine. <indecipherable>…[b]ecause we're Space-Truckers. It's what we do."

Space-Trucker Chung is a sterling example of what it means to be a Space-Trucker, but in all fairness, there's a dark side to the business. What isn't publicized is the high rate of turnover among Space-Truckers. Some go mad from the experience of being alone among the stars, while others simply refuse to go back out after their run. Others depart from one place never to arrive at their intended destination.

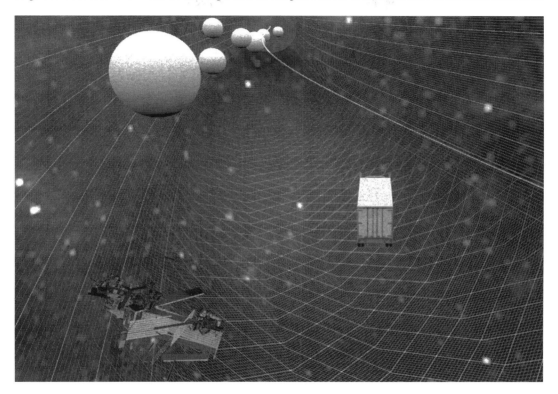

Figure 1.3 – Space-Trucking is dangerous business

Sure, computers can help, and other technologies also contribute to help make Space-Trucking safe and dependable. However, no amount of hardware or software compares to the wetware of the human mind when it comes to dealing with unanticipated situations, and that's why Space-Truckers need to be behind the wheel of their Space-Rigs.

Before any space wheels can hit the space pavement, our driver needs to know where to go. Space-Dispatch is here to help with Route Planning services, and with their detailed orbital and launch simulation, different potential routes to the cargo's destination can be evaluated and tried without risk to the Space-Trucker.

Figure 1.4 – Planning a route involves timing the launch as well as properly
aiming it. The left-side bar controls the launch impulse – higher is faster

Despite the risks, the potential rewards are quite high. Completing a Space-Haul has a variable payout for the Space-Trucker, with space-bucks being awarded or demerited based on the driver's performance in the field. Factors from the simulated route include the total transit time, how much fuel (launch force) is consumed, and the total distance traveled.

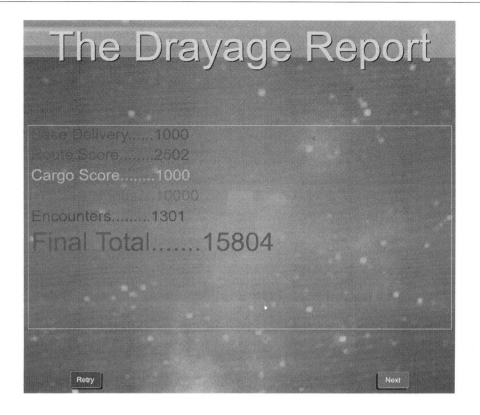

Figure 1.5 – Space-Trucking pays well when things go well

Many different obstacles can be encountered, and no two routes are the same, but the scoring factors ensure that when it comes to comparing runs, the High Scores board is the ultimate arbiter of the G.O.A.T Space-Truckers.

> **Note**
>
> G.O.A.T. is not referring to any animal in this context. The Greatest of All Time Space-Truckers are a select and elite group – show proper respect!

Timing is of the essence in Space-Trucking, but so is safety. By being mindful of the latter in service of the former, the Space-Trucker stands the best chance of completing their Space-Haul and getting the opportunity to spend their payday on the Space-Beach.

Never forget, Space-Trucker – the cold, hard equations of planetary motion have no concern for whether you've got enough air to breathe or heat to stay warm. Keep your slide rule handy in case of instrument failure and go forth to find your fortune slinging cargo!

Figure 1.6 – Recovered image of a "Space-Trucker" and their "Space-Rig." The Space-Trucker is the small figure in the foreground

END TRANSMISSION

The life of a Space-Trucker certainly must be full of glamorous riches and perilous travels for those folks to send a recruitment leaflet all that distance! Stepping back to the real world is hard, but it's important that we break down the various elements of how Space-Truckers is designed and put together. Ideally, as you progress through this book, you'll have this foundation to help you stay grounded with where everything goes and fits together.

Space-Truckers: The Video Game Design

The basic idea behind Space-Truckers is simple: get stuff from Point A to Point B, in spaaace! (It's not required to draw out that last word, but it helps set the mood.) As a game, it is separated into several distinct phases or states:

- Landing (Home) Screen
- Splash Screen
- Menus (inc. High Scores)
- Route Planning
- Driving + Scoring

Each of these screens (used as a synonym for "state" here) will be established, then later enhanced over the course of this book along with an underlying application to support and coordinate between them.

Landing

This is the first thing that a player sees when they navigate to space-truckers.com (or the beta testing site, dev.space-truckers.com). It's an HTML page with a simple Call to Action: "Launch." Under the hood, however, the HTML page is the host for the main application canvas – the WebGL context onto which all the rendered outputs are painted. It is responsible for loading the packaged web application as well as registration of a Service Worker (see *Chapter 13, Converting the Application to a PWA*) to manage and pre-fetch assets. As the DOM host, it provides access to the web browser and through it the host machine's resources, such as the ability to play sound or read input from gamepads or VR hardware. Learn more about this in *Chapter 3, Establishing the Development Workflow*.

Splash Screen

In music and comedy, a warm-up act precedes the main headline performance as a way to put audiences into a particular frame of mind or mood. After all, it's much easier to crank things up past 10 on the volume dial when you're already at 7! The Space-Truckers Splash Screen serves that purpose, as well as giving us an opportunity to showcase the underlying framework and proclaim that this game is **Powered by Babylon.js**. Once the short, animated content completes, the application enters "attract mode" to entice players to continue.

Menus

The transportation hub of the game, the Main Menu, is where players will start a new game, view high scores, exit back to the landing page, and potentially do more. Sound effects and an animated selection icon bring a bit of motion to a twinkling background. The menu system is initially covered in *Space-Truckers: The Main Menu* section of *Chapter 4, Creating the Application*.

Route Planning

One of the two main game phases, the Route Planning Simulation, is where players become content creators. Using a top-down map view, drivers plan their route before embarking on their journey. From an initial starting orbit close to the inner-most planet, players must balance how much launch force is used with aiming and timing to put the simulated cargo on a path to the destination planet. Once launched, the cargo is entirely at the mercy of gravity and Sir Isaac Newton. Pro tip: aim ahead of where you want to end up but be sure to account for the pull of the sun. Because it is a simulation of a route, there are no consequences for failure – the player is free to try as many times as they want to find the perfect route to drive in the next phase.

Driving and Scoring

After planning out the desired route, it's time for players to then take the wheel and guide their Space-Truck through the transit corridor while avoiding collision with the random events that have been recorded during the route planning phase. The player's unit drifts in free-fall, so velocity accrued in any given direction will remain unless later canceled out by opposing acceleration. Collision results in damage, and with enough damage, the truck and its cargo are destroyed.

Figure 1.7 – Collisions during the driving phase have consequences

On a brighter note, completing the course results in the player's score being calculated. Several different factors contribute to the overall total final score. The length of the route, the time it took the simulation to complete the route versus the time the player took, and the initial launch velocity in route planning are all some of the factors involved in scoring. If a player's score is high enough, then it will displace one of the previous high score holders to place the player's selected initials into the hall of legends.

This is the game in a nutshell. As with any such high-level overview, it is necessarily lacking in some detail, but it provides a holistic picture of what we're going to be developing over the course of this book. To get into more detail, we're going to need to first get an understanding of where we can find those details as well as where and how to pick up supporting context in the GitHub repository for Space-Truckers.

Space-Truckers: The Repository

Exploration is an important learning tactic for the discovery of new knowledge. Its converse, exploitation, is an equally important tactic used to convert passing knowledge into actionable skills. The key to maximizing learning is the proper application of each type of learning at the appropriate level and time. With tight iterative exchanges between the two, it is possible to learn a lot in a little amount of time.

Our journey has many stops and signposts along the way to help assist and guide us toward our destination, and in the spirit of maximizing learning, each chapter represents an evolution toward our goal that includes live, runnable examples (exploration) along with the exact source code for the application at that point of the journey.

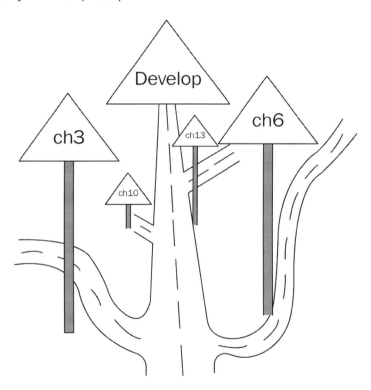

Figure 1.8 – View the application source in context with the stage of your journey

We accomplish this in a simple fashion via the use of Git branches – one for each chapter involving the application code. In addition, each chapter may have one or more Playground snippets (see *Chapter 2, Ramping up on Babylon.js*, for more on the Playground) specific to the content covered in that chapter. Snippets are neat in a lot of ways and one of those is that they can have multiple revisions. Toggling between different revisions of a snippet is a great way to visually see how an example has evolved and can help bring insights as to why a particular piece of code behaves as it does.

Maybe things were going OK but then you've found yourself stuck on something that you just can't figure out. That's OK too – there are places you can go for help! Create a post or add to an existing one in the Discussions board over at `https://github.com/jelster/space-truckers/discussions` for questions, comments, or concerns about content in the repository and/or book. Questions more general to BJS can be posted over at the BJS community forums – `https://forum.babylonjs.com`. Creating an account for both GitHub and the BJS Forums can be relatively quick and painless.

> **Tip**
>
> If you are planning to create both a BJS Forum and a GitHub account login, save yourself half the effort by signing up for GH first. Then, when you create your forum account, you can select the **Login With GitHub** option, supplying the information for your newly created GH account.

The Space-Truckers repository has more than just the source code and discussions, though. It also hosts the Issue Tracker for the game (`https://github.com/jelster/space-truckers/issues`), which is where people can request a new feature or file a bug report – it's also where folks looking to contribute to the project can peek to find something suitable to their abilities.

> **Tip**
>
> Another pro-tip offered pro rata via the cost of this book: Scan through issues with the labels **good-first-issue** and **needs-help**. Those are ones the repository's maintainers either need assistance with or feel that the issue represents a gentle introduction to the code base.

Community contributions are what **Open-Source Software** (**OSS**) is all about, but because they are largely volunteer-driven, there's always more work than there are people that can get that work done. Consequently, most maintainers are thrilled whenever somebody submits a Pull Request – a set of changes to be incorporated into the code base – to the project that resolves an existing issue!

> **Tip**
>
> Getting tired of these yet? Fair enough. Final tip: Even projects like BJS with many maintainers working full time on it have this problem. The maintainers might not be having to scrounge donations to keep servers on, but they do have to scrounge for the time to accomplish everything that we want them to!

It can be difficult to synthesize and learn new things when it feels like you're in drinking all the newness through a firehose. That's why the Space-Truckers code base is branched by chapter. Though an individual chapter won't necessarily resemble the current, final game as represented in the main or develop branches (production and beta environments, respectively), each branch has as much complexity as it needs to have for that point in the book and no more. To put it differently, the evolution of the application will mirror the evolution of our journey as it unfolds.

Summary

The next thirteen chapters each represent their own signpost denoting the progress of our journey, and there is much yet to see and accomplish. Pulling onto the Space-Highway, it can appear like the space-road ahead is stretching out toward infinity. The truth is every road seems that way at the start of a trip. By keeping the focus on what's immediately ahead, the infinite can become finite, and overwhelming complexity becomes manageable tasks.

Much like this book is separated into sections and chapters, Space-Truckers is separated into distinct phases or states. The Landing Page is the launchpad (pun intended) for starting the game, while the Splash Screen prepares the audience and sets the mood. Meanwhile, the Main Menu Screen serves as a navigation hub between the main gameplay states and the others.

There are two(ish) phases to the gameplay. Route Planning is where players use an orbital mechanics simulation to plot a course for their Space-Cargo to get from the origin to the destination planets. The direction and force of the launch are set by the player prior to launch, with the timing of the launch also a major factor in how players dictate their route.

Having planned a route, the next game phase sees that route being used to create a tunnel filled with obstacles (random encounters) that the player now must navigate their Space-Truck through to reach the end point. Time matters, but so does bringing the cargo to its destination in as good a condition as possible. Once the destination has been reached, a third, pseudo-game phase enters the stage.

Scoring is done using several factors that will be outlined in detail as part of *Chapter 9, Calculating and Displaying Scoring Results*. Players' decisions from Route Planning impact the final scores in multiple ways ranging from time goals to fuel costs. Only the top scores get persisted into the High Score Screen, a feature available in both the web and PWA versions of the application.

The place where all the work around Space-Truckers is tracked and managed is in **Space-Truckers: The GitHub Repository.** Additionally, each chapter of the book (with a few exceptions) has its own branch in the source code. This allows you to view the state of the overall application in context with the content of the corresponding chapter. Additional assistance can be found by posting in either Space-Truckers: The Discussion Boards or on the BJS official community forums.

Next, we'll start by gradually building some momentum through a back-to-basics review of the BJS framework and ecosystem. We'll look at some of the tools, resources, and techniques and if necessary (re)introduce ourselves to how rendering in BJS works. We'll learn about the Playground and begin the process of building our application by creating a simple loading animation. Buckle up, Space-Trucker – we're hitting the road!

2
Ramping up on Babylon.js

At the risk of sounding hyperbolic, **Babylon.js** (**BJS**) is nothing short of incredible in how fast effortless, and **fun** it can be to work with 3D graphics and games. Most game and graphics engines come with sizable footprints in terms of size and computing resource requirements, but BJS is different because it can run in a web browser. The BJS team has created a rich web-based tooling ecosystem that covers a wide range of development workflows and use cases to support developers and designers from many different angles. After establishing some shared vocabulary and reviewing some basics, we will begin our journey with the **Babylon.js Playground** (**PG**). After this chapter, we'll have laid the foundations for Space-Truckers by creating and rendering a basic animated scene that uses the PG along with content from the asset library.

In order to get from where we are to where we want to be, we'll divide the work into these sections:

- Catching up or Refreshing on Babylon.js
- Building Our Scene in the Playground
- Animating Orbits
- Extended Topics

Technical Requirements

Like most things in software, you'll get the best results with Babylon.js. PG snippets requires only a web browser supporting **WebGL**, but a desktop-based browser is required for some BJS web-based toolsets such as the **Node Material Editor** (**NME**). A keyboard is highly recommended for typing code into the PG. With regards to browser support, while there are some exceptions around specific devices and platforms the latest versions of Edge, Chrome, and Firefox all support WebGL2, with ever-growing support for the newer WebGPU functionality. See `https://caniuse.com/webgl2` for the most up-to-date list of browser vendors supporting WebGL2.

Catching up or Refreshing on Babylon.js

When starting a new project, it's easy to get overwhelmed by the sheer number of different things that need to be done. Throw unfamiliar technologies or domains into the mix, and even the most seasoned software veteran might blanch a bit at the challenge. That's an okay feeling to have! The key to overcoming and moving past it is both difficult and simple at the same time: you just need to find an atomic, well-defined task and then just do that task. After tackling a few of these tasks, you can take a step back to reassess things in light of what you now know. Most likely, you will find that the work you originally thought was needed isn't.

Whether you're a veteran game developer exploring the possibilities of BJS or someone who has never programmed a game before, a strategy of starting simple and building iteratively can be the best way to get usable, immediate results. Let's start with the basics. The following screenshot is part of the BJS 4.2 release content that demonstrates simply how BJS can render scenes with high visual fidelity.

Figure 2.1: A real-time interactive demo from the Babylon.js home page. Semi-transparent shadows, reflections, and refraction are clearly visible along (and inside) the bottle and table, just as different substances cast different shadows in the real world. (https://playground.babylonjs.com/#P1RZV0)

The Basics of BJS

BJS is a WebGL-based, full-featured 3D rendering engine written in TypeScript and compiled to JavaScript. Although commonly accessed via a web browser, current versions do not require an HTML DOM or Canvas elements, meaning that it can run "headless" on a server. The BJS team has a very clear vision and mandate, as illustrated from the BJS home page (`https://www.BJS.com`):

> *"Our mission is to create one of the most powerful, beautiful, and simple Web rendering engines in the world. Our passion is to make it completely open and free for everyone. We are artists, developers, creators, and dreamers and we want to make it as simple as possible to enable everyone to bring their ideas to life."*

BJS supports a wide range of both input and output scenarios, from game pads and accelerometer-based input to single- or multiple-viewport output (e.g., VR/AR). A full list of the engine's specifications is available at `https://www.babylonjs.com/specifications`. Something that's less obvious from the specifications is that support for WebGPU is limited only by the implementation of the standard by browser vendors, so if you read news about WebGPU support being released for a browser, you can be confident that BJS will be able to take full advantage of it without needing you to do anything at all!

> **Tip**
>
> Something I always forget to apply to when I'm working with imported assets being from other 3D/image editing tools such as Blender is coordinate conventions. The 3D coordinate system used by BJS is "left-handed," meaning that the positive y-axis will (by default) point in the "up" direction, the positive x-axis to the "right," and the positive z-axis "toward" the camera.

Get Started with Getting Started

Something that will quickly become apparent to anyone browsing the documentation for BJS is how thorough and comprehensive that documentation is. Given the high quality of the Getting Started content there, it would be a pointless waste of precious space in this book to attempt to recreate the basic tutorial at `https://doc.babylonjs.com/start`. If this is your first time adventuring with game development, BJS, or JavaScript, it is *highly* recommended that you take the time to at least browse through the Getting Started tutorial linked earlier. Don't worry about leaving – everything will still be here right as you left it when you get back!

Tools for the Toolbox

One of the advantages of being JavaScript-based is that it is very easy to make web-based tooling available that allows users to code and render in real time in a tight iteration loop. The BJS **Playground** (**PG**) is probably the most prominent member of the BJS toolchain, but that should not diminish the utility and importance of the other tools that we're going to cover. The following table summarizes the various tools available and their purposes:

Tool	How to Access It	Purpose
Playground (PG)	`https://playground.babylonjs.com.`	Writing, running, and debugging runnable snippets. Saving and sharing snippets.
Sandbox	`https://sandbox.babylonjs.com.`	Viewing 3D models, and computing environment textures for PBR/IBL.
Node Material Editor (NME)	`https://nme.babylonjs.com.`	Creating, saving, and sharing custom shaders made via a GUI. Custom materials, texture shaders, post-processes, and more.
Inspector	Invoked via code or PG.	Visual debugging and modification of running scene.
Sprite Editor	Built-into inspector.	Create and share snippets for sprites. Manage and debug sprite properties.
GUI Editor	`Built-into inspector – standalone tool forthcoming .`	Visually create and manage GUI elements.
Particle Editor	Built-into inspector.	Create, manage, and debug particle systems.
Texture Editor	Built into inspector.	Upload, view, and modify textures in a scene.
Skeleton Viewer	Built into inspector.	Display skeleton info of models in scene.

Throughout this book, we'll be making heavy use of the PG; we'll use it to quickly put together a piece of code or test a concept before integrating it into our application code. Not to be left out, the **Inspector** (and its accompanying tools) is also going to see heavy usage for its powerful scene-debugging capabilities. Finally, the NME will be covered later in this book as we dive into the making of Space-Truckers.

> **Note**
> The typical usage of the word **Game** in this book denotes the portion of the overall **Application** that is devoted to the game mechanics, logic, and loops.

The Asset Types of BJS

Many different types of files and formats are supported by BJS, either directly or indirectly (via exporter plugins). When selecting and/or creating assets for your game, it's important to put together a production workflow that minimizes the amount of friction without sacrificing quality – something we'll learn more about in the next chapter. Here are a few of the most commonly encountered third-party tools and file types that BJS supports:

- Textures/Images:
  - DDS (DXT1, 4bpp, and RGBA)
  - PNG/JPEG/BMP
  - TGA
  - HDR

- 3D Models:

    - GLTF (preferred)

    - OBJ

    - STL

    - BLENDER/3DS Max/Maya (exporter plugins)

- Sounds:

    - WAV

    - MP3

    - MP4

    - M4A

- Fonts:

    - TrueType

    - OTT

More relevant to our immediate purposes, however, is the BJS **Asset Library**. You can see the asset categories and browse entries by category at `https://doc.babylonjs.com/toolsAndResources/assetLibraries`, but the true power of the Asset Library comes from being able to reference and load them from the PG! Let's start off our scene creation by doing just that. Open up your browser of choice and head to the BJS PG: `https://playground.babylonjs.com`.

Building the Playground Scene

The **Babylon.js Playground** is designed around providing users with the easiest, shortest possible path to rendering content in the scene. Open your web browser of choice and navigate to `https://playground.babylonjs.com/` and you'll see the basic outline of a snippet. This basic template snippet simply creates a new **scene** and a **camera** that renders it, but it's as good a starting place as any!

On the left of the playground is the code editor and on the right the render canvas. The important thing to know about the playground is that each snippet is unique in two ways, both contained within the URL to the snippet. The characters after the first hash (#) symbol are the snippet's ID, the number after the second hash the revision. Every time a snippet is created it is assigned a unique identifier, and every time that snippet is saved a new revision is created. For example, **#L92PHY#36** points to a sample showing multiple viewports in an FPS camera, with the current revision being 36. Thus, it's possible to step incrementally through a particular snippet's revision history simply by changing the URL.

> **Note**
>
> The completed playground snippet for this chapter is **#0UYAPE#42**. That is, snippet **0UYAPE** at revision **42**.

Because we are going to be using snippets from the PG in our game though, we're going to want to do a little bit of preparatory structuring so that we can easily and reliably transfer code between our PG snippets and the source repos (more on this in *Chapter 3, Establishing the Development Workflow*). Throughout the book and in snippets, we will be using **ES6** syntax where possible. This gives us access to some important language features that we'll be leveraging to help keep our code readable and maintainable.

> **Tip**
>
> ES6 recommendation: choose `let` over `var`.
>
> It's all about hoisting and closures. Variables declared using the `var` keyword are valid in their declaring scopes, but also potentially in a/their containing scope (known as "hoisting"). Additionally, you can reference a `var` prior to its usage without throwing a runtime error. When a variable is declared with the `let` statement, it is only available in the declared scope, and it must be declared prior to usage; otherwise, an error will be thrown. Generally, you should prefer the use of `let` over `var` because it will more easily prevent and expose all-too-common-but-potentially-quite-subtle defects. Of course, if you aren't going to be changing the value, you should use `const` over `let`.

Establishing the AppStartScene

A new PG snippet starts with a single block of code – the `createScene` function. As the code comments also indicate, the `engine` and `canvas` global variables are available in the window's context.

> **Important Note**
>
> The HTML Canvas element has been removed as a dependency in BJS 4.2+, but for backward compatibility reasons, methods involving the HTML Canvas element will still function as expected.

Modifying the createScene function

To make the reuse of code easier, we will make a small change to the initial function template. Instead of putting all of the scene's logic into the same `createScene` function, we're going to subdivide the logic into atomic functions as much as possible. The initialization routine will be done in a new function, which will return an object containing the populated scene objects:

```
let createScene = function () {
    let eng = engine;
```

```
        let startScene = createStartScene(eng);
        return startScene.scene;
};
```

A sharp observer will notice that we have not as yet implemented the `createStartScene` function, which is of course the next step. Its purpose is to create and initialize the scene and its elements – see the following list. Low-friction change is critically important, so to make it easier to change them later we're going to place each piece of functionality into its own function (pun intended):

- ArcRotateCamera

- Point light

- Star (sun)

- Skybox for background

- Planets – four rocky and one gas giant

It's time to fill out our add and populate this new function, `createStartScene`. First, we are creating the scene and camera, specifying some specifics before making calls to soon-to-be-written functions (in bold) that create their respective elements:

```
function createStartScene(engine) {
    let that = {};
    let scene = that.scene = new BABYLON.Scene(engine);
    let camAlpha = 0,
        camBeta = -Math.PI / 4,
        camDist = 350,
        camTarget = new BABYLON.Vector3(0, 0, 0);
    let camera = that.camera = new BABYLON.
ArcRotateCamera("camera1", camAlpha, camBeta, camDist,
camTarget, scene);
    let env = setupEnvironment(scene);
    let star = that.star = createStar(scene);
    let planets = that.planets =
populatePlanetarySystem(scene);
    camera.attachControl(true);
    return that;
}
```

To save you the effort of doing the math in your head, the camBeta (or, the latitudinal position in radians of the camera from the target) value comes out to around 0.785 rad - 45 degrees, between the equator and the pole of an imaginary circle around the target of camDist radius. Of course, this code won't compile or run yet because we haven't yet defined setupEnvironment, createStar, or populatePlanetarySystem. Add stub implementations for these functions to make sure that the code runs as expected. The resulting scene is empty, but it's a good checkpoint in our progress. It's time to fill in the stubs and make our scene come to life! Don't forget to save (*Ctrl + S*) your snippet before continuing.

Setting up the Environment

The default environment is pretty bland and dark. The primary source of lighting for the scene is going to be a **Point Light** positioned at the center of the star system, while a skybox gives the scene perspective. The texturing of the skybox is of particular interest, because an attractive-looking skybox tends to be quite large in terms of file size. We care about this because we are going to use this scene as a loading graphic, meaning that it needs to load and begin rendering as quickly as possible. Loading a large texture over an internet connection is unlikely to help us with that goal, so instead we will create the texture on the fly using the **Starfield Procedural Texture** from the Babylon.js **Procedural Textures Library** (see https://doc.babylonjs.com/toolsAndResources/assetLibraries/ proceduralTexturesLibrary for the full list of available procedural textures).

> **Tip**
> Every **procedural texture** may or may not have its own set of input parameters that can be set to modify the output rendering of the texture. For the **Starfield** Procedural Texture, we are setting just two out of many available properties: darkmatter, which controls the lacunae (voids), and distfading, which governs the sharpness or blurriness of the rendered texture. The values in the code listed in the following code were arrived at after trial-and-error, so experiment to see what you like the best!

PointLight is, as the name implies, a source of light that radiates in a spherical shell from a single point in space. Because of the darkness of the scene and its large-ish size, the intensity of the light gets a bump before setting some sun-like colors for the diffuse and specular color channels. We use the **Scene's** createDefaultEnvironment method along with some previously defined options to create the skybox and accompanying background material. That method returns an EnvironmentHelper instance, which we will kindly return to the original caller of setupEnvironment:

```
function setupEnvironment(scene) {
    let starfieldPT = new BABYLON.
StarfieldProceduralTexture("starfieldPT", 512, scene);
    starfieldPT.coordinatesMode = BABYLON.Texture.FIXED_
EQUIRECTANGULAR_MIRRORED_MODE;
    starfieldPT.darkmatter = 1.5;
```

```
    starfieldPT.distfading = 0.75;
    let envOptions = {
        skyboxSize: 512,
        createGround: false,
        skyboxTexture: starfieldPT,
        environmentTexture: starfieldPT
    };
    let light = new BABYLON.PointLight("starLight", BABYLON.
Vector3.Zero(), scene);
    light.intensity = 2;
    light.diffuse = new BABYLON.Color3(.98, .9, 1);
    light.specular = new BABYLON.Color3(1, 0.9, 0.5);
    let env = scene.createDefaultEnvironment(envOptions);
    return env;
}
```

Clicking **Run** should now show a nifty-looking starfield in a skybox you can pan around. If everything is working correctly, now is a good time to save your work.

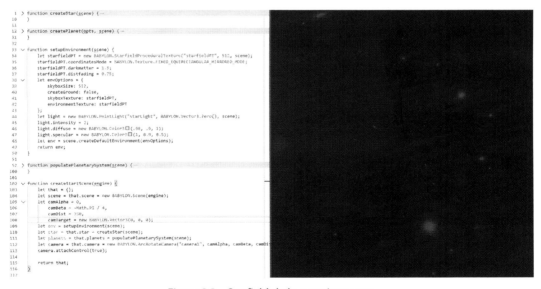

Figure 2.2 – Starfield skybox environment

Birthing a Star

The mesh for our star is a simple sphere, but when we add the standard material and some color channels, the result is a single-toned, flat-appearing circle – not very "star-like." We can get a more nuanced look with very little effort by combining an **emissive** (or, the color of light emanating from the object) color with a **diffuse** (a color map of light reflected off the object non-directionally) texture containing some noise or distortion. Fortunately, the BJS **Texture Library** contains a **distortion** texture that should do perfectly. Because we're loading from there, we can simply specify a relative path to the specific filename of the desired texture in the constructor for BABYLON.Texture:

```
function createStar(scene) {
    let starDiam = 16;
    let star = BABYLON.MeshBuilder.CreateSphere("star",
        { diameter: starDiam, segments: 128 }, scene);
    let mat = new BABYLON.StandardMaterial("starMat",
        scene);
    star.material = mat;
    mat.emissiveColor = new BABYLON.Color3(0.37, 0.333,
        0.11);
    mat.diffuseTexture = new BABYLON.Texture
        ("textures/distortion.png", scene);
    mat.diffuseTexture.level = 1.8;
    return star;
}
```

Without changing the diffuseTexture.level value, the emissiveColor tends to either wash out the distortion or be extinguished entirely by the diffuse texture's pixel values. The level, 1.8, was a product of trial-and-error (as is the case with many of these "magic numbers" that tend to show up during app design/game development). This is a good checkpoint for **saving** your progress if you haven't recently.

Figure 2.3 – Emissive color combined with a diffuse distortion texture

Producing Planets

There's only one remaining top-level scene element that we still need to create, and that's the populatePlanetarySystem function. The implementation for this is a classic example of the power of compositional software patterns – a topic we will be returning to later. There's what you might think of as a central control logic in the form of populatePlanetarySystems, which is responsible for defining the number and unique properties of the various planetary bodies. It then asks another function, the new createPlanet method, to take care of how the actual object is constructed. Finally, it collects the planets into an array that it returns to the caller.

We want to be able to create different types of planets with different properties, so in our populatePlanetarySystems method, we create an array of objects that define each planet. For the full listing of planetary data, see https://playground.babylonjs.com/#0UYAPE#26:

```
let hg = {
    name: "hg",
    posRadians: BABYLON.Scalar.RandomRange(0, 2 * Math.PI),
    posRadius: 14,
    scale: 2,
```

```
      color: new BABYLON.Color3(0.45, 0.33, 0.18),
      rocky: true
}; //...
```

The posRadians property generates a random value between 0 and 360 degrees (in radians), whereas the posRadius property specifies the distance from the origin the planet should reside – how far away it is from the sun. The overall size of the planet is determined by its scale factor, while the **specular** and **diffuse** color channels of the material are populated with the eponymous color property. We'll cover the final property in a moment. Scaling of a scene can be tricky, but you can use relative scale guides to help come up with appropriate ranges of numbers.

You don't have to stick to realistic numbers – have you ever been told that "Space is Big. Really Big"? It is, in fact, quite too big to fit in our tiny viewport, so when choosing posRadius for the planet, it might be easier to approach coming up with a figure from a different direction. By looking at the orbital radius in terms of the relative steps between planets, we can come up with a decent-looking (but probably not realistically stable) system of planets. Our starDiameter is 16, giving us a radius of 8 units. Our inner-most planet, "hg", needs to be at least 8 + 2 = 10 units to avoid intersecting the star; putting it at 14 units seems about right. Moving to subsequent planets, by placing each planet around 1.5–1.8x, the orbital radius of the previous planet will give nice-looking results that aren't too far from the ratios found in our own Solar System – that's how you know it will be interesting!

This leaves us with the rocky property. This flag will signal our logic that it needs to apply a different set of textures to the **Standard Material** the planet model uses to be rendered. With this data in hand, we push new items returned from createPlanet into the planets array before returning the populated array:

```
planets.push(createPlanet(hg, scene));
planets.push(createPlanet(aphro, scene));
planets.push(createPlanet(tellus, scene));
planets.push(createPlanet(ares, scene));
planets.push(createPlanet(zeus, scene));
return planets;
```

The final sub-task needed to display our planetary system is to implement the createPlanet function. In this method, we do the following:

1. Create a new Sphere **Mesh** using the **MeshBuilder**.
2. Create a new **StandardMaterial**, assigning diffuseColor and specularColor to the passed-in Color3 value.
3. Assign textures based on the value of the rocky flag.

4. Assign the material to the mesh.

5. Scale and position `planet` according to the passed-in `scale`, `posRadians`, and `posRadius` values.

It may not be immediately obvious, but we are also setting the material's `specularPower` to zero. This is because we will otherwise get very shiny spots on our planets, making them look more like billiard balls than rocky or gaseous spheres. For rocky planets, we are pulling in both `bumpTexture` (a.k.a. a **Normal Map**) and a regular `diffuseTexture` from the BJS **Textures Library**. For planets with no visible surface, we use the distortion texture to add the appearance of cloud bands in the atmosphere:

```
function createPlanet(opts, scene) {
    let planet = BABYLON.MeshBuilder.
        CreateSphere(opts.name, { diameter: 1 }, scene);
    let mat = new BABYLON.StandardMaterial(planet.
        name + "-mat", scene);
    mat.diffuseColor = mat.specularColor = opts.color;
    mat.specularPower = 0;
    if (opts.rocky === true) {
        mat.bumpTexture = new
            BABYLON.Texture("textures/rockn.png", scene);
        mat.diffuseTexture = new
            BABYLON.Texture("textures/rock.png", scene);
    }
    else {
        mat.diffuseTexture = new BABYLON.Texture
            ("textures/distortion.png", scene);
    }
    planet.material = mat;
    planet.scaling.setAll(opts.scale);
    planet.position.x = opts.posRadius *
        Math.sin(opts.posRadians);
    planet.position.z = opts.posRadius *
        Math.cos(opts.posRadians);
    return planet;
}
```

With that code in place, you should be able to **Run** the scene and get a most excellent result, showing our central star with four various-sized and colored planets at varying distances from the star.

Figure 2.4 – Star system with planets and a skybox

Save the snippet and strap in, because next, we're going to learn two different ways and styles of making our planets move.

Animating the Orbits

BJS has many different ways of accomplishing any given task; animating objects in a scene is no different. Some of the different ways to animate in BJS include the following:

- Define a reusable `BABYLON.Animation` object that will interpolate specified properties between an array of **keyframes**.

- Import pre-built Animations from a file – BABYLON, GLTF, GLB, OBJ, and so on.

- Use `OnPreRenderObservable` to update object properties (e.g., position, rotation, color, and so on) before each frame is rendered.

For our title screen animations, we will be using the first and third methods to animate the rotations and circular orbits of our little solar system, respectively. In later chapters, we will see more of the second.

Putting Spin on the Star and Planets

The rotation of stars and planets is pretty simple, but it can serve as a good review of the principle and practice of keyframe animation. Since animations can be looped or cycled, it's often unnecessary to need a large number of frames for a given animation. We'll follow a few easy steps to add a createSpinAnimation function that returns a new **Animation** instance.

First, we figure out what/which properties of the animation's target will be changing. In this case, it is just the target node's rotation.y value. We can say that our animation should complete a full circle (360 degrees or 2 * Pi radians) in 2 seconds. Next, determine how many frames the animation should comprise in total, the number of **frames per second (fps)**, and the length of time you want the animation to last. A framerate of 30 fps is sufficient, so our total number of frames is 2 s * 30 fps = 60 frames. Just two keyframes will suffice: one showing the rotation's initial value and the other at the end point of Scalar.TwoPi. This is all we need to implement the code to create and set the animation properties:

```
function createSpinAnimation() {
    let orbitAnim = new BABYLON.Animation("planetspin",
        "rotation.y", 30,
        BABYLON.Animation.ANIMATIONTYPE_FLOAT,
        BABYLON.Animation.ANIMATIONLOOPMODE_CYCLE);
    const keyFrames = [];
    keyFrames.push({
        frame: 0,
        value: 0
    });
    keyFrames.push({
        frame: 60,
        value: BABYLON.Scalar.TwoPi
    });
    orbitAnim.setKeys(keyFrames);
    return orbitAnim;
}
```

The createSpinAnimation method is called from createStartScene to make the spinAnim variable available to the rest of the scene's controlling code.

Once the animation has been created, it can then be added to one or more different `mesh.animations` arrays. This attaches the animation to that particular **mesh**, but you might notice that the `Animation` object has no `start` function or equivalent. That is because the Animation itself is agnostic of its target, allowing it to be used across any arbitrary number of different meshes. Starting with `star` and then looping through our `planets` array, we add `spinAnim` to each mesh:

```
let spinAnim = createSpinAnimation();
star.animations.push(spinAnim);
scene.beginAnimation(star, 0, 60, true);
```

To start an animation, you call the `scene.beginAnimation` function, passing the start frame, the end frame, and the speed parameters along with the animation object. We want it to loop, so we pass `true` as our final parameter to the method:

```
planets.forEach(p => {
    p.animations.push(spinAnim);
        scene.beginAnimation(p, 0, 60, true,
            BABYLON.Scalar.RandomRange(0.1, 3));
});
```

When the scene is run, the animation automatically starts and you can observe the rotation of all the bodies.

Making Orbital Motion

Unlike the **Animation**-based keyframing we did for the planetary rotation, the circular motion of the planets around the star will be performed by computing the planet's new position prior to being rendered on every frame. We can do this by adding an observer function to `scene.onBeforeRenderObservable`. In the context of the game engine loop, this is where the update logic happens. At the end of `createPlanet`, we will add code to attach the event listener along with additional data that tracks the planet's orbital parameters:

```
planet.orbitOptions = opts;
planet.orbitAnimationObserver =
    createAndStartOrbitAnimation(planet, scene);
```

Our `createAndStartOrbitAnimation` method needs to derive a number of values. Two of these, the orbital radius (`posRadius`) and the angular position (`posRadians`) are added to `planet` as the `orbitOptions` property.

The `period` orbital is the amount of time it takes for the planet to make one complete revolution (360 degrees or 2 * Pi radians) and is measured in seconds. We want each planet to have a different period, with distant bodies taking longer than closer ones to complete an orbit, but we don't want to laboriously tweak values until they look good. Physics – or, more specifically, Newtonian mechanics – gives us the equations to compute a planet's orbital speed given its distance (radius) from a given massive body. Knowing the rate of position change over time, it's possible to calculate the angular velocity:

```
function createAndStartOrbitAnimation(planet, scene) {
    const Gm = 6672.59 * 0.07;
    const opts = planet.orbitOptions;
    const rCubed = Math.pow(opts.posRadius, 3);
    const period = BABYLON.Scalar.TwoPi * Math.sqrt
        (rCubed / Gm);
    const v = Math.sqrt(Gm / opts.posRadius);
    const w = v / period;
    const circum = Scalar.TwoPi * opts.posRadius;
    let angPos = opts.posRadians;
```

The `Gm` constant is more or less arbitrarily chosen to ensure a smooth distribution of orbital velocities as the radius changes. The state variable needed is `angPos`, which is incremented by w every frame and kept within a valid range by wrapping the statement in a call to `Scalar.Repeat`. In general, it's useful to think of the angular components of these kinematics as being counters or watch dials; incrementing the angular position by the angular velocity over time and computing position components completes the logic:

```
let preRenderObsv = scene.onBeforeRenderObservable.add(sc => {
    planet.position.x = opts.posRadius * Math.sin(angPos);
    planet.position.z = opts.posRadius * Math.cos(angPos);
    angPos = BABYLON.Scalar.Repeat(angPos + w,
        BABYLON.Scalar.TwoPi);
});
return preRenderObsv;
```

Returning the `preRenderObsv` object isn't needed to make this work, but it's a good practice so that we can later on cleanly dispose of the observer when it's no longer needed. Now, when the scene is run, the planets all circle around the sun in a unique fashion. This is all looking great, but there's one last thing we can do to really spice things up before we move on. Mash **Save** and let's move on to the finale.

Orbit Lines

To cap off this animation, we're going to add lines to each planet's orbit using a **TrailMesh**. This is a built-in mesh type that attaches to a given **Transform Node** or **Mesh** and follows it as its position changes, extruding a variable width and length ribbon as it does. The createAndStartOrbitAnimation method is a good place to do this. We declare our TrailMesh and pass it planet to attach to along with the circum orbital (length) of the trail ribbon, also specifying that we want the trail to start immediately. At the same time, we also create a new material and associate it with the Trail Mesh:

```
planet.computeWorldMatrix(true);
let planetTrail = new BABYLON.TrailMesh(planet.name +
    "-trail", planet, scene, .1, circum, true);
let trailMat = new BABYLON.StandardMaterial
    (planetTrail.name + "-mat", scene);
trailMat.emissiveColor = trailMat.specularColor =
    trailMat.diffuseColor = opts.color;
planetTrail.material = trailMat;
```

Before adding the trail mesh, we need to force recomputation of the planet's **World Matrix**; otherwise, the trail will have artifacts from the origin to the planet's location. That's it! The orbits trace out nice circles as they move, but it still feels as if the scene were a bit dark and washed out.

Shining up with GlowLayer

By default, BJS does not add the emissive color channel of a material to the lighting computations – emissive textures and colors don't brighten up a scene. Making objects glow is easy; just add this line to the createStartScene method:

```
let glowLayer = new BABYLON.GlowLayer("glowLayer", scene);
```

Unless otherwise specified, the GlowLayer will impact every mesh in the scene. We don't want the planets to glow, so while we're looping through the planets to animate their rotation, add the planet to the mesh exclusion list of the GlowLayer:

```
planets.forEach(p => {
        glowLayer.addExcludedMesh(p);
        p.animations.push(spinAnim);
        scene.beginAnimation(p, 0, 60, true,
            BABYLON.Scalar.RandomRange(0.1, 3));
    });
```

Click **Run** to view the results. If you're not satisfied with how things look, you can tweak the camera altitude and angle (**beta** and **alpha** respectively), distance, and so on. Make sure to save the snippet in any case and enjoy the fruits of your labor. Once you're done admiring your work, post your snippets on the boards at `https://github.com/jelster/space-truckers/discussions/21`, where you can look at other folks' creations, share, and discuss – but don't forget to come back here, there's still more work to be done!

Figure 2.5 – Completed orbital animation with GlowLayer and Trail Meshes

Extended Topics

The completed snippet meets the immediate needs of our application, but that doesn't mean that there aren't ways to improve it! The following are a few ideas you might pursue on your own that could enhance the scene. Join the BJS and the Space-Truckers community by posting and sharing your snippets over at the Space-Truckers Discussions board (`https://github.com/jelster/space-truckers/discussions`) or over on the BJS forums (`https://forum.babylonjs.com/`). The discussion boards and forum aren't just there to share your accomplishments, however. They're a place where you can post questions or issues you're encountering, with a thriving community that loves to help.

You could do the following:

- Remove the helix-like appearance of the planet trails. The spin animation and the trail mesh are both parented to the planet. As the planet rotates, the trail mesh gets twisted around. One approach to fixing this could be to add a **TransformNode** to the scene and parent the planet to it. Keep the spin animation on the planet, but associate and point the **TrailMesh** and the orbital animation at the **TransformNode**.

- Replace the star's current texture with a particle system. The **ParticleHelper** has a **sun** effect that can bring a cool effect to the scene. The docs on this are at `https://doc.babylonjs.com/divingDeeper/particles/particle_system/particleHelper`, where there's also useful information on how to create your own custom **ParticleSets**. The easiest (and perhaps the best) option for creating custom particle systems is to use the NME (`https://nme.babylonjs.com/`) in **Particle** mode. The NME is to shaders as the PG is to scenes, meaning that just as you can save and share PG snippets, you can also save and share NME snippets. The difference between them in this context is that you can use NME snippets in the PG but not vice versa.

- Add a comet on an **inclined** orbit that brightens and shows a tail as it gets closer to the star on its elliptical path through the scene. An inclination simply means that the object includes the y axis as it "bobs" up and down through the orbital plane. An elliptical orbit has the same period as a circular orbit, with an orbital radius that's the same as the ellipse's **semi-major axis** (the length of the line dividing the ellipse along its long side), but the difference is that rather than having a constant velocity along its path, objects moving in an elliptical orbit travel fastest at their closest approach (**apopse**).

- Give the outer-most gas giant planet a ring system. One way to approach this would be to create a flat torus mesh using the MeshBuilder, and then use BJS **Parenting** to attach the rings to a planet. Another approach that builds on the prior would be to use the **Solid Particle System** (**SPS**) to generate tens or even hundreds of small rocks to comprise the rings. Consider it a preview of what's coming up: in the next chapter, we'll be using the SPS to create an asteroid belt.

- Add clouds specular, terrain bump (normal) map to a rocky planet to make it look like real-world planets. The BJS **Asset Library** has a height map of the earth's terrain along with various textures for cloud and ground effects. The **Materials Library** also has some interesting options to explore for making the planets unique and attractive – have fun!

- Make the camera pan and zoom around the system cinematically. Choose one of the animation methods we discussed previously, targeting the scene's `camera`. Depending on your methods and plan, you may want to unset or change the camera's target to be a **TransformNode**. This new, non-rendered node acts as a sort of "mark" that can be moved around to change the camera's view as the position changes. Another option is to explore a different type of camera than the current **ArcRotateCamera**.

Summary

Over the course of this chapter, we've refreshed and ramped ourselves up on BJS by creating a simple scene in the PG. We learned about different ways of animating a scene along with how to load textures and other assets from the BJS Asset Library. Hopefully, we've had a little bit of fun along the way, but this is just the tip of the iceberg when it comes to what's in store in later chapters. If you needed a little bit of a refresher on BJS, hopefully this has gotten you warmed up and ready to go. If you're new to BJS, then I hope this has empowered you to push onward to the next chapter. Coming up in the next chapter, we will begin Space-Truckers in earnest by setting up a local development environment along with source control and debugging.

Further Reading

The BJS documentation site contains an enormous wealth of knowledge and content. Here are some relevant pages from the docs that go into more detail on the topics covered in this chapter:

- Once you've gotten how to do individual Animations, read about Animation sequencing, grouping, and combining, starting at `https://doc.babylonjs.com/divingDeeper/animation/sequenceAnimations`.

- Learn about importing different files types of assets into a scene and how loaders work at `https://doc.babylonjs.com/divingDeeper/importers/loadingFileTypes`.

- The Diving Deeper: The Mesh section has details on how the GlowLayer works at `https://doc.babylonjs.com/divingDeeper/mesh/glowLayer`.

- For details on the different types of cameras and their properties, see `https://doc.babylonjs.com/divingDeeper/cameras/camera_introduction`. Something that is worth mentioning is that whenever you see the docs mention `FreeCamera`, `TouchCamera`, or `GamepadCamera`, you should instead substitute or use `UniversalCamera`, as it supersedes those three, which are retained for backward compatibility reasons.

Establishing the Development Workflow

While it is an extremely versatile and powerful tool for developing, running, and sharing a working 3D rendered scene, the **Babylon.js Playground** (**PG**) also has a place in the development workflow of a traditional web application. Effective software development is effectively enabled by the removal of friction. Friction in this sense is anything that presents an obstacle between writing code and executing the results and can take almost any form, from the mundane to the obscure. As an example, say it takes an hour between the time a change is made in code to the time that changed code is running in the developer's web browser. The developer will then be compelled to include as much as possible in every new build, which then makes it more difficult to understand the effects of any one change on the application's behavior. Focus is diluted and progress is incremental and not in proportion to the effort required in these situations, which is why small tweaks to a development workflow can yield large gains. We're going to examine one out of many potential **Babylon.js** development workflows during the course of this chapter, and by the end of it, you will have the tools to rapidly and efficiently build games that can evolve as rapidly as you can think of designs!

Everyone is going to have a different way of approaching the structure and process of development, and that's OK. Each of these sections illustrates an aspect of the workflow that seeks to maximize developer efficiency and quality while minimizing tech debt and uncertainty:

- Setting up the Environment
- Crafting a Playground Snippet
- Transitioning from the Playground to the Application
- Constructing the Landing Page

Technical Requirements

The base set of requirements for running the BJS PG are detailed in *Chapter 2, Ramping up on Babylon.js*, but in addition to those requirements, there are some additional development tools that we're going to be using.

> **Important Note**
>
> Although the examples and such are all based on a Windows-based developer experience, there are no Operating System requirements to follow along with this book. All of the tools discussed are available on multiple platforms and any differences in syntax or usage will be highlighted or called out where feasible.

The specific usages of each individual item will be covered during the accompanying chapter material, and it is assumed that you have some familiarity with the tools and/or usage. For information on setting up and configuring a given tool, please see the corresponding link to the tool's documentation.

- **Visual Studio Code** is our IDE of choice, is available on all platforms, works wonderfully, and is free: `https://code.visualstudio.com`

- **Node.js v14.15.4 (LTS)** or greater: `https://docs.npmjs.com/`

- **Node Package Manager (npm) CLI v6.x (LTS Release)** or greater, installed via a node version manager listed at `https://docs.npmjs.com/cli/v6/configuring-npm/install`

- **Git** SCM client. Also, to be able to submit **Pull Requests**, file **issues**, or participate in **Discussions**, a valid GitHub account is required: `https://github.com`

A Note for TypeScript Users

Should you prefer to do all your coding in **TypeScript** as opposed to straight-JavaScript, that's great! Babylon.js itself is written in **TypeScript** and is fully supported for developing in BJS. Following along with the code in this book is possible, and any differences in syntax and structure aren't always going to be explained or called out. That said, the code should be largely compatible between the two languages, keeping in mind the following two primary changes:

1. Playground snippets should use TypeScript mode. This has a slightly different template. Start at `https://www.babylonjs-playground.com/ts.html#` and click **New** The `createScene` method is encapsulated as a **static method** within a class called `Playground`. Declare new classes and use them in the `createScene` method similar to how you would in regular JavaScript.

2. When integrating classes written in the PG, it's important to add the **export** modifier to your **class** declaration, (e.g. `export class Foo { //... }`). Since you will be using the **tsc** (**TypeScript Compiler**) to output JavaScript, there are times when you'll need to **import** certain Babylon.js modules for their **side effects**. Please see `https://doc.babylonjs.com/divingDeeper/developWithBjs/npmSupport#typescript-support` for more on how to configure **TypeScript** for use with Babylon.js

Setting up the Environment

Effective software development relies on being able to confidently introduce changes to an application's construction. Confidence in introducing, changing, or removing code comes from a) being able to run the code using the new changes, and b) through not being in a position where undoing changes imposes risks of its own. Let's park that thought for a moment to back up and start from the beginning.

Preparatory Steps

The *a priori* assumption going into this step is that you have **Git, VSCode, Node.js**, and **NPM** all set up and ready to go. A linting tool such as **ESLint** is also recommended. If you know what you're doing, go ahead and get those tools set up and configured now. No rush, it's just the rest of the book that's waiting is all – this has been speculated to go faster if you work while humming *The Girl from Ipanema* to yourself. **VSCode** has a rich ecosystem of extensions that can make your life easier. Here is a list of some of the ones you'll want to install (or their equivalents). Go to the **Extensions** panel in **VSCode**, then search for the appropriate item's **Marketplace ID**:

Extension	Description	VSCode Marketplace
Live Server (opt.)	A simple local web server with live reload	ritwickdey.LiveServer
Node.js Extension Pack	A bundle of extensions relevant to Node.js development	waderyan.nodejs-extension-pack
ESLint	Performs design-time checks for potential issues with JavaScript code. Bundled with the Node.js Extension Pack.	dbaeumer.vscode-eslint
NPM Intellisense	Provides autocompletion for npm modules in `import` statements. Bundled with the Node.js Extension Pack.	christian-kohler.npm-intellisense
JavaScript (ES6) Snippets	Snippets of ES6 code for common tasks. Bundled with the Node.js Extension Pack.	xabikos.JavaScriptSnippets
Npm	Validates package.json dependencies and integrates npm scripts with VSCode Command Pallet. Bundled with the Node.js Extension Pack.	eg2.vscode-npm-script
Path Intellisense	Autocompletion extension for filenames in the current project. Bundled with the Node.js Extension Pack.	christian-kohler.path-intellisense
Debugger for Chrome Debugger for Edge Debugger for Firefox	JavaScript debugging in Chrome, Chromium Edge, Firefox, EdgeHTML	msjsdiag.debugger-for-chrome msjsdiag.debugger-for-edge firefox-devtools.vscode-firefox-debug

Figure 3.1 – List of useful VSCode extensions

If you're not quite there yet when it comes to knowing where and how to do this sort of thing, here's what you can do. Ignore the elevator muzak, tie a bandana around your forehead, and dive straight into an 80s movie montage sequence. You will probably want to set a bookmark on this page first – the montage features a series of vignettes of you flipping to the *Further Reading* section at the end of this chapter, reading and following the links, culminating in a triumphantly successful installation… and then flipping back to your bookmark, ready to continue the journey.

Initialize All the Things

There are a number of unflashy tasks that go on here – things such as creating a new Git repository in GitHub and cloning it locally, which would take up too much space to go through in detail. Instead, here's a rough checklist of what to expect to do as part of this step:

1. Create a new **Git** repository. If created in **GitHub**, you may need to **clone** the repos locally.

2. Add a .gitignore file to the repos – the only contents it really needs at this point are entries for the output dist/ folder and for the node_modules/ folders.

3. Create some folders – src, dist, public, and assets – to hold the source code, the packed output, and game assets, respectively.

4. Run npm init to create a package.json for the application.

5. Install webpack and core Babylon.js libraries and dependencies as developer dependencies with this command:

    ```
    npm install --save-dev webpack webpack-cli webpack-
        dev-server webpack-merge clean-webpack-plugin file-
        loader html-webpack-plugin source-map-loader url-
        loader eslint `@babylonjs/core
    ```

6. Install additional Babylon.js modules that we'll be using:

    ```
    npm install -save-dev @babylonjs/materials
        @babylonjs/loaders @babylonjs/gui
        @babylonjs/procedural-textures @babylonjs/post-
        processes @babylonjs/serializers
        @babylonjs/inspector
    ```

With the package dependencies squared away, it's time to add a few more foundational pieces to our nascent application.

Scripts and ESLint Configuration

At some point in the very near future, we're going to want to be able to add some automation around our application's build and deployment tasks. The key to making this as frictionless as possible is to leverage as much of the (and similar) application infrastructure as possible. Keeping it simple and focusing scripts on a single task will allow for easier automation in the future.

package.json Scripts

There are three basic commands that we want to start out adding to our `package.json` file. These are simple scripts that will allow both local and production builds and linting of source. We'll address dev versus production builds in an upcoming section, but for now, add these scripts to the `package.json` file:

- `start`: The webpack dev server and related packing processes for local development. Command: `npx webpack serve --mode development`

- `build`: Runs webpack in production configuration. Command: `npx webpack --mode production`

- `lint`: Makes sure our code doesn't have any big "whoopsies!". Command: `npx eslint`

Check your work for typos, and make sure that you save and commit both your `package.json` and your `package.lock.json` files. At this point, we're still a couple of items short on our checklist to set up the application, so let's get them knocked out so we can press forward on our journey!

Important Note

While it is possible to simply reference and load the entire Babylon.js library into the application, it is incredibly inefficient to do so – because BJS does so much, there's a lot to the libraries, meaning they're quite large in size and complexity. Clients are forced to download the full bundle of JS before the application can become responsive to input, reducing a user's perception of an application's performance. One of the most modern and effective ways to reduce an application's footprint is by leveraging a feature of **ES6** called **tree shaking**. The process of tree shaking results in code output that includes only dependencies that are actually used in the code, resulting in smaller, faster, and more efficient JavaScript modules.

What's the downside? As you'll see, every imported type must have its own `import` statement, but in addition, the full path of the type must be specified – not just the containing package. Still, the benefits can be substantial – as I commented in this pull request: `https://github.com/jelster/space-truckers/pull/15`. The start scene was reduced in size from 8.91 MB to 3.11 MB, a more than 50% reduction!

Babylon.js has been around longer than ES6 modules have been supported, and the team has made a firm commitment to support backward compatibility in the engine. That's why you'll notice there are some places where compromises in that vein result in the need to import modules purely for side effects – the **MeshBuilder CreateXXXX** APIs are a prominent example of this. The BJS docs have more information located at `https://doc.babylonjs.com/divingDeeper/developWithBjs/treeShaking` that can explain more about why and what modules behave in this fashion.

The PG examples we've looked at previously haven't required anything special in the way of building, but that's because the PG is built towards a different goal than what we're looking to accomplish. We're building a complete application that needs to not be dependent on the same luxuries (such as a CDN for grabbing the Babylon.js libraries) as the PG. To do that, we will sacrifice the flexible but inefficient load-everything approach of the PG for the compactness and efficiency of a webpacked application.

Adding Configuration for ESLint

Add a new file using VSCode to the root folder of your repository, named .eslintignore. This is a text file that we'll use to exclude certain directories from being checked by the lint tool, improving responsiveness and reliability. We don't want our node_modules directory to be checked since we're not working on those libraries. Neither do we care about JavaScript that's already been packaged and output – anything in our dist/ folder. Add the following lines to the .eslintignore file you've just created:

```
node_modules
dist
```

Save and close the file.

Configuring Webpack

Add another new file to the root directory and name it webpack.common.js, then create another two named webpack.dev.js and webpack.prod.js. We'll put the base webpack config in the webpack.common.js file and merge environment-specific config at script runtime using webpack-merge. At the same time, create a new empty file in src and name it index.js along with an empty index.html in the public/ directory. This will serve as a placeholder for future work while allowing us to test and validate our current config.

> **Note**
>
> **Webpack** has a lot of different ways and means of configuration, which can sometimes make it hard to figure out which way, or how, to approach a particular scenario. Always keep in mind what you want to accomplish and finding a path can be much easier. In this case, the end goal of using **Webpack** is to identify, aggregate, and compress the source code for our application into an atomic set of bundled JavaScript written to our dist/ folder. Other related assets may also be affected in ways ranging from generating correct URL paths to rendering markup templates into output directories and more. Check out the **Webpack** repos along with the docs at https://github.com/webpack/webpack to learn more about configuration and plugin options.

Development versus Production Modes

When running in a production build context, there are really only two things we need to happen. First, Webpack does its thing, bundling and packaging up all the .js scripts in the src/ folder, outputting the results to the dist/ folder. Second, a script reference to the application's entry point – index. js – is injected into an index.html file that is what gets served to web browsers.

Local development has a slightly different set of needs than a production build. We want to be able to make changes to our code and see the results of those changes as quickly as possible, which rules out the potentially lengthy process of re-bundling everything from scratch upon a change. Instead, the **webpack development server** is smart enough to both cache build output and selectively rebuild only what's been changed. A **WebSocket** connection to the browser is used to automatically refresh the page when a new bundle is compiled, helping further to close any gaps in iteration. We also want to emit JavaScript **source maps** to aid in debugging as well as to specify content paths for non-bundled content served by our development server.

Common Webpack Config

Regardless of whether webpack is being run for development or production usage, we always want to make sure that our destination directory is cleaned of any old or potentially stale source files. We'll use the CleanWebpackPlugin for that purpose, and the HtmlWebpackPlugin to inject the proper script references into our index.html template.

Back to the webpack.common.js file, let's add some import statements and define the module. exports stub function:

```
const path = require("path");
const HtmlWebpackPlugin = require("html-webpack-plugin");
const { CleanWebpackPlugin } = require("clean-webpack-
  plugin");
const appDirectory = __dirname;
module.exports = env => {
    return {
    };
};
```

You may notice that unlike the rest of our application, our webpack configuration isn't using **ES6 module syntax**. This is one you'll probably just need to get over for now, because although there are workarounds, it's overall more trouble than it's worth to use ES6 syntax in just a couple of files that aren't part of the build output. The configuration requires an entry object that designates the script that will serve to launch our application on the client; it will be injected into a <script> tag in the site's default index.html landing page.

> **Important Note**
>
> File and folder paths can be tricky to navigate when working in a cross-platform environment. The __dirname webpack-provided variable is a good way to avoid problems in the first place because it will correctly and consistently represent the equivalent of fs.cwd().

The entry item and potentially other config elements will need to know what base paths to use when reading and writing files, so we designate and compute that value. While we're at it, we might as well add the output entry to our config. This object specifies where to emit the packed results, and to help identify it among potential other scripts we name it babylonBundle.js. Finally, we instantiate new instances of our CleanWebpackPlugin and HtmlWebpackPlugin modules.

> **Important Note**
>
> The order that plugins are added to the plugins array is important! Make sure that your CleanWebpackPlugin is always at the top of the plugin list so that it runs first.

The HtmlWebpackPlugin is given the path to our publicly served HTML index.html page and told to inject the proper script tags for the bundle into the document. Once that is done, we'll test our config quickly before completing the common (and also the biggest) configuration setup:

```
module.exports = {
    const appDirectory = __dirname;
    return {
        entry: "./src/index.js"),
        output: {
            filename: "js/babylonBundle.js",
            path: path.resolve(appDirectory, "./dist")
        },
        plugins: [
            new CleanWebpackPlugin(),
            new HtmlWebpackPlugin({
                template: path.resolve("public/index.html"),
                inject: true
            })
        ]
    };
};
```

By specifying an `assetModuleFilename` pattern, we are instructing **WebPack** to output any assets resolved (see the next section) into the output's `assets` subfolder with the original file name, extension, and any query string parameters. To test out our configuration, make sure you've saved everything and enter the following command in a terminal window (make sure your working directory is the same as the root of the repository):

```
npx webpack –config webpack.common.js
```

If everything goes well, you should see a bunch of text in your command window, some green text, and no errors. That's great, but there's not much of anything going on so we can't take a break quite yet – we're very close to finishing this section!

Resolver and Loader Configuration

As part of processing your source code, Webpack will compile a list of all the various **import** (or require for CommonJS modules) and invoke a processing pipeline that uses matching rules to select the appropriate logic to resolve the location for the request.

> **Note**
> This is an area where **TypeScript** users will see significant differences between their implementations and this ES6 (-ish) one. **Raanan Weber** of the BJS team has made a TypeScript starter repository available at `https://github.com/RaananW/babylonjs-webpack-es6`. The TypeScript Webpack code listed here is modeled to be as similar as possible to Raanan's starter template to make transitioning between reading this text and your code easier.

To avoid the need to have to code for environmental differences in static asset URLs, we use **asset loader** to serve up various types of asset files from the assets folder as described previously. The `source-map-loader` helps to match symbols from runtime code with locations in the source code. Before that though, our config needs a `resolve` object that specifies an array of `extensions` to enable searching through. Add this as a property of the returned config, just below the `output` property. Here's what that part of the config might look like:

```
// entry, output, etc...
    resolve: {
        extensions: [".js"],
        fallback: {
            fs: false,
            path: false,
        },
    },
    module: {
```

```
        rules: [
          {
            test: /\.(png|jpg|gif|env|glb|stl)$/i,
            use: [
              {
                loader: "url-loader",
                options: {
                  limit: 8192,
                },
              },
            ],
          },
// plugins, etc.
```

The list of `rules` in the `modules` property define what constitutes a separate module in the eyes of **WebPack**. Each of these has their own configuration that defines a **regular expression**-based `test` to perform to see whether the given loader will handle the request. The long regular expression for the asset/resource module type is essentially a list of all the different file extensions that we want to be considered as assets, which are copied without further processing into the output directory.

Webpack Development and Production Configurations

In our `webpack.dev.js`, we're going to make use of the `webpack-merge` add-on to webpack. This handy utility will merge two webpack config objects together, returning the combined result. Why is this handy? Because we'll be able to have separate development and production configurations without needing to hardcode their names into the `webpack.common.js` or the `package.json` scripts. If we want to add another environment configuration, all we need to do is add the new webpack config file, merge our common config, and then point our `npx webpack --config` parameter at the appropriate file.

There are really only two things we need from our dev config that we don't have in common. First, configuration for the web server launched with `npx webpack serve`. Second, we specify that we want our source maps to be sent inline with our scripts. The top-level mode of "development" ensures that various production-suited optimization paths are not taken by webpack. This is what our `webpack.dev.js` looks like when we're done:

```
const { merge } = require('webpack-merge');
const common = require('./webpack.common.js');
const path = require('path');

const appDirectory = __dirname;
```

```
const devConfig = {
    mode: "development",
    devtool: "inline-source-map",
    devServer: {
        contentBase: path.resolve(appDirectory, "public"),
        compress: true,
        hot: true,
        open: true,
        publicPath: "/"
    }
};
module.exports = merge(common, devConfig);
```

Creating webpack.prod.js is even simpler since we don't need the dev server configuration, and it shares the same set of top-level require statements as our dev configuration. To reduce the size of our script packages, we will choose not to emit source maps, and other than setting the mode to **production**, that's the only difference:

```
const { merge } = require('webpack-merge');
const common = require('./webpack.common.js');
const prodConfig = {
    mode: "production"
};
module.exports = merge(common, prodConfig);
```

Before we shift our focus a bit, let's get some markup into our public/index.html file. We don't need much right now, so let's start with this simple markup:

```
<!doctype html>
<html lang="en">
<head>
  <meta charset="utf-8">
  <title>Space-Truckers: The Video Game!</title>
    <style>
      html,
      body {
        overflow: hidden;
        width: 100%;
```

```
        height: 100%;
        margin: 0;
        padding: 0;
      }
      canvas {
        width: 100%;
        height: 100%;
        touch-action: none;
      }
    </style>
  </head>
  <body>
  </body>
</html>
```

This is enough for us to check our progress by making sure all files have been saved before running npm run start. Success is indicated by the launching of your web browser and a console output similar to this screenshot:

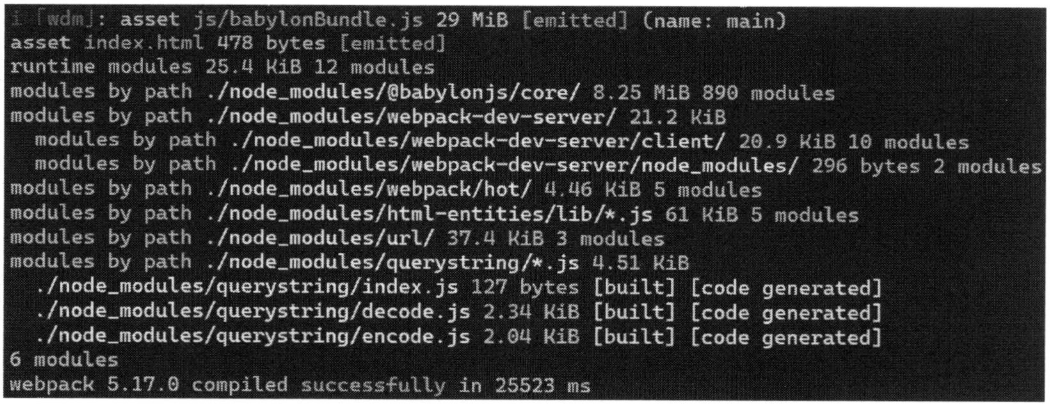

```
i [wdm]: asset js/babylonBundle.js 29 MiB [emitted] (name: main)
asset index.html 478 bytes [emitted]
runtime modules 25.4 KiB 12 modules
modules by path ./node_modules/@babylonjs/core/ 8.25 MiB 890 modules
modules by path ./node_modules/webpack-dev-server/ 21.2 KiB
  modules by path ./node_modules/webpack-dev-server/client/ 20.9 KiB 10 modules
  modules by path ./node_modules/webpack-dev-server/node_modules/ 296 bytes 2 modules
modules by path ./node_modules/webpack/hot/ 4.46 KiB 5 modules
modules by path ./node_modules/html-entities/lib/*.js 61 KiB 5 modules
modules by path ./node_modules/url/ 37.4 KiB 3 modules
modules by path ./node_modules/querystring/*.js 4.51 KiB
  ./node_modules/querystring/index.js 127 bytes [built] [code generated]
  ./node_modules/querystring/decode.js 2.34 KiB [built] [code generated]
  ./node_modules/querystring/encode.js 2.04 KiB [built] [code generated]
6 modules
webpack 5.17.0 compiled successfully in 25523 ms
```

Figure 3.2 – Webpack output after successful bundle

While the webpack development server is running, any changes you make to your source code will automatically refresh your browser. Leave the dev server running, because we're going to start making use of it!

Crafting a PG Snippet

Before we can use our PG code in our application, we're going to need to do some light refactoring. A little bit of preparation can save a lot of time later! The things we're going to change are select pieces of code that could vary between the PG and local environments, such as texture paths and URLs, along with some minor structural modifications. For your convenience, here's a link to the refactored snippet. If you are just joining us here in the journey, use the link below. If you've been following along, substitute your own snippet URL for the following one. Start by opening your favorite browser and navigating to either your own snippet or to `https://playground.babylonjs.com/#0UYAPE#42`.

Cleaning up the BABYLON Namespace Prefix

One of the things that you may have found annoying about coding in the PG is how in the PG it's necessary to always prefix BJS types with the BABYLON namespace. This is not ideal, but we can get rid of the need for them by adding an alias to all the various types we're using to the top of our snippet. The alias in our PG snippet will be defined as a `const` assembled from the various BJS types used:

```
const { Mesh,
MeshBuilder,
StandardMaterial,
// ...
} = BABYLON;
```

We can then do a Find and Replace (*Ctrl + F* or *Command + F*) for the string `BABYLON.` (don't forget the period!) and that will complete our work on this section. To preview where this is headed, when we move this into our VSCode environment, we'll convert this to an `import` statement. Doing this refactoring after the fact, like we are in this case, isn't ideal; in the future, we will start our snippets out with this construct and build it over time. That way, it won't be nearly as much effort!

Extracting Magic Strings

There are three separate textures (not including the procedural one) in use in our snippet, and we want to make it easier to change the specific URL or file path. We begin that by defining a set of `const` strings in the PG to contain the PG-specific paths:

```
const distortTexture = "textures/distortion.png";
const rockTextureN = "textures/rockn.png";
const rockTexture = "textures/rock.png";
```

We can then go into the `createStar` and `createPlanet` functions and replace the hardcoded paths with our constant expressions:

```
mat.diffuseTexture = new Texture(distortTexture, scene);
```

Once you've replaced all of the hardcoded string values, click **Save** and refresh the page to make sure the snippet still runs OK, paying attention to any missing textures, and fixing any missing references that may pop up. With these changes in place, it will be a smooth transition from running this in the PG to using it in our application.

Transitioning from the PG to the Application

The PG is a rich, robust, and extensible way to quickly get started writing and running code, but our application has different needs from the PG that we will need to account for and fulfill. We want to make sure that our code is both easy to change and easy to understand, but fortunately, there are small steps we can take that will make a large difference later on.

Creating the Engine Instance

Now, the immediate question is this: how do we take our plucky snippet here and plug it into our application without turning it into an exercise in both masochism and self-discipline? The secret lies in preparation. When we built our PG snippet, we structured logic as atomically as possible into various discrete **functions**, which have all their **dependencies** passed in as **parameters**. This will help us "lift-and-shift" the code into our application. First, though, we need to add some code to our `index.js` that will take the place of the PG's `engine` initialization. Add this to the file below the part where we created the `canvas` element:

```
let eng = new Engine(canvas, true, null, true);
let startScene = createStartScene(eng);
eng.runRenderLoop(() => {
    startScene.scene.render();
});
```

This is a pretty bog-standard Babylon.js `Engine` initialization. The `Engine` constructor has a number of interesting different parameters and configuration options that we'll explore further on down the road. For now, we are mostly using the engine defaults except for enabling **anti-aliasing** (the second parameter) and instructing the engine to adapt automatically to the device's viewport ratio (the last parameter). Although it's not yet part of the project, we've added the necessary call to `createStartScene` in anticipation of its imminent arrival.

Adding and Importing the StartScene

Create a new file in your project's `src` folder and name it `startscene.js`. Copy and paste everything from the PG snippet into this new file *except* the `createScene` function. A couple of minor modifications are all that's needed thanks to the groundwork we previously laid down!

Change the `const` to `import`, also replacing the `=` with `from "@babylonjs/core"` as the name to source imports. The `StarfieldProceduralTexture` isn't a part of the core BJS framework, so we'll also need to pull that entry out of the import list and give it its own entry: `import { StarfieldProceduralTexture } from "@babylonjs/procedural-textures";`.

The final change is to replace our `const` texture paths with `import` statements pointing to the appropriate texture in our `/assets/textures` folder.

> **Important Note**
>
> If you don't already have the three textures downloaded and in the asset directory, now would be a good time to do it. The URL prefix for textures is just `https://www.babylonjs-playground.com/textures/`, followed by the name of the texture with the extension, (e.g., `rock.png`). We want to be able to use consistent paths to refer to assets throughout the application, so we are using **Webpack** to resolve and supply the runtime URL to a given asset. The way we are telling Webpack to provide these URLs is via the `import` statement.
>
> Why don't we just use the online version of the resource instead of duplicating it locally? Good question. Later on in the book, we'll cover how to make Space-Truckers into a **Progressive Web Application** (**PWA**), and how to make assets available for offline use.

When the **Webpack bundle** is created, any assets referenced in one of these `import` statements will be included in the build output. In addition, the asset is assigned a unique filename that helps bust aggressive caches when assets are modified:

```
import distortTexture from
  "../assets/textures/distortion.png";
import rockTextureN from "../assets/textures/rockn.png";
import rockTexture from "../assets/textures/rock.png";
```

Exporting and Importing the Start Scene

One last item to add to our `startscene.js` and we'll be ready to finish wiring it into the game! If we reflect back on the overall design of our snippet's functions, we can readily see that the only "public" function need be the `createStartScene` function. Let's make that function available to consumers by adding `export default` to the function declaration:

```
export default function createStartScene(engine) {
```

Save the file and switch back to your `index.js`. Since we've already added the invocation of the `createStartScene` and the following **render loop**, all we need to do to make this complete is to add the following `import` to the top of the file's import list: `import createStartScene from "./startscene";`. Save the file and check that the **Webpack output** doesn't contain any errors. When your browser refreshes, you should see a familiar scene being rendered. Go ahead and give yourself a pat on the back – you've completed pulling in our main application background scene! There's something still missing, however, and that's something for visitors to see when they first arrive at the web page but before they launch the game. It would be sort of rude to just take over a visitor's browser and start downloading MBs of content without asking first, so we are going to put out a welcome mat in the form of the landing HTML page.

Constructing the Landing Page

Although it is web-based and hosted by a web server, there is a critical principle at play for Space-Truckers: the game that we haven't done much but hint at previously. That principle is that we want to, by all means necessary, avoid using the HTML DOM in the game. Now, to be fair, it's not a total blanket ban on using HTML or CSS anywhere, just anywhere important. The reason for this is we want to give our future selves a gift that makes it seamless to target Space-Truckers to Babylon Native; code that uses the HTML DOM isn't compatible with BJS Native. That said, there is still the need to do a little bit of HTML and CSS work to make the landing page a little bit more hospitable to visitors.

The Concept (Art)

When Space-Truckers was just in the process of being conceived as an idea, early concept sketches were useful in helping to establish various different aspects of the look, feel, and setting of the game. The following figure depicts what we want our landing page to look like:

Figure 3.3 – HTML landing page design

When a user navigates to the Space-Truckers website, they'll be presented with a centered image that functions in the same way that a book cover attempts to convey some sense of the book's content. A Call-to-Action button to Launch the game sits prominently and visibly in the center of the viewport, enticing the visitor to click the button and play the game. Lastly, we have a small site footer with the standard privacy, support, repository, license, copyright notices, and so on.

> **Note**
> We will want to structure our markup such that it will display appropriately on-screen dimensions ranging from the high dpi (but small screen size) of a smartphone or tablet to the much larger but lower resolutions offered by large-screen TVs and display monitors. Aspect ratios are important too!

Sticking the Landing

If all goes well, we'll end up with something similar to this for our landing page. We're not going to worry about fonts or background images right now as much as we want to get more of a sense of how we want to lay out and design various elements.

Figure 3.4 – The Space-Truckers landing page. Behind the foreground content are the animated orbiting planets created in Chapter 2, Ramping up on Babylon.js

To achieve this, there's some HTML markup along with CSS styles that need to be added to the /public/index.html page. There's an additional small change we'll need to make to the index.js file that will add a class of background-canvas to the newly created HTML Canvas that is appended to the document with canvas.classList.add("background-canvas");, so get that change out of the way and open up the public/index.html file in VSCode. There's enough that needs to be added that it would take up a prohibitive amount of page space, so at this point, you have a couple of options:

- Take the homework assignment and build out the HTML/CSS to get to the preceding screenshot

- Grab the finished files (there will be two or so in total, in addition to the index.js change) from https://github.com/jelster/space-truckers/tree/ch3-final

There isn't any right or wrong answer; it's whatever you will enjoy and learn from the most in the amount of time you have available that means the most and you're the only one who can decide what that is! Each chapter in this book has an accompanying branch (and tag) in Git. The purpose of leaving the entire branch with its commit history in place is to give you the opportunity to see how the code evolves, commit by commit, while avoiding adding too much noise to the main branch's commit history.

Summary

In a whirlwind of Webpack, ES6 Imports, and CSS shenanigans, we've completed a key process that started with a simple PG snippet and finished with an animated landing page. Along the way, we set up our local development scripts so we can take advantage of modern JavaScript features such as tree-shaking to optimize our package bundle sizes, while still being able to quickly integrate and view changes into the application.

What's next from here should be fairly obvious to anyone who has ever stood in front of a Big Red Button labeled "Launch". It's time to Push the Button, and make it do interesting things! Yes, we will be implementing our application's Launch-time experience, which involves establishing some mechanics of state in the application. Don't worry if you're not through with this section yet, there's more to be done!

Extended Topics

For the person looking to make the launch page their own or who wants to dive deeper into the potential possibilities opened up by this chapter, here are some things you might consider doing:

- Add a cool hover-in/out effect to the launch button so that when the cursor hovers over it, a color and/or animated effect is applied. Do the same for clicking the button.

- Improve the landing page's navigational structure with links to the GitHub repos, and so on.

- Make the central hero area into an image carousel that can be populated with additional concept art, screenshots, gameplay videos, and so on.

- Use CSS to blend the canvas animation with the hero image in an interesting fashion. You can do different types of blending, such as difference, exclusion, screen, and so on, along with other cool transformations.

4
Creating the Application

The Space-Truckers application needs to be capable of maintaining and transitioning between a set of discrete states that correspond with different screens, such as a Menu screen and a Game screen. Transitions between application states typically occur as a result of user interaction (e.g., the user selects a menu item) or as part of something such as an application launch or exit. Here, we derive our basic application flow, which we then use to build a basic framework for presenting and transitioning between arbitrary screens.

In the first chapter, we saw the complete Space-Truckers game in all its glory and beauty. We then immediately went on to create the loading screen's animation in the Playground before slowing down a bit to build out the supporting application infrastructure that the game will need. It may feel seem to be a bit of a let-down that we've been focusing so much on things that aren't part of the game's design, and it's natural to want to focus on activities such as bringing in 3D models and textures or programming game mechanics. Fear not – we will be getting there in the not-too-distant future! *Part 2: Constructing the Game* is all about those sorts of topics, but without the work from this chapter and the accompanying ones, there would be nothing to tie together a thematically connected collection of interesting Playground snippets and code fragments.

> **Important Note**
>
> This chapter will represent even more of a shift in how the code and content are presented. From here on out, code listings will tend towards displaying fragments or highlighting interesting areas of a larger piece of code. A link to the repository or Playground will always be provided so you can check your work or use the code to skip ahead!

The work of this section and chapter is to build the necessary pieces of software and logic to allow a cohesive and compelling experience to emerge from the individual pieces. Over the course of this chapter, we will write code to implement state management and transitioning logic to support the future development of the core game mechanics under these headings:

- Adding a Custom Loading UI
- Space-Truckers: The State Machine
- Space-Truckers: The Main Menu
- Integrating the Main Menu

Technical Requirements

For this chapter, we'll continue to use the development process covered in *Chapter 3, Establishing the Development Workflow*. If you're just joining us on the journey or haven't been writing code on your own, you can catch up by cloning or checking out the `ch3-final` tag from Space-Truckers: The GitHub Repository at `https://github.com/jelster/space-truckers/tree/ch3-final`. Before writing any code for the material in this chapter, it's typically a good idea to create a new **git** branch that tracks the previous chapter's **branch** or **tag**. This is unusual, as you would normally set up your branch to track **develop** or **main**. In this case, however, you want to be comparing commits from a specific point in the repository's commit history prior to where you're starting, and not everything that comes afterward has been covered yet.

Adding a Custom Loading UI

As we start to gain some traction and therefore momentum, we first have to let our engines rev up before we can think about shifting gears. A short exercise in code management is just the thing to get those RPMs up! Once we've hit our sweet spot, we're going to cruise straight into leveraging that work to build our loading screen. Remember, as we progress through the metaphorical gearbox of complexity, we'll be seeing fewer details such as the following while at the same time covering greater amounts of ground.

Solo Exercise: Refactoring the StartScene to Extract the AstroFactory

To lay the groundwork for this and some future features, we want to extract all the logic involved in creating new planets that aren't specific to the scene from the **startScene**. That logic goes into a new **astroFactory** class. The essentials of this refactoring are straightforward, but the key to it all is going to be creating an array of planetary data objects, then looping through that array, calling the **AstroFactory**'s various methods to compose the scene's objects. Consider performing this refactoring a bit of a special exercise or challenge, but don't sweat it too much. The idea is to try and apply the new knowledge, not to assign passing or failing grades! Alternatively, if you don't feel you need the practice or want to skip this exercise, start your code by checking out and examining the patch diff at the following commit URL: `https://github.com/jelster/space-truckers/commit/9821811`. Take the time you need to understand the material, but don't forget to come back for the rest of the chapter and book!

The CustomLoadingScreen Type

Babylon.js provides a default loading UI that appears automatically during **AssetContainer** operations, or manually by calling the `engine.displayLoadingUI()` method. Either way that it is invoked, we're going to replace the default loading UI with one of our own devising. The Babylon.js docs specify the specifics of the **LoadingScreen** TypeScript interface that will be implemented in JavaScript, but there are really only two that are required: `displayLoadingUI()` and `hideLoadingUI()` – do those look familiar or what? Add a new JS file to the project's source and name it **SpaceTruckerLoadingScreen**. Before declaring the **class**, add an **import** for the `createStartScene` function from our old friend, **startscene.js**.

The **CustomLoadingScreen** we'll be implementing will use it to host the planets animating on the render canvas during loading operations. Declare the **SpaceTruckerLoadingScreen** class and define a constructor for it that takes an `engine` instance (required by the `createStartScene` method). In the constructor, we'll initialize and assign some class-level properties for later use – including `_startScene`:

```
constructor(engine) {
    this._totalToLoad = 0.00;
    this._loadingText = "Loading Space-Truckers: The Video
        Game...";
    this._currentAmountLoaded = 0.00;
    this._engine = engine;
    this._startScene = createStartScene(engine);
}
```

That takes care of constructing the loading screen. Now, we need to implement the LoadingScreen interface's members to show and hide the UI at the appropriate times. This is just done by having the show and hide methods toggle an `_active` Boolean flag; we'll let other code that we'll write shortly decide what to do about it:

```
displayLoadingUI() {
    this._active = true;
}
hideLoadingUI() {
    this._active = false;
}
```

The last thing needed is to conditionally render the scene. Since we have the engine instance passed into the constructor, we will add a simple render routine to call `runRenderLoop` at the end of the constructor:

```
engine.runRenderLoop(() => {
    if (this._startScene && this._active === true) {
        this._startScene.scene.render();
    }
});
```

We've gotten the bulk of the work done, but there's still a bit more to do before we can call this a done task.

Enhancing the Loading Screen with Progress Display

We've added what is called a non-deterministic progress bar, but what if we want to display some text along with a percentage of assets loaded? Though our project doesn't quite yet have said assets, it soon will. Fortunately, there are only a couple of small things we need to do in order to support this when it's needed.

Adding Property Getters

The **SpaceTruckerLoadingScreen** class already contains definitions for properties to hold the data we're interested in, but it makes for a lot more maintainable design if we make these fields available as properties. The only one we need to make available in this fashion is `loadingUIText`; it will be potentially invoked or queried by external code. While we're at it though, let's add additional getters as follows:

```
get progressAvailable() {
    return this._progressAvailable;
}
get currentAmountLoaded() {
    return this._currentAmountLoaded;
}
get totalToLoad() {
    return this._totalToLoad;
}
get loadingUIText() {
    return this._loadingText;
}
```

A sharp eye may notice that the `progressAvailable` getter uses a field we didn't define in the constructor. The place where this is set and managed is the same place where `currentAmountLoaded` and `totalToLoad` get their values from – the `onProgressHandler` function.

Handling Progress

`onProgressHandler` is an event handler that gets subscribed to HTTP and other Progress events emitted by various Babylon.js components such as `AssetManager` and `SceneLoader`:

```
onProgressHandler(evt) {
    this._progressAvailable = evt.lengthComputable === true;
    this._currentAmountLoaded = evt.loaded || this.
        currentAmountLoaded;
    this._totalToLoad = evt.total || this.
        currentAmountLoaded;
    if (this._progressAvailable) {
        this._loadingText = "Loading Space-Truckers:
            The Video Game... " + ((this._current
                AmountLoaded / this._totalToLoad) * 100).
                    toFixed(2);
    }
}
```

The `evt` event data object is used to set the `progressAvailable` property value. If the progress event doesn't have a computable length, `currentAmountLoaded` is set to 0 (false) if incomplete and 1 (true) if complete. Otherwise, it's set to the number of bytes loaded. If we can calculate the percentage loaded, we do so and set the `loadingUIText` backing field accordingly. The final piece of the loading screen is displaying `loadingText` and the progress string (if it's available).

Displaying Loading Text and Progress

To display text in our scene, we'll use the Babylon.js **2D GUI** system. There's going to be a lot more on this later in this chapter, so for now, copy and paste this at the end of the constructor for **SpaceTruckerLoadingScene**:

```
this._textContainer = AdvancedDynamicTexture.CreateFullscre
    enUI("loadingUI", true, this._startScene.scene);
const textBlock = new TextBlock("textBlock", this._
    loadingText);
textBlock.fontSize = "62pt";
textBlock.color = "antiquewhite";
```

```
textBlock.verticalAlignment = Container.VERTICAL_ALIGNMENT_
    BOTTOM;
textBlock.paddingTop = "15%";
this._textContainer.addControl(textBlock);
```

All we're doing here is creating a new `AdvancedDynamicTexture` sized to the render canvas, then adding a **TextBlock** that we apply a couple of size, color, and placement adjustments to before adding it to the texture's control collection.

> **Note**
> `onProgressHandler` will update the `loadingUIText` value if it's available.

We've completed the loading screen functionality, now it's time to wire it up globally in the `index.js` component. This is just one line of code that is added right after the `eng` instance is created:

```
const eng = new Engine(canvas, true, null, true);
logger.logInfo("Created BJS engine");
eng.loadingScreen = new SpaceTruckerLoadingScreen(eng);
```

That's all there is to it! Now, any time that a piece of code asks the Engine to show the loading UI, our little planet animations will be shown. Though it may seem to be a minor piece of functionality, completing this part of the application leaves us ready to change the pace a bit and examine the ins and outs of how we're going to manage the overall behavior of Space-Truckers: The Application.

Space-Truckers: The State Machine

People who have some familiarity with game development may be familiar with the idea of a game being structured around a series of loops. An Update loop runs the simulation and physics, moving objects and applying effects according to the latest update. A render loop is when the scene is actually drawn to the screen. We've seen examples of this previously, such as when we add event observers for the **scene.onBeforeRenderObservable**, but that's at a lower level than what we're looking at currently. Our application is going to be a host for multiple different BJS scenes and it will therefore need a way to periodically update the application's state as well as tell the active scene to render. Finally, it must be able to manage to transition between different scenes.

An application of the kind we're building has some implicit requirements when it comes to how it responds to input and evolves its internal state over time. For instance, when a player selects a menu item or exits their current game, the system must respond by altering (or "mutating") its data to fill and render a submenu, or by returning to the main menu. Implicit requirements make for poorly designed software, so we're going to start by making the implicit explicit.

Logging Interlude

Our application is about to get more complex, so it's a good time to begin adding basic instrumentation and debugging messages – we can always enhance and refine the logging routines later, but not having them at all is a much more difficult place to begin the more code we write. The source file `logger.js` with its exported class, `ConsoleProxy`, is an incredibly basic wrapper around the console object that provides functions to log different levels of log messages (INFO, WARN, ERROR, and FATAL) to the console (if present). Each of the different logging methods has an identical body (if this bothers you, fix it and open a PR! The beauty of open source software in action), so in the interest of saving space, only one of the functions will be shown in the following code:

```
class ConsoleProxy {
    constructor(console) {
        this._console = console;
        this._consoleIsPresent = this._console == true;
        this._messageBuffer = [];
    }

    logInfo(message) {
        const logObj = { type: "INFO", message: message};
        if (this._consoleIsPresent) {
            this._console.log(logObj);
            return;
        }
        this._messageBuffer.push(message);
    }
// ...
}
const theProxy = new ConsoleProxy(console);
export default theProxy;
```

Most of the preceding code is pretty bog-standard – the sort of thing you'd see in almost any home-brew application framework. The `constructor` accepts a `console` parameter, which it uses to set a presence flag. This is because it's not always guaranteed that the `console` object will be available, and we don't want any logging calls to fail and cause problems with the rest of the application if that were to be the case. The `_messageBuffer` array is used as a fall-back when the console isn't available. In this case, application logging can still be accessed by attaching a debugger and reading the contents of the log array. Should it be required, this can easily be extended to suit the scenario at hand. Outside of the **class** definition, a new const instance, `theProxy`, is instantiated before being exported as a single object. Consumers of the logger don't instantiate a new log instance – they just call **logger.logXXX**. When using this logger in Playground snippets, don't forget to omit the last `export default` line and change `theProxy` to `logger`. We'll want to have this handy for the next part so that we can easily test and verify proper code behavior, or you can refer to snippet **#EK321G** as a starting reference template.

Generators and function* Iterators

From the perspective of software design, we will be thinking about our State Machine as a type of **iterator**, or a type of looping construct where each iteration **yields** the next (or current) state, also allowing callers to specify state conditions. The JavaScript language construct that gives us this functionality is known as a **Generator** function, or a **function***.

The MDN Web Docs at `https://developer.mozilla.org/en-US/docs/Web/JavaScript/Reference/Statements/function*` say this about Generators and their behavior:

> *"Generators are functions that can be exited and later re-entered. Their context (variable bindings) will be saved across re-entrances…"*

> *"When the iterator's* `next()` *method is called, the generator function's body is executed until the first* `yield` *expression, which specifies the value to be returned from the iterator"*

> *"Calling the* `next()` *method with an argument will resume the generator function execution, replacing the* `yield` *expression where an execution was paused with the argument from* `next()` *"*

> *"A* `return` *statement in a generator, when executed, will make the generator finish"*

Writing a Generator function

It's more helpful to see actual code than it is to read descriptions of it, so let's start up a new Playground Snippet and lay down some code. Using the base PG snippet (**#EK321G**), add some room in the createScene function for our Generator function stub:

```
function* appStateMachine() {
    let currentState = "INDETERMINATE";
    yield currentState;
    yield currentState + "-POST";
    yield "DONE";
}
```

Remember that when the body of this function is executed, control is transferred any time a yield statement is encountered. The value is returned by the iterator – in the form of an object with a structure that looks as follows: { value: <yielded value>, done: false|true }. In the preceding code, we define and set a local variable, currentState, before **yielding** its value. Execution stops in this method until **next** is called on the **iterator**, at which point the code immediately yields back a modified version of the currentState variable. After execution resumes, the code once again yields back – this time with the phrase "DONE" before implicitly **returning**.

Using the Generator

To best illustrate some of the non-intuitive behavior of **iterator functions**, let's write two different ways of using the appStateMachine Generator we just defined. Follow along in your own Playground or skip ahead and load up the result of this sub-section as the next snippet revision (we started with 0) – **#EK321G#1**.

The first – and arguably the simplest – method of using our appStateMachine Generator is to use the **for…of** ES6 iteration construct to progressively swap execution through each yield statement:

```
let index = 0;
const asm = appStateMachine();
for (const a of asm) {
    logger.logInfo("Index " + index++, a);
}
```

In the previous snippet, the value of the index variable is logged to the console before being incremented as a convenient way of displaying the behavior of the code. Open your browser's Developer Tools and look at the console output after clicking **Run**. The output should look similar to this:

```
{type: "INFO", message: "Index 0"} "INDETERMINATE"
{type: "INFO", message: "Index 1"} "INDETERMINATE-POST"
{type: "INFO", message: "Index 2"} "DONE"
```

You can see from the progression of the Index value from 0 to 2 shows how the yield statement is switching the code execution between the generator function and the for...of loop. This means of iterating over the generator works best for situations where the looping logic doesn't need to do a lot of heavy lifting or if the code that you're writing needs to coordinate many different asynchronous operations in the correct order and you don't need fine control over the iteration.

An alternative use instead of iterating over the generated function is to manually call the next() function to transfer control. Each time it is called is equivalent to an iteration of the looping construct discussed previously, but recall that the difference is that instead of directly getting whatever value was part of the yield statement, an iterator object is returned with value and done properties:

```
const asm2 = appStateMachine();
let s0 = asm2.next();
let s1 = asm2.next();
let s2 = asm2.next();
let s3 = asm2.next();
logger.logInfo("s0", s0);
logger.logInfo("s1", s1);
logger.logInfo("s2", s2);
logger.logInfo("s3", s3);
```

Running this leads to an identical output to the prior code, but with an extra value. Instead of only having three separate index values, this approach leaves you with four:

```
{type: "INFO", message: "s3"} {value: undefined, done: true}
```

This "s3" object doesn't have a value, and it has the done flag set to true, indicating the sequence is complete. Any further calls to asm2.next() will return the same undefined value and true flag. The advantage of this approach is that consumers of the Generator have a lot of control over when and how to call next(), which is a critical feature that we're about to use when we create our first State Machine.

The Definition of a State Machine

A core concept in computer science a **Finite State Machine (FSM)** – or just a **State Machine** – is defined and characterized, for our purposes, by these important attributes:

1. The system can only ever be in one state at any given time.

2. The State Machine has a finite number of possible states. For practical purposes, at a minimum, there is an initial state and a final state for the system.

3. Transitions between states are triggered in response to commands, external input, or other changes in the environment (e.g., time passing).

4. Before a frame is rendered, the State Machine should be updated with the latest information about the state.

Let's look at each of these points in some more detail.

One State at a Time

This is pretty self-explanatory. A given state machine may only be in a single state, no matter how many possible states could be valid – there is no mixing, aggregated, or hybrid types of state. In code terms, this means our state machine will have a single field or property to represent its current state. This is not to say that a particular state machine can't have attributes that themselves have their own states (e.g., an animation might be in the RUNNING state), just that the state machine as a whole will only be classified as being in a single state at any given time. At the time of writing, quantum computing has not yet reached mainstream availability, neatly avoiding any discussion of potential eigenstates – a probabilistic combination of potential states – and keeping the subject matter firmly rooted in classical computational theory.Phew, what a relief!

Finite Number of States, Start and Finish

There needs to be an initial state for the machine to begin in and there should also be an end state. Technically, the end state and the initial state can be the same, but it doesn't make for very interesting or relevant software. In between the start and finish can be any number of states, although to keep things practical, we'll only be looking to define a small handful of them.

Transitions Happen When Something Happens

It sounds silly, but it's true. During the course of a given Update cycle, the application or game logic may receive input events that trigger a state transition. Part of our FSM's definition is the logic to invoke any given state transition. That implies our code will contain methods for transitions that have names such as `goToMainMenu`.

> **Note**
>
> If it helps, try to think of a state as being a short-hand way of describing a single, discrete combination of the system's internal data. State transitions are the logic controlling the mutation of one combination of internal data into another different arrangement of data.

Updating the State Machine

Wrapping it all up is the mechanism by which we can progress or evolve the machine's state on a frequent basis. Because we're going to be managing multiple scenes, we can't use something such as `scene.onPreRenderObservable`, as we've already done for things such as animating the planetary orbits. Instead, we'll make use of the `engine.runRenderLoop` callback as a way of ensuring that our update logic is invoked no matter which scene is being rendered. This also fulfills the requirement of updating the state before rendering the frame quite nicely.

> **Important Note**
>
> If you need to ensure that animations and physics are synchronized or if you need framerate-independent rendering, you'll need to ensure that you do both of the following things:
>
> a) Set the `deterministicLockstep` flag of the options parameter when creating the Engine instance
>
> b) Use `onBeforeStep` along with the `onAfterStep` observables instead of the `onPre/onAfterRenderObservable` sets to perform state updates

With the knowledge of how we're going to build the next part of our application, it's time to look at the specifics of our design and start to prototype the Playground snippet.

Space-Truckers: The Application State Diagram

Before we dive into writing code for our FSM, we should take a moment to figure out just what it is that we're going to need to build. An important distinction we need to make out of the gate is between the gameplay and non-gameplay sections of the application. The gameplay will have its own state machine to manage the different phases of play, and each phase in turn can have its own mini-state machine. It's state machines all the way down! The following diagram shows each state and how they transition between them. The circles in the diagram represent events or transitions triggered by external input, such as a user clicking a button:

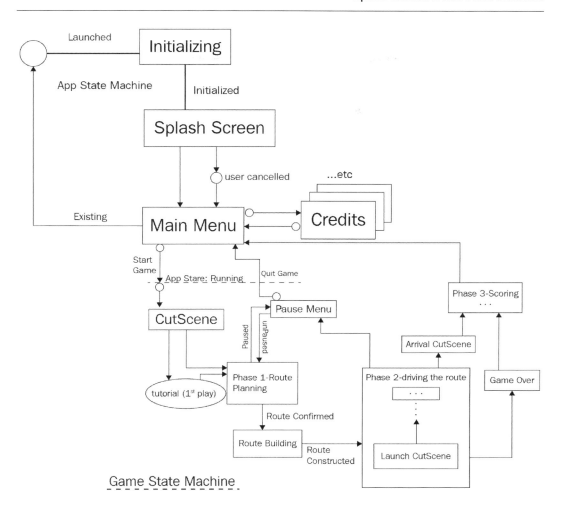

Figure 4.1 – A State diagram, from the early Space-Truckers design process, showing the
application and game state – transitions between states (lines and arrows) happen sequentially
(such as Initialized) or as the result of an input event (such as user Cancelled)

For now, we'll disregard the lower portion of the diagram. Being an early iteration, some of it (that is, the cut scenes) is at any rate aspirational. Looking at the diagram's upper portion, if we consider that the Loading Screen is in the **Initializing** state then we can see a 1:1 correspondence between the states and application screens. It should also start to become clearer how each screen also corresponds to a BJS scene. Reasoning along these lines, we can generalize the different **CutScene** and **Splash Screen** items as simply being two separate instances of the same thing (save with different actual content, but that's not relevant here). Here are the screens and scenes from the diagram that we've identified so far:

App State	Screen/Scene	Transitions From	Transitions To
CREATED	n/a	n/a	INITIALIZING
INITIALIZING	Loading UI	CREATED	CUTSCENE
CUTSCENE	Splash Scene	INITIALIZING	MENU
MENU	Main Menu	CUTSCENE	CUTSCENE
CUTSCENE	Intro Scene	MENU	RUNNING
RUNNING	Varies	CUTSCENE	MENU
EXITING	n/a	MENU	n/a

Figure 4.2 – A table of application-level states and transition rules

This may look like a lot to take in, but it's really not as complicated as it seems. It's time to open up **VSCode** and start adding some new code. You can either follow along here or if you would rather just copy, paste, and modify existing code, go to snippet **#EK321G#6**. Bear in mind that you'll need to make similar types of adaptations to the snippet as we made in the previous chapter as you progress through incorporating the snippet into your code.

Almost Infinitely Looping State

The first thing we're going to add to our project is the **AppStates** enumeration. This is a simple object defining constants and values for the different states in the preceding table. Add a new file, appstates.js, to the project's /src directory. Since this is a very simple and unchanging object, we can use Object.freeze to ensure that the values aren't changed at runtime:

```
export default Object.freeze({
    CREATED: 0,
    INITIALIZING: 2,
    CUTSCENE: 3,
    MENU: 4,
    RUNNING: 5,
    EXITING: 6
});
```

After adding the **AppStates** enumeration, add a new file, spaceTruckerApplication.js, to contain a class definition named (surprise!) SpaceTruckerApplication:

```
class SpaceTruckerApplication {
}
```

This class is the central class of this application (as the name implies). It will be growing much larger as time passes, so treasure it in all of its adorable brevity while you can before breaking ground on it by defining our `appStateMachine` function*. Add a function* definition inside the class for it.

As we discussed earlier, a state machine needs to have one and only one current state. It becomes very useful in state calculations to be able to compare the present state to whatever value the previous state was, so in the body of the function* Generator, add a couple of variable declarations to contain those values, along with a helper function to change them:

```
function* appStateMachine() {
        let previousState = null;
        let currentState = null;
        function setState(newState) {
            previousState = currentState;
            currentState = newState;
            logger.logInfo("App state changed. Previous
                state:" + previousState + "
                    New state: " + newState);
            return newState;
        }
}
// … create scene, camera return scene
```

We can now turn our attention to the state machine's output – what it will yield back to callers. Our little sample earlier would simply stop (returning `done: true`) once it had reached the end of its sequence, but we want our FSM to run for as long as the application is running, and we don't know ahead of time how many times that means calling the Generator's `next()` method. The way we address this is by placing that call inside of an infinite loop.

Each time, the loop first starts by receiving input from the caller to indicate the desired `nextState` – the caller does this by passing the value as an argument to **next** – and assuming the state is valid, then our `setState` method makes the actual state change. Once that happens, the code checks to see whether the conditions have been met to reach the end state (`AppStates.EXITING`), returning the `currentState` if so – otherwise, it will `yield` back to the caller at the top of the loop:

```
while (true) {
    let nextState = yield;
      if (nextState !== null && nextState !== undefined) {
            setState(nextState);
            if (nextState === AppStates.EXITING) {
                return currentState;
```

```
            }
        }
    }
```

Our state machine implementation is done (for now), and now it's time to hook-up the supporting application logic.

Adding the Constructor and Supporting Logic

We need to initialize the state machine by creating a function from our Generator along with other creation tasks, so add a constructor to our new class. Because we are creating and managing scenes with this class, we need to take in **BABYLON.Engine** as a parameter in the constructor and initialize the private property, _engine, with it. While we're here, we might as well call the Generator and add a field for tracking which scene to render. Finally, the last action in the constructor is to transition the state of the application from its previous value of undefined to CREATED. We'll do this by invoking the to-be-created moveNextAppState function (see the following code block):

```
constructor(engine) {
    this._engine = engine;
    this._currentScene = null;
    this._stateMachine = this.appStateMachine();
    this.moveNextAppState(AppStates.CREATED);
}
```

It can be cumbersome to have to write statements such as this._stateMachine.next(). value, and worse, it reveals the internal implementation details to code that doesn't need to know about that sort of stuff, making it harder to make changes in the future. Let's insulate the rest of our code from having to deal with that by adding some accessor properties to retrieve currentState and activeScene. Also as mentioned previously, we will add the moveNextAppState helper method to help us to hide the passing of values to and from the state machine:

```
    get currentState() {
        return this._stateMachine.next();
    }

    get activeScene() {
        return this._currentScene;
    }

    moveNextAppState(state) {
```

```
        return this._stateMachine.next(state).value;
}
```

Something important to note before we move any further is that the application must respect its boundaries as far as not trying to perform heavy loading tasks during construction time.

That type of task is reserved for `AppStates.INITIALIZING`, and the reason for this is crucial to the user experience. We don't want to do anything that might transfer large amounts of data to the client until they've affirmatively decided to launch the game. That respects people who might be curious about the game and are on limited data or a limited bandwidth connection and enforces a clean separation between the HTML-based landing page and the WebGPU or WebGL-based game.

> **Important Note**
> The state diagram we looked at earlier *starts* when the user clicks the **Launch** button on our landing page.

The effect of clicking the landing page's **Launch** button is a mini-transition in and of itself – a transition between the DOM-focused HTML page and the Canvas-rendered game application. The first step towards implementing this is to add a new function we'll name `run` to the `SpaceTruckerApplication` class. This is the place where we hook the engine's `runRenderLoop` callback up with our `applicationStateMachine`:

```
run() {
    this._engine.runRenderLoop(() => {
        // update loop
        let state = this.currentState;
        switch (state) {
            case AppStates.CREATED:
            case AppStates.INITIALIZING:
                break;
            case AppStates.CUTSCENE:
                break;
            case AppStates.MENU:
                break;
            case AppStates.RUNNING:
                break;
            case AppStates.EXITING:
                break;
            default:
```

```
                    break;
            }
        this._currentScene?.render();
    });
}
```

Within the runRenderLoop callback, we retrieve the currentState by using the getter method to call the _applicationStateMachine.next() function without any parameters. There's not much to see at the moment, but the stubbed-out switch statement shows where each state is handled. The first two, CREATED and INITIALIZING, are grouped because they are not rendered – or at least in the case of INITIALIZING, the loading UI is the rendered output of that state. Once scene selection and management have been completed, the render() method of the _currentScene (if present) is called.

Wiring the initial call to run is done with two lines that we'll add to the index.js file. There's some cleanup of now-obsolete code needed too – we don't want index.js calling createStartScene, nor do we want it interacting with the engine's render loop. After creating and setting up SpaceTruckerLoadingScreen, declare and instantiate a new instance of SpaceTruckerApplication. Since it's pretty well named as a type, just call it theApp. Next, add a line to invoke theApp.run() in the **Launch** button's click handler. It can be useful to add logging statements at key areas in the code to help in understanding the app's runtime behavior during development, so make liberal use of them! This is the basic framework for our application's state management functionality all wired up and ready to be filled with more interesting states and behaviors. To that end, it's time to start fleshing out these states and behaviors as we get ready to build the Main Menu.

Writing the Initialize logic

Returning to the State Diagram, once the application has finished initialization, it should transition to displaying the opening splash screen (cut scene) before transitioning to the Main Menu again. This is a nice linear progression, so it is simple to implement with the aid of the await ES6 feature.

Since the INITIALIZING state is the first state after construction, it should be the first thing that happens in the run() method. With this change, we'll also need to mark the run() method as async to allow us to use this language feature, so change the first few lines of the function to match the following:

```
async run() {
    await this.initialize();
    // ...
```

Now, add the function for `initialize`. We want this method to accomplish several tasks, some of which we will be simulating for the time being. Another method stub, `goToMainMenu`, helps us to complete the first part of the state diagram with what we will build next:

```
async initialize() {
    this._engine.enterFullscreen(true);
    this._engine.displayLoadingUI();
    this.moveNextAppState(AppStates.INITIALIZING)
    // for simulating loading times
    const p = new Promise((res, rej) => {
        setTimeout(() => res(), 5000);
    });

    await p;
    this._engine.hideLoadingUI();
    this.goToMainMenu();
}
```

First, we request a fullscreen session from the engine. This is equivalent to the user selecting their web browser's fullscreen option, which we want to do before we have to do any serious rendering – applying canvas scaling or a size change is faster when there's not anything being rendered yet. Next, we want to display the engine's Loading UI – which if you recall, we've replaced with our own custom loading UI in our codebase.

> **Note**
> When running this in the Playground, the default Babylon.js loading UI will be displayed instead of our customized one.

After that, we are officially into the `INITITIALIZING` state, so we transition to that state by calling `moveNextAppState` with the new state. Lastly, we are simulating a 5-second load time by creating a new `Promise` that resolves after the timeout period. We `await` this to occur before hiding the loading UI and then initiating the next state transition to the `MENU` state.

Transitioning to the Main Menu

The goToMainMenu function definition is very simple, as it has a very specific task. It needs to create an instance of the (soon-to-be-created) MainMenuScene class before transitioning to the MENU state. Add the following function definition to the class:

```
goToMainMenu() {
    this._engine.displayLoadingUI();
    this._mainMenu = new MainMenuScene(this._engine);
    this._engine.hideLoadingUI();
    this.moveNextAppState(AppStates.MENU);
}
```

There's one more change needed before we can finish wiring up our state machine. In our main Update loop, under the AppStates.MENU case statement, we need to set the _currentScene value to our Main Menu's scene:

```
case AppStates.MENU:
    this._currentScene = this._mainMenu.scene;
    break;
```

Of course, this doesn't currently exist, and now's a good time to address that deficiency! Create another new JS file, mainMenuScene.js, and add a stub class to the snippet called MainMenuScene. Implement its constructor to take an engine instance; it should also create a new **Scene** instance that is exposed via a public **get** accessor named scene. To keep the scene happy, create a new ArcRotateCamera, using the final parameter of its constructor to set the camera as the scene's default. To blend with the existing background, we'll also set scene.clearColor to an opaque black with **RGBA** values of 0, 0, 0, and 1 respectively. The camera distance parameter is set to -30 and seems somewhat arbitrary – however, the value will be important soon when we are rendering an animated background. This is how your class definition should look after putting in the basic elements (don't forget to add import statements for Scene, Vector3, and ArcRotateCamera, and to add from "@babylonjs/core" to the top of the file and export default MainMenuScene to the bottom!):

```
class MainMenuScene {
    get scene() {
        return this._scene;
    }
    constructor(engine) {
        this._engine = engine;
        let scene = this._scene = new Scene(engine);
```

```
            const camera = new ArcRotateCamera("menuCam",
                0, 0, -30, Vector3.Zero(), scene, true);
        }
    }
export default MainMenuScene;
```

Check to make sure there aren't any syntax errors or other issues, and make sure to save and commit your work. Things are about to get more interesting here!

The final listing for our basic state machine is in snippet **#EK321G#6**. Don't be fooled by the seeming lack of accomplishment – it's not always wise to gauge progress using visual indicators. We've laid the foundations with this groundwork that will help with our future efforts, which will make more sense as we seek to coordinate between multiple scenes and screens. The first screen that we're going to build is the Main Menu, which on our diagram isn't the next state in the sequence – the splash scene is what comes next on it – but we will be returning to that after we've built some of the display and transitioning logic that we're going to need as part of building cut scenes.

Space-Truckers: The Main Menu

One of the primary features that pretty much every single video game in existence has in common with each other is that they all have a Main Menu. Space-Truckers is to be no exception, but we first have to sit down and figure out how we want our menu to look before we can make it. We start with a basic concept sketch of the layout and elements of the menu, which we'll then use as a guidepost for building out a PG snippet of the menu. From the background to the foreground, we'll build up a GUI menu display progressively, adding containers, a title block, and then buttons that will be ready to practically drag and drop into the codebase!

Basic Design

Firstly, let's think about the application's navigational structure. Consulting our State Diagram (*Fig. 4.1*), we can see that there are a couple of different branches that the state can transition to from the Menu AppState. With the exception of the initial transition into the Main Menu, each of the paths represent a different menu item or selection option:

- Transitioning from **MENU** to **Running** will be user-triggered by clicking a **PLAY** button.

- Exiting the application is triggered by clicking an **EXIT** button.

- Additional menus are accessed by clicking their respective buttons. Initially, we'll only be creating a **High Scores** sub-menu.

Appearance-wise, we want to make the menu functionally attractive and to show a bit of dynamic behavior over time, both in the foreground and the background. Another consideration is that because players may be using a gamepad or controller instead of a keyboard and mouse, we'll want to have a **selection indicator** that shows the player which menu item will be invoked by clicking or pressing the appropriate button on their controllers. The following sketch shows how this may look without any background:

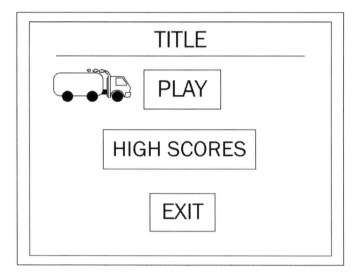

Figure 4.3 – A Main Menu design sketch

To help the menu stand out against the background, we'll fill it with a gradient or other semi-opaque image, as well as give the container a border.

The background doesn't need to have a lot going on – time and bandwidth constraints are likely to put this particular piece of content on a low-priority track. That's OK because we can quickly and easily put something in place that looks pretty good and does what we want – do you remember our old friend the **Starfield Procedural Texture** (**PT**)? We'll use it to give the menu a cool space-themed background, and then we'll animate it to give the illusion of travel.

Switch back to the Playground in your web browser and click the **New** icon to create a new snippet for our Main Menu.

Setting up the Main Menu snippet

Knowing how we plan to transport the code in our snippet into our codebase at some point is a great opportunity to invest the time and effort into making the process as quick, reliable, and accurate as possible.

We can start with this by defining some aliases for the various BABYLON components and namespaces at the top of our snippet, just as we did back in *Chapter 3*, *Establishing the Development Workflow*:

```
const {
    Color4,
    Vector3,
    ArcRotateCamera,
    Scene
} = BABYLON;
```

There will be more items to add to this list as we involve additional **Babylon.js** APIs, so don't forget to update this list when that happens! Below the alias declarations in the snippet, copy and paste just the MainMenuScene class definition from your local file.

> **Note**
> The items in the alias list that we just defined will need to be converted into **import** statements when integrated into the codebase.

When we're ready to integrate and commit our changes, we'll update the local files by essentially performing the same thing in reverse. In the snippet's createScene function, instantiate a new instance of MainMenuScene and return its scene property, and that will hook up our budding MainMenuScene class into the snippet's rendering loop:

```
var createScene = function () {
    const mainMenu = new MainMenuScene(engine);
    return mainMenu.scene;
};
```

Short and sweet, we don't have to think about this part of the snippet ever again.

Building the Background

We'll start with the general environment and background setup for the scene, so scroll back up to the class definition and add a new instance method named _setupBackgroundEnvironment. This is where we will instantiate and configure the Starfield PT that serves as the background for the screen. It's also where we'll set up the texture to animate gradually over time to give the illusion of traveling through the starfield.

Invoke `this._setupBackgroundEnvironment()` at the end of the constructor so we can use the run button immediately to see results. Before coding the body of the function though, add these types to the top alias definition list:

- `HemisphericLight`
- `StarfieldProceduralTexture` (put on its own line, you'll thank yourself later)
- `StandardMaterial`
- `CylinderBuilder`
- `Texture`

The scene already has a camera placed at -30 units from the origin and pointing at the origin, but it's going to need a light and something for that light to illuminate as well. Instead of using a cubical mesh as a skybox, as we did with the Loading Screen, we'll create a conical sort of shape made by making a tube with different radii for each end cap. Applying the Starfield PT to the interior of the cylinder requires us to set `backFaceCulling` to `false`, since we want to see the interior faces. To animate the starfield, we can simply increment the `time` property of `StarfieldProceduralTexture` before every frame is rendered:

```
_setupBackgroundEnvironment() {
    const light = new HemisphericLight("light", new Vector3
        (0, 0.5, 0), this._scene);
    const starfieldPT = new StarfieldProceduralTexture
        ("starfieldPT", 1024, this._scene);
    const starfieldMat = new StandardMaterial("starfield",
        this._scene);
    const space = CylinderBuilder.CreateCylinder("space",
            { height: 64, diameterTop: 0, diameterBottom: 64,
                tessellation: 512 },
            this._scene);
    starfieldMat.diffuseTexture = starfieldPT;
    starfieldMat.diffuseTexture.coordinatesMode = Texture.
        SKYBOX_MODE;
    starfieldMat.backFaceCulling = false;
    starfieldPT.beta = 0.1;
    space.material = starfieldMat;
    return this._scene.onBeforeRenderObservable.add(() => {
        starfieldPT.time += this._scene.getEngine().
            getDeltaTime() / 1000;
```

```
    });
}
```

`HemisphericLight` is a type of light source in Babylon.js that simulates an ambient environment type of lighting. There are a ton of interesting effects that you can achieve by messing around with the combination of **diffuse**, **specular**, and, unique to this type of light, **groundColor**, but we don't need to do that right now since our needs are pretty simple.

> **Important Note**
> Dividing the scene's delta time by 1,000 is what sets the rate at which the starfield twinkles and shifts. Try removing the division statement and see what happens!

Finishing up the function, we are following a similar pattern to what we did when we created the planetary orbits animation for the Loading Screen by registering an **observer** in `onBeforeRenderObservable` and returning the **observer** for tidy later disposal. If all went well, clicking the **Run** button should display a nice picture of our starfield, twinkling and glittering as it slowly shifts.

Click **Save** and let's move on! If you find that your snippet isn't working the way it should be, or are having any other trouble, pull up Playground snippet #16XY6Z to see the full code for this snippet at this point in development.

Creating the AdvancedDynamicTexture and GUI

There can be a lot to take in when it comes to the extensive functionality present in the Babylon.js 2D GUI system. More extensive documentation on the GUI APIs can be found at `https://doc.babylonjs.com/divingDeeper/gui/gui`, but what we're about to do with it now should either refresh your memory or provide enough of a foundation to begin learning. Add new types to the alias list, but instead of putting them in the `BABYLON` object, add a new `BABYLON.GUI` entry that is similar to the `BABYLON` entry, with the following types from the `BABYLON.GUI` namespace:

- `AdvancedDynamicTexture`
- `Rectangle`
- `Image`
- `StackPanel`
- `TextBlock`
- `Control`

Add a new method called `_setupUi` to `MainMenuClass`, and add a line in the constructor to invoke it at the bottom of the function.

We're not going to try to do anything fancy with the menu UI right now, so the first thing the _setupUi function needs to do is to create an instance of the BABYLON.GUI.AdvancedDynamicTexture class in the (default) fullscreen mode. This results in a 2D texture the size of the render canvas, with the controls painted on it, which is rendered on top of the scene in turn. One minor tweak we'll make is to tell the texture to render at its ideal size – this will help avoid fuzziness in rendered text caused by down- or up- sampling effects. To allow other class instance methods to access the texture, assign it to the _guiMenu property:

```
const gui = AdvancedDynamicTexture.CreateFullscreenUI("UI");
gui.renderAtIdealSize = true;
this._guiMenu = gui;
```

Next up, we need to add a Rectangle control to contain the actual menu items. We don't want it to be completely opaque, but it should have a contrasting background color or gradient.

Adding the Menu Container and Background

For web developers and designers, there are a lot of what are hopefully comfortingly familiar concepts at play. A GUI control tree is a hierarchy similar to an **HTML DOM**, where controls can be nested inside of each other, with siblings inheriting some of their layouts from the parent element or control. In order to be rendered, a control needs to be able to trace its parentage back to AdvancedDynamicTexture either directly or indirectly. It's often easiest to show this rather than describe it, so add the following code to define our menu's container and basic appearance:

```
const menuContainer = new Rectangle("menuContainer");
menuContainer.width = 0.8;
menuContainer.thickness = 5;
menuContainer.cornerRadius = 13;
this._guiMenu.addControl(menuContainer);
this._menuContainer = menuContainer;
```

The width is set as a percentage of the canvas size (0.8) so that the menu doesn't cover the entire background, while the border width (thickness) is in pixels and the corner radius is specified in degrees – got all that?

> **Tip**
> Intellisense can be your best friend in providing quick descriptions of the numerous properties available on GUI controls, particularly when it comes to determining which units are in use (e.g., pixels or percentage).

Next, we want to add an Image control to hold the background of the menu. Apropos of the Image, it's easy to create a nice background image texture, but what use is it if it can't be seen in the Playground? So, it's time for a magic trick…

Image Aside: Bringing in External Content

The Babylon.js Playground has a feature configured in its web server's configuration to allow **Cross-Origin Resource Sharing** (**CORS**) of content served from a number of well-known and established repository hosts, such as GitHub. By crafting the appropriate URL to our source repository, we can load textures, sounds, and models in our Playground snippet – just as with the **Babylon.js Asset Libraries**! By way of demonstrating how this works, add the following line to the very top of the snippet (first line):

```
const menuBackground = https://raw.githubusercontent.com/
jelster/space-truckers/ch4/assets/menuBackground.png
    + "?" + Number(new Date());
```

Breaking the URL down, here's how you can apply this tactic to any publicly hosted GitHub repository:

1. Starting with the base URL of `raw.githubusercontent.com`, add the path segments (in order) for the repository owner (or owning Organization) name, and the name of the repository itself – for example, `raw.githubusercontent.com/jelster/space-truckers`.

2. Next, add a path segment for the name of the branch or tag from which to retrieve the asset. For this book, the assets will be listed in their chapter's respective branch, but for many other repositories, this will be `main`, `master`, or possibly `develop`.

3. Finally, add the rest of the path to the asset, including the file extension. Because there are pretty robust caching headers accompanying the responses for these files, it's often a good idea during active content production to append a cache-using string such as the current date and time to the end of the URL so that you can be sure you're always seeing the most current version of the file.

Using the `menuBackground` URL, create an `Image` and add it to the `menuContainer` we previously added:

```
const menuBg = new Image("menuBg", menuBackground);
menuContainer.addControl(menuBg);
```

Test out your progress by clicking **Run**, fixing any issues, then of course make sure to **Save** the snippet. To check yourself or to start with the latest snippet for this chapter, use **#16XY6Z#1**. This is how it should look:

Figure 4.4 – The main menu at #16XY6Z#1 has the Starfield PT background and
a semi-opaque gradient-filled rectangle that will contain menu items

Laying out the Title and Menu Items

Referring back to *Figure 4.2*, we can see that the menu screen can be divided up into a grid with two rows – one for the title and one for the menu items. To ensure that the buttons and selection icons all line up the way we want them to, we'll need the grid to have three columns, each one-third of the width of the grid (which itself has a width of 0.8 or 80%). **Grid** has the addColumnDefinition and addRowDefinition methods to accomplish this, making the setup very simple to add to our _setupUi method:

```
const menuGrid = new GUI.Grid("menuGrid");
menuGrid.addColumnDefinition(0.33);
menuGrid.addColumnDefinition(0.33);
menuGrid.addColumnDefinition(0.33);
menuGrid.addRowDefinition(0.5);
menuGrid.addRowDefinition(0.5);
menuContainer.addControl(menuGrid);
this._menuGrid = menuGrid;
```

The title text is an important factor in defining a game or application's look and feel through its font and display, but we're going to be circling back to that topic in *Chapter 7, Processing Route Data*. For now, we'll use the default font and ensure that it auto-sizes the text as needed. Vertically aligning `TextBlock` with the top of the grid will ensure that no matter how many buttons there are, the title will always stay where it belongs. A bit of styling to add shadows and padding results in code similar to this:

```
const titleText = new TextBlock("title", "Space-
    Truckers");
titleText.resizeToFit = true;
titleText.textWrapping = GUI.TextWrapping.Ellipse;
titleText.fontSize = "72pt";
titleText.color = "white";
titleText.width = 0.9;
titleText.verticalAlignment = Control.
    VERTICAL_ALIGNMENT_TOP;
titleText.paddingTop = titleText.paddingBottom =
    "18px";
titleText.shadowOffsetX = 3;
titleText.shadowOffsetY = 6;
titleText.shadowBlur = 2;
menuContainer.addControl(titleText);
```

Check your work by running it and then save your progress. For those following along, this can be found at **#16XY6Z#2**. The next task is to write some functionality to populate the menu with selectable button items. We'll be doing a bunch of these, so the less we have to repeat ourselves, the more keystrokes we can save.

Populating the Menu with Items

Similar to how we added and then implemented the `_setupUi` function, we'll start our latest task by adding an `_addMenuItems` function and constructor invocation expression to our class. We know that we want all the buttons of the menu to share a certain subset of property values, but not all of them. The properties that are unique to a given instance of a menu item can be defined by a simple object such as the following one defining the **Play** button's properties:

```
const pbOpts = {
    name: "btPlay",
    title: "Play",
```

```
        background: "red",
        color: "white",
        onInvoked: () => console.log("Play button clicked")
    };
```

A button needs to have a unique name and it also needs some text to display. The foreground and background colors ought to be specific to each item, and of course, the action that is taken when the button is selected certainly qualifies as being specific to a given button. Within the _addMenuItems definition but before the pbOpts expression, add this local helper function to create and populate a button control with the given properties:

```
function createMenuItem(opts) {
    const btn = Button.CreateSimpleButton(opts.name || "",
        opts.title);
    btn.color = opts.color || "white";
    btn.background = opts.background || "green";
    btn.height = "80px";
    btn.thickness = 4;
    btn.cornerRadius = 80;
    btn.shadowOffsetY = 12;
    btn.horizontalAlignment = Control.
        HORIZONTAL_ALIGNMENT_CENTER;
    btn.fontSize = "36pt";

    if (opts.onInvoked) {
        btn.onPointerClickObservable.add((ed, es) =>
            opts.onInvoked(ed, es));
    }
    return btn;
}
```

With the button returned from our helper method, there's just the matter of adding it to the menu grid:

```
const playButton = createMenuItem(pbOpts);
this._menuGrid.addControl(playButton, this._menuGrid.
    children.length, 1);
```

Unlike the same functions of its **Control** relatives, the addControl function of **Grid** accepts an optional **row** and **column** assignment as its second and third parameters, respectively. This lets us insert an item in the last row without knowing its index by getting the count of its child rows. We want buttons to be centered, so the column will always be the same – one.

Finish the buttons by adding an exit button according to these options, and don't forget to **Save**! To compare with the checkpoint snippet, see **#16XY6Z#3**:

```
const ebOpts = {
    name: "btExit",
    title: "Exit",
    background: "yellow",
    color: "black",
    onInvoked: () => console.log("Exit button clicked")
}
```

We've come a long way in this chapter, but we're not quite done yet. There's been a lot of different things that we've been juggling so far, and all of the functionality we plan to build is completed – now, we just need to incorporate this functionality into the rest of our code.

Adding Menu Item Selection and Indicators

Although there are a chunk of players who will want to and enjoy using a keyboard and mouse to play Space-Truckers, it should also be an enjoyable experience with a gamepad. In the next chapter, we'll look at how to work with gamepad input in more detail, and to prepare for that, we need the main menu's items to be selectable without invoking their actions and without the presence of a mouse pointer hovering over them. A selection indicator icon will serve this purpose, displaying the icon next to the currently selected menu item and showing the player what command or option will be invoked on the appropriate button press.

Before we get to the visual aspect of the selected item, let's add some supporting properties to our class in the form of a get and set pair of functions that we'll call selectedItemIndex. Retrieving the value is simple using return this_selectedItemIndex. Setting it is a little bit more complicated. We want to ensure that the index doesn't exceed the number of menu items and that upon reaching the end of the menu items, we want it to start over at the first item. There are other things that we want to enact when the selected item index changes, but a set method is not the place to do anything more than simple logic, as follows:

```
    get selectedItemIndex() {
        return this._selectedItemIndex || -1;
    }
    set selectedItemIndex(idx) {
```

```
        const itemCount = this._menuGrid.rowCount;
        const newIdx = Scalar.Repeat(idx, itemCount);
        this._selectedItemIndex = newIdx;
        this._selectedItemChanged.notifyObservers(newIdx);
    }
```

We saw the usage of Scalar.Repeat earlier, when animating planetary orbits. Then, we used it to ensure that the radian values stayed smoothly circular. Similarly, we want the selection to loop around smoothly once it reaches the end. The new item (highlighted in the preceding code) is for a class member that we haven't yet declared, the _selectedItemChanged Observer.

Indicating Selection and Reacting to Change

Calling the **Observer** something new is a bit of a misnomer; we've been using the Babylon.js **Observable** since the very second chapter, when we used scene.onBeforeRenderObservable. This time, however, we're not using a built-in observable on a BJS object, but one that we're declaring ourselves. The usage semantics are exactly the same as they are for the other ones we've used – calling the add() method to register a function to be invoked whenever the observable is triggered. Creating the observable is just as simple, done by creating a new **Observable** instance. At the end of the MainMenuScene constructor, add code to create the _selectedItemChanged observable, then call its add method to register our selection's changed logic:

```
this._selectedItemChanged = new Observable();
this._selectedItemChanged.add((idx) => {
    const menuGrid = this._menuGrid;
    const selectedItem = menuGrid.getChildrenAt(idx, 1);
    if (selectedItem[0].isEnabled !== true) {
        this.selectedItemIndex = 1 + idx;
    }
    this._selectorIcon.isVisible = true;
    menuGrid.removeControl(this._selectorIcon);
    menuGrid.addControl(this._selectorIcon, idx);
});
```

When the selection changes, the event handler is passed the newly-selected item's index – its row in the grid. Sometimes, we might want to display non-selectable menu items, so we retrieve the selected item and then check the item retrieved from the second column of the selected row to see whether it's isEnabled. If that's not the case, then we increment selectedItemIndex – making sure to use the property setter and not directly changing the backing field's value. The last part of our event handler again represents something we haven't added yet – the selection icon. This hides the icon first before removing it from the grid and re-adding it at the new position. Moving backward now, again, add a method call to this._createSelectorIcon() to the constructor, then add the eponymous function declaration to the class. Here's how the body of the function should look:

```
_createSelectorIcon() {
    const selectorIcon = new BABYLON.GUI.Image
        ("selectorIcon", selectionIcon);
    selectorIcon.width = "160px";
    selectorIcon.height = "60px";
    selectorIcon.horizontalAlignment = Control.
        HORIZONTAL_ALIGNMENT_CENTER;
    selectorIcon.shadowOffsetX = 5;
    selectorIcon.shadowOffsetY = 3;
    selectorIcon.isVisible = false;
    this._menuGrid.addControl(selectorIcon, 1, 0);
    this._selectorIcon = selectorIcon;
}
```

This creates a new GUI.Image using the final undeclared constant, the selectionIcon URL string. The rest of the method is boilerplate code we've written in the not-so-distant past.

> **Note**
>
> To avoid ambiguity with the HTML DOM Image type, the fully-qualified name is used in the Playground.

Wrap up the penultimate task of this section by adding the selectionIcon URL string at the top of the snippet:

```
const selectionIcon = "https://raw.githubusercontent.
com/jelster/space-truckers/ch4/assets/ui-selection-icon.
PNG" + "?" + Number(new Date());
```

Feel free to substitute your image of choice for the one in the repository, and if you want to see it used in the production game, send us a **Pull Request** with it! Finally, we want to automatically select the first item in the menu, but only after the scene has completely finished loading and is waiting for user input. We do that by adding a simple line to the end of our constructor:

```
scene.whenReadyAsync().then(() => this.selectedItemIndex = 0);
```

Clicking **Run** should show a finely crafted main menu – click **Save** and congratulate yourself. Look at how much you've accomplished during just this one pretty small section of one chapter of a (relatively) short book and contemplate how far you'll be by the end! To compare your code for troubleshooting or catching up, see snippet **#16XY6Z#4**. The Main Menu looks nice, but despite the starfield twinkling in the background, it still needs a little bit of motion to give it some life and energy. Let's be honest too – hornet yellow for the **Exit** button isn't really the look we're aiming for either, so let's take a moment to correct those matters before moving on.

Visual Improvements and Animating the Selection Idle

The easiest change we want is to set the color property of our ebOpts object, all the way down in the _createMenuItems method, to the string color **black**. For the next change, we will add a small animation to the selection icon to make it look as though the truck is floating next to the menu item. This is a two-step process and the components of each individual step should be familiar from recent usage.

First, we need to track the current animation frame for the icon with a class member named _selectorAnimationFrame. Second, we need to register an onBeforeRenderObservable that will execute a new function, _selectorIconAnimation, before every frame is rendered in the scene. In that function, we increment the current frame (looping around if necessary) and use that value to compute the position of the icon along the vertical axis according to our circular standby – the **sine** function. This is what the animation function should resemble:

```
_selectorIconAnimation() {
    const animTimeSeconds = Math.PI * 2;
    const dT = this._scene.getEngine().
        getDeltaTime() / 1000;
    this._selectorAnimationFrame = Scalar.Repeat(this._
    selectorAnimationFrame + dT * 5, animTimeSeconds * 10);
    this._selectorIcon.top = Math.sin(this.
        _selectorAnimationFrame).toFixed(0) + "px";
}
```

The total time that it takes to go through a complete animation cycle is given by the first expression, while the amount of time (in seconds) elapsed since the last frame was rendered is given by the second. As we did before with **Scalar** in set selectedItemIndex, we loop _selectorAnimationFrame here when it reaches the frame count, but we are scaling some values by arbitrary factors at the same time to yield the new top position (in pixels) that is set in the final line. Running this should result in a much more pleasing color for the **Exit** button as well as displaying a nice subtle floating appearance for the truck selection icon.

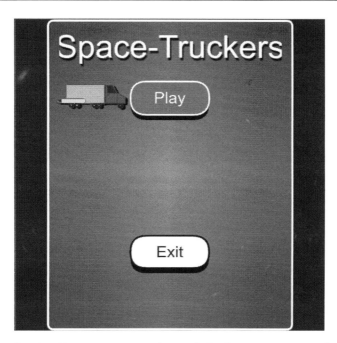

Figure 4.5 – The Main Menu snippet complete with the floating animation of a truck icon

If this is starting to feel repetitive, then that's good, because it means that the material in this book is starting to sink in! Snippet **#16XY6Z#5** has the latest code; if you've not prepared your own, then navigate to this one and make sure you have VSCode open and ready to accept the application's sparkling new Main Menu.

Integrating the Main Menu

Despite the potentially intimidating heading, there's really not a whole lot we'll need to do in order to incorporate all of the work from our snippets into the application's code structure. In fact, after all of the effort and journeying we've done throughout this chapter, it may feel a bit anti-climactic when we finish this part of the work.

The most straightforward and simple way to do it is to copy and paste the whole of the MainMenuScene class from the snippet into your local file, making sure to *entirely* replace the existing class declaration. You'll need to only slightly adjust your import statements; here are the two most relevant lines where this changes:

```
import { Scene, Vector3, Scalar, Observable, Sound,
HemisphericLight } from "@babylonjs/core";
import { AdvancedDynamicTexture, Rectangle, Image, Button,
Control, TextBlock, Grid, TextWrapping } from "@babylonjs/gui";
```

For the selection icon image asset, download the one at the snippet's URL or make your own. Either way, add an import statement for it as well:

```
import selectionIcon from "../assets/
    ui-selection-icon.PNG";
```

Either wait for the development webpack output to finish or run the webpack process to test your changes, and don't forget to commit and push your work – there's no reason to lose work due to the omission of a few keystrokes. Earlier, when we went over our State Machine, we learned that in addition to the state behaviors, it's important to define the transitions to and from those states.On the topic of transitions, here's one now!

Entering and Leaving Transitions

When we're looking at the integration of our Main Menu with the SpaceTruckerApplication State Machine, there are two functions that we've yet to implement and wire up. Those functions are the two transition functions for the main menu. In other words, we need to define the logic for what happens when we transition to the MENU state, as well as out of that state. Naming these new functions is actually pretty easy for once – _onMenuEnter and _onMenuLeave. While there might be more involved behavior we'd like to implement later, for now, we will say that when the menu either starts or ceases to be the current state of the application, we want it to fade in or out accordingly.

The simplest way to accomplish this is by animating the menuContainer.alpha property between either 0 to 1 (entering) or 1 to 0 (leaving). As with the selection icon animation, we'll need to store the current frame of fadeIn and fadeOut. Unlike the selection icon animation, we have a finite amount of time that the animation should last, so we also need to store the total duration value of the transition. Between every frame, we should set the current alpha value to one that is only slightly different from the previous value, so the transition appears smooth. Finally, when the animation ends, we want to (in the case of the leaving transition) set the menu's visibility to false, along with any other clean-up that needs to happen. Interestingly enough, the logic for the enter and leave transitions is identical save for swapping the ranges in the SmoothStep function used to interpolate the alpha value. Here's the _onMenuEnter function:

```
_onMenuEnter(duration) {
    let fadeIn = 0;
    const fadeTime = duration || 1500;
    const timer = BABYLON.setAndStartTimer({
        timeout: fadeTime,
        contextObservable: this._scene.
            onBeforeRenderObservable,
        onTick: () => {
            const dT = this._scene.getEngine().
```

```
              getDeltaTime();
          fadeIn += dT;
          const currAmt = Scalar.SmoothStep(0, 1, fadeIn
              / fadeTime);
          this._menuContainer.alpha = currAmt;
        },
        onEnded: () => {
            this.selectedItemIndex = 0;
        }
    });
    return timer;
}
```

Instead of using the standard timer creation method in JavaScript of calling `setTimeout`, we're using the `BABYLON.setAndStartTimer` utility function. By attaching `contextObservable` to `scene.onBeforeRenderObservable`, the `onTick` method is called consistently before each frame is rendered. The `onEnded` function is invoked when the name implies – after the timer has completed. In our case, we want to wait until the menu has transitioned in fully before showing the selection icon, so we set the `selectedItemIndex` there. In the constructor, we can replace the callback used with `scene.whenReadyAsync` to call our `onMenuEnter` function as follows:

```
scene.whenReadyAsync().then(() => this._onMenuEnter());
```

Save the file and run the app. You should see the menu fade in over the course of a couple of seconds before the selection item shows up. Learn more about this and other related functionality at `https://doc.babylonjs.com/divingDeeper/events/observables#setandstarttimer`, but maybe wait a tiny bit to do that – it's time to finish off this chapter!

The `onMenuLeave` function is, as was mentioned earlier, almost identical to its `onMenuEnter` counterpart (with the exception of the `onEnded` callback), just swapping terms in `SmoothStep` (as follows). Add the `onMenuLeave` function with the changed expression:

```
const currAmt = Scalar.SmoothStep(1, 0, fadeOut / fadeTime);
```

Hooking up the **Exit** button to `onMenuLeave` is easy: in the `_addMenuItems` method's `ebOpts` object definition, change the `onInvoked` function to look something similar to the following:

```
onInvoked: () => {
    console.log("Exit button clicked");
    this._onMenuLeave(1000);
}
```

Save again and test your work to ensure it's behaving as expected. This is looking and behaving excellently, but before we can pull over and rest, there's one last thing left to accomplish.

Menu Finishing Touches

It's a bit too quiet here for what should be an engaging and interesting main menu screen. We can fix that though, with the power of music! Although we'll be covering the playing of sounds and music in more detail later, it's too simple to pass the opportunity up, so here's the quick and dirty version in as few words as possible:

Add an import statement

```
import titleMusic from "../assets/sounds/space-trucker-title-
theme.m4a";
```

Load and play the music from the constructor

```
this._music = new Sound("titleMusic", titleMusic, scene, ()
=> console.log("loaded title music"), { autoplay: true, loop:
true, volume: 0.5 });
```

Enjoy the vibes

```
<enjoy the music>
```

OK, so maybe the last part is getting a bit carried away; we do want to stop the music at some point. In the onEnded callback of _onMenuLeave, call this._music.stop() to stop the sound from playing when the **Exit** button is clicked. Once you've run the app and corrected any issues, it's time to commit changes to source control and have a nice refreshing beverage – we've completed the chapter!

Summary

What a journey we've taken during this chapter. Some might prefer to think of it as more of a slog, and that's not unfair – we've been wading through some pretty dense material here! Despite there being a fair bit of theory and high-level concepts tossed around, think back to what's been accomplished over the course of this chapter – where we started was with a landing page that launches into an animation. Now, we have a landing page that launches into an *application*.

Coming up next, we're going to look at how to address the problem of accepting different forms and methods of input in a way that produces consistent and predictable behavior from the application – stick with us, and don't be afraid to take your time to go back and re-read anything you didn't understand the first time around. It's amazing how much comprehension can require multiple passes to really take hold, but if that's not working and you find you're struggling to understand or follow along, no worries. Navigate to the Space-Trucker Discussions or the Babylon.js forums and post your question or problem to the community – you aren't alone!

Extended Topics

Things are just getting some momentum, but that doesn't mean there isn't more to explore and extend what we've got already! Here are some ideas for things that you might look at, explore, or build into this chapter's code:

- Create or extend the regular Babylon.js **Animation** type's capabilities to include 2D **GUI** controls – or – implement a class that mimics the behavior of the Animation object with **GUI** controls.

- Can you spot the defect in the `SpaceTruckerLoadingScreen.js` code? It's a bit subtle if you're reading through it in your head, but there's definitely a logical defect in the code. Running it won't cause any errors to be thrown but it does have effects that are visible at runtime under the right conditions.

- Instead of using a single, full-screen `AdvancedDynamicTexture`, use one or more mesh-attached textures that are painted onto the meshes in the scene, which can then be animated in interesting ways.

- Add an attract mode that engages after the Main Menu has been displayed without user input for more than 30 seconds. An attract mode was an arcade game feature that puts the game into a non-interactive demo mode intended to catch the attention of passers-by. What is your idea for an attract mode?

5
Adding a Cut Scene and Handling Input

Much of the work we've completed so far has contributed to the whole largely unseen and unheard. The only action we've required – or even listened for – from users is a single button click. How boring – and quiet. That's all about to change, though! In this chapter, we're going to add some flavor to our app's launch by adding a Splash Screen that tells the world that everything they're about to see is "Powered by Babylon.js" in the process of providing players with their first experience with Space-Truckers. We'll also be giving users agency in the game world by adding inputs for multiple different device types, along with the logic to process inputs into actions in the game.

This seems like a lot to cover in such a short chapter, but thanks to how easy it can be to accomplish tasks in Babylon.js, progress can come faster than you might think.

In this chapter, we will cover the following topics:

- Space-Truckers – the Splash Screen
- Designing the Input System

Everything we'll be doing will build from the work we've done in previous chapters, but it's OK if you're just picking things up from here – read on for technical details on how to obtain the source code to complete this chapter.

Technical Requirements

This is the first time that we're going to be expanding the technical requirements, but it should hardly be a surprise to anyone that to work with a particular type of input device – be it a mouse and keyboard, Xbox™ controller, Sony PlayStation™ controller, or even a VR joystick – it is necessary to either have one of such devices handy or (worst case) download and install a suitable emulator/simulation app. That said, Space-Truckers should be playable with the following input types:

- Keyboard and mouse
- Virtual joysticks/touch screen
- Xbox™ controller
- Sony PlayStation™ controller
- Generic gamepads

An appropriate audio output device will be needed to play music and sounds.

This chapter will follow a similar pattern as previous chapters, where we will build out one or more PlayGround snippets before integrating them into the application's code base. The code we'll be starting from is at `https://github.com/jelster/space-truckers/tree/ch4` if you want a reference point or a place from where you can start your journey. Now, with that squared away, we can turn our full attention to our first task: building the Splash Screen!

Space-Truckers – the Splash Screen

Nothing gets the attention of an audience better than a splashy entrance, and nobody knew this better than good ol' William Shakespeare. A glance at the first few pages of any of his plays uncovers a host of different exciting scenes from a street brawl between rival gangs in *Romeo and Juliet* to an interrupted wedding in *A Midsummer Night's Dream*. The Bard knew how to get the attention of his audiences – a notable feat in those times – and just as he shamelessly plundered history and mythology (sometimes both at the same time!) for his stories, we're going to shamelessly plunder the techniques he used in our work.

The specific inspiration from Mr. S. that we will examine is the idea of engaging the attention of an audience to prepare and prime them for what they're about to experience. We don't have a fancy fight scene or a fantasy wedding in the cards for Space-Truckers, but we do have our Splash Screen!

Looking at the Splash Screen in context, the user has just clicked the **Launch** button on the regular HTML web page, transitioning the page over to WebGL and rendering the animated Loading Screen we built back in *Chapter 2, Ramping up on Babylon.js*. Immediately following the completion of the Splash Screen (either because it ran to the end or because the user chose to skip through it), the user will be taken to the **Main Menu** screen that we built out in the previous chapter. Through a series of animated sequences and in conjunction with the audio soundtrack, users will be put solidly into the mood of a Space-Trucker.

Storyboarding the Scene

While it's easy to let the mind wander off into the potential avenues that a splash scene might show, we'll Save It For A PR™ and instead start with something incredibly simple that we can then use as a base for expansion. A storyboard doesn't have to be an immensely complicated and planned-out artifact. Time spent storyboarding is time that isn't being spent trying out the ideas laid out by the storyboard, so don't worry about making it look good, worry about the boards capturing a set of snapshots of what you want to happen. The following diagram shows the sketched-out series of panels that comprise the Splash Screen storyboard:

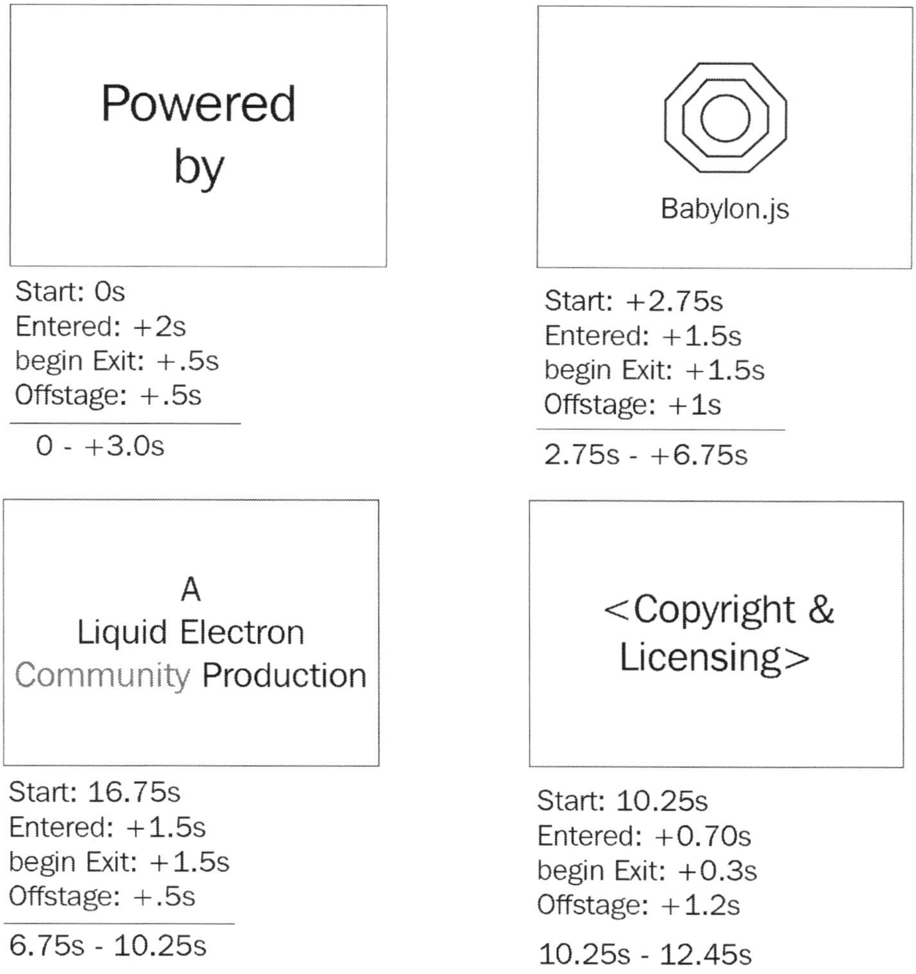

Powered
by

Start: 0s
Entered: +2s
begin Exit: +.5s
Offstage: +.5s

0 - +3.0s

Babylon.js

Start: +2.75s
Entered: +1.5s
begin Exit: +1.5s
Offstage: +1s

2.75s - +6.75s

A
Liquid Electron
Community Production

Start: 16.75s
Entered: +1.5s
begin Exit: +1.5s
Offstage: +.5s

6.75s - 10.25s

<Copyright &
Licensing>

Start: 10.25s
Entered: +0.70s
begin Exit: +0.3s
Offstage: +1.2s

10.25s - 12.45s

Figure 5.1 – Storyboard for the Splash Screen sequence. Being a sketch, the numbers given for timings should not be taken at face value

Let's break this diagram down a bit by walking through the scene in a temporal order. At time = 0, we have a blank stage (screen). After 2 seconds have passed, the first panel with the words "Powered By" is fully visible. Half (0.5) a second after that (or T+2.5s) marks the beginning of the exit sub-sequence, which completes with the panel fully hidden another half a second later. The total amount of time that the first panel depicts is 3 seconds. Armed with that explanation, the other three panels should also make sense. Each panel progresses the scene forward, starting at the top-left, moving right, and wrapping back to the left panel, respectively. The image shown in a panel fades in and out according to the given timings, but those numbers should be used as rough guide markers only – it's important to tweak the values to what you like.

If you were to compare the storyboard with the final splash screen sequence, there are some gross similarities; the panels are all mostly the same and in the same order, the timings notated are roughly the same, and more. That shows the evolution of the design from start to finish and serves to drive home a central point of storyboarding – the boards are not the whole story! These admittedly crude sketches serve the purpose of putting a stake in the ground, giving loose definition to the basic elements and timings involved so that we can focus on other aspects of implementation – such as the code.

Building the Scene

There is only one new concept that we haven't encountered yet that we'll need to learn to build out the Splash Screen in code. Everything else will use a combination of techniques that we've used in previous chapters in one way or another, so hopefully, this will seem pretty easy! For this part of the chapter, we'll be working exclusively in the **PlayGround** (**PG**) – if you're following along, this is where you'll want to load up the PG with a new snippet.

> **Important note**
>
> Code listings will continue to become less complete and more focused on specific aspects or areas of the code under discussion that are important, tricky, or non-obvious. The complete code for this chapter can be found at `https://github.com/jelster/space-truckers/tree/ch5`. Don't hesitate to pull it up to compare your progress against it or check your work – sometimes, an explanation just won't cut it and you need to see working code!

When we break out the various animated sequences outlined in the storyboard, there's an immediate structure or way of ordering the cut scene that sticks out right away. Each board in the storyboard represents a distinct snapshot of what is happening at a given time in the scene, so we need to come up with a way to represent these cut scene segments in code. We want it to be a reusable component, and we want to be able to use The Power of **Composition** to assemble multiple segments into a greater whole. As with any flexible programming language, there are many ways we might fulfill these requirements. A class-based approach leverages ES6 language features to make it quick and easy to create new instances of a `CutSceneSegment`, and a new `SplashScene` class can be used to compose and manage those segments with proper timings and transitions.

The CutSceneSegment Class

The `CutSceneSegment` class is a simple container that can represent an atomic portion of the scene's sequence, but although it is simple, it isn't devoid of any behaviors. A `CutSceneSegment` should be able to `start` and `stop` its sequence, potentially looping playback. Similarly, other components may need to know when a segment completes, so a `onEnd` observable will make it easier for us to write controlling logic to manage multiple segments in sequence. Because we don't hate ourselves and we don't want to spend time debugging mysteriously misbehaving code, we'll treat an instance of a `CutSceneSegment` as **immutable**. That is, once we've created the object, we're not going to try to change it by say, swapping out the contained animations.

> **Important note**
>
> Can you keep a secret? Those who have experience with JavaScript may be thinking that the word "immutable" is incorrectly being applied. While it is true that from a strictly technical sense, the objects we're dealing with are not immutable, the idea is that we simply pretend it is immutable. If we're using it as-is, and if nobody tells, does it matter whether an object is immutable or not? Be warned, though – it's easy to lose the distinction between ways of thinking about software and expressing those concepts in code, so don't mistake this for language-specific guidance!

Although it would be useful to be able to control multiple target scene elements in a single `CutSceneSegment`, we don't need that complexity to implement the scene from our storyboards. This decision, in conjunction with the previous decision regarding immutability, has two important implications for how we will write our classes' **constructor**.

First, we'll need to get a `target` against which the segment will operate. This can be anything capable of being animated, so, pretty much any BJS type you may want to animate can be used here (with the notable exception of the types in **BABYLON.GUI.Controls**). Second, the constructor will need to accept an array of arbitrary individual **Animation** instances as an `animationSequence`. Of course, the "ctor" (as the cool kids all call it) will need to take a reference to the current scene, which gives us the following signature for the method:

```
class CutSceneSegment {
    //loopAnimation = false;
    //animationGroup;
    //onEnd = new Observable();
    constructor(target, scene, ...animationSequence) { ... }
```

You may be unfamiliar with the highlighted language construct. That's OK because although it's not uncommon, it's also not something that you might encounter in your everyday JavaScript. The three periods (`.`) before `animationSequence` indicate that the parameter is treated as an arbitrary params-style array. This is merely a convenient piece of "syntactic sugar" that allows callers of the function to avoid the need to create and pass an `Array` and instead pass a comma-separated list of the elements comprising the Array. The following code fragment shows arrays being passed as the trailing three parameters:

```
new CutSceneSegment(billboard, scene, fadeAnimation,
  scaleAnimation, rotateAnimation);
```

In the `CutSceneSegment` constructor, there are two primary things we need to accomplish:

1. Create a `TargetedAnimation` from each Animation in `animationSequence`.
2. Add the TargetedAnimations to a new `AnimationGroup`.

Going in reverse order, `AnimationGroup` is something new to the project. Do not try to overthink it – it is and does exactly what its name suggests. Next, because we already have animations that just need targeting, we can loop through the `animationSequence` collection and use AnimationGroup's `addTargetedAnimation` method to complete the binding. The Babylon.js Docs site at `https://doc.babylonjs.com/divingDeeper/animation/groupAnimations` has more information on different aspects of the `AnimationGroup` properties and methods, but other than the previous looping logic, the usage of an `AnimationGroup` is very similar to an individual `Animation`. Having accomplished these tasks, all that's left for the constructor is to delegate the `CutSceneSegment.onEnd` member property to `AnimationGroup.onAnimationGroupEndObservable`. Here's what the entire `constructor` looks like:

```
constructor(target, scene, ...animationSequence) {
    this._target = target;
    let ag = new AnimationGroup(target.name +
      "-animGroupCS", scene);
    for (var an of animationSequence) {
        ag.addTargetedAnimation(an, target);
    }
    this.animationGroup = ag;
    this.onEnd = ag.onAnimationGroupEndObservable;
    this._scene = scene;
}
```

Finishing the `CutSceneSegment` class are the `start` and `stop` methods. These are extremely simple, and just call the appropriate function of `this.animationGroup`. When we want to loop a `CutSceneSegment` – not a typical usage – we can set the `loopAnimation` flag to true before calling `start`:

```
start() {
    this.animationGroup.start(this.loopAnimation);
```

```
}
stop() {
    this.animationGroup.stop();
}
```

This completes the `CutSceneSegment` class. It's ready to be used in the code we're just about to write for the `SplashScene` class, where we'll be creating a segment for each panel in the storyboard before playing them in sequence. First, though, let's add another set of building blocks for our scene – the animations driving the scene's visuals.

The Animations

There are only three separate types of animations that we need for the scene. The keyframes and targets may be different, but the base property being animated is the same. Separate from any class declaration, add declarations for `flipAnimation`, `fadeAnimation`, and `scaleAnimation`. To keep the frame rates the same, we declare `animationFps` as `const`:

```
const animationFps = 30;
const flipAnimation = new Animation("flip", "rotation.x",
  animationFps, Animation.ANIMATIONTYPE_FLOAT,
  ANIMATIONLOOPMODE_CONSTANT, true);
const fadeAnimation = new Animation("entranceAndExitFade",
  "visibility", animationFps,
  Animation.ANIMATIONTYPE_FLOAT,
  Animation.ANIMATIONLOOPMODE_CONSTANT, true);
const scaleAnimation = new BABYLON.Animation("scaleTarget",
  "scaling", animationFps, Animation.ANIMATIONTYPE_VECTOR3,
  Animation.ANIMATIONLOOPMODE_CYCLE, true);
```

This should be pretty familiar by now, except for the highlighted `true` parameter; this instructs the Babylon.js animation engine to enable the animation to be blended with others. It's not necessarily something we're leveraging immediately in the scene, but it's important to configure it correctly at the outset for when it's needed.

> **Important note**
> In the BJS PlayGround, IntelliSense may sometimes confuse the `BABYLON.Animation` type with browser or DOM types with the same name. Adding the `BABYLON` prefix can help clear up confusion, but remember to remove it later – you won't need it when the code is integrated locally.

The pieces have all been prepared and moved into place for us to start constructing the `SplashScene` class, where we'll create and assemble CutSceneSegments into a complete scene.

The SplashScene Class

When designing a class or component's code structure, a good way to start can be simply identifying and capturing any currently known variables of the state as class members, even if the value won't be set until later. One such example of this is `currentSegment`. This property holds the currently playing `CutSceneSegment`. We'll populate the various segments in the constructor, but by declaring the members outside of `constructor` (as opposed to defining it in the **ctor** – for example, `this. foo = 3`), we improve the readability of the code – something that is incredibly important in any code destined for production! Here are the class members that we'll want to define:

- `currentSegment`
- `poweredBy`
- `babylonBillboard`
- `communityProduction`
- `dedication`
- **`onReadyObservable = new Observable()`**
- **`skipRequested = false`**

Each of the preceding segments (save the highlighted ones, for obvious reasons) corresponds to a panel on the storyboard – in order of execution to help with readability. Though we won't use it until later in this chapter, `onReadyObservable` is there to signal that all the assets have finished loading and the cutscene is ready to start. It's a similar situation with `skipRequested` – later in this chapter, we'll add the ability for players to skip the cut scene, so adding this now is legitimate. Adding the small pieces of code to hook it up is trivial too since we're already working in that area, and it's one less thing to worry about later.

There will be enough setup code in the constructor as it is, so a forward-thinker might consider adding method stubs to encapsulate each segment's setup process! Turning our attention to the `createScene` function, we want to start seeing things as soon as possible, so let's hook up one end of the logic, which will allow our segments to transition between each other.

Just as our previous PlayGround snippets have been structured, the `SplashScene` constructor needs a `BABYLON.Engine` instance passed as a parameter, which it uses to create the scene. Also similar is the sparse and simple `createScene` function, which is used purely in the PlayGround. In case a refresher is needed, here's how to hook up the code with the Playground in the body of `createScene`:

```
const splashScreen = new SplashScene(engine);
splashScreen.onReadyObservable.add(() =>
  splashScreen.run());
return splashScreen.scene;
```

We need to be able to discretely control when SplashScene starts and stops, so the constructor isn't going to be the place to start playing CutSceneSegments. Instead, we'll add a run method (highlighted in the preceding snippet) to perform those duties in response to a signal from onReadyObservable. Now, as we enhance and expand SplashScene, we'll be able to build off from this without having to worry about getting everything to start at the same time.

The SplashScreen.run() function looks very similar to the run function of the Space-TruckerApplication run function if you squint enough and possibly stare unprotected at the sun for a bit.

> **Important note**
>
> Do not look directly at the sun without proper eye protection! Sunglasses, even ones that block UV radiation, are not sufficient protection for eyes, and permanent damage may result. On a related note, never take advice on what to do in the outdoors from a technical book on programming. HTH.

The reason they look similar to each other is that they both serve similar duties. Similar problems face similar solutions and all, so here we are:

```
run() {
    this.currentSegment.start();
    let prior, curr = this.currentSegment;
    this.onUpdate = this.scene.onBeforeRenderObservable
    .add(() => {
        if (this.skipRequested) {
            this?.currentSegment.stop();
            this.currentSegment = null;
            return;
        }
        curr = this.currentSegment;
        if (prior !== curr) {
            this.currentSegment?.start();
        }
    });
}
```

Even though this scene doesn't use the function* generators that we saw in the previous chapter, it still qualifies as a simple type of state machine. The current state (represented by currentSegment) is polled on every frame and compared with the previous frame's value. If they are different, then it means that a new segment has been swapped in and must have its start method invoked to continue the sequence. Because it's so straightforward, and again because we're already here, the logic for managing the use case where the player wishes to skip the cutscene and go straight to the Main Menu gets added as well. The only real items of note are the combination of setting `this.currentSegment = null` with the `?.` operators to prevent any attempt to call a method on an undefined value; if `currentSegment` is null (from the viewpoint of the code), then the cutscene either hasn't started yet, or it has finished.

To provide a stable platform for creating the CutSceneSegments, there are still a few things that we need to add to the constructor logic, as shown in the following code:

```
const scene = this.scene = new Scene(engine);
scene.clearColor = Color3.Black();
this.camera = new ArcRotateCamera("camera", 0, Math.PI / 2,
  5, Vector3.Zero(), scene);
this.light = new HemisphericLight("light", new Vector3(0,
  1, 0), scene);
this.light.groundColor = Color3.White();
this.light.intensity = 0.5;
const billboard = this.billboard =
  PlaneBuilder.CreatePlane("billboard", {
    width: 5,
    height: 3
}, scene);
billboard.rotation.z = Math.PI;
billboard.rotation.x = Math.PI;
billboard.rotation.y = Math.PI / 2;
const billMat = new StandardMaterial("stdMat", scene);
billboard.material = billMat;
```

Setting up the scene, camera, and light should be pretty standard by now, and although the `billboard` **Plane** isn't new either, it's understandable to wonder at what role it plays in the scene. It's pretty simple if you think about it. There's `camera` to render the scene, there's `light` to illuminate `billboard`, and there's `billboard` to display our content – whatever that may be! We want the billboard to face perpendicular to the camera's view, hence setting the initial rotations. The values may seem a bit weird, but they will all make sense shortly. Now that we have the framework to render the cutscene, it's time to start defining the cutscene segments! We've gone quite a bit without saving (or not, if you're well disciplined!), so now's a good time to run the snippet and check for any obvious issues or errors before saving it for posterity.

The "Powered By" CutScene Segment

Referring to our initial storyboard, as our first segment, we've got a billboard displaying a stylized "Powered By" image. The timings make sense, and it's perfectly serviceable. However, the problem with it is that it's just plain outright *boring*. Let's spice it up a bit by having the billboard spin around slowly throughout the segment using `flipAnimation` we created earlier. At the same time, we'll apply `fadeAnimation` to fade the billboard in and out at the appropriate times. To keep the constructor to a manageable size, add a new class member function to `SplashScene` and call it `buildPoweredByAnimations`. Then, in the body of the function, start by declaring constants for each of the key timing events of the segment:

```
const start = 0;
const enterTime = 2.5;
const exitTime = enterTime + 2.5;
const end = exitTime + 2.5;
```

The values in the preceding snippet were arrived at through experimentation, so feel free to try out other values until you find something that works right for you. With absolute timing values computed, we can also compute the associated frame number for each timing event:

```
const entranceFrame = enterTime * animationFps;
const beginExitFrame = exitTime * animationFps;
const endFrame = end * animationFps;
```

These frame numbers are important when we want to define the animations' **key frames** array. Each separate animation will need a set of keyframes defined for it, so we'll need a fade-in and fade-out set of keyframes and a set of rotation – or "flip" – keyframes. Remember, the value for fade animations corresponds to the **alpha** property, so it will be between 0 (completely transparent) and 1 (completely opaque). The `flipKey` values represent the **y** component of the target's **rotation**:

```
const keys = [
        { frame: start, value: 0 },
        { frame: entranceFrame, value: 1 },
        { frame: beginExitFrame, value: 0.998 },
        { frame: endFrame, value: 0 }
    ];
    fadeAnimation.setKeys(keys);
    const flipKeys = [
        { frame: start, value: Math.PI },
        { frame: entranceFrame, value: 0 },
        { frame: beginExitFrame, value: Math.PI },
```

```
                { frame: endFrame, value: 2 * Math.PI }
        ];
        flipAnimation.setKeys(flipKeys);
```

After defining each of the relevant keyframes according to the computed frame timings, it's important to pass those keyframes onto the animation by calling setKeys. This works with our plan for reusing Animations because the keyframes are copied into the resulting TargetAnimation instance created when associated with its target; we can just call setKeys again with a new set of keyframes whenever needed.

> **Important note**
> The pattern that we're establishing here for this CutSceneSegment will be used for the rest of the segments. In other words, this will be on the test!

The final thing our buildPoweredByAnimations function needs to do is create and return a new CutSceneSegment that puts everything together:

```
const seg0 = new CutSceneSegment(this.billboard,
    this.scene, fadeAnimation, flipAnimation);
return seg0;
```

Back in the SplashScene constructor is where we'll invoke the buildPoweredByAnimations function to create a poweredBy object variable. Assigning poweredBy to this.currentSegment will ensure that when run is called, the sequence is started. Following that, we need to load up the "Powered By" image as a texture that we can use with billMat. Since this involves an external image asset, add top-level declarations for the full URL to the image files (see the previous chapter for more on constructing the full GitHub URL for an asset). In this initial case, it'll be a file called https://raw.githubusercontent.com/jelster/space-truckers/develop/assets/powered-by.png. Use that URL to construct a new **texture**, then assign the new **texture** to the previously-created billMat.diffuseTexture property.

> **Important note**
> Make sure you load the texture before assigning it to the material!

When running, you should see the image on the surface of the billboard plane, which is a good way to test your work before saving it!

Transitioning to the Next CutSceneSegment... and Beyond

When a `CutSceneSegment` begins running, it may make certain assumptions about the current state of the different actors and set pieces involved in a scene. For instance, a lighting animation that dims a light in a specific pattern may need the intensity values to start at a specific level. At the same time, a given segment can't "know" anything about other segments or their relationships – with a single crucial, albeit caveated exception. Upon completion of a `CutSceneSegment`, the `onEnd` **observable** notifies any interested parties of the fact, but the observer itself doesn't know anything about its subscribers. This is why adding a delegate to handle the `onEnd` observable is the ideal solution – and at the same time is also the caveat! To keep some local variables in the constructor conveniently in scope, we can call `onEnd.addOnce(() => { ... })`. The body of the function is where we want to tidy up objects in the scene, along with designating the next segment in the Splash Scene sequence:

```
poweredBy.onEnd.addOnce(() => {
    console.log("powered End");
    billMat.diffuseTexture = babylonTexture;
    billboard.rotation.x = Math.PI;
    this.light.intensity = 0.667;
    billboard.visibility = 0;
    this.currentSegment = babylonBillboard;
});
```

In our immediate case, the next segment is going to be the `babylonBillboard` segment, so make the last statement be `this.currentSegment = babylonBillboard` in the `poweredBy.onEnd` handler. Before that expression, we need to reset the **rotation** of the **billboard** to be front (perpendicular) facing to the camera, as well as swap `billMat.diffuseTexture` for the Babylon.js logo texture.

> **Important note**
>
> Before moving on to the next segment, it's a good idea to try and run the PlayGround snippet to see how it looks and test it for any major errors. Opening the browser's Dev Tools to see logged messages can help you gain a sense of timing!

What's that? The new segment doesn't exist and neither does the **Texture**? That's right – it's time to Repeat the Process that we just did but this time, apply it to the next panel in the scene! "Repetition is the key to learning" is how the phrase commonly goes, and because it gets repeated so much it has got to make sense, so take the opportunity to review what we've just done and apply it using these values for the logic of the `buildBabylonAnimation` function: for the texture, use `https://raw.githubusercontent.com/BabylonJS/Brand-Toolkit/master/babylonjs_identity/fullColor/babylonjs_identity_color.png` and for `animationSequence`, use `fadeAnimation`:

Attribute	Timing	Keyframe Value
Start	0	0
Entrance	2.5	1.0
BeginExit	Entrance + 3	0.998
Exit	BeginExit + 2.5	0

After adding the buildBabylonAnimation method, make sure to call it in the constructor so that you can subscribe to the new segment's onEnd observable. In the babylonBillboard.onEnd handler, there's no need to reposition the billboard since it didn't move during this segment, but there is the matter of teeing up the next one, in what is hopefully a familiar cadence.

The next segment is called communityProduction and is functionally identical to the previous segment save for a different texture, located at https://raw.githubusercontent.com/jelster/space-truckers/develop/assets/splash-screen-community.png. It is also just using fadeAnimation. Here are the main relevant timings and numbers needed:

Attribute	Timing	Keyframe Value
Start	0.0	0
Entrance	4.0	1
BeginExit	Entrance + 2.5	0.998
Exit	BeginExit + 3.0	0

Just like the previous segment, the communityProduction.onEnd handler will be responsible for setting the next segment – callToAction – and swapping billMat.diffuseTexture to the next one, which for lack of any better name will be called rigTexture. This texture is rendered onto the billboard mesh, where after fading in we'll apply a looping animation to its scaling property to make it look more dynamic.

> **Important note**
>
> The storyboard indicates this panel is where copyright notices and such would go, but there's no reason those can't go someplace else that's equally useful but less prominent. Instead, we'll make the panel contain a Space-Trucker image, with the image slowly pulsing the scale and opacity in a ready-wait indication state, waiting for the player to interact.

In a short while, we will be adding some input management. To prepare for that, we're going to need a way to display some appropriately formatted Text. In a block. A sort of TextBlock, as it were. Our SplashScreen is going to need to use the **BABYLON.GUI**.

The Last Segment

Our final CutSceneSegment – callToAction – follows a similar path that the others have taken, in that we use billBoard to display a diffuseTexture that fades into the scene. Here is where the segments start to diverge because instead of fading out again, we want it to fade in and then loop around without ever completely fading away. At the same time, we will use $scaleAnimation$ to vary the scale of the $billboard$ mesh along its X- and Z-axes. This will give the two-dimensional flat image a fake appearance of depth and scale as the animation cycles, which means that it looks cool! Here are the timings for each animation in the segment:

Attribute	Timing	Fade KFV	Scale KFV
start	0	0	(1, 1, 1)
enterTime	3.0	1	(1.25, 1, 1.25)
exitTime	enterTime + 2.5	0.998	(1.5, 1, 1.5)
end	exitTime + 3.0	1	(1, 1, 1)

When the end timing is reached, we want our **Call To Action** (CTA) text to be made visible, inviting us to press a key or tap their touch screen to continue. In another of the Bard's favorite tricks, here is some foreshadowing (not of the shading variety, the literary kind) – the **CTA** serves the subtle purpose of allowing the application to figure out what type of input the player wants to use. It's an incredibly direct means of communication between two entities that otherwise have almost zero capability to understand each other, and it works because its binary (the irony! It burns!) simplicity conveys a user's preference simply by them picking up the device and engaging an input.

Before we go there, we need to wrap up the implementation of the constructor by creating BABYLON. GUI.AdvancedDynamicTexture mentioned earlier: callToActionTexture. Creating, configuring the properties of, and adding a TextBlock to a GUI is a familiar exercise by now (though stick around for *Chapter 10, Improving the Environment with Lighting and Materials,* where we'll introduce the GUI Editor!), so the next listing should require very little explanation:

```
// ... create billboard textures used in segments
let callToActionTexture =
    this.callToActionTexture =
      BABYLON.GUI.AdvancedDynamicTexture.
      CreateFullscreenUI("splashGui");
let ctaBlock = new TextBlock("ctaBlock",
    "Press any key or tap the screen to continue...");
ctaBlock.textWrapping = BABYLON.GUI.TextWrapping.WordWrap;
ctaBlock.color = "white";
ctaBlock.fontSize = "16pt";
ctaBlock.verticalAlignment =
    ctaBlock.textVerticalAlignment =
      TextBlock.VERTICAL_ALIGNMENT_BOTTOM;
ctaBlock.paddingBottom = "12%";
```

```
ctaBlock.isVisible = false;
callToActionTexture.addControl(ctaBlock);
// ... call the builder functions
// ... Attach onEnd delegates
```

One thing not to forget is to set the initial visibility of `ctaBlock` (highlighted) to `false`. If you want to display it sooner than in the handler for `callToAction.onEnd`, go ahead – it's your game! Once you've gotten everything added to the constructor, give it a whirl and fix any errors that come up. Hit **Save**, then make sure you either put on headphones or can otherwise crank up your computer's audio – it's time to put in the theme song!

Fading in the Title Music

After working on this `SplashScene` for so long by now, it's probably started to feel a bit bland, and that is something we will not accept any longer. In *Chapter 4, Creating the Application*, we added the Space-Truckers main theme song to the **Main Menu**. Here, we'll be doing something very similar, but with a `SplashScene` twist.

Recall what was hopefully not-so-long-ago, when you read this gem?

> *"Though we won't use it until later in this chapter, onReadyObservable is there to signal that all the assets have finished loading and the cutscene is ready to start."*

Well, "later in this chapter" starts right now. Since we've already put everything else into place, there are only four tasks left to wrap up this bad boy and take 'er home:

1. Add a string to hold the URL to the song (or substitute your own) at `https://raw.githubusercontent.com/jelster/space-truckers/develop/assets/music/space-trucker-title-theme.m4a`.

2. Create a new **Sound** in the constructor, calling `SplashScene.onReadyObservable.notifyObservers` in the **Sound's** `readyToPlayCallback`. Set the volume really low – `0.01` works nicely – to give the volume room to grow.

3. Add a call to `this.music.play()` in the `SplashScene.run` method.

4. Crank up the volume (also in the `run` method) over some time by calling `this.music.setVolume(0.998, 500)`.

Do the usual drill of running, fixing issues, repeating as needed, and then saving. If you run into trouble or want to compare your results with a known "working" snippet, check out `https://playground.babylonjs.com/#DSALXR`. Still can't seem to get things working? Head over to the Space-Truckers GitHub Discussion boards at `https://github.com/jelster/space-truckers/discussions` and get help from the community, leave feedback or bug reports, and catch any updates to the code since this book was published. Having a runnable sample of what you want to accomplish in the PG is a great way to play around with ideas and concepts, but now, it's time to metaphorically remove our more abstract and theoretical game designer's hat and put on our more concrete and pragmatic software engineer's work helmet – we'll need those qualities as we integrate our PG code with the application.

Integrating the SplashScene

The integration phase of the work is where the shiny, pretty, elegant PG Snippet meets the hard-faced ugly truth of reality. It's the part where things are most likely to go wrong, and also where bugs in the application code can be uncovered. The reason this happens has little to do with the character and attributes of the person writing the code, even though it might feel that way sometimes. Any bugs or defects uncovered at this point are reflections of what wasn't known at the time the original code was written, and that means there's an opportunity to improve it!

Seeing the Difference

Because you have the benefit of this text to help guide your efforts, you'll be spared having to track down and fix two issues uncovered in the `SpaceTruckerApplication.js` component, along with some other changes we'll make structurally to the class. Including the two issues just mentioned, here is a list of the things we need to do to integrate `SplashScreen`:

- Add new files to `/src` - `cutSceneSegment.js` and `splashScene.js`
- Add appropriate imports to new files and copy over class definitions

The `spaceTruckerApplication.js` file will see the greatest changes with these tasks:

- Remove the placeholder `Promises` that were used to simulate loading times in `spaceTruckerApplication`. With those gone, we can also remove the `async` designator from their hosting functions.
- Instantiate the Scenes in the `initialize` method instead of previous locations.
- Register an Observer in `goToOpeningCutscene` that listens for the **SplashScreen's** `onReady` event.

And finally, the two issues that would otherwise prevent the application from correctly progressing and rendering are as follows:

- (Issue) `AppStateMachine` should yield `currentState`.
- (Issue) Logic in the `engine.runRenderLoop` callback needs to be a class-level function to access `this` properly. The problem can be resolved by extracting the arrow function into a class-level function – that is, `this._engine.runRenderLoop(() => this.onRender());`.

The best way to visualize the changes is to view a **diff**, or difference, report between two revisions. The Git **Source Control Management (SCM)** system offers a huge amount of functionality when it comes to comparing the contents of a repository at two (or more) points in time, so let's leverage that to help understand what needs to change to integrate `SplashScreen` into the app.

However it is accessed, the range of revisions we need to compare can be represented with the `ch4...6db9f7e` expression. Use this as an argument to `git diff` or paste it into a browser as the trailing path to `<repo URL>/compare/<revision range>`, or in this case, `https://github.com/jelster/space-truckers/compare/ch4...6db9f7e`.

Depending on the particulars of your development environment, a **diff** will be displayed in a varying number of (pardon the pun) different ways. Regardless of the specific tool, almost every **diff** will organize its report by individual files that have changed between the given range of revisions. **VSCode's Timeline** feature will show the commit history for an opened file; the diff can be viewed by clicking the revision in the **Timeline** pane.

> **Tip**
>
> Making a habit of examining these diffs closely before each commit or merge can improve your coding abilities, together with the quality of your code. A good sign that you are trying to do too much in a single commit is having a complicated and long changeset. Break the work into smaller components and commit each separately, and not only will any reviewers of your **Pull Request (PR)** thank you, but you'll find yourself moving faster and with greater confidence.

The **GitHub** web interface can also be useful for viewing differences between **revisions**, **branches**, and even **forks** (also known as **upstream repositories**). Navigating through and understanding the different reports is a key skill for people who wish to become skilled in software development, but it can be tough to block out the inevitable noise that comes with viewing so much information. GitHub will try to do some of this for you, by collapsing large diffs by default, for instance, but the best way to deal with poor a signal:noise ratio is unfortunately not retroactive; it is only useful when applied at the time of **commit** or **push**. This solution is to be mindful of and structure commits with a high signal:noise ratio from the beginning. Here are some tips for helping with that:

Instead Of...	Try Doing...
Waiting until a feature is finished before committing	Commit atomic groups of changes at regular intervals
Leaving no or a cryptic commit message	State the effect of applying this commit to the code
Mixing unrelated changes in the same commit	Always try to make a particular commit about one single thing

Using the diff as a reference guide when needed, try to accomplish the activities listed earlier on your own. Of course, since you're already looking at the diff, you should feel free to simply pull down the code at **commit 6db9f7e** if you'd simply like to resume following along right away. The following figure shows a still capture of where you should end up after running the application, clicking the **Launch** button, and after the conclusion of the Splash Screen:

Figure 5.2 – Splash Screen finished and waiting for user input

We'll get into the nitty-gritty details of all of the items – some familiar, some new – contained in that commit's **patch** soon enough, but before we do, let's quickly recap what we've accomplished so far.

Starting with a set of storyboard panels depicting snapshots of the scene at various points in time, we used the boards to pin down timings for the various animations and transitions involved. Then, we crafted some reusable code to define a CutSceneSegment, along with other logic relating to animating objects. Finally, we wrote the containing SplashScreen class and its attendant asset and CutSceneSegment orchestration logic that comprises the full timeline of the scene. That's a lot to accomplish – don't neglect to acknowledge that!

Next, we'll be moving on to one of the more under-appreciated areas of game development: input systems. Because of its importance, we'll be devoting the rest of this chapter to going over how the Space-Truckers input system functions and how it is implemented.

Designing the Input System

The topic of the **User Interface** (**UI**) often focuses quite heavily on visual elements, layout, and design. For the majority of web applications, the basics of tracking a pointer, touches, or taps along with keyboard input are handled by the web browser, which in turn delegates many responsibilities, such as hardware driver interfacing to the underlying **Operating System** (**OS**). When using a web-native application library such as Babylon.js, developers can take advantage of these already-present abstractions to make it quick and easy to add user interaction elements to their scenes. In this section, we'll learn how to add the application scaffolding that can support multiple types of inputs on-the-fly, followed by implementing a way to map arbitrary inputs to actions or commands in the game.

It's said that imitation is the sincerest form of flattery, so let's flatter the Babylon.js team by "stealing" (called "researching" in polite company) the camera input management code. Using the **FreeCamera** as an example (read about it at `https://github.com/BabylonJS/Babylon.js/blob/master/packages/dev/core/src/Cameras/Inputs/freeCameraGamepadInput.ts`), here is how the data flows between the controller and the application:

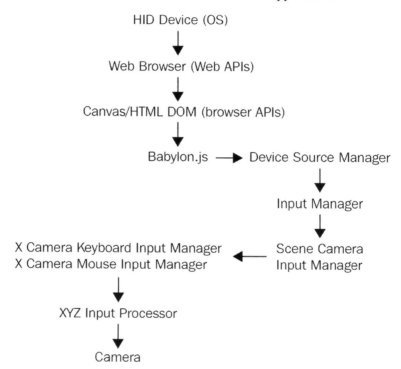

Figure 5.3 – Flow of input from a Human Input Device (HID) through the Web Browser's APIs, to the HTML/Canvas and into Babylon.js and the various components of the FreeCamera's input system

Data starts at the top with the device itself sending data to the connected host OS, which (via its device driver interface) translates that raw input data into structures compatible and familiar to the web browser or native host interfaces. Eventually, it makes its way into Babylon.js, where it is massaged, processed, filtered down, and passed around until it reaches the target of its affections: the **FreeCamera**. Here is a PG that represents a slightly simplified version of the actual input system we'll be discussing now – use it as a working reference if you get lost: `https://playground.babylonjs.com/#78MJJ8#64`.

Defining the Main Menu Control Scheme

Although we won't be defining control maps for the game phases at this time, the foundations we'll establish with this pattern will make it quick, painless, and easy to add whatever arbitrary control maps later as they become necessary. The table shows the various inputs and actions that we'll be interested in handling in the Menu system:

GamePad	Key(s)	Action
D-Pad Up/L. Stick	W, Up Arrow	MOVE_UP
D-Pad Down/L. Stick	S, Down Arrow	MOVE_DOWN
D-Pad Left/L. Stick	A, Left Arrow	MOVE_LEFT
D-Pad Right/L. Stick	D, Right Arrow	MOVE_RIGHT
A/X	Enter/Return	ACTIVATE
B/Circle	Backspace/Delete	GO_BACK
B/Circle	Space bar	ACTIVATE

Figure 5.4 – Menu controls mapped to various inputs

When it comes to the basic keyboard and (mouse) pointer interactions, the Babylon.js **Scene** offers the `onKeyboardObservable` and `onPointerObservable` properties to allow subscribers to be notified of keyboard and mouse (touch) interactions, respectively. `GamepadManager` (accessible from a scene's `gamepadManager` property) and `VirtualJoystick` are useful for adding gamepads and their virtual touch equivalents for when mouse and keyboard aren't the goal. You can read more about these in the Babylon.js docs at `https://doc.babylonjs.com/divingDeeper/input/virtualJoysticks` and `https://doc.babylonjs.com/divingDeeper/input/gamepads`.

> **Important note**
>
> As alluded to earlier, the topic of input handling is sufficiently complex that it would take a great deal of the finite space available in these pages to review all the code line by line, so the code that is listed will be highlighted in sections under a particular area of discussion. Don't worry about not being able to follow along, though – you can still examine the full source code and the links to PG snippets won't be going away either!

Mapping Input Data

Although the table of controls from the previous section is something that would work well in the game or application's user manual, it's less clear how the information in that table can be leveraged in this application.

A JavaScript **object map** (or **hashmap**) refers to a regular JS object where the string name for each property is the key to its value. Using object-key notation (for example, accessing an object's values, as in foo["property"]), indices will be represented in the new source file we'll call inputActionMaps.js. In it, we will define all the various object constants and helper functions relating to – as suggested by the name – mapping inputs to actions:

```
const inputControlsMap = {
    /* Keyboard Mappings */
    w: 'MOVE_UP', 87: 'MOVE_UP',
    s: 'MOVE_DOWN', 83: 'MOVE_DOWN',
    a: 'MOVE_LEFT', 65: 'MOVE_LEFT',
    d: 'MOVE_RIGHT', 68: 'MOVE_RIGHT',
    //...
    PointerTap: 'ACTIVATE',
    //...
    button1: 'ACTIVATE', buttonStart: 'ACTIVATE',
    buttonBack: 'GO_BACK', button2: 'GO_BACK',
    dPadDown: 'MOVE_DOWN', lStickDown: 'MOVE_DOWN',
};
export default { inputControlsMap, ...};
```

On the left-hand side (the property name or **key**) of the object map is every unique potential input index that we are interested in handling. We include every potential combination of input codes that should apply to this action; this includes the integer codes, as well as the character keys, to allow interchangeability between different types of keyboard input events; this will also make it easier to add additional input methods in the future. You'll notice that we've defined our own input indexes as well, in the form of the button1 and buttonStart members. Although it seems duplicative and redundant, having a layer of indirection between the actual device codes and the logic handling them gives the system a ton of flexibility.

When it comes to handling the various types of gamepad input, indirection comes in handy once again. The BABYLON.DeviceType enumeration defines constants for each supported type of gamepad device. We'll use another object map to store how each particular device's inputs matches up to our defined inputControlsMap:

```
const gamePadControlMap = {
    /* deviceType */
    2: [
        { 0: 'button1' }, // BABYLON.Xbox360Button.A
        { 1: 'button2' },
```

```
        { 2: 'button3' },
        { 3: 'button4' }
    ]
};
```

The preceding code is what the mapping for the Xbox360 controller looks like at a very basic level. As the comment indicates, each object in the `deviceType` array corresponds to a different input index on the controller.

In a moment, we'll learn how to use this mapping information at runtime to resolve inputs from connected devices, but first, let's get a bit of a wider perspective by taking a small step back – not too far, we don't want to get overwhelmed in it all! The following diagram illustrates the different concerns we'll need to address to be able to handle input in Space-Truckers:

Figure 5.5 – Handling input Part 1 of 4. This section covers mapping input data from multiple devices and types into standardized structures that can be resolved to game or application-level actions

Entire books can be written just on the topic of designing the input models and such, but the important thing to take away here is that the goal of the code we're writing or are about to write is to hide away (or **abstract**) the details of how inputs are processed from the game's core logic. The game logic doesn't care or need to know about whether a user wants to move their truck with a keyboard or a gamepad – it just needs to know that the user wants to move their truck and in what direction!

Input Management

When it comes to managing the specific inputs and devices, `SpaceTruckerInputManager` (follow along with the code at `https://github.com/jelster/space-truckers/blob/ch5/src/spaceTruckerInput.js`) is responsible for managing the lower-level device management tasks of subscribing and unsubscribing to/from device events, retrieving input from the underlying Babylon.js input abstraction layers, and preparing it for being processed into actions.

Coalescing, or aggregating input from multiple devices, can be both tricky and tedious – not the best combination for anything requiring concentration and recall as coding does. Tackling the tricky part by breaking down the complexity is the first step; the second step is paradoxically (or perhaps ironically) more complicated than the first step because it is more up to the individual involved to find ways to keep chugging through to the end.

Addressing Inputs

One of the most common decisions that needs to be made about a potential software design is where (in the code) to assign various responsibilities. It can sometimes be tempting to just put all the logic, data, and code into a single file for convenience's sake, but unless this is all taking place in the PG, enhancing and maintaining the application will quickly become an uncontrollable nightmare in every practical respect.

One way that the **SpaceTruckerInputManager** (**STIM**) manages complexity is by maintaining individual and separate device-specific registration logic. Different devices present their data in different ways; some types of inputs lend themselves to Observables that can be subscribed to receive input events:

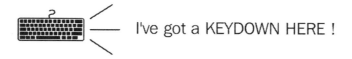

Figure 5.6 – Observables propagating events – onKeyDownObservable in this case

Others are more suited to have their state polled on a frame-by-frame basis:

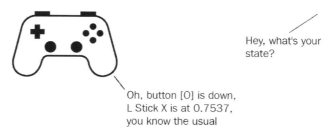

Figure 5.7 – Analog inputs (joystick axis, triggers, and more) need
to be polled to get the current state of the device

To make things more fun, many devices mix paradigms, with some inputs exposed via observable events and some only available via polling! All this data is aggregated into an `inputMap` **hashmap** (there it is again!) that contains the current state of all registered inputs.

The Input Manager must deal with either scenario with aplomb and grace according to Etiquette, and so it shall. Leaving a subscription dangling after the subscriber has gone away is considered poor form, so we must ensure the Input Manager also cleans up after itself like a good houseguest. That means we need to track our subscriptions and their sources so that we can use `Observable.remove`. Fortunately, we also have a parallel need for the Input Manager to have access to a given Scene.

Input Registration

Whenever a **Scene** wants to be able to accept input, it must register that intent. From the perspective of `SpaceTruckerInputManager`, it doesn't matter who is invoking `registerInputForScene`, it just needs `sceneToRegister` into its `inputSubscriptions` array. The object map that's added to the list is keyed by the scene being registered because the lifetime of `SpaceTruckerInputManager` follows a **Singleton** pattern (for example, there is only one instance of the **STIM** in the application). We do this because we want to be able to control when and how a particular scene is routed input at runtime, and to be good neighbors, we hook ourselves up to `Scene.onDisposeObservable` (highlighted). The subscriptions array contains the returned set of **Observers** from each of the enabled device types (`enableKeyboard`, `enableMouse`, and `enableGamePad`):

```
registerInputForScene(sceneToRegister) {
    logger.logInfo("registering input for scene",
      sceneToRegister);
    const inputSubscriptions = this.inputSubscriptions;
    const registration = {
        scene: sceneToRegister, subscriptions: [
            this.enableKeyboard(sceneToRegister),
            this.enableMouse(sceneToRegister),
            this.enableGamepad(sceneToRegister)
        ]
    };
    sceneToRegister.onDisposeObservable.add(() =>
      this.unregisterInputForScene(sceneToRegister));
    inputSubscriptions.push(registration);
    sceneToRegister.attachControl();
}
```

The aforementioned device-enable functions return an object with a very specific shape – and that shape is one of the keys (pardon the deep-running pun here) to making everything come together smoothly.

Checking Inputs

To deal with inputs requiring polling, each type of device needs to have a checkInput method that knows how to retrieve input and place it into the SpaceTruckerInputManager.inputMap hash map. For devices that exclusively utilize observables in their input surfacing, the checkInput function can be a no-op or empty function that does nothing. Devices with mixed or solely axis inputs (for example, thumbsticks, joysticks, triggers – any input type that returns an input that isn't always a 0 or 1) implement checkInput to read the gamepad's state every time it is called (every frame). Since things such as normalizing input are concerns shared across different models of gamepads, the utility functions in inputActionMap.js (referenced as SpaceTruckerControls in the following code block) are leveraged to ensure that axis input values are in the range of *-1 <= value <= 1*. Other functions take those normalized values and map them to a particular input direction based on the inputs crossing a threshold value:

```
const checkInputs = () => {
    const iMap = this.inputMap;
    if (!this.gamepad) { return; }
// handle quantitative or input that reads between 0 and 1
//(on/off) inputs are handled by the onButton/ondPad
Observables

    let LSValues = SpaceTruckerControls
        .normalizeJoystickInputs(this.gamepad.leftStick);
    SpaceTruckerControls
        .mapStickTranslationInputToActions(LSValues, iMap);

    let RSValues = SpaceTruckerControls
        .normalizeJoystickInputs(this.gamepad.rightStick);

    SpaceTruckerControls
        .mapStickRotationInputToActions(RSValues, iMap);
};
```

The preceding code block is from spaceTruckerInput.js and is contained as part of the checkInputs function object defined in the enableGamepads method. For any type of analog input device, there will be a certain amount of imprecision and noise in the inputs. To deal with that, the input is "normalized" (that is, values that are reported are in the range of -1 <= x <= 1) using static methods.

Disposing Input Subscriptions

The other property of the `enableDevice` contract is the `dispose` method. This is a function, like `checkInputs`, that contains all the specific logic needed to unsubscribe any observers and clean up after itself. Those two properties allow the consumers of `inputManager` to remain completely ignorant about the specifics of how input is collected by the application. This makes the code simpler and gives us more attention to focus on accomplishing other things (such as getting through the rest of this chapter). This is what the return value of the `enableGamepad` method looks like:

```
return {
        checkInputs,
        dispose: () => {
            this.gamepad = null;
            manager.onGamepadConnectedObservable
                .remove(gamepadConnectedObserver);
            manager.onGamepadDisconnectedObservable
                .remove(gamepadDisconnectedObserver);
        }
    };
```

All this talk about observers, observables, and subscriptions can be confusing. That's the complexity you're tasting, but hopefully, that taste will yield to a more pleasing robust, functional flavor as we discuss the final piece of the **STIM**: the `getInputs` method.

The getInputs Method

Although we want a scene to check inputs every frame, we haven't defined what will invoke that logic yet, or where it will occur in the application. For the **STIM**, that is a largely irrelevant question. The `getInputs` function takes a Scene as its sole parameter. The **Scene** is used to look up the inputSubscriptions registered to that scene, captured as the `sceneInputHandler` local constant. Each of the subscriptions in the `sceneInputHandler.subscriptions` array has its `checkInputs` function invoked as part of a `forEach` loop; recall that each subscription represents a specific input type and that the `checkInputs` function populates `SpaceTruckerInputManager.inputMap` with the latest values.

With `inputMap` containing all the various inputs to the Screen, an array of entries is iterated across and mapped into an input event structure containing the **action** name or **key**, along with any contextual event information in the form of the `lastEvent` property:

```
getInputs(scene) {
    const sceneInputHandler = this.inputSubscriptions
        .find(is => is.scene === scene);
    if (!sceneInputHandler) {
        return;
    }
    sceneInputHandler.subscriptions
        .forEach(s => s.checkInputs());
    const im = this.inputMap;
    const ik = Object.keys(im);
    const inputs = ik
        .map((key) => {
            return {
                action: controlsMap[key],
                lastEvent: im[key]
            };
        });
    if (inputs && inputs.length > 0) {
        this.onInputAvailableObservable
            .notifyObservers(inputs);
    }
    return inputs;
}
```

The resulting inputs array is then returned to callers, as well as getting syndicated via `onInputAvailableObservable` (currently unused). Note the large gap in this discussion, namely the question as to where and who calls the `getInputs` function. This is indeed a good question, but it is not one that `SpaceTruckerInputManager` needs to concern itself with – that is a matter for our next topic: Input Processing:

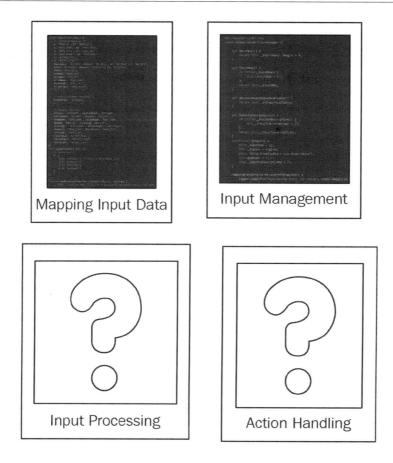

Figure 5.8 – Two of the four components covered so far

Input Processing

Mapping raw inputs to game or application inputs is a crucial part of Input Management, the two components of our input system that we've covered so far. That's potentially enough to be sufficient for a relatively simple application or game, but Space-Truckers has different needs. It needs to be able to selectively route the input to Screens without needing to know anything about the details of that input. It also needs to handle input state – not just the current, but past as well.

There is a point whereupon it becomes rude to ask additional favors from a distinguished houseguest, and if our houseguest is `SpaceTruckerInputManager`, then asking it to take on these responsibilities is… well, it's just too much. We need another component to take up the burden: `SpaceTruckerInputProcessor`.

Attaching Controls

Similar to the `registerInputForScene` and `unRegisterInputForScene` methods of its sibling, `SpaceTruckerInputManager`, the **SpaceTruckerInputProcessor** (**STIP**) has the `attachControl` and `detachControl` functions. Unlike its sibling, though, the STIP functions do not accept a **Scene** as a parameter. That is because a given STIP instance is tied to a given **Screen** that it will be performing input processing against. It is the `SpaceTruckerInputProcessor.attachControl` method that calls `registerInputForScene` in the first place:

```
attachControl() {
    if (!this.controlsAttached) {
        this.scene.attachControl();
        this.inputManager.registerInputForScene(this.scene);
        this.onInputObserver =
            this.inputManager.onInputAvailableObservable
        .add((inputs) => {
            this.inputAvailableHandler(inputs);
        });
        this.controlsAttached = true;
    }
}
```

Also, as part of attaching control to the Screen, `inputManager.onInputObservable` gets `SpaceTruckerInputProcessor.inputAvailableHandler` subscribed to be notified when a new set of inputs has been received. It's a simple little method that just pushes received inputs into `inputQueue`, which is processed as part of the `update` method.

Update

This is where the magic happens. After a quick check to ensure that it's OK to be handling inputs, `inputManager.getInputs` is invoked, which, in turn, triggers an out-of-function process that ends up populating `inputQueue` with information. This may not happen in time for the rest of the update function logic, but that's OK because it will just be handled in the next frame:

```
update() {
    if (!this.controlsAttached) {
        return;
    }
    this.inputManager.getInputs(this.scene);
    this.lastActionState = this.actionState;
```

```
    const inputQueue = this.inputQueue;
    while (inputQueue.length > 0) {
        let input = inputQueue.pop();
        this.inputCommandHandler(input);
    }
}
```

The current map of actions to state (`this.actionState`) is copied into `this.lastActionState` to preserve it for later usage in processing inputs. Then, `inputQueue` is drained of items one by one and dispatched by `inputCommandHandler`.

InputCommandHandler

This deceptively simple method does a lot more than it might seem at first glance. That's all due to the power of (third time's the charm!) **hashmaps**. In this case, there are a couple of layers of this type of shenanigans going on, but right now, we'll focus solely on `actionMap`. The `actionMap` class member is an object map that relates a game action (`ACTIVATE`) to an executable function in the hosting Screen – a topic we'll delve into shortly – which it uses to look up and invoke the game logic attached to the given action:

```
inputCommandHandler(input) {
    input.forEach(i => {
        const inputParam = i.lastEvent;
        const actionFn = this.actionMap[i.action];
        if (actionFn) {
            const priorState = this.lastActionState
                ? this.lastActionState[i.action] : null;
            this.actionState[i.action] =
                actionFn({priorState}, inputParam);
        }
    });
}
```

By convention, we pass an object with `lastActionState`, along with the event object passed along from `inputManager`, and store the return value in a previously mentioned object map, `actionState`. Each individual `actionFn` decides what to return, as well as what to do with the passed-in state value without `inputProcessor` ever needing to deal with the specifics – nice and tidy!

The buildActionMap Function

What `buildActionMap` does is what is known as **metaprogramming** or writing code that writes code. Going through each of the action parameters passed in `actionList`, the `actionDef.action` string property is used to look up a function with the same name in the `SpaceTruckerInputProcessor. screen` object:

```
buildActionMap(actionList, createNew) {
    if (createNew) {
        this.actionMap = {};
    }
    actionList.forEach(actionDef => {
      const action = actionDef.action;
        const actionFn = this.screen[action];
        if (!actionFn) {
            return;
        }
        this.actionMap[action] = actionDef.shouldBounce() ?
            bounce(actionFn, 250, this) : actionFn;
    });
}
```

If located, `actionMap` is populated with the located function after optionally wrapping it with a pre-processing bounce function to prevent it from being invoked too many times in a given period… which brings us to the final component of our input system: Action Handling:

Mapping Input Data

Input Management

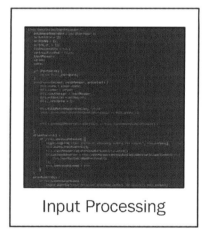
Input Processing

Action Handling

Figure 5.9 – Input Processing, Input Management, and Mapping of
Input data covered. Just Action Handling remains

Action Handling

We've spent the last few pages diving through multiple levels of abstraction and indirection, and we're now finally at the point where it all starts to do something – the Action Handling. While the previous steps were confined to a specific class or instance type, the action handlers are the screens themselves.

Conventional Actions

Sounds like the name of a bad early 2000s cover band, but it's a term for how we go about naming and describing our action functions on a given screen. It's a lot simpler than it sounds: for every action that a **Screen** would like to handle, create a **function** with the same name as the action. If you want to track the previous state of the given action, accept a `state` parameter. Should you need to get more information about the input event, add a second parameter to the function to accept an `inputEvent`.

> **Important note**
>
> Remember, an action is a game-specific concept, such as MOVE_UP, or ACTIVATE. Those are just the names given for this game; you are free to name them whatever you want!

Using `SpaceTruckerMainMenuScreen` as an example, the MOVE_UP and MOVE_DOWN actions should increment or decrement `selectedItemIndex` for the menu items. An ACTIVATE action should invoke the menu item. Here's what that looks like when we code up the MOVE_UP action:

```
MOVE_UP(state) {
    logger.logInfo("MOVE_UP");
    const lastState = state.priorState;
    if (!lastState) {
        const oldIdx = this.selectedItemIndex;
        const newIdx = oldIdx - 1;
        this.selectedItemIndex = newIdx;
    }
    return true;
}
```

Similarly, `ACTIVATE` retrieves `selectedItem` before simulating a click event by calling its `onPointerClickObservable.notifyObservers` method to invoke whatever result is indicated by the particular button selected.

Skipping the Splash Screen

As part of constructing the Splash screen earlier in this chapter, we added a `skipRequested` flag to the scene, but there wasn't ever anything that would change that value… until now! The ACTIVATE action doesn't need to know what key was pressed – it only needs to know that it happened at all; just that a key was pressed in the first place. That makes this a pretty simple piece of logic:

```
ACTIVATE(state) {
    const lastState = state.priorState;
    if (!this.skipRequested && !lastState) {
```

```
        logger.logInfo("Key press detected. Skipping cut
          scene.");
        this.skipRequested = true;
        return true;
    }
    return false;
}
```

The `SpaceTruckerSplashScreen.update` function, where the `actionProcessor.update` function is invoked, is, in turn, called during `SpaceTruckerApplication.Render`, but only if it is the currently active screen.

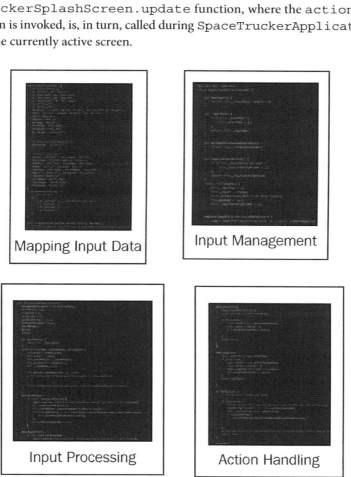

Figure 5.10 – All four components of the input system

Summary

Glancing back through the previous pages in this chapter, it might be easy to think that we haven't accomplished a whole lot, but never sell yourself short – the things we've covered in this chapter aren't the most straightforward to understand or wrap your brain around! Constructing and orchestrating the sequencing of `SplashScreen` starts to ramp up the complexity of our code, not counting the mental whiplash induced by pivoting from that to input in the space of a page.

As stated earlier and not redundantly stated again now, entire thick textbooks can and have been written on the topic of input handling, something we're trying to cram into a mere fraction of that. Not only that, but we are now able to approach future features with a much clearer picture of how all of the non-game-specific tasks are to be managed and handled.

That statement could be expanded to cover this and the other chapters in this section as well – we've gotten much of the supporting application in place now, which leaves us far more attention to focus on the topics in our next section! In section two, we'll build the gameplay mechanics, set up lighting and materials, and much, much more.

Extended Topics

Where to start? There are simply so many interesting things and possibilities to explore! Here are just a few ideas for things you can do to further your learning and enhance `SplashScreen`:

- Add a camera animation to the beginning portion that has the camera moving and rotating along a path in such a way that the `billboard` panel grows in apparent size at about the same rate as the volume of the music rises

- Add background environmental effects to the Scene, similar to what we did with the Main Menu and the Procedural Starfield texture

- Replace the final static image with a mesh, texture, material, or something else

The input system is also a great source of ideas. Here are a few to consider:

- Implement support for your favorite gamepad or joystick device. Use this testing site to see the various inputs and values emitted by your device: `https://luser.github.io/gamepadtest/`

- Modify the input system to allow for multiple simultaneously connected users – that is, local multiplayer

- Expose the joystick sensitivity settings to the application so that they can be edited in-game by the player

Part 2: Constructing the Game

In this second part of the book, we will build on the foundations of the first part to implement the primary components that comprise **Space-Truckers: The Video Game**. The pace picks up, as there's far more material to cover than there is space to contain it.

This section comprises the following chapters:

- *Chapter 6, Implementing the Game Mechanics*
- *Chapter 7, Processing Route Data*
- *Chapter 8, Building the Driving Game*
- *Chapter 9, Calculating and Displaying Scoring Results*
- *Chapter 10, Improving the Environment with Lighting and Materials*

6

Implementing the Game Mechanics

The focus of the previous chapters was solidly on building an application foundation for **Space-Truckers**. Now, it's time to shift gears (as it were) and look at the way we want to implement the game for its first phase: **Route Planning**. As we usually want to do when faced with a single, daunting, complex problem, we break down this part of the game into two principal facets: simulation and game elements. Throughout this chapter, we'll start by looking at the simulation part of the game before layering the game mechanics on top of the simulation in a way that gives us the freedom to iterate.

It's a common tactic of reality shows and gameshows where the host will give a wind-up speech that seems to indicate that they're about to get to the big reveal, but then instead the show cuts to a commercial. This is relevant because we're going to perform a similar *headfake* – instead of diving directly into the exciting simulation and game mechanics, we're going to first take a short detour so that we can learn about how to manage music and sounds in Space-Truckers. Though a short one, it will be a handy addition as we continue integrating more and more functionality into the application.

In this chapter, we will cover the following topics:

- A Detour into Sound Management
- Designing the Game Elements of the Route Simulation
- Creating the Orbital Mechanics Simulation
- Defining the Rules – Game Mechanics

Technical Requirements

The first section of this chapter deals with audio files and playing them, so it's helpful but not necessary to have speakers or some other way of hearing sound output. As always, the source code is available on GitHub at https://github.com/jelster/space-truckers/tree/ch6.

As you might expect, most of the technical requirements from previous chapters apply to this one since we're continuing the work that started there.

Helpful Things to Know

The following are helpful things to know:

- Outside of the technical realm of software, there are some concepts and skills that are helpful to have previous knowledge of coming into this section. Don't worry if you don't recognize or aren't familiar with this stuff – that's the whole reason you're reading this book in the first place – to learn! This includes vector operations in 3D space, addition, subtraction, multiplication, and so on, as well as the difference between normalized (1- unit) and non- normalized vectors.

- Basic kinematic physics – calculate the velocity or position of something based on time, with and without including acceleration.

- Familiarity with force and momentum relationships.

> **Note**
> Computers are supposed to be the ones who are good at crunching numbers, not you. Don't freak out if you don't consider yourself a math person – we've got you covered!

Useful Links from the Babylon.js Docs

The following are some useful links:

- Physics Engine and Forces: `https://doc.babylonjs.com/divingDeeper/physics/forces`

- Mesh Copies, Clones, and Instances – look at the **Solid Particle System** (**SPS**), Instances, and Thin Instances: `https://doc.babylonjs.com/divingDeeper/mesh/copies`

- Environment Skyboxes (which we will get more into in *Chapter 10, Improving the Environment with Lighting and Materials*): `https://doc.babylonjs.com/divingDeeper/environment/skybox`

- Events and Actions: `https://doc.babylonjs.com/divingDeeper/events/actions`

A Detour into Sound Management

The topic of playing music and sound FX has come up previously in our journey – the theme song sound is played as part of the Splash Screen that we built in *Chapter 5, Adding a Cut Scene and Handling Input*, after all. The sound plays just fine, and everything seems to work, so what need is there to *make things more complicated* for no apparent reason? This is an excellent point to raise because, in software, the best approaches tend to also be the simplest, and simple is good because it means fewer things can go wrong (by definition). When fewer things can go wrong in software, it's easy and cheap to make changes, additions, and enhancements and that is good for both Engineering and Accounting – a two-for-one special!

What all of that is getting to is that even though it works fine in isolation to load and directly play the `BABYLON.Sound` instance directly in the Screen itself, things break down when more than one Scene and Screen become involved. The main reason for this has to do with the fact that `AudioEngine` is independent of the Scene, but the Sound is not. This causes issues when we want to coordinate the starting, stopping, and volume levels of multiple Sounds across multiple different Scenes.

Sounds, SoundTracks, and the AudioEngine

Analogous to how the **WebGL2/WebGPU** canvas is used to perform rendering, the underlying audio engine used in Babylon.js is based on the **Web Audio** specification. If you're interested in diving into that, and/or if you have insomnia, check it out at `https://webaudio.github.io/web-audio-api/`. To read more details on the abstractions built on top of that specification, the relevant Babylon.js API docs can be found at `https://doc.babylonjs.com/typedoc/classes/babylon.sound`.

To boil down our requirements when it comes to audio, we need the application to be able to do the following things or have the following qualities:

- We need to be able to control the collective volume (gain) level for groups of related types of sounds, such as background music, UI feedback sounds, and game sound effects

- It should be easy to change out the underlying sound assets without needing to change any of the consuming components' code

- Consumers of the audio component should be able to easily access the underlying `BABYLON.Sound`

- The asynchronous loading of audio assets should be coordinated to ensure all of a Scene's assets have completed their tasks before signaling readiness

To accomplish the first item, we'll leverage the functionality of `BABYLON.SoundTrack`. This type is well named because it tells you what it does in the name! Instances of a Sound are associated with a `SoundTrack` via the `SoundTrack.addSound` function. The collective volume of any Sounds belonging to a given `SoundTrack` is controlled with the `setVolume` function. There are other methods in `SoundTrack` of course, but the two mentioned functions are the ones that we're interested in now.

Looking back at the list of requirements, the third can be provided by a property accessor, while the second requirement is fulfilled by creating a mapping between a *friendly* string identifier and an object map (see *Chapter 5, Adding a Cut Scene and Handling Input*, the *Designing the Input System* section for more examples of this). The last requirement can be satisfied easily with the use of the functionality of the JS-standard `Promise` object. We'll see how these all work together shortly, but it's worth taking a moment to step back from the detailed requirements discussed previously to understand how this fits into the bigger picture.

A helpful way of identifying missing requirements and potential opportunities to solve problems relating to those requirements is to mentally picture a concrete scenario involving the matter at hand. In this case, picture the gameplay screen. Things are happening in it – the player inputs commands, the application responds to acknowledge entry, and events happen in-game. At the same time, music is playing in the background underneath the mechanical whines and screeching put out by the player's cargo pod as it is launched or as it crashes. There is a multitude of audio samples being played at any given time, but they all have different volumes appropriate to their category or type of sound. Keep that goal in mind because as we dive into the details, this overall *big picture* will help guide and keep us on track.

SpaceTruckerSoundManager

The first two steps – design and build – concern the specifics of how we will use the audio features of Babylon.js to create our audio component, while the third concerns how we will make use of that component. The full code for the following snippets can be found in this chapter's branch of the Space-Truckers GitHub repository at `https://github.com/jelster/space-truckers/blob/ch6/src/spaceTruckerSoundManager.js`.

Design

We need a bit of helper logic that will wrap the Babylon.js objects and help us manage their lifetimes and behavior. Because we're so very imaginative, we'll call it `SpaceTruckerSoundManager` – catchy, right? There are probably a lot of different ways that this can be constructed, but we want *The Simplest Thing That Could Possibly Work*, and that is `spaceTruckerSoundMap.js` and its `soundFileMap`:

```
const soundFileMap = {
    "title": { url: titleSongUrl, channel: 'music',
      loop: true },
    "overworld": { url: backgroundMusicUrl,
      channel: 'music', loop: true },
    "whoosh": { url: uiWhooshSoundUrl,
      channel: 'ui', loop: false }
};
```

The URL for each sound file is supplied by an associated `import` statement, with the object key being an arbitrary (but unique) string name. `SoundTrack` that the sound will be added to, as well as the `loop` flag to control auto-looping, are the two other data pieces rounding out `soundFileMap`, so let's move on to how `SpaceTruckerSoundManager` uses it.

Build

Each instance of `SpaceTruckerSoundManager` is initialized with the associated scene, along with a list of one or more `soundId`. These are stored in the `registeredSounds` object map, which can be used to retrieve a given Sound by calling the `sound(id)` accessor function:

```
registeredSounds = {};
sound(id) {
    return this.registeredSounds[id];
}
```

The three different `SoundTrack`s are stored in the `channels` property and initialized in the constructor:

```
constructor(scene, ...soundIds) {
    this.channels.music = new SoundTrack(scene,
      { mainTrack: false, volume: 0.89 });
    this.channels.sfx = new SoundTrack(scene,
      { mainTrack: true, volume: 1 });
    this.channels.ui = new SoundTrack(scene,
      { mainTrack: false, volume: 0.94 });
```

As mentioned previously, `constructor` takes `scene` and a list of `soundIds`; what was not mentioned previously was that after the constructor finishes, the component will not be ready for use yet – the `onReadyObservable` property of the component will notify subscribers when `SpaceTruckerSoundManager` has finished loading and preparing all its child `Sound` instances:

```
Promise.all(onReadyPromises).then(readyIds =>
  this.onReadyObservable.notifyObservers(readyIds));
```

The bulk of the constructor's logic is taken up by a loop over the list of `soundIds`. Inside the loop is logic charged with the business of instantiating and managing how that Sound is loaded, the state of which is represented by `prom`. When the Sound's `onLoaded` callback fires, the newly loaded Sound is added to the appropriate channel, `SoundTrack`, and the promise is resolved successfully:

```
const onReadyPromises = [];
soundIds.forEach(soundId => {
    const mapped = soundFileMap[soundId];
```

```
const chan = this.channels[soundId] ??
    scene.mainSoundTrack;
// guard logic omitted for length
const prom = new Promise((resolve, reject) => {
    const sound = new Sound(soundId, mapped.url, scene,
        () => {
          chan.addSound(this.registeredSounds[soundId]);
          resolve(soundId);
        }, {
          autoplay: false,
          loop: mapped.loop,
          spatialSound: mapped.channel === 'sfx'
    });
    sound.onEndedObservable.add((endedSound, state)
      => {
            this.onSoundPlaybackEnded
                .notifyObservers(endedSound.name);
        });
    this.registeredSounds[soundId] = sound;
    });
    onReadyPromises.push(prom);
});
}
```

The individual asynchronous `Promises` are coordinated in two ways: first, an array of promises is constructed containing all of the different asynchronous calls that need to be resolved before continuing. Second, the `Promise.all` method takes that array of Promises and returns another `Promise` that, when resolved, will contain the results of each `Promise` contained in the array. In other words, it waits until everything has finished and then announces its completion.

Because we can't mark the constructor as `async`, we can't await the Promise results. Instead, we attach a function to the `Promise.then` chain, which, in turn, signals readiness via `onReadyObservable`. What's notable is the absence is any sort of error or exception handling or catching – something that we will want to include in a more production-hardened application!

Integrate

The Splash Screen (see *Chapter 5, Adding a Cut Scene and Handling Input*) already plays a Sound, so we'll want to replace that with a `SpaceTruckerSoundManager` instance that is initialized in the constructor:

```
this.audioManager = new SpaceTruckerSoundManager
    (scene, 'title');
this.audioManager.onReadyObservable.addOnce(_ =>
    this.onReadyObservable.notifyObservers());
```

The Scene will have completed loading and initialization long before `audioManager.onReadyObservable` fires, so we will use that event to signal the Screen's overall readiness. To make the refactor seamless and easy, the music field of `SplashScene` is changed into the `get music()` accessor, which retrieves the *title* Sound from the underlying `audioManager`:

```
get music() {
    return this.audioManager.sound("title");
}
```

As a result, no other code changes are necessary to retrofit `SpaceTruckerSoundManager` into `SplashScreen` – it's good to go! This brings our little detour to its end, but this won't be the last time we see this since we're going to be making direct use of it later in this chapter. For now, however, we're going to be shifting topics to look at the route simulation and how it is constructed.

Designing the Game Elements of the Route Simulation

The Helios star system is the setting for Space-Truckers, but up until now, we haven't gotten into what that entails. A topic covered in exhaustive detail in other books both fiction and non- is the well-known fact that Space Is Big. Like, Really Big. At the scale of a solar system, distances involved are so large compared to relative sizes of things that trying to represent this huge scale accurately in our game will neither be fun nor performant.

An Overview of the Helios System

The following diagram is a rather stylized view of the Helios system – the home setting for Space-Truckers – from a bird's-eye view. Bracketed planetary bodies show the two different start and end route possibilities –outward going in toward the sun and vice versa. In the following diagram, the different shaded regions correspond to different potential encounters for players during the driving phase:

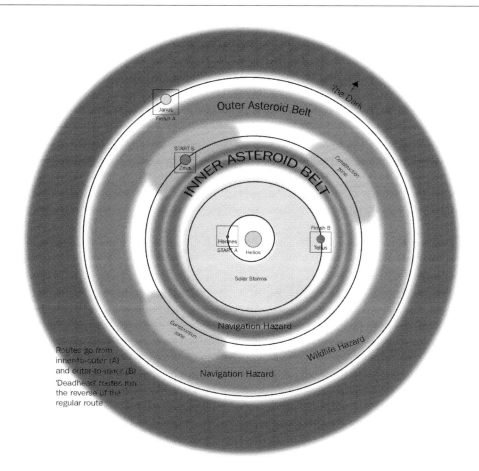

Figure 6.1 – Depiction of the route planning gameplay map

The closest planet is Hermes, so-called because it speeds around in its tight orbit of Helios. In the game world, it's the primary starting position for route planning. Routes originating from Hermes will end at the busy hive of construction at Zeus. The alternative, the *B* route, starts a bit further out from the star around the planet Tellus and has as its destination as the distant ice factories of Janus.

In between either set of origins and destinations are a whole solar system's worth of potential hazards and obstacles. Close to the turbulent star, solar storms are common. They can ruin a Space-Trucker's Day by twisting and curling the Space-Road and forcing operators to steer their vehicle and cargo through them to maintain accurate navigation. A bit past the orbit of the blue-and-green jewel Tellus is another navigation hazard in the form of a dense asteroid belt.

In the real world, there's no such thing as an asteroid belt thick enough to be a meaningful navigation hazard, but in the world of Space-Truckers, decades of asteroid mining operations have littered and set loose enough debris to make it a real problem for vessels aiming to pass through the rocky hazards.

Past the asteroid belt lies the gas giant Zeus, the titan of planets in the Helios system, where a hive of industrial activity sparkles and glimmers around the clock. The busy factories require a constant supply of raw materials, spare parts, and supplies, and that's where Space-Truckers come in. Getting straight to Zeus isn't always as easy as it may seem, though.

Not content to confine their industries to merely the orbit of the giant planet, recent engineering projects at the leading and trailing LaGrange points take advantage of the rich resources present in the so-called *Trojan* and *Greek* families of asteroids. Anyone familiar with road construction knows the delays, detours, and occasional flag-waver directing traffic that has been diverted, and those construction zones are no different in space!

Past the glowing forges and factories of the Zeus system, things start to get dark and cold. The ice giant Janus sits at the gateway between the warm buzzing of activity of the inner system with the quiet darkness of the outer. Space-Truckers arrive and depart from the area on journeys to deliver stored energy gathered in the brightness sunward, departing with full loads of icy volatiles vital to sustaining life in the inner system. However, they are not alone out there – large herds of simple space-life roam these cold and distant plains. Not used to seeing visitors, they present a navigational hazard for the unwary Space-Trucker on the tail-end of a long haul.

Putting everything together, the following screenshot shows what the system looks like when the route planning begins:

Figure 6.2 – The ReadyToLaunch phase of the route planning screen. This shows most of the actors involved, including the Star, destinationMesh, planets, launchArrow, and cargo

Now that we've looked at the system from the big picture perspective, it's time to break out the individual actors and look for commonalities between them. This allows us to start creating game components that will help service the game concepts that in a way is kind of like putting together a list of job requirements.

Actors and Their Behavior

Before we get into the specifics of the different objects and components that will comprise the route planning screen, let's take a look at what our object hierarchies look like concerning our game objects. The basic idea is that there are several pieces of data and behaviors that we know our game objects will need, but at the same time, we want to avoid writing repetitive code. We need to be able to update or advance the simulation, sometimes at a very fine-grained level, so we will generally avoid having components register their own `onBeforeRender` handlers and instead provide an `update(deltaTime)` method that will serve the same purpose. Here is one way of depicting how our various components interact with each other, with data, and with the application:

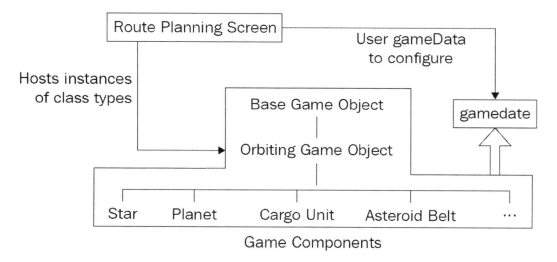

Figure 6.3 – A class diagram of the Game Components involved in RoutePlanningScreen

In the preceding diagram, the abstract hierarchy of classes is in the center. `BaseGameObject` is the least derived (for example, it doesn't extend any other type), while the various classes for the game concepts are the most derived. `RoutePlanningScreen` hosts the various instances of those game component classes, managing their behavior in a fashion that is like the overall rendering pipeline:

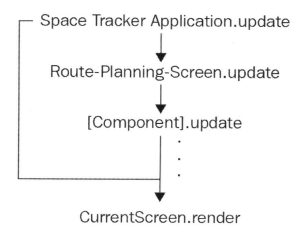

Figure 6.4 – The SpaceTruckerApplication update and render cycle, simplified

Each frame that the `RoutePlanningScreen.update` method is invoked by `SpaceTrucker-Application`, `RoutePlanningScreen` goes through its own child components and (optionally) calls their update methods. When all of those have been completed and `RoutePlanningScreen` has finished its update cycle, the screen is finally rendered. There are a few steps that are missing in this diagram, such as the before and after physics steps, but that is the mechanism for how our game's underlying state can change and evolve. That's how we describe the most primitive behavior needed by our game objects, so let's use that knowledge to code it up!

Abstracting the BaseGameObject Class

The `BaseGameObject` class (see `https://github.com/jelster/space-truckers/blob/ch6/src/baseGameObject.js` for its source) is what provides that shared, low-level functionality that we don't want to have to duplicate across game objects. It is the least common denominator for any object that we may want to render in a `Scene`. Many of the properties of `BaseGameObject` are simple proxies that allow access to the underlying properties of the different Babylon.js components comprising the game object, such as the `Vector3` rotation property accessors:

```
get rotation() { return this.mesh?.rotation; }
set rotation(value) { this.mesh.rotation = value; }
```

In addition to consolidating access to the various component and data properties, `BaseGameObject` provides two crucial behaviors: `update` and `dispose`.

`update` doesn't seem to do much in this base class, since all it does is update the `lastSceneTime` property, but it's an important role; many types of behaviors require tracking not just the amount of time since the last frame was rendered but also the previous value to properly integrate things such as velocity and acceleration.

> **Important note**
>
> If an extending class depends on the `deltaTime` and/or `lastSceneTime` value, make sure to call `super.update(deltaTime)` as the *first* thing it does in its `update` method.

For folks with experience in traditional **Object-Oriented Programming (OOP)** languages, the usage pattern might be familiar: an abstract base class provides common functionality to its more derived classes. An example of how this works is in the orbital mechanics simulation that we've implemented.

Defining the Orbital Mechanics Simulation Elements

The `Planet` class (covered shortly) builds off the `OrbitingGameObject` class (`https://github.com/jelster/space-truckers/blob/ch6/src/orbitingGameObject.js`), which, in turn, is derived from the `BaseGameObject` prototype. `OrbitingGameObject` provides a base suite of data and behavior about the various calculations involved in both orbital motion and gravitational acceleration – the nerdy but interesting physics and math stuff we'd otherwise end up repeating across multiple places in the code base. Though it isn't intended for objects of this type to be rendered directly, it would still be possible to do so by simply setting the `mesh` and `material` properties appropriately. The following table summarizes the data and behavior of `OrbitingGameObject`:

Function/Property	Type	Use
angularPosition	Property	Updated every frame when autoUpdatePosition = true. Provides the current position of the object in terms of its orbit in radians.
angularVelocity	Property	Calculated from base values. The speed, in radians, of the object's circular motion as it orbits.
orbitalPeriod	Property	Calculated from base values. The amount of time it takes for the object to complete an entire orbit of 2π radians.
orbitalRadius	Property	Initial value. The linear distance from the center of the system to the object's circular orbit.
gravConstant, primaryReferenceMass	(gameData.js)	Newton's Gravitational Constant, along with the mass of the star, are two of three needed values for most orbital calculations.
calculate/setOrbitalParameters	Function	Functions that compute and set the various orbital parameters for the object based on either object data or from parameter overrides.
updateOrbitalPosition(deltaTime)	Function	Called by the update method when autoUpdatePosition = true. Combines angularPosition, angularVelocity, and deltaTime to compute the current position of the object.
calculateGravitationalForce(position)	Function	Given a world position, it calculates the direction and magnitude of the gravitational force imparted to an object of negligible mass at that position. This only applies if a mass value from physicsImpostor is present. See this chapter's section on *Creating the Orbital Mechanics Simulation* for more.

Figure 6.5 – Summary of the behavior and data of the OrbitingGameObject component

By abstracting away the details of the orbital and gravitational calculations, more derived classes are much easier to understand, build, and maintain. A great example of how this can be leveraged is the Planet class.

Implementing the Star and Planets

The bulk of the constructor logic for the Planet class (https://github.com/jelster/space-truckers/blob/ch6/src/route-planning/planet.js) is devoted to the pertinent needs of reading the input planData and then instantiating and configuring the render-specific aspects of the component – tasks such as creating materials and loading and applying textures. Notice that there is no mention in the Planet class file of anything relating to our orbital simulation – only the specifics that make a given Planet instance different from another.

To aid in this effort, the class is data-driven: `planData` passed into the constructor function contains all the data needed. That's the beauty of the mixed inheritance/composition patterns that we've been applying; each of our components only needs to concern itself with the specific tasks that it has been designed to accomplish and nothing more! As a result, this is what a typical `planData` looks like:

```
{
        name: "tellus",
        posRadians: Scalar.RandomRange(0, 2 * Math.PI),
        posRadius: 750,
        scale: 30,
        color: new Color3(0.91, 0.89, 0.72),
        diffuseTexture: earthDiffuseUrl,
        normalTexture: earthNormalUrl,
        specularTexture: earthSpecularUrl,
        lightMapUrl: earthCloudsUrl,
        mass: 1e14
    }
```

Perhaps this looks familiar? Back in *Chapter 2, Ramping Up on Babylon.js*, we saw a very similar structure that was used to generate the orbiting planets of the Loading Screen – with a few new members (such as mass). Similarly, the `Star` class (`https://github.com/jelster/space-truckers/blob/ch6/src/route-planning/star.js`) can be very short and sweet since although it does not orbit like other game objects, it does participate in gravitational calculations.

By setting `autoUpdatePosition = false`, the star will not move in its central position in the world space. This makes the constructor and subsequent class quite simple:

```
constructor(scene, options) {
    super(scene, options);
    this.autoUpdatePosition = false;
    const starData = options;

    this.mesh = MeshBuilder.CreateSphere("star",
        { diameter: starData.scale }, this.scene);
    this.material = new StandardMaterial("starMat",
        this.scene);
    this.material.emissiveTexture = new
        Texture(starData.diffuseTexture, this.scene);
}
```

The last two actors of our dramatis personae are the player's avatar, also known as **the cargo**, and the hazardous collection of boulders that form the asteroid belt. We'll cover the cargo later because we have a major new concept to cover first in the Asteroid Belt – **Thin Instances**. If you have a phobia of numbers and math (and it's OK if you do!), fair warning – there be matrices and quaternions ahead, but there's no need to worry – you won't have to sweat any of the hard *maths*. All of the hard work and heavy thinking is done by functions in Babylon.js, so all we need to do is understand when and how to use them!

Procedurally Generating the Asteroid Belt

Before we talk about the particulars of the `AsteroidBelt` class (`https://github.com/jelster/space-truckers/blob/ch6/src/route-planning/asteroidBelt.js`), we should review some definitions and concepts in the context of rendering meshes. Firstly, it's important to understand what a **mesh** is at its simplest level. Starting with the simplest explanation, a mesh is a bunch of points set up in a particular order in 3D space. More in-depth, a mesh is a collection of points in 3D space that can be positioned, rotated, and scaled together. To describe it in extremely precise terms, a mesh is an array of vectors grouped as a set of matrices that represent the position, translation, and rotation of each part of the 3D model, respectively. While a mesh's geometry is sent to the GPU once, that same geometry can be linked (reused) by the GPU to render as many additional instances as are required.

In the case of regular instances, it is important to understand that although the mesh geometry is not duplicated in the GPU, there is still a CPU (JavaScript) overhead stemming from the need to iterate over each instance every frame for processing. That's the price of being able to retain control over individual instances, but some situations may not require that much control. That's where Thin Instances come into play.

> **Note**
> If you've used 3D Modeling tools such as Blender, Thin Instances in Babylon.js are referred to as linked objects in Blender.

The essential concept that we're focusing on here is the idea that there are circumstances where we might need hundreds, thousands, or even tens of thousands of individual copies of a given mesh to be rendered in a particular Scene, but we don't want to incur the memory or CPU overhead of having to process and maintain multiple copies of that mesh's geometry. Think trees in a forest (for example, `https://playground.babylonjs.com/#YB006J#75`), or an ocean comprised of LEGO® (for example, `https://playground.babylonjs.com/#TWQZAU#3`), or, as is relevant to our case, a large number of asteroids – giant, floating space rocks (for example, `https://playground.babylonjs.com/#5BS9JG#59` – with a tip of the hat to Babylon.js community member *Evgeni_Popov*).

The key limitations to keep in mind when thinking about (Thin) Instances are as follows:

- All instances, Thin or not, must share the same Material

- Although much more efficient than cloning a mesh, Instances are still both CPU- and GPU-bound

- For Thin Instances, you must manipulate an individual Instance's properties (for example, position, scaling, rotation, and so on) by manually manipulating the specific Instance's matrix values

- All Thin Instances are always drawn (or not) – there is no way to hide or skip the rendering of an individual Thin Instance

- Thin Instances check collisions as a single, giant mesh; there is no way to register collision detection for individual Instances

Even with those limitations in mind, it makes sense to use Thin Instances to render the Asteroid Belt – we want at least a thousand (or so...) of them, so we don't need to exercise much control over them, and since we want them to look relatively homogenous, it's OK for them to share the same Material. We'll get more into the Material we'll use for the asteroids later, so for now, let's look at how we are creating each asteroid's Thin Instance through the power of Analogy.

> **Important note**
>
> We are operating under the assumption that an instance has the same sign for its scaling, position, and rotation components (this is known in matrix jargon as having the same sign *determinant*). You should not directly mix elements with opposite signs. For example, the following statement results in a mixed determinant sign:
>
> ```
> Matrix.Compose(new Vector3(-1, 1, 1),Quaternion.Identity(),
> newVector3(2, 1, 0))
> ```
>
> This is because the negative sign in the first argument conflicts with the positive 1 that an Identity Quaternion represents.

Astrophysicists who study black holes have an interesting way of describing the properties of their scientific studies.

The idea is that, any given black hole only has three observable properties – electric charge, mass, and spine that uniquely defines it, whereas things like people, stars and plants, have quite a few additional attributes making them – and you – uniquely special. Like this **no-hair theorem**, as it's called, each Thin Instance of our asteroid will be distinguished apart from its brethren by just their properties of **position**, **rotation**, and **scale**. We will define values for each of these properties, for each instance individually, storing the arrays as class members. Thus, the algorithm for generating the asteroids can be relatively quite simple: declare the matrices, quaternions, rotations, scalings, and position arrays. Then, allocate a Float32Array to use as the matrix buffer. The size should be nine times the count of asteroids to create to hold the resulting data.

For every asteroid that we want to create, we must do the following:

1. Generate a set of three vectors, one each for the position, rotation, and scale.
2. Randomly set the component values of each vector to a number in limits.
3. Add the new vectors to their respective arrays.
4. Create and add a new, empty Quaternion, Matrix to arrays.
5. Convert the rotation vector into a Quaternion.
6. Use vectors and quaternions to compose the Matrix.
7. Copy the matrix elements to the matrix buffer.
8. Set the `thinInstance` buffer on the target mesh to the instance from the matrix buffer.

When we randomly generate the values, we need to ensure that the values are all within valid parameters, and we can do this in several different ways. The first is used for the scaling and rotational vector values and helps to create the rough, rock-shaped surface of what started as a smooth `IcoSphere` mesh. Because `Math.random()` returns a floating-point number between zero and one, we scale that number out by a factor representing the maximum in the range of values we want to see generated – in other words, when the random value is equal to one.

Since it's also possible to get zero as a value, the scale has an additional additive constant to ensure at least a minimum value. A similar, though more simple expression, generates rotations for each axis. The scaling `Vector3` works well for defining the scale and rotation of the asteroid instance, but specifying the position requires another approach.

Once again, we must shift from thinking in linear terms to that of angular. Using the Babylon.js `Scalar.RandomRange()` utility function, we can generate a random point somewhere in the torus (donut shape) by defining `innerBeltRadius` and `outerBeltRadius` – that is, we generate a random number (`rTheta`) that is then combined with another random number between 0 and 2 * π.

> **Note**
>
> Recall that the sine and cosine functions take their inputs in radians, and a full circle is described by 2 * π or approximately 6.28319 radians.

The X and Z-axis values for the world position of the asteroid are computed by converting the radial (angular) value into world coordinates – for example, `Math.sin(theta)` or `Math.cos(theta)` – which yields a normalized value, then multiplying that by our randomized scale constant to properly place the object in the world. Because we are using a very simplified mathematical model to distribute the asteroids in space, we can treat the vertical Y-axis by multiplying half of a random number by the density configuration constant:

```
this.positions.push(new Vector3(
    Math.sin(theta) * rTheta,
```

```
    (Math.random() - 0.5) * density,
    Math.cos(theta) * rTheta
));
```

Updating an asteroid's rotation, position, or scale is a two-step process. The first step is for the `AsteroidBelt` class to modify values in the desired array at the index corresponding to the desired asteroid instance. In the update loop, each asteroid's rotation values are tweaked by a small random amount by modifying `this.rotations[i]`.

Once that has been completed, the second step is the same as the original generation algorithm, conveniently factored out into the `updateMatrices` function of the class. The only difference between creating and updating the thin instance data is that when we update, we use `mesh.thinInstanceBufferUpdated` instead of `mesh.thinInstanceSetBuffer`.

Note

For more on the technical aspects of using Babylon.js with meshes, Instances, and the GPU, see the official docs at `https://doc.babylonjs.com/divingDeeper/mesh/copies/instances` and `https://doc.babylonjs.com/divingDeeper/mesh/copies/thinInstances`.

It is finally time to put everything we've been looking at together into one and begin our examination of the actual **Route Planning Screen**. Although it may seem a bit confusing due to an apparent lack of *big-picture focus*, we didn't have the proper context established yet to take that picture in. Still, it can be difficult to follow along with this type of overview, so here's yet another occasion where the PG comes in handy. As shown previously, this snippet (`https://playground.babylonjs.com/#5BS9JG#59`) is a preliminary, basic implementation of the planet simulation, and although not 100% identical to the game's code, it's illustrative of all the concepts described previously, as well as some we have yet to cover!

Adding the CargoUnit Class

The `CargoUnit` class is this part of the game's projection of the player into the game world. It derives from `OrbitingGameObject`, but it does not automatically have its position updated – just like the `Star` class we just finished looking at. Unlike the `Star` class, there's a little bit more happening.

Starting with the data, the `CargoUnit` class tracks several pieces of game-specific in-flight information, such as `timeInTransit` and `distanceTraveled`. The `isInFlight` Boolean flag is implicitly correlated with `PLANNING_STATE.InFlight`, if that wasn't apparent already. These and other pieces of data are consumed by both `RoutePlanningScreen` and `PlanningScreenGui` (more on that later) and get updated as part of the hopefully now-familiar update method pattern shown in the following code.

During the update, there is some logic to point the cargo unit's rotation in the direction of flight, which involves a tiny bit of vector math, but more importantly, there is logic to apply the current frame's accumulated gravitational forces to the box. Since force is calculated in terms of effect per second, it must be scaled to the amount of time that has passed since the last frame, using `deltaTime`. After the force is applied, we clear the `currentGravity` field to prevent forces from infiltrating across rendered frames:

```
update(deltaTime) {
    super.update(deltaTime);
    if (this.isInFlight) {
        this.lastGravity = this.currentGravity.clone();
        const linVel =
            this.physicsImpostor.getLinearVelocity();
        this.lastVelocity = linVel.clone();
        linVel.normalize();

        this.timeInTransit += deltaTime;
        this.distanceTraveled +=
            this.lastVelocity.length() * deltaTime;

        this.rotation = Vector3.Cross(this.mesh.up,
            linVel);
        this.physicsImpostor.applyImpulse(this.
            currentGravity.scale(deltaTime),
            this.mesh.getAbsolutePosition());
        this.currentGravity = Vector3.Zero();
    }
}
```

A vector cross-product is a mathematical operation that takes two orthogonal vectors (that is, two vectors perpendicular to each other) and yields a third, new vector that points in a direction perpendicular to *both* of the inputs. By inputting the (normalized) physical velocity of `cargoUnit` along with the local *Up* axis, we are given the resulting rotational coordinates that `cargoUnit` must adopt to point itself in the direction of travel.

> **Note**
>
> A force applied to an asymmetrically massed body such as `cargoUnit` will cause angular rotation, or torque, causing the unit to spin wildly around its center of mass. This is not as bad as the game crashing, but not great, especially when paired with `TrailMesh`! By setting the rotation to point in the direction of travel, we are ensuring that gravitational forces transfer to the unit's linear – not angular – velocity. Also, we prevent `TrailMesh` from twisting itself up into knots – a factor that is critical when generating the next phase's route.

Defining the CargoUnit's behaviors is the last thing to cover before we shift focus. In addition to the update behavior, only three other actions are implemented by the class.

The `reset`, `launch`, and `destroy` actions are fairly self-explanatory from their names. The `reset` method is called any time the simulation is being restarted, such as when the player presses the *Delete* key on their keyboard. It clears all of the stored state data from `CargoUnit` before moving itself back to its initial start location and setting the `isInFlight` flag to `false`. The `launch` function is where `TrailMesh` is instantiated, along with the initial *kick* from the launcher; it is responsible for setting the `isInFlight` flag appropriately. Lastly, the `destroyed` function is called whenever `SpaceTruckerApplication` has determined that `CargoUnit` has been officially *destroyed*, for example, when encountering an obstacle that is not amused by the impact. It is responsible for making sure that `CargoUnit` doesn't fly off at infinite velocity after a collision and instead stays put where it is.

That was certainly a large number of different concepts and classes to go over in such a short space, but there is so much more to see we can't possibly stay on this topic any longer. We have mentioned several times that we would eventually go into some detail regarding how the flight mechanics are implemented with the physics engine, and we've almost got to the point where we can create a critical mass of contextual knowledge. This knowledge will propel us toward a greater understanding and progress – hang in there!

Establishing the Basic Route Planning Screen

Of all the different things we've worked on to date in Space-Truckers, `SpaceTruckerPlanningScreen` (`https://github.com/jelster/space-truckers/blob/ch6/src/route-planning/spaceTruckerPlanningScreen.js`) is by far the most complex. We've come prepared to manage that complexity by looking at the individual components first; with fewer things to have to try and keep track of, it's much easier to stay focused on the topic at hand. Let's break down the different aspects of the screen to make it a bit more manageable. There are three basic categories or facets that we'll focus on – this should start to be getting familiar by now – data, behavior, and state transitions. Each has a distinct role to play, and by understanding each, in turn, we will be prepared to take the next steps toward creating the simulation.

Developing the Data

A lot of different pieces of data are needed to both run the simulation and embody the game mechanics. Some of them, such as `launchForce`, `origin`, and `cargo`, deal with the game mechanics, while others, such as the `planets` array and the `asteroidBelt` and `star` objects, store information needed for the gravitational simulation. `onStateChangeObservable` is used by other components (for example, the `PlanningScreenGui` class at `https://github.com/jelster/space-truckers/blob/ch6/src/route-planning/route-plan-gui.js`) to respond to changes in the `gameState` property, an enumeration value of one of the `PLANNING_STATE` keys:

```
static PLANNING_STATE = Object.freeze({
        Created: 0,
        Initialized: 1,
        ReadyToLaunch: 2,
        InFlight: 3,
        CargoArrived: 4,
        GeneratingCourse: 6,
        CargoDestroyed: 7,
        Paused: 8
    });
```

Rounding out the defined data for this Screen is `preFlightActionList` (see *Chapter 5, Adding a Cut Scene and Handling Input*), which specifies the names of the input actions this class should handle, as well as whether the input should be *bounced*, or prevented from repeating for a brief time:

```
const preFlightActionList = [
    { action: 'ACTIVATE', shouldBounce: () => true },
    { action: 'MOVE_OUT', shouldBounce: () => false },
    { action: 'MOVE_IN', shouldBounce: () => false },
    { action: 'GO_BACK', shouldBounce: () => true },
    { action: 'MOVE_LEFT', shouldBounce: () => false },
    { action: 'MOVE_RIGHT', shouldBounce: () => false },
];
```

In this particular instance, our actions will be linked to the previously mentioned factors such as `launchForce`, allowing players to choose their launch direction, timing, and speed using whatever input method has been configured – except for touch and visual controls (those must be created and hosted in the GUI).

As you may expect, the constructor is where the majority of the Screen's objects are initialized. Game Components such as soundManager, actionProcessor, camera, lights, skybox, and so on are all created and configured there. For lighting, we use a PointLight with the intensity cranked up to a cool ten million – the vastness of space is dark – and we want to make sure the light of star can light up the scene in the way we want. That covers many of the familiar happenings occurring in the constructor, but there's a lot more going on that falls outside of the familiar.

Driving Behavior with Data

An important factor driving the code design is the need to drive the behavior of the simulation via data as much as possible (without going overboard). This means that instead of hardcoding values directly into SpaceTruckerPlanningScreen, we define the gameData file to hold our configuration values. By reading through the configuration data passed into the constructor, it is easy to run the simulation using arbitrary, easily changed values (more on refactoring to accommodate iteration will be covered shortly). Factors such as the origin planet and the destination planet are stored in gameData, along with physical information about the system (for example, PrimaryReferenceMass, or how much the central star weighs).

Some components of SpaceTruckerPlanningScreen are defined internally to the class. An example of this is the launchArrow mesh, which was created using a combination of the arrowLines Vector3 array, and MeshBuilder.CreateDashedLines functions, which returns a mesh from a passed-in array of points. Other meshes are much simpler, such as destinationMesh – a sphere parented to a Planet that's used for visual and collision purposes.

Preparing for the implementation of the game mechanics is part of our task here, so we will create and set up destinationMesh with an ActionManager that will look out for intersections with cargo.mesh (the player's cargo unit), invoking the cargoArrived function if that does happen:

```
this.destinationMesh.actionManager = new ActionManager(this.
scene);
this.destinationMesh.actionManager.registerAction(
    new ExecuteCodeAction(
        {
            trigger:
              ActionManager.OnIntersectionEnterTrigger,
            parameter: this.cargo.mesh
        },
        (ev) => {
            console.log('mesh intersection triggered!', ev);
            this.cargoArrived();
        }
    ));
```

The purpose of `cargoArrived` is to set the current state for `Screen`, along with any other needed state-change-related actions to stop the simulation. For now, this is enough, but later, we will be adding additional behavior to this function.

Similar to how `SpaceTruckerApplication` takes different sets of actions in its per-frame `update` method, (see *Chapter 3, Establishing the Development Workflow*), switching on `currentState` to control its behavior, `SpaceTruckerPlanningScreen` does so as well. The first thing to do is calculate the number of milliseconds since the last time the frame was rendered, which we can do using the `deltaTime` parameter (for testing) or retrieve using `scene.getEngine().getDeltaTime()` if missing. After that, `actionProcessor` updates its list of inputs and mappings to actions. Now, it's time to `switch` on `gameState`:

```
switch (this.gameState) {
    case SpaceTruckerPlanningScreen.PLANNING_STATE.Created:
        break;
    case SpaceTruckerPlanningScreen.
        PLANNING_STATE.ReadyToLaunch:
        this.star.update(dT);
        this.planets.forEach(p => p.update(dT));
        this.asteroidBelt.update(dT);
        this.cargo.update(dT);
        this.cargo.position = this.origin.position.clone().
          scaleInPlace(1.1, 1, 1);

        break;
    case SpaceTruckerPlanningScreen.
        PLANNING_STATE.InFlight:
        this.star.update(dT);
        this.planets.forEach(p => p.update(dT));
        this.asteroidBelt.update(dT);
        this.cargo.update(dT);

        let grav =
          this.updateGravitationalForcesForBox(dT);
        this.cargo.physicsImpostor.applyImpulse(grav,
          this.cargo.mesh.getAbsolutePosition());
        break;
    // ...and so on
}
```

Looking at the statement, it's easy to see that when gameState is in the ReadyToLaunch or InFlight stages, the various celestial bodies get their update methods called. In other words, the simulation is only advanced when the game state is either ReadyToLaunch or InFlight. This brings up the overall question of how we will implement the signature feature of this Screen: **the orbital mechanics simulation**.

Transitioning States

As implied in the previous discussion about the cargoArrived function, changes in the Screen's gameState are triggered by cargoArrived and similar functions. Here is a summary of the different state changes, the functions initiating the change, and their usage:

Ending State	Change Initiated By	Usage/Trigger
Initialized	constructor	Signals that the scene objects have been created. Does not guarantee all resources have finished loading.
ReadyToLaunch	setReadyToLaunchState	Resets the simulation to its initial state, including physics.
InFlight	launchCargo	Flings the cargo unit on its launch path. Signals to run and update the physics simulation every frame.
CargoArrived	cargoArrived	Triggered by the destinationMesh. actionManager event (described previously) when the cargo intersects destinationMesh. Signals successful route simulation.
CargoDestroyed	onCargoDestroyed	Player failure caused by "lithobraking" – a collision with a planetary body. Triggered by the cargo physics impostor via registerOnPhysicsCollide.
Paused	togglePause	Signals that the application should pause processing the simulation and input to it.

Except for the setReadyToLaunchState function, all of the state changes in this Screen arise from either events happening in the game or via direct user input. The reason that setReadyToLaunchState is the exception is that while the Screen is created as part of the overall application initialization process, certain things can't happen until the Scene is being rendered. In addition, we need to be able to arbitrarily reset the screen to its initial state so that players don't have to restart the entire application when they want to try a new route. Here's what a very basic success route looks like with the CargoArrived state:

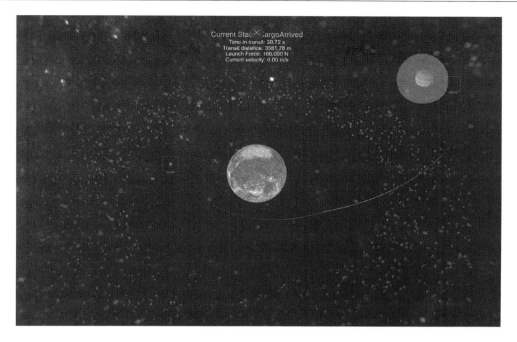

Figure 6.6 – The Route planning screen after a successful cargo arrival at the Destination planet. The trail mesh shows the path of the cargo from start to finish

On the topic of routes, it can be difficult at first to figure out how to get a successful cargo launch, so here is a quick tip – aim in the opposite (retrograde) direction to the direction of the orbital motion to get a more direct flight path. As depicted in the preceding screenshot, you can see the trail of the cargo unit going in a counterclockwise direction to the camera while the planets all orbit clockwise.

Understanding the three facets we examined for the Route Planning Screen helps make the connection between the inputs and how the application should behave as a result (its outputs). Behaviors are defined to be dependent upon data to drive the specifics of that behavior. Game data specifies how far planets might orbit from their star, their mass, and more, but the application state is what ultimately controls and decides whether and how much to move them in their celestial dance.

Creating the Orbital Mechanics Simulation

When thinking about the various components involved in `SpaceTruckerPlanningScreen`, it's important to consider how the simulation runs. Every frame (actually, it could be potentially more than once per frame, but for simplicity's sake, we'll go with once per frame), the physics simulation updates its own internal state. That state is largely opaque to us – though if needed we can always access it – but is manifested through the post-physics step changes that are made to an object's position and/or rotation. To make our `CargoUnit` perform the necessary gravitational boogie, we need to tell the physics simulation the force it should impart, calculated from the accumulated gravitational forces of the system.

Though very similar in appearance, the `InFlight` game state has two major differences from `ReadyToLaunch`: when we are `InFlight`, we want the cargo to be affected by the gravity of all the different massive bodies in the system. To keep things tidy, we wrap up the task of summing together all these forces into the `updateGravitationalForcesForBox` function:

```
updateGravitationalForcesForBox(timeStep) {
    const cargoPosition = this.cargo.position;
    let summedForces =
        this.star.calculateGravitationalForce(cargoPosition);
    this.planets.forEach(p => summedForces.addInPlace(p.
        calculateGravitationalForce(cargoPosition)));

    return summedForces.scaleInPlace(timeStep);
}
```

What's nice about this function is that it can leverage the base functionality provided by `OrbitingGameObject` to obtain each component's contribution to the overall forces experienced by the cargo unit, even though we are mixing different types of objects such as *stars* and *planets*. The returned `Vector3` is passed to `physicsImpostor` (see the *Understanding the Physics* section) as an impulsive *shove* imparted to the cargo object. From there, we let the physics engine take over the task of updating the CargoUnit's position and velocity.

Understanding the Physics

Most people are familiar with the apocryphal story of how Isaac Newton came up with his Theory of Gravity after getting hit on the head by a falling apple, and of how he changed how we think about the world we live in and the universe we inhabit. We don't need to have memorized the equations to experience the effects of gravity – being a law of nature and all, it doesn't care one way or another how someone feels about it. Stars wheel and twinkle around the night sky as planets spin in a celestial dance, and all of it – at least from the viewpoint of a 17th-century scientist – can be described with just a few equations.

> **Important note**
> We will be diving a bit into some physics and algebra here, but greatly simplified from what a more realistic simulation would require. For example, by assuming that our planets all have perfectly circular orbits, we obviate the need to implement the more complicated equations needed to support elliptical ones. Another example of how we're simplifying this is that the force calculations are only being performed on `cargoUnit` and not between each massive body, as would be the case in the real world.

The first and most fundamental is known as Newton's First Law of Motion. It describes the relationship between an object, a force applied to that object, and the object's resistance to being accelerated – its inertia:

$$\vec{F} = m\vec{a}$$

Figure 6.7 – Newton's First Law of Motion. The force (a vector) on an object is equal to the object's mass times its current acceleration. This is commonly re-arranged to solve for either m or a unknowns

Since force is what we ultimately want to calculate when we are running the simulation, we can replace the left-hand side of the preceding equation with the following equation. The two values for the object's mass cancel each other out, leading to a rather curious conclusion – the only mass that matters for our calculations is the mass of the larger body. The mass of cargoUnit does not factor in at all:

$$-F = G\frac{m_1 m_2}{r^2}, \qquad G = 6.67 \times 10^{-11}$$

Figure 6.8 – Newton's Law of Universal Gravitation. Implemented in OrbitingGameObject. The value of the Gravitational Constant (G) has been experimentally verified to many decimal places

In conversational language, the equation can be phrased thus: the force (F) experienced by an object of a given mass ($m1$) at a distance of r from another mass ($m2$) is equal to a constant value (G), times the product of the two masses divided by the square of the distance between them. In computational terms, we separately compute the direction of the force (via a vector subtraction of the two object's positions) and its magnitude (via the preceding equation), or scale, before combining and returning a final result vector.

The choice of units can be arbitrary but must be consistent; the metric system is assumed throughout this text because sanity is a prized possession and should be treasured. Therefore, masses are in kilograms, and the radius is in meters. This makes the resulting Force a value with units of $kg * m/s^2$. Put alternatively, this is the measure of how fast a 1 kg mass is accelerated in 1 second by the applied force and is known as the N, or Newton, for obvious reasons. What is much less obvious are some of the implications of the equation.

First, the force, F, is a vector value, not a scalar. This means that there are both direction and magnitude components to the force.

Second, unlike electrical and magnetic forces, which have positive or negative *charges*, gravity is always positive. Because mathematicians are constantly trying to prove their theory that they have a sense of humor, this fact is denoted in the equation by the negative sign, indicating that objects are always pulled toward the gravitational mass, never pushed away.

Third, the force experienced by the object is dictated by the sum of all the forces from each mass capable of influencing the object. This means that the overall force may be lessened to a degree or even canceled out altogether from equal or stronger resulting forces at opposing positions from the object under scrutiny.

A final note on this topic aimed at those who might have some knowledge of calculus and numerical integration: though our time step between physics calculations may be around 1/60th of a second, the straightforward integration via summation is inherently inaccurate. It is accurate enough, however, to allow the simulation to exhibit the type of emergent behavior that we're looking to see using our simplified orbital physics model. The full implementation of the gravitational force calculation for a single pair of bodies is contained in `OrbitingGameObject.calculateGravitationalForce(position)`. The code can also be viewed at `https://github.com/jelster/space-truckers/blob/8a8022b4cac08f1df9e4c7cfc8ff7c6275c71558/src/orbitingGameObject.js#L72`.

Hopefully, that little digression into abstract equations wasn't too intimidating, because that was the worst of it (for now…) and understanding how those equations are structured helps to clarify the simulation's `InFlight` behavior. But before the simulation can perform any `InFlight` calculations, the physics engine and the data it depends upon must be initialized and configured.

Driving the Simulation's Physics

The Babylon.js distribution contains built-in support for four separate physics engines: **Cannon**, **Oimo**, **Energy**, and **Ammo**. Each of them has pros and cons, and though not perfect, the **Ammo** physics library is what is being used in Space-Truckers. The choice comes down to an individual project's needs and the developer's preferences, but there are some practical matters relating to the developer's experience that are worth understanding.

The team behind Babylon.js is fiercely dedicated to maintaining backward-compatibility support for users. As we discussed in *Chapter 3, Establishing the Development Workflow*, the Babylon.js ES6 libraries retain some of the prior versions' patterns in use at the time, such as the use of side-effect only `import` statements. Further complicating matters is the fact that the Babylon.js team doesn't own or maintain any of the physics engines themselves – only the Babylon.js plugin wrapper for the library – yet the CDN and *full* Babylon.js distributions come bundled with all supported engines.

Because the point of tree-shaking with ES6 modules is to only package and load the source files needed, it is necessary to add a `package.json` reference to one or more physics engines. Unfortunately, none of the libraries with available Babylon.js plugins currently have a trusted, verified, and up-to-date package published to the NPM, but the GitHub repository for Ammo shows the most consistent activity over the last few years, indicating that it is likely to continue active development on updates, bug fixes, and feature enhancements, which is where Node's support for referencing a package directly from a GitHub repository is very handy.

> **Important note**
>
> The initialization of the Ammo.js physics library is **asynchronous** (this is a breaking change from the previous 4.X version of the library), meaning that it is necessary to resolve or somehow `await` the Ammo promise. To ensure that the library has been properly initialized and loaded, a wrapper is needed. The `/src/externals/ammoWrapper.js` module first imports the `ammo.js` library, and exports two variables: `ammoModule` itself along with an `ammoReadyPromise` that populates `ammoModule` before resolving.
>
> In `SpaceTruckerPlanningScreen`, `ammoReadyPromise` is imported and resolved as part of the constructor logic, ensuring that by the time `initializePhysics` is called, `AmmoJsPlugin` has everything it needs to do its job (see the next section for more on `initializePhysics`).

The great thing about using a physics engine that has already been built and proven is that there isn't much to do other than set up the desired parameters for the physics simulation. This is done in the `SpaceTruckerPlanningScreen.initializePhysics` method.

Configuring the InFlight Physics Simulation

The `initializePhysics` method is not invoked during object construction because we know the screen won't initially be shown to players, and we want to make sure that the scene has been completely set up with all the meshes involved before doing anything with the physics engine. It is invoked by `setReadyToLaunchState`, and since that method can be called several different ways, the `initializePhysics` function can't make assumptions about the current state of the engine. That is why the physics engine is reset and cleared before every flight – keeping the interface between the engine and game opaque makes for simpler code.

The first thing we want to make sure and do is set `scene.gravity` to `Vector3.Zero` – otherwise, it would default to the Earth-normal value of `(0, -9.8, 0)`. This is a space simulation, and it wouldn't pass muster to have players falling at the wrong speed and direction! Next, we must dispose of any existing physics impostors before disabling the engine entirely. That paves the way for the newly-created `AmmoJSPlugin` to get passed into the `scene.enablePhysics` method. Let's slow down for a moment – what is a `PhysicsImpostor`?

Most meshes (or at least most interesting meshes) are going to have complicated geometries. The overall shape of the mesh may not be symmetric on all axes, and there may be convex or concave surfaces that can obscure or hide other parts of the geometry, depending on the angle in question. Some meshes may also have dense geometries, with vertice counts in the hundreds of thousands or more. Performing physics – and when we mention physics in this context, what we are referring to are collision calculations for the most part – against such complicated geometries is complicated, inaccurate, and untenably slow.

To make these calculations work in the short amount of time available between frames, we must substitute a much simpler geometric shape that can approximate the actual mesh's shape in place of the original. This approximation is generally a simple shape, such as a `Box`, `Sphere`, or `Cylinder`. The challenge for the developer is to select the most appropriate impostor type for the mesh getting physics applied.

The physics Impostor sounds pretty cool as a name, but in terms of its functionality, it might also be thought of as being a proxy object to act on behalf of the Mesh when dealing with the Physics engine. It holds information such as mass, linear and angular velocities, and friction values, as you might expect, but there's also logic for controlling how the Impostor syncs data between engine and mesh.

After enabling the physics engine with `AmmoJSPlugin`, every `planet`, as well as `star` and `cargoUnit` have their `physicsImpostor` properties populated with appropriate values read from the `gameData` configuration, similar to the one shown here:

```
this.star.physicsImpostor = new
  PhysicsImpostor(this.star.mesh,
  PhysicsImpostor.SphereImpostor, {
    mass: this.config.starData.mass,
    restitution: 0,
    disableBidirectionalTransformation: false,
}, this.scene);
```

Once the impostors have been created, `cargoUnit.physicsImpostor` is subscribed to the `onCargoDestroyed` method handler, which is responsible for transitioning the game state from `InFlight` to `CargoDestroyed`.

This was a big lead-up to what is a bit of an anti-climax – shouldn't complex stuff like physics and gravity be a lot more complicated? Perhaps it should be, but thanks to the hard work of a LOT of people over a very long time, it isn't anymore! That's a fortunate thing indeed because that allows us to pay more attention to the game mechanics and how they fit on top of the orbital simulation.

Defining the Rules – Game Mechanics

Typical business application development focuses on dividing the responsibilities of the application into logical segments that layer on top of one another, with the user on one side and the application's foundational infrastructure on the other. Data and commands pass sequentially from one layer to another as user-initiated events propagate in concert with system and application events. Ideally, the code has the qualities of both being loosely coupled and tightly cohesive.

This may sound like a paradox or contradiction – how can something be both loose and tight at the same time? The answer is that it can be both because the two qualities tend to be inversely correlated with each other. Loose coupling between components means that making changes to one has little to no effect on the other. A tightly cohesive system is one where functionality is confined to a small number of code or application components; everything needed to accomplish a particular task is close at hand.

When developing a game, we strive to factor it in a similarly well-structured fashion – not because it looks nice in a class diagram but because it makes it easy to change, extend, fix, and enhance. Now, let's provide a summary of the basic game mechanics (also known as **Business Rules**) that are applied to `RoutePlanningScreen`.

Controllable Launch Parameters

A key part of the principal game loop in route planning is that the player should be able to control the timing, angle, and velocity of their launch. This only applies in the `ReadyToLaunch` phase. A minimum and a maximum launch velocity should be enforced, with the specific values for the minimum and maximum determined by empirical iteration (for example, trial and error).

The player should be able to visually gauge the launch factors, with or without the help of seeing the underlying data. If the player isn't satisfied with their alignments or they want to start over, they should be able to reset to starting parameters. In the *Supporting Input Controls* section, we'll look at the input mapping to see how players should interact from their end of things. Next, we'll talk about how a player might succeed or fail at the game along with what defines a particular scenario.

Going Places and Crashing EVERYWHERE

A given game playthrough should have an `origin` and a `destination` Planet designated in the scenario's `gameData`. These should be visible to the player so that they know where they are and where they need to be. Potential hazards and obstacles should be made visible to players. After the player has elected to launch their cargo into its ballistic trajectory, the game ends in a losing state (`CargoDestroyed`) if `CargoUnit` contacts our `Star` or any `Planet`.

If the player can align their launch so that it intersects the destination within a certain radius, they will be considered to have successfully planned their flight route. If the player chooses to reject the given flight plan, the simulation is reset in the same way as it is elsewhere. Should the player accept the flight plan, gameplay moves to the next phase.

Future game phases, along with the game mechanics of scoring, will be covered later in this book. To read more about the basic game design, the original game design docs for Space-Truckers can be found at `https://github.com/jelster/space-truckers/blob/develop/design/game-design-specs.md`. While mostly out of date, it can provide further insights into how the game's elements have evolved and grown over time, in addition to potentially deriving some degree of amusement by looking at the various concept sketches.

Supporting Input Controls

In the previous chapter, we looked at the input processing and control system. That system defines an `inputActionMap`, with every potential input getting mapped to the name of an Action (Command). The specific meaning and effect of a given action is determined by whatever code implements that action and is specific to the Screen.

Let's look at the Route Planning's control scheme in its entirety. Some entries are new since the preceding chapter; the pointer (touch/mouse) operations are assumed to be centered around GUI elements (see the *Showing Game Information with the GUI* section) and the camera controls are using native keymaps unless otherwise noted:

Effect	Action	Keyboard	Gamepad
Rotate camera	N/A	Arrow keys	Right Stick
Pause	PAUSE	'p'	Button Start
Rotate launcher	MOVE_XXXX	'w', 'a', 's', 'd', 'q', 'r'	Left Stick
Launch cargo	ACTIVATE	Enter, Space, Return	Button1
Add launch force	MOVE_IN	Shift	Right Bumper
Subtr. launch force	MOVE_OUT	Control	Left Bumper

The `GamePad` control scheme is oriented toward an Xbox® controller, but other types of controllers can still be supported with little effort – see *Chapter 5, Adding a Cut Scene and Handling Input*, along with the `gamePadControlMap` constant in the `inputActionMap.js` file at `https://github.com/jelster/space-truckers/blob/ch6/src/inputActionMaps.js`.

For the most part, we've already covered the function implementations for each of these actions separately in earlier sections of this chapter, so we aren't going to spend time on how that operates because we've only looked at half of the feedback loop by looking at user input. We need to close that loop by examining the sorts of information that the game presents back to the user.

Showing Game Information with the GUI

When folks think about **UIs**, the first thing that comes to mind are those of a graphical nature – web pages, start menus, and the like. While the visual medium is one of the dominant means of communication between person and computer, audio and other channels of output are definitely on the docket for us to look through – just not at this time. We'll be beefing up the environmental effects both visually and audibly in the next chapter. For now, let's look at how the GUI is structured.

Unlike the **Splash** and **Main Menu** Screens, the **Planning Screen** screen doesn't directly create or manage its UI. As you may recall, we've been using the Babylon.js GUI's AdvancedDynamicTexture to render our GUI elements, and that isn't going to change. What is different, however, is that SpaceTruckerPlanningScreen hosts an instance of PlanningScreenGui (see https://github.com/jelster/space-truckers/blob/ch6/src/route-planning/route-plan-gui.js). In turn, PlanningScreenGui takes the SpaceTruckerPlanningScreen instance in its constructor, allowing it to access all of the data it needs to dynamically update the GUI. We need to perform our UI initialization and configuration after the Scene has finished loading and the Screen is completely constructed; otherwise, our GUI will need to contain an eventual spaghetti-flavored mess of conditional and null checks.

Avoiding that is straightforward: listen for scene.onReadyObservable and then use that to instantiate the GUI. To provide additional flexibility in separating construction from configuration time, the bindToScreen function creates the actual UI components, links display objects with meshes from the Screen, and performs other boilerplate-type creation tasks. This completes the static configuration of the GUI, but we want – no, demand – that the GUI should update in more-or-less real time with the latest data from the simulation and game. That's where our double-fisted combination comes in handy!

The first punch is given by the event subscription to SpaceTruckerPlanningScreen.onStateChangeObservable with the onScreenStateChange function:

```
this.planningScreen.onStateChangeObservable.add(state => {
    const currentState = state.currentState;
    this.onScreenStateChange(currentState);
});
```

This ensures that the GUI is informed whenever the game state changes, such as from ReadyToLaunch to InFlight. The logic in that method looks at newState to determine which controls should be visible, and what color the text should be. That handles the problem of needing to coordinate UI changes with state changes, while the other side of this pugilistic analogy is the knock-out blow of per-frame updates to controls done as part of the update method.

In the update method, numbers are formatted for display, controls update their text properties, and the Launch Arrow gets scaled according to the current launch Force. Essentially, anything that doesn't directly affect the game gets updated in this method. The problem of needing to display dynamically updated data has been solved as well – we can cease our unyielding demands and claim victory!

It's a great thing that we've knocked out the rest of this chapter, not only because of the great amount of information we've covered in quite a small amount of text but because the boxing analogy is very off-brand for Space-Truckers and it was wearing quite thin. Let's review what we've just gone over and look at some ideas for what you can do to practice working with the concepts.

Summary

We started this chapter having freshly completed the **Main Menu** Screen, and we've finished it having implemented the **Route Planning** Screen and the bulk of its core game loop – that's quite the trip for how short a time we've been traveling! `SpaceTruckerSoundManager` maintains an internal catalog of all sound assets and makes those assets available to hosting Screens that want to play sounds. Although it seems like it does a lot, when it comes to actual Babylon.js Sounds, it likes to delegate responsibility to the Sound.

The ability to mix different sounds and sources is provided by the different SoundTracks defined by `SpaceTruckerSoundManager`, and they make it very easy to have background music playing at the same time as a game sound effect without having to code logic around volume levels. This is because each soundtrack has a volume (gain) control.

After reviewing the `GameObject` class hierarchy, we dove – or more appropriately, fell – into the specifics of how the rendered actors are constructed. Toolbox ready, we created `SpaceTruckerPlanningScreen` and set up a set of states and transitions between them. From there, we danced over basic gravitational physics – doesn't that sound cool? Find a way to work into your next conversation that you know gravitational physics and stroke your chin thoughtfully.

Then, we learned a bit about how the `Ammo.js` physics engine is set up and configured with our project. Having set the planets in motion, we shifted our focus to layering on some of the gameplay elements. Player-controlled launch parameters, collision detection, and showing players their stats all went quickly to our enlightened senses, leaving us facing the path forward.

In the next chapter, solar flares and prominences will erupt from the particle systems we'll put in place.Later, we will explore encounter zones and focus on capturing route data as we flesh out route planning and prepare for the next phase of gameplay.

Extended Topics

Are you not feeling quite ready to move on to the next chapter? Are you having trouble figuring out how all of what you've just read works? Jump over to the Space-Truckers discussion board (`https://github.com/jelster/space-truckers/discussions`) to search for answers or post your questions so that others may be able to help answer them. Not ready to move on but feel like you've got a good grasp of things? Why not try enhancing the Screen with some of these ideas:

- When the game begins, have the camera start somewhere far out before pulling in toward the star, giving a tour of the system as it does so, before ending in the starting camera position. There are lots of ways to accomplish this, but one potential approach would be to create an animation and set of keyframes that dictate the camera's position. Another might be to use `autoFramingBehavior`, along with tweaking the camera's inertia and other related values.

- Make the gamepad's triggers usable for adjusting the launch force; pulling on the left could decrease the force while pulling on the right could increase the force. Essentially, this would work the same way as the current button presses do, except that the constant value being incremented is scaled or replaced by the trigger value instead (the trigger is the positive axis, while the other is negative).

- Think the physics calculations are too inaccurate? Do you sneer at the idea of matrix math being *complex*? Do you begin to question your existence when someone says that you're *irrational*? OK, here's a challenge: add a basic numerical integrator to the part of the simulation where the forces are scaled according to `deltaTime`.

  (Easier) Use Euler's method to calculate the cargo unit's new/future position using the current velocity and the frame's `deltaTime` combined with the previous frame's velocity and position (`https://en.wikipedia.org/wiki/Euler_method`).

  (Harder) Use Verlet integration to do the same (`https://en.wikipedia.org/wiki/Verlet_integration`).

- OK, so maybe the last one was a bit too hardcore, but there's still the urge to do something to make the code suck a little bit less… here's a challenge that doesn't specifically require knowledge of any of the aforementioned topics but does require engineering savvy and great source code literacy: integrate the core gravitational simulation into the Babylon.js physics plugin/engine.

- If you accomplish any of these things, be sure to share your work with the world by posting links on the Space-Truckers discussion, the Babylon.js Forums, and/or by opening a Pull Request!

7
Processing Route Data

Although we won't be looking at the transition between route planning and route driving quite yet, in the big picture of where things stand, generating a route is an integral piece of the Space-Truckers gameplay. In this chapter, we're going to stick with the previous practice of taking a brief detour into a tangential topic – in this case, that topic will be spiffing up the Sun rendering with some Particle Systems.

Following our detour into particle systems, we'll dive straight into how to capture, crunch, and consolidate the data from route planning into a rich set of encounters based on location, which will then drive player challenges in the next phase.

What makes this all possible is a technique that has its roots in the earliest days of the RPG – when dark Dungeons filled with dangerous Dragons saw players rolling dice against encounter tables that would determine their fate. The encounter tables for Space-Truckers are categorized by zoneand play a similar part in determining a Space-Trucker's fate. Each zone has a list of potential encounters along with a base probability or chance of that encounter happening. Most encounters carry potential hazards the player must act upon to avoid or mitigate, while, more rarely, other encounters may have beneficial effects (if managed correctly).

In this chapter, we will cover the following topics:

- A Detour into Practical Systems
- Marking Out the Route
- Defining the Encounter Zone
- Selecting Encounters
- Adding Encounter Visuals

By the end of this chapter, we'll have prettied up the route-planning environment a little, but for the most part, the areas of the application being covered won't have as much tangible effect on the end user experience. That's OK – it will end up having a huge effect later! For this to become the case, though, we must build up some logic to process and prepare the route for encounters.

Technical requirements

The technical prerequisites are not a whole lot different in this chapter, but there are some concepts and techniques that may have utility for the topics in this chapter.

Here are some topics to research if you're feeling lost, overwhelmed by complexity, or having trouble with a particular area:

- Particle System: `https://doc.babylonjs.com/divingDeeper/particles`
- Torus Set Shape: `https://doc.babylonjs.com/divingDeeper/mesh/creation/set/torus`
- Torus (maths): `https://www.mathsisfun.com/geometry/torus.html`
- More torus maths: `https://www.geeksforgeeks.org/calculate-volume-and-surface-area-of-torus/`

The source code for this chapter is located at `https://github.com/jelster/space-truckers/tree/ch7` and contains all the work in this chapter and previous ones. In addition to that, there are several improvements, bug fixes, and tweaks that have been introduced separately from what's been covered previously in this book. While it would be great if we could include and discuss each of these in greater detail, that's not possible in the space and time available! Where relevant, though, these changes will be called out. For the most part, however, the changes aren't introducing any new concepts or techniques, but just refining, fixing, or enhancing what's already present.

A Detour into Particle Systems

Particle systems are an area of graphics programming that, like the topic of input processing, can have entire books devoted to covering particle systems from basic theory to concrete implementation. We're not going to get into that level of detail here, because we've got a lot of other things to do in addition to learning about particle systems! Here's what you need to know about particle systems in general. In a moment, we'll look at their relationship to Babylon.js and how we can use them for fun and profit.

Think back to the last video game you played. If it was a text-based game, then think of the last game you played that wasn't text-based. Did the game have explosions? Are there magic fireballs exploding? What about fireworks or campfires? Each of these is an example of where a particle system might be employed by a game developer.

Let's back up a bit. A particle is a single entity with a discrete life cycle of creation and death. It is usually represented not with a single mesh but with a texture, for most particles are 2D billboard textures or sprites. The texture or image has transparency properties blended into the rest of the scene in a varying number of ways. If "transparency properties" is confusing, it can be helpful to recall that transparency refers to the alpha channel, and the properties of this channel are the instructions to the engine on how to blend or mix that channel with overlapping colors. This means that often, a particle will always be oriented so that it is always directly facing the camera, and that it will have the ability to fade in and out of view.

A particle system is more than just an aggregation of particles. A particle system is what defines and controls the entire life cycle of its constituent particles. It does this through a few primary mechanisms:

- **Emitter(s)**: The mesh or node where a particle begins its life. Different properties of the emitter allow granular control over parts of the mesh and the shape of the emission, as well as the number of particles emitted and the rate of emissions.

- **Particle properties**: Both visual and behavioral, these include size, scaling, rotation, color, and speed for the former, and lifetime for the latter.

- **Animations, noise, and blending effects**: Adding noise to the system enhances the realism of the particle system, while animations provide a dynamic look and feel to it.

If a particle system is comprised of particles, then what about a collection of particle systems? That is what's called a Particle System Set, and that is also what we will be employing to give the Sun of Space-Truckers a bit of "flare!"

> **Important note**
> That last sentence may have been a pun too far.

The advantage of using a Particle System Set is that we can use a single consolidated piece of logic to load, start, and stop all the systems at once. Although we'll be using the Particle System Set in our imminent future, there are a couple of other different but related means of generating and managing particles in Babylon.js.

The Disparate Particle Systems of Babylon.js

The family tree of BJS particle systems isn't nearly as complex as the Greek pantheon, but what it does share with that fabled genealogy is a separation of generations.

The "Classic" CPU Particle System

This is what everyone knows, loves, and is familiar with. The vanilla flavor of the three, this offers the greatest amount of end developer (that is, you) programmatic control over every aspect of the particle's behavior. Because it runs on the CPU every frame, it must share time in the frame budget with everything else the game needs to happen between frames. If the target framerate is 60 FPS, then the intra-frame budget is just 1/60s or just under 17 milliseconds. As any middle-child sibling knows, compromise is key!

The "New Wave" GPU Particle System

Since graphics accelerators have become pretty much ubiquitous in today's computing environment (evidenced by a certain Web-GPU JavaScript framework…), so have the tools needed to program them to become more powerful. Later, in *Chapter 11, Scratching the Surface of Shaders*, we'll take a closer look at how we can easily and effectively leverage this power for fun (and profit!), but for the present moment, the relevant fact is that the same particle systems that we used to run on the CPU are now executed and updated directly on the GPU. The biggest effect of this change is that the number of particles available to use has gone up drastically. Instead of worrying about the effect of a few hundred particles on performance, the same concerns only start to appear when particles number in the tens of thousands – quite a large improvement!

The "Hard Core" Solid Particle System

When the pedal hits the pavement and things get real, it's time to pull out the big guns. A **Solid Particle System** (**SPS**) is constructed not from a point-like particle but from a three-dimensional mesh. Each particle instance must share the same material as the other SPS instances, but the other attributes such as position, scale, rotation, and others are all controlled by the developer. SPS particles can be physics-enabled, along with providing support for collisions. The downside of this level of control and detail is that each property must also be set and controlled individually – unlike a regular particle system that evolves according to the various attribute values associated with it. Hard-coding the individual values for a system is tedious, error-prone, and not very fun to maintain. It's fine to do that for Playgrounds and prototypes, but for our application, we're going to want to be able to represent our Particle Systems as data that we can manage separately from the behavior of the application.

Loading Particle Systems From Saved Data

When dealing with CPU or GPU Particle Systems, it can be extremely tedious and error-prone to type and tweak each specific property through code. The almighty Babylon.js Inspector (praise be its crazy good nature!) is probably the quickest way to iterate against different property values to see what they look like in real time, but how to effectively capture the current state of every property for every particle system in a Particle System Set may appear, at first, to be elusive. However, like many things in Babylon.js, there are multiple ways to accomplish the same goal. Fortunately, though, there are multiple ways to get the same result; each of them makes use of different methods of the

ParticleHelper. All three are available to use in the Inspector (see *Figure 7.2*), which can be used to choose the most appropriate method for the requirements of the project.

ExportSet/Save to File (Inspector)

First up is the purely programmatic approach of calling `ParticleHelper.ExportSet(setA, setB,...)`. The output of the function is a JSON string, which can then be saved to a file or stored somewhere else. It's easiest to use this method in the Playground after putting together multiple systems. Using the Inspector, it's possible to save a single system to JSON by selecting the desired system in the Scene Explorer, then clicking the **Save…** button under the **FILE** heading. This is useful for single-system setups, but for saving multiple systems to file, the **ExportSet** is the best option.

Saving a Snippet to the Snippet Server (Inspector)

With the Babylon.js Playground open in a browser – here's one for reference: `https://playground.babylonjs.com/#735KL4#15` – notice how the specific Playground is identified by a unique combination of a hash (the #735KL4 part) and a revision (#15). Well, the idea of making Playground resources referenceable in that fashion worked so well that the concept has been extended to many other areas of Babylon.js.

Want to load up a GUI setup in the **GUI Editor**? Use a snippet! How about that fancy procedural texture created in the **Node Material Editor**? Snippet's got you! The Particle System Set JSON's too big a drag to include? Snippet's. Got. You. Like the **Save to File** option, but under the **Snippet Server** heading, click the **Save to Snippet Server** button to do what it says on the box. Loading can be done by clicking the **Companion** button manually or programmatically by calling `ParticleHelper.CreateFromSnippetAsync`. You can read more about the Snippet Server for Particle Systems in the official docs: `https://doc.babylonjs.com/divingDeeper/particles/particle_system/particle_snippets`.

Using a Built-In Particle System Set

Aristotle was an influential guy even during his time, and his idea that things are made of four "elements" – air, earth, fire, and water – was widely accepted as being true, mostly due to good marketing. In that spirit, Babylon.js provides a basic "elemental" catalog of particle system sets for you to use. Here are the available effects (see more about them in the docs at `https://doc.babylonjs.com/divingDeeper/particles/particle_system/particleHelper#available-effects`):

- **Explosion**: Good for blowing stuff up.
- **Rain**: For that extra bit of melancholy.
- **Smoke**: Useful to signal the selection of a new Pope, but also for a lot of other things. Just remember, where there's smoke, there's often…

- **Fire**: Whether it's a campfire, a torch, or a good old-fashioned house fire, this is the place to start.

- **Sun**: Jackpot! This particle set includes flares, a dynamically evolving surface, and the hazy glare of a coronasphere. There's just one problem…

> **Note**
>
> There was another theory floating around that things are made of these tiny, indivisible particles called (ἄτομος, or *atomos*), but its main proponent, Democritus, wasn't as popular as Aristotle, so nobody listened to him. Who's got the last laugh now, Aristotle?

What's this problem mentioned? It's not a big one. It's kind of – no, it's exactly the opposite of a big problem. It's a small problem, one of scale. The Sun effect is perfect for our needs, but it's way, way, way too small. We need to be able to scale it up to match our astronomical proportions, but it's not going to be precise in how or where things are scaled – that will take some experimentation. The Playground at `https://playground.babylonjs.com/#J9J6CG#9` shows the tweaks involved that were eventually incorporated into the JSON data committed to the Space-Truckers code repository.

> **Note**
>
> Though it would be ideal to include all the various game design aspects and decisions involved in this book, it isn't possible to anticipate everything ahead of time. There are also pragmatic limits as to how large this book can get. Therefore, where applicable, links will be provided to GitHub Issues that provide details about the feature or part of the game. Issues in GitHub can be linked to other Issues and to Pull Requests (among other things), which makes it easy to quickly assess and evaluate the code associated with a given Issue or feature. Relevant to our current work, this issue – *Star should have occasional flares and activity* (`https://github.com/jelster/space-truckers/issues/71`) – aggregates links from the Babylon.js docs and from Playground snippets to provide insight into the desired outcome. Comments and linked Pull Requests show the history and evolution of the issue. This isn't to say that we're not going to cover the game design or details of it – far from it! Simply put, things in software evolve and change at a vastly disproportionate rate to that of other goods and industries, such as publishing. Those wishing to see how the game has evolved can do so by reading through the Issues documenting that change.

Before we can get into those changes, we must figure out how to load and start the Particle System Set from a JSON file. There is friction in attempting this. The **ParticleHelper** is designed and built with the focus on removing complexity for developers, certain aspects of which can be obstacles to our goals.

Parsing From a JSON File

One of those convenient features that ends up becoming a bit of an obstacle is that the `CreateAsync` method of `PracticalHelper` takes just a string representing the type of the system to create – that is, "rain," "smoke," "Sun," and so on. This string is then used in conjunction with `ParticleHelper.BaseAssetsUrl` to construct the full URL for the JSON file. Unless explicitly overridden, `BaseAssetsUrl` has a value of `https://github.com/BabylonJS/Assets/tree/master/particles/`. The structure of the folders places the JSON files in a `/systems` subfolder and textures in the `/textures` subfolder – a nice consistent convention that works great for most use cases, save ours. The main conflicts with our setup are as follows:

- Our folder structure is different from what the convention assumes

- Multiple assets need to use the same textures

- We are using webpack to bundle and manage our assets and dependencies, so our design-time folder structures vary slightly from that of runtime

- Relying on external sources for core game assets and data complicates and prevents offline/native/PWA-type scenarios

The first and last items can be mitigated, to an extent, by using relative paths and by overriding `BaseAssetsUrl` and making it something like `document.baseURI`. The middle two, however, require a bit more thinking to resolve. Examining the **ParticleHelper** source code (see `https://github.com/BabylonJS/Babylon.js/blob/master/packages/dev/core/src/Particles/particleHelper.ts`) reveals that there's no practical way to override the conventional logic that computes the URL of the JSON file. However, once past that step, parsing and hydrating the particle system set is very straightforward. The problem here isn't that we can't use the conventional approach, it's that because of webpack, we don't need to figure out how to load the JSON data – we already have it, while the **ParticleHelper** expects to have to retrieve the same. It's time to start thinking like everyone's favorite field engineer from the mid-1980s, MacGyver.

What would MacGyver do (WWMD)? MacGyver's greatest strength wasn't that he was big and brawny, or that he could kick bad-guy butt in a fistfight. It wasn't even his luxurious mane of hair that would make an Olympian God (or Goddess!) jealous. No, MacGyver's greatest strength was that he could build, hack, or otherwise science his way out of pretty much any situation he found himself stuck in. By paying attention to his surroundings and then applying his (extensive) knowledge of subjects far and wide, he proved that a sharp eye and a clever mind can overcome almost any obstacle. Let's look at this problem through a MacGyver-tinted lens:

"We need to get a ParticleSystemSet before the bomb goes off! The JSON data is loaded, but the ParticleHelper needs the URL string, and there's only one minute left until everything goes boom… What else do we have, let's see… ah! Pass the object data to ParticleSystemSet.Parse and bypass the ParticleHelper entirely but do it quickly – we're running out of time!"

So, according to MG up there, we don't want to use the **ParticleHelper** at all and instead directly pass the loaded object data to `ParticleSystemSet.Parse`, since that's what the **ParticleHelper** ends up doing anyway. How did he know to try this? He traced down the different ways the Babylon.js source code APIs allow a **ParticleSystemSet** to be created until he came across the `Parse` method (`https://doc.babylonjs.com/typedoc/classes/babylon.particlesystemset#parse`). Knowing that we were starting with a plain old JavaScript object deserialized from the correct definition file, he made the rather obvious (in hindsight, natch) conclusion that since the result (a **ParticleSystemSet**) was all that mattered, there was no need to involve the **ParticleHelper** since the only additional action it takes other than loading the data file is to specify the `name` property. Thanks to MG, we have the tools we need to be able to integrate the Sun particle system set with our application!

Adapting the Sun Particle System Set

The proof-of-concept Playground (`https://playground.babylonjs.com/#J9J6CG#9`) gave us a general idea of where to scale things in the game, but there's more to be done to get the Sun system working the way we want it to. The Playground only has one of the three particle systems – the flare system – while there are two others; that is, the Sun and glare systems. These must also be properly scaled and configured. The best way to get it done is by following these steps:

1. Go to the Babylon.js assets repository and save the needed JSON and texture files to the local repository. For example, the Sun set is located at `https://github.com/BabylonJS/Assets/blob/master/particles/systems/sun.json`.

2. Open the `sun.json` file and change the texture paths to reflect the project's folder structure. Use relative paths, but make sure to consider the relative path of the consuming script, not the path of the JSON file. In the `Star` class, add the necessary code to load and start the set (see `https://github.com/jelster/space-truckers/blob/ch7/src/route-planning/star.js#L26`).

3. With the application running and on the appropriate screen, open the **Inspector** window by pressing the appropriate key combination (*Shift* + *Alt* + *I* by default). Modify the properties of the systems and wait for the changes to take effect.

4. Update the properties of the various systems so that they match the desired values.

5. GOTO (3).

The result will be whatever you think looks the coolest, but if you want to start with or just go with the existing definition, you can find it at `https://github.com/jelster/space-truckers/blob/ch7/src/systems/sun.json`:

Figure 7.1 – After the Sun particle system has been adapted to the scale of Space-Truckers. The Inspector window is crucial to being able to see the effect of different values in real time

In general, the particle counts may need to be increased for the Sun and glare particles, but whatever the change, make sure to wait a few seconds for it to propagate to newly spawned particles, since some may have lifetimes measured in the low 10s of seconds!

In this section, we've learned about the different types of particle systems available in Babylon.js, as well as some techniques to quickly iterate toward finding our desired look and feel. Hopefully, we've made ol' Mac proud by channeling his clever knack for finding solutions to the problem of loading up and adapting the Sun **ParticleSystemSet** to the game. As we pull away from this detour, let's turn our gaze to what's coming up next – building the foundation for tracking our `CargoUnit` as it traverses the system in its flight.

Marking Out the Route

A key aspect of the gameplay of Space-Truckers is how the path taken by `CargoUnit` in the route planning phase affects the challenges – and the rewards – of the driving phase. We've already tackled the ballistic flight mechanics of the route planning, so now, we need to capture that route and data about the environments it traverses. The following diagram shows the primary properties of our route and how they might be represented:

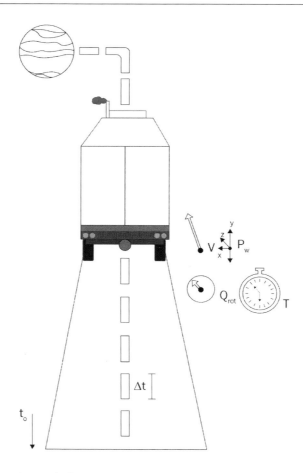

Figure 7.2 – Various pieces of telemetry are captured during the in-flight part of route planning. The Position, rotation, velocity, and a timestamp are all collected for each sample

Here, the idea that `CargoUnit` is what is responsible for saving its path, which translates out to the `CargoUnit` class, thus gaining a new `routePath[]` property along with associated logic in the `reset()` and `update()` methods to clear and update the path, respectively. The data itself is simple, though we'll get into the `encounterZone` field in a bit:

```
let node = new TransformNode("cargoNode", this.scene,
    true);
node.position = this.mesh.position.clone();
node.rotationQuaternion = this.mesh.rotationQuaternion?.
    clone() ??
    Quaternion.FromEulerVector(this.rotation.clone());
```

```
node.scaling = this.lastVelocity.clone();
node.velocity = this.lastVelocity.clone();
node.gravity = this.lastGravity.clone();
node.time = this.timeInTransit;
node.encounterZone = this.encounterManager.
    currentZone?.name;
```

A `TransformNode` is a non-rendered object in the **Scene** that is a **superclass** of the more-derived **Mesh** type. We'll look at one way that storing this data as a `TransformNode` is useful in the *Adding Encounter Visuals* section. Because they implement everything needed to calculate and place the node's position in the world of the Scene, `TransformNodes` are useful in a lot of different applications. This includes the ability to both be a parent and/or a child to other objects within the Scene. Some examples include a "camera dolly" made by parenting a **camera** to a node, a source for **particles**, and scaffolding to hold a `PhysicsImpostor`.

Since this code comes right after we've freshly calculated the velocity, gravity, and rotation properties, we're ensuring that we have the latest and most up-to-date values. Why are we storing the rotation as a **Quaternion** rather than the **Vector3** representation we already have? The reason is that we are going to want to perform some mathematical transformations against mesh vertices in a **local space**, rather than **world space**, and having the quaternion already computed makes for more simple calculations, as well as being more efficient.

> **Important note**
> Don't forget that JavaScript reference types assign by reference, not by value – hence the need to clone the Vector3 property values.

Although that's all there is to capturing the path telemetry data, there's still more work to do before this will start to be useful in the game. One of those pieces of work is to implement the concept of an **Encounter Table** and its concomitant **Encounter Zones**. After that, we can start to put the two together into the **SpaceTruckerEncounterManager**. If you want to get more in-depth into the history and linkages between the different components we'll be talking about and their high-level design, `https://github.com/jelster/space-truckers/issues/70` is a good place to start.

Defining the Encounter Zone

An **Encounter Table** is what it says on the box: it's a tabular format of probabilities for certain events to occur based on a random factor. In tabletop and RPG-style games, the random factor is provided by rolling one or more dice of various numbered sides. In computer-based games, the same thing applies, except that instead of tossing physical dice, we'll generate encounters based on the output of a random number generator.

Like much of the rest of the game objects, the **Encounter Zones (EZs)** are updateable game components, while each Encounter serves as a container for data defining that encounter. This allows the **EncounterManager** to choose which EZ should be responsible for running encounter checks, simplifying the logic required in the EZ. Easy, right?

Encounters Overview

The structure of an Encounter table is simple. Down each row is a specific event or encounter that the game designer wants to make possible. A probability column in the table indicates the likelihood of that event occurring in the form of a number between 0 (no chance whatsoever) and 1 (guaranteed). This is a good start, but we need to be able to further group encounters by their spatial locations in the world; it wouldn't make much sense to encounter a solar flare in the dark reaches of the Outer System, would it? That's where the concept of an Encounter Zone comes in.

Encounter Zones and Encounter Tables

An Encounter Zone is an Encounter Table scoped to a specific spatial location in the game world, as alluded to previously. From the Inner System to the Outer Reaches, each Encounter Zone has a unique set of potential encounters for the player to deal with – or benefit from! The following is a table of encounters grouped by zone that was part of the Space-Truckers game design specifications. Incomplete and purposefully vague on specifics, it still provides a clear picture of how the feature should work and interoperate with other features:

Zone	Encounter	Effects	Probability
Inner System	Solar Flare	Drags CargoUnit up, around, down, and so on, potentially off-course	Somewhat common
Inner System	Coronal Mass Ejection	Pushes CargoUnit outward from the star	Uncommon
Asteroid Belt	Rock Hazard	Damages CargoUnit, potentially destroying it	Common
Asteroid Belt	Rock Monster	Attempts to entrap CargoUnit for later feasting	Rare
Construction	Lane closure	Gets stuck in traffic and misses the rendezvous	Uncommon
Construction	Detour	Navigates a path around ongoing work	Uncommon
Construction	Nav Flagger	Follows the guide vehicle to maintain the flight path	Rare
Outer Reaches	Space-cow (single)	A collision that causes damage and obscures vision	Uncommon
Outer Reaches	Space-cow (herd)	A collision that causes significant damage and completely obscures vision	Rare

Figure 7.3 – Design for the Space-Truckers encounter. Source: `https://github.com/jelster/space-truckers/issues/65`

When implementing encounters, there will be different needs and thus differently structured solutions for each type of encounter. Fortunately, we don't need to define those specifics quite yet, so we'll park it for the moment and take a step back to look at how the **Encounter Zone** can track **CargoUnit**.

Tracking Intersections

Each EZ needs to register the intersection exit and enter triggers for the `CargoUnit` mesh's Action Manager, but we don't want to have to write code to do that for each Zone – what if we change the number of `EncounterZones`, or want to change the way intersections are used? Thankfully, this problem can be solved easily.

When the `initialize` method of `SpaceTruckerEncounterManager` is invoked, the list of `encounterZones` is iterated across in a `forEach` loop. Among other actions, each zone is passed by `cargo.mesh` as a parameter to its `registerZoneIntersectionTrigger` method. This function performs the intersection registration on `meshToWatch.actionManager`, which hooks up the corresponding `OnIntersectionExitTrigger` and `OnIntersectionEnterTrigger` to the EncounterZone's `onExitObservable` and `onEnterObservable`, respectively.

> **Note**
>
> `SpaceTruckerEncounterManager` is a member of `CargoUnit`.

The primary purpose of `SpaceTruckerEncounterManager` is to (as the name implies) manage encounters in its constituent Zones but to be able to do that, it needs to know which EZ `cargoUnit` is currently transiting. You may initially surmise that because `EncounterZone` has a torus shape, nested (but not overlapping) zones should fire their intersection triggers only when the mesh is crossed, but that's not the case in practice.

Performing intersection calculations against a complex mesh is a very computationally expensive process, making it not very suitable for real-time processing applications. Instead, what Babylon.js does is use the much less expensive and computationally efficient bounding box intersection calculations. Though fast, they do not mimic the actual geometries being tested very accurately, resulting in a problem wherein the cargo unit appears to the application as if it is within not just the zone at its location but all other zones that are nested around it!

To resolve this, `SpaceTruckerEncounterManager` keeps track of all triggered intersections with the `inAndOut` field. Incremented whenever a zone signals the entrance, and decremented for the converse, it is an integer that represents an index to `currentZone` that's offset by the total number of encounter zones:

```
get currentZone() {
    let zidx = this.encounterZones.length - this.inAndOut;
    return this.encounterZones[zidx]?.zone;
}
```

This property is used in several areas, from `CargoUnit` to the Route Planning GUI, but the underlying zones in the encounter manager need to be populated ahead of time with data defining the boundaries and characteristics of each zone.

Encounter Zones and Game Data

An **Encounter Zone** (like most software components) is defined by its behaviors and data. The data comes from the encounter zone's definition and looks something like this:

```
asteroidBelt: {
    id: "asteroid_belt",
    name: "Asteroid Belt",
    innerBoundary: 1000,
    outerBoundary: 1700,
    encounterRate: 0.2,
    colorCode: "#ff0000",
    encounters: [
        { id: 'rock_hazard', name: 'Rock Hazard', image
            hazard_icon, probability: 0.90 },
        { name: '', id: 'no_encounter', probability: 0.1,
            image: '' }
    ]
}
```

At construction time, `SpaceTruckerEncounterZone` uses this structure (passed as a parameter to the constructor) to initialize and configure the EZ. Some properties are self-explanatory, but `innerBoundary` and `outerBoundary` warrant explicit definitions, along with `encounterRate`. Once we've covered those, we'll dive into the encounters array and how it works.

The `innerBoundary` field is the **radius** (remember that for later) of the innermost circle of a torus – a donut shape – making this value the radius of the donut hole, while `outerBoundary` is the radius of the outer circle described by the torus. Though this makes sense from a conceptual viewpoint, it is a bit different from how the Babylon.js **TorusBuilder** API approaches the subject. When calling the `createTorus` method, the primary "knobs and switches" available to control the size of the mesh are the `diameter` and `thickness` parameters. These two values sound like they would work well if we were to pass `outerBoundary` and (`outerBoundary` - `innerBoundary`), respectively, but closely reading the parameter descriptions tells us a different story.

The best way to picture how the various parameters all fit together is by taking a length of wire and forming it into a half-circle of some radius, **r**. The diameter is $2 * r$. Now, picture taking a small paper coaster of the radius, **R**, and poking the wire through the center of it while joining the two ends of the wire to make a complete circle. So, the thickness of the torus described by the coaster around the wire is 2 * R. The outer boundary of the torus isn't the same as the diameter parameter – it's equal to the diameter plus one-half the thickness. The inner boundary is equal to half of the diameter minus half the thickness. That's not the best way to picture this, but it is one way to describe it! Here's something better than a description – a visualization for that analogy, available at the Playground link in the caption:

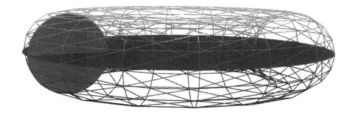

Figure 7.4 – The properties of a torus. The diameter is depicted by a solid circle with its thickness described by a second smaller circle. This Playground can be found at `https://playground.babylonjs.com/#P2YP2E#1`

Why are we going through these hoops? Because by structuring it in this way, we can quickly and easily compare and align encounter zones with planetary orbits, as defined in **gameData**.

Finally, getting back to the EZ data, the `encounterRate` field is a percentile (0 – 1) number indicating how often encounters happen in general for the zone. Each zone independently keeps its own encounter table, which it then uses to determine what, if any, encounter might occur. Since we're on the topic of encounters and random numbers, we might as well try to gain an understanding of exactly how to go about implementing the logic of picking entries from the Encounter Table. For that, we need to talk about something called a **Cumulative Distribution Mass Function**.

Selecting Encounters

A developer implementing this kind of functionality for the first time might devise a simple function, `getEncounter`, that picks a random number to serve as a dice roll before searching through an array of encounters for the first one with a probability less than or equal to the dice roll. To that developer's chagrin, this simple approach would also be incorrect! Though this approach works when rolling to determine the chance of a singular Encounter, it won't work when there are multiple potential encounters. Here's what the Asteroid Belt **Encounter Table** looks like in simplified form:

```
encounters: [
            { id: 'rock_hazard', name: 'Rock Hazard',
                image: hazard_icon, probability: 0.90 },
            { name: '', id: 'no_encounter', probability:
```

```
            0.1, image: '' }
    ]
```

Each entry in the encounter table has an associated probability factor, the total of which will usually (but doesn't have to due to some code we'll write shortly) equal 1 (100%). When you want to pick a random entry from the table, it's necessary to consider all the potential other events that might take place. The fancy-pants way of referring to the process of computing an event output in response to a random number input is a **Cumulative (Mass) Distribution Function** (**CMDF**). In the **EncounterZone** source (see `https://github.com/jelster/space-truckers/blob/ch7/src/encounterZone.js#L44`), the CMDF is implemented in the constructor as a two-step process.

Summing the Probabilities

In step one, we take the sum of all the individual encounters' probabilities. This step is what will allow the application to handle scenarios where the individual probabilities don't all add up to 1 and is used by step two. While we're there, the encounter table gets populated from the definition:

```
var total = 0;
definition.encounters.forEach((e, i) => {
    total += e.probability;
    this.encounterTable.push(e);
});
```

The point of this step is that while we can't necessarily guarantee that the total of the probabilities will come to one, we can normalize that sum in the next step so that each entry in the table is correctly and proportionally represented in the CMDF.

Populating CMDF Results

Step two involves looping through the list of `encounters` again (after pre-baking the first element of the `cumulativeDistribution` array) and populating entries into a second array – the aforementioned `cumulativeDistribution` array. This collection's entries represent the **CMDF** over its entire space and can therefore be used as an index to look up values for arbitrary inputs:

```
this.cumulativeDistribution[0] = this.encounterTable[0].
    Probability / total;
for (var I = 1; i < definition.encounters.length; i++) {
    this.cumulativeDistribution[i] =
        this.cumulativeDistribution[i - 1] +
            definition.encounters[i].probability / total;
}
```

Note that because the loop looks backward, the first element is calculated outside of the loop, which then starts at the **second** element. Essentially, the current element of the loop's value (`this.cumulativeDistribution[i]`) is equal to the previous element's value added to the current encounter's share of `probability` toward `total`. This only needs to happen once, upon initialization. Once in place, it is now possible to "roll the dice" and implement a more correct form of `getEncounter`.

Rolling an Encounter Check

Every time **EncounterZone's** `update` method is called, the logic will evaluate whether an encounter happens before deciding which encounter is going to take place. It needs to consider how much time has elapsed since the last frame, as it would then tie encounters to a player's frame rate – not what we want! Once that is considered, and if there is indeed an encounter indicated for the zone, the `getEncounter` method is called to retrieve a random entry from `encounterTable`. The encounter retrieved is then passed as the event parameter for `onEncounterObservable`, letting any subscriber know about `encounter`:

```
const encounterProbability = this.encounterRate * deltaTime;
if (Math.random() < encounterProbability) {
    let encounter = this.getEncounter();
    console.log('encounter ' + encounter?.name);
    this.onEncounterObservable.notifyObservers(encounter);
}
```

That's the update loop in its entirety. If only life could always be as elegant and simple as these solutions, maybe people would get along better, because the `getEncounter` method boils down to a single line of correct, though slightly esoteric, JavaScript:

```
for (var i = 0; i < this.cumulativeDistribution.length &&
  (diceRoll > this.cumulativeDistribution[i]); i++) {};
```

The reason this is a bit esoteric is that, as you might have noticed, the `for` loop has no body! There isn't a body in the loop because, simply put, there isn't a need for any. The purpose of the loop is to find the index (`i`) that conforms to the **CMDF**, given the input random `diceRoll` number. Once that condition has been fulfilled, the `i` value sticks around due to being declared with `var` rather than with `let`. The encounter itself is retrieved as an index and returned to the calling method for distribution.

Listening for Encounters

Once the **EncounterZone** has notified its subscribers of the **onEncounterObservable's** new event, its role in the encounter journey has ended. It doesn't need to know anything about who is listening to that event or what happens as a result of it, which allows our code to be more resistant to change (robust) and to be simpler and easier to understand (maintainable). This is one of the many strengths that can be leveraged from an event-driven system. The primary subscriber of these events is SpaceTruckerEncounterManager, which then acts as a broker and aggregator for distributing the news of Encounter throughout the application in its onEncounter observer method. The same observer is subscribed to all the zone's onEncounterObservable, which is what gives us the aggregation of these events that we need, along with the **CargoUnit's** lastFlightPoint telemetry package.

Both the encounter and cargoData are then bundled together and pushed into the encounterEvents array for future reference. The index of the newly added element is what is then propagated to observers of onNewEncounterObservable:

```
const cargoData = this.cargo.lastFlightPoint;
const idx = this.encounterEvents.push({ encounter,
    cargoData });
this.onNewEncounterObservable.notifyObservers(idx - 1);
```

The reason we are passing an index (or pointer) to the encounterEvents collection is that we want to ensure that we can dispose of those objects cleanly and at any time; if the object were passed in the event, it might not be possible for the system to determine whether memory can be freed up from disposed-of objects – a condition known as a memory leak.

At this point, we have finished inspecting and discussing the underlying infrastructure needed to define, locate, and generate encounters of different types. These encounters will be brought to life later in this book when we get into the driving phase game logic for each encounter. However, while our understanding of encounters is fresh, let's look at how encounters might be used and presented within the context of the route planning screen.

Adding Encounter Visuals

This is where our previous work in the *Marking Out the Route* section comes into play. Recall that as our CargoUnit falls through its trajectory, it is constantly laying down a line of breadcrumbs to mark out its path. This is visualized by the CargoUnit.trailMesh component, which other than needing to be initialized and disposed of during scenario resets, takes care of itself without much need for us to intervene. We need an equivalently hands-off way to similarly render visualizations for encounters when and where they occur along the route, and that's precisely what the work we just covered is meant to enable.

> **Important note:**
>
> While the following section is ultimately cut from the game, the technique demonstrated is helpful to have in your pocket.

Putting 2D Labels into 3D Space

Although there is a 3D GUI system in Babylon.js, our current needs don't require the use of a full 3D UI. Still, one of the advantages of a 3D GUI is that it is easy to position elements within the World Space – for reasons that should hopefully be obvious.

> **Note**
>
> Unlike jokes, there's no risk of ruining this with an explanation. The obvious reason is that positioning 2D elements concerning a 3D world-space point can get tricky because of the need to combine camera position, world position, and screen position transformations to get the correct coordinates as opposed to a 3D GUI system operating in the same coordinate space.

Much of the complexity inherent in coordinate transformations is, fortunately, hidden away from the developer by the BJS GUI framework – `linkWithMesh` and `moveToVector` both allow callers to place a GUI control somewhere in the **World Space**. That's good for part of the way, but we still need to have someplace to hang the visuals as well as provide a base for future enhancements and behaviors.

If you've come back to this section after a break, you can thank your Past Self for putting all the pieces into place. If you've been binging through this chapter (don't stop – won't stop – can't stop!) then take a moment to pat yourself on the back. It's important to take the time to properly acknowledge yourself and the impact of previous actions on present situations – both good and bad! This is going to be easy, in other words.

Remember how we used a `TransformNode` to track our cargo's flight path? This is where that decision is finally justified. Most **Controls** in the **Babylon.js GUI** system have the `linkWithMesh` function, whose name implies that you must only pass a Mesh. This would be a wrong, though understandable, conclusion to make that can be remedied by studying the method's documentation and seeing that while the name of the parameter is `mesh`, the expected type of the parameter is our old friend **Transform Node**!

> **Note**
>
> The documentation isn't wrong, strictly speaking, because **Mesh** extends the `TransformNode` type.

The `PlanningScreenGui` component already has access to the `encounterManager` property of the `planningScreen` field in its constructor, so we can subscribe to its `onNewEncounterObservable` to be notified when a new encounter happens. In the observer function, we get the image URL from the encounter itself and use it to create Babylon.js GUI elements that are then linked to the associated `TransformNode` of the flight path:

```
const encounter = evt.encounter;
let panel = new Rectangle("panel-" + encounter.name);
let image = new Image("image-" + encounter.name,
    encounter.image);
image.alpha = 0.68;
panel.addControl(image);
panel.thickness = 0;
this.gui.addControl(panel);
this.encounterPanels.push(panel);
panel.linkWithMesh(evt.cargoData);
```

That's the visual placed in the correct spot and with the right image, so now, let's think about what else is involved with displaying an encounter. First, we want there to be a sound effect that plays. This can be done by registering `SpaceTruckerPlanningScreen` to `onNewEncounterObservable`, as shown in the following code:

```
this.encounterManager.onNewEncounterObservable.add(enc =>
        this.soundManager.sound("encounter").play());
```

While we're not currently using the actual encounter index now, this approach allows it to be easily extended in the future – to allow individual encounters to specify their own sound to play, for instance. When an encounter occurs, we don't want an icon to simply appear, with no fanfare. We want to make sure the player's attention is called to it, but only momentarily. One way to accomplish that is to initially render the panel so that it's much larger than its eventual size and then animate the panel so that it's shrinking to its final size and position.

Animating the Encounter Panel

In *Chapter 4*, *Creating the Application*, we saw how to statically define an **Animation** that was later targeted to a specific object as part of an **AnimationGroup**. We will use the same technique here to define the animations involved in shrinking the encounter panel.

> **Important note**
>
> Even though it may not seem like it, almost any object can be the target of an **Animation** – including GUI components! You just need to know the specific name(s) of the properties to animate. In our case, those are the `scaleX` and `scaleY` properties of the `GUI.Image` component.

Note that there are two separate animations involved – one each for the *X* and *Y*-axes – since an **Animation** can only target a single property. Though there are separate animations for each mentioned axis, they have the same set of keyframes. In our encounter observer function, we can create an `AnimationGroup` and use `addTargetedAnimation` along with the target `panel` and `panelShrink` Animation, after which the animation is started:

```
let animationGroup = new
AnimationGroup("shrinkAnimationGroup-"+ encounter.name,
    this.scene);
animationGroup.addTargetedAnimation(panelShrinkX, panel);
animationGroup.addTargetedAnimation(panelShrinkY, panel);
animationGroup.start(false, 1.0, 0, 180, true);
```

This gives us a nice presentation for the encounters, leaving just one more use case that we have yet to cover – resetting the route planning screen.

Clearing Encounter Panels

The list that encounters the GUI elements that are collected in anticipation of just this scenario is the `encounterPanels` array. Since each GUI control implements a `dispose` function, we reset the encounters UI by simply looping through the array and calling `dispose` on each element in turn. To avoid the need to anticipate every single place we need to do this, we can add the logic to the place it makes the most sense – the `onScreenStateChange` observer function. Whenever it executes logic to transition to the `ReadyToLaunch` state, the encounter panel is cleared of any elements and all children are disposed of:

```
this.encounterPanels.forEach(panel => {
    panel.children.forEach(child => child.dispose());
    panel.dispose();
});
```

That's all there is to it.

> **Important note**
>
> Of course, that's *not* all there is to it! There is much, much more that can be done and is being done in the context of Encounter visuals, but by and large, all of this is based on the same concepts presented throughout this section and chapter. If you haven't already, don't forget to remind yourself: game development is hard and there are a lot of moving parts!

Although we have only covered how the encounter GUI panels are cleared, this pattern completes the circle of creation and destruction.

Registering to listen for `EncounterManager.onNewEncounterObservable` informs components of new encounters, while setting `SpaceTruckerPlanningScreen.onStateChangeObservable` to the `ReadyToLaunch` state clears any existing ones.

Summary

Let's take a step back and review what we've covered in this chapter. First, we took another side route to visit the various Babylon.js particle systems, making use of and adapting the Sun Particle System Set for our purposes.

We can look at particle systems in three rough categories of distinction – the "Classic", "New Wave", and "Hard Core" monikers. Each references the always-available CPU-bound Particle System, the GPU-bound GPU Particle System, and the mixed **Solid Particle System** (**SPS**). While the first two systems are based around 2D billboards and sprites – characteristics that can animate via sprite sheets and the like – an **SPS** uses a source mesh to generate particles, which can, in turn, be assigned any type of Material desired (we'll get more into **Materials**, the different types, their properties, and more in *Chapter 10, Improving the Environment with Lighting and Materials*).

Loading a custom Particle System Set involves capturing a serialized JSON file containing the specific parameters for each Particle System involved in the appropriate structure. This can be done by calling `ParticleHelper.ExportSet(setA, setB,…)`. Loading saved JSON from a URL is easy but loading it from a local URL gets a bit more complicated. However, by falling back to the `ParticleSystemSet.Parse` function, we can load data for the **ParticleSystemSet** in any way we please!

Following our detour into Particles, we examined the telemetry data our **CargoUnit** captures during its flight, and how we can use **TransformNodes** to represent spatial locations. This proves to be crucial for making it easy to display visuals without writing a lot of code and provided a good on-ramp to get into how Encounter Zones work.

Each **Encounter Zone** can be thought of as a unique biome or environment in the world of *Space-Truckers*. From the toasty **Inner System** to the frosty **Outer System**, each Zone has its own set of potential Encounters players might face. Defined by an inner and outer Boundary, some light math is involved in converting those handy **gameData** figures into parameter values used to create a set of nested Torus meshes to represent the zones. Not rendered, these meshes' **ActionManagers** are used to register **IntersectionEnter** and **IntersectionExit** triggers against the **CargoUnit**. As it traverses the system, the **SpaceTruckerEncounterManager** keeps track of which Zone the player's **CargoUnit** is currently transiting.

While transiting a given zone, the Zone's `update` method makes a weighted random check every frame to decide whether there should be an Encounter, selected from the Zone's Encounter Table. The Encounter Zone's constructor pre-computes the **Cumulative Mass Distribution Function** values for every entry in the Table, normalizing the probabilities so that the total adds up to 1. If an encounter is "rolled," the value of the roll (a number between 0 and 1) is used as an input to the function, which returns an index to the indicated event. **SpaceTruckerEncounterManager** listens for these Encounter Zone events.

Responsible for aggregating Encounter data with **CargoUnit** data and informing subscribers of where to find the resulting encounter data, the **onNewEncounterObservable** is the primary means for components such as the **PlanningScreenGui** to update themselves without needing to pepper appropriate logic throughout the application's components. Within the **PlanningScreenGui**, techniques first perfected during the construction of the Splash Screen come in handy. Here, we can define some Animations that target the Encounter's Image panel to give it a shrinking effect as an entrance.

Within the **onNewEncounter** observer, targeted animations are generated from the **Animations** and put into an **AnimationGroup** associated with the new GUI display elements. Our previous planning in the *Marking the Route* section pays off here as well, as we can ensure that the UI element is correctly positioned by calling `linkWithMesh` and passing in the **TransformNode** captured from the flight telemetry.

As usual, the code discussed in this chapter is available at `https://github.com/jelster/space-truckers/tree/ch7`, and while the game is still incomplete at this point in its history, we can point to concrete and valuable progress through the course of this chapter – never forget to give yourself credit for progress made on a journey! The Discussions board at `https://github.com/jelster/space-truckers/discussions` is a good place to post questions about the code, book, or application. Want to contribute? Navigate to the Issues at `https://github.com/jelster/space-truckers/issues` and browse for open ones that catch your fancy, or create a new Issue to discuss your enhancement, bug, or new feature. In the next chapter, we're going to make good use of the route and the encounters generated to build the driving mini-game. Along the way, we'll learn how to shift camera perspectives to a first-person view, apply decals to meshes, and more!

> **Note**
>
> There's an entire category of Issues aimed at first-time contributors and people lacking experience or familiarity with Babylon.js and/or Space-Truckers – it's called **Good First Issue**. Want to make MacGyver proud and fix Issues that nobody else can fix? Check out the **Help Wanted** label!

Extended Topics

There is always more content and ideas than there are time and space to implement them, so here are some ways that you can push yourself further with the content from this chapter. Before moving on to the next chapter, or at any time later, think of these as launch pads for you to clarify and fold the lessons learned here in the forge of experience:

- Add a new particle system based on the Sparks particle sample that is triggered when the cargo collides with something during the route planning's flight phase.

- The world of Space-Truckers is rich and varied, and the game could display more of that richness. Use an animated particle system to bring these areas to life:

  - Orbital manufacturing might look like a series of flashing lights from maneuver thrusters and welding torches clustering around shadowed block structures

  - Traffic in the Space-Construction and Space-Highway zones could similarly be approximated with clusters of flashing lights zipping around

- Add the capability to load encounter lists from external sources other than the **gameData** file. The source can be a relative or remote path, with CMDFs being recomputed for the new list for each zone.

- Make an enhanced random number generator that will weigh or re-roll random values to avoid returning the same value more than X times in Y rolls.

- Random numbers generated by computers tend to cluster and clump unrealistically – the Asteroids are a great demonstration of that. There are other ways to weigh and generate random series of numbers, though. Sneak to the `ch10` branch of the Space-Truckers source code on GitHub to see how the `randomGenerator` module implements `getGaussianRandom` for one example.

Building the Driving Game

It may not be easy to believe it, but we are officially past the halfway point – while the end is still not in sight, we've made so much progress it's tough to see our starting point. In the previous six chapters, we built out a huge amount of functionality encompassing an almost breathtaking diversity of subjects. The following figure shows where we were before and where we are now:

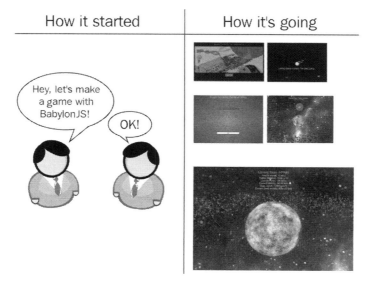

Figure 8.1 – How it started versus how it's going. A montage of screenshots showing our progress

From setting up the basic web application to implementing random encounters, a lot has gone into our code base to get to this point, but we're not stopping or even slowing down any time soon! Making it this far into this book shows admirable persistence and determination – this chapter is where all of that will pay off. One of the more enjoyable aspects of game development is also one of the more obvious ones – the part of getting to work on the core gameplay and logic code. Unfortunately, and as people with experience of developing and shipping software will attest, all the other activities that go into building and delivering software tend to take up the lion's share of available project time.

Throughout this chapter, we're going to be building out the driving phase of Space-Truckers. Along with some of the techniques we learned earlier, we're going to introduce a few new tools for the ol' toolbox. We're going to take things up a notch by adding a second camera to our scene that will render the **Graphical User Interface (GUI)**. We'll generate a route based on the previous phase's simulated route and allow players to drive their trucks along it, avoiding obstacles (if they can). Our scene will use physics as the previous phase does, but instead of mainly using it as a gravitational simulation, we're going to make use of the physics engine's capabilities to simulate the results of collisions, friction, and more. Some things we're going to introduce but defer more detailed examination until upcoming chapters – when this is the case, the relevant chapters and sections will be linked for easy reference.

All those exciting topics will hopefully more than make up for the more mundane but no less important task of building the necessary logic ahead of us. By the end of this chapter, we'll have a playable driving game that sets us up for the following chapter, where we will continue to finish the overall game's life cycle as we learn how to calculate and display scoring results.

In this chapter, we will cover the following topics:

- Prototyping the Driving Phase
- Integrating with the Application
- Adding Encounters
- Making the Mini-Map

Technical Requirements

Nothing in this chapter is required from a technical perspective that hasn't already been listed as being needed for the previous chapters, but there are some technical areas where it might be useful to have working knowledge as you read through this chapter:

- **MultiViews**: `https://doc.babylonjs.com/divingDeeper/cameras/multiViewsPart2`
- **Layer Masks**: `https://doc.babylonjs.com/divingDeeper/cameras/layerMasksAndMultiCam`
- **In-Depth Layer Masks**: `https://doc.babylonjs.com/divingDeeper/scene/layermask`
- **Loading Any File Type**: `https://doc.babylonjs.com/divingDeeper/importers/loadingFileTypes`
- **Polar Coordinates**: `https://tutorial.math.lamar.edu/Classes/CalcII/PolarCoordinates.aspx` and `https://math.etsu.edu/multicalc/prealpha/Chap3/Chap3-2/`

Prototyping the Driving Phase

There's a lot to do, so let's dive right into it. Due to the way the driving phase is designed, players must navigate their trucks along a route that's been pre-determined by the players in the previous game phase. The nature of the overall planned route determines similar overall characteristics of the driving route. Factors such as total transit time, distance, and velocities all fall into that kind of characteristic. Others, such as random encounters along the path, are more localized to a specific portion of the path. The behavior of each encounter is variable, but all will have a general form of forcing the player to make choices to avoid/obtain a collision while piloting their space-truck. Capturing the correlations between the two phases is an important design specification that will be useful – here's what is listed on the Space-Trucker Issue created for that purpose:

Planning Phase	Driving Phase
Distance traveled	Length of the course
Launch velocity	Initial speed parameter
Encounters	Obstacles/events
Instantaneous velocities	Track diameter
Total transit time	Target time to finish

Figure 8.2 – Comparison of Route Planning versus driving phase variables. Source: https://github.com/jelster/space-truckers/issues/84

Some of the properties have a direct 1:1 correlation between phases, such as total transit time and distance traveled. Others are used as scale or other indirect influencing factors, such as the point velocity affecting the route's diameter. This will all be quite useful a bit further down this chapter's journey, but for now, we will turn our attention to building out a Playground demonstrating the core principles of the driving phase.

Playground Overview

Prototyping in software is all about reducing a particular problem or area of interest to its bare essence. It forces us to ask the question – what is the smallest set of characteristics, attributes, features, and so on needed to evaluate the viability of a particular approach? In the case of our driving phase prototype, we don't need to play through the planning phase to accomplish our goals – we just need to be able to process the route data generated by that phase. Focusing in, the problem of hooking up our route data to the driving phase isn't the problem we're trying to solve right now (though we can certainly do our future selves a solid by structuring our code in ways that facilitate building that logic!). This saves mental bandwidth and energy that can be put to good use elsewhere, which is where we will begin.

> **Important note**
>
> The Playground at `https://playground.babylonjs.com/#WU7235#49` is the reference for this section of this chapter.

We'll need physics to be working so that we can playtest the interactions and relationships between the truck, obstacles, and velocities. We need to determine the proper scaling, orientation, and import settings for loading the first 3D asset model into the game – the semi-truck. Finally, we need to figure out how we're going to plot oncoming obstacles in the radar GUI presented to the player. This seems like quite a lot to take on, but thanks to the functionality built into Babylon.js there's much less complexity than it might seem. The following screenshot illustrates how these elements all come together in the Playground demo:

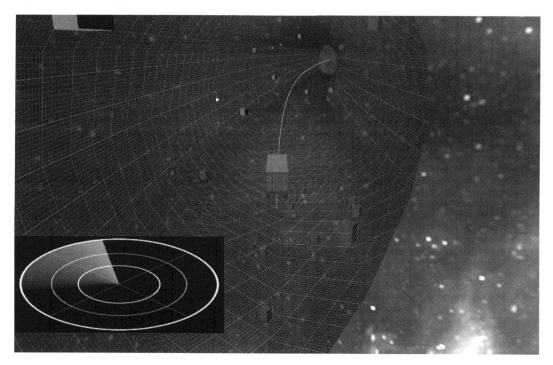

Figure 8.3 – Space-Truckers driving phase Playground at `https://playground.babylonjs.com/#WU7235#49`

In the center of the viewport is our game's protagonist, the eponymous space-trucker. The space-road stretches out in front of them, littered with the untextured blocks that are filling the place of encounters. In the lower-left part of the screen, a radar display sweeps in a circle, revealing upcoming obstacles as blips. The camera is chained to the truck so that the player's perspective is always behind and a bit above the truck – the classic Third-Person Perspective. The controls are simple – *W* and *S* accelerate and decelerate in the truck's forward direction, while *A* and *D* accelerate to the left and right, respectively. Vertical acceleration is managed with the *up arrow* and *down arrow* keys, and rotation with the *right arrow* and *left arrow*; resetting the demo is done by pressing the *Delete* key. Try to make it to the end of the path as fast as you can!

Let's swap over to looking at the code for the demo, and how the demo is structured. Right away, we can see some similarities but also some differences from how we've structured our previous Playground demos. At the very top are the various asset URL and **BABYLON** namespace aliases; moving down, we have a rather hefty `gameData` object, and then we get to the most striking difference yet: the `async drive(scene)` function.

This is, as implied by the `async` prefix, an **asynchronous** JavaScript function. Its purpose is two-fold: one, to allow the use of the `await` statement in expressions within the function body, and two, to provide a container for closure over all the **var**-ious objects and values used by the demo.

> **Note**
> The editors of this book apologize for subjecting you to the inredibad pun that was just made.

Furious punning discharged, we will continue with the first few lines of the PG above the `drive` function. To load our route data, we'll choose the simple approach of wrapping a call to `jQuery. getJSON` in a promise that resolves to the array of route path points:

```
var scriptLoaded = new Promise(
    (resolve, reject) =>
        $.getJSON(routeDataURL)
            .done(d => resolve(d))
);
```

This requires us to specify our `createScene` method as `async`, allowing us to write a simple harness to instantiate and return the Playground's Scene after doing the same for the driving phase initialization logic:

```
var createScene = async function () {
    var routeJSON = await scriptLoaded;
    var scene = new BABYLON.Scene(engine);
    const run = await drive(scene, routeJSON);
    run();
    return scene;
};
```

The `drive` function is responsible for creating and/or loading any type of asset or resource that might require a bit of time to complete, so it is also marked as async. There's a ton of code that goes into this function, so to make it easier to work with, the logic is split up into a few helper methods. Before those, the logic for basic scene and environment setup is constructed or defined. These are elements that might be needed by any or all the (potentially asynchronous) helper functions that include the invocation of those helper functions in the proper order. Once those tasks are complete, the `run` function is returned:

```
await loadAssets();
initializeDrivingPhase();
initializeGui();
return run;
```

We'll cover the `initializeGui` method in this chapter's *Making a Mini-Map* section after we establish a bit more context. Earlier in the `drive` function is probably the most important helper function that we want to prove out in the Playground, and that is the `calculateRouteParameters(routeData)` method. This is the workhorse function of the driving phase's world creation and has probably the largest impact on how gameplay evolves in the form of dictating the properties of the route driven by the player.

Generating the Driving Path

In *Chapter 7, Processing Route Data*, we set up `cargoUnit` to log `routeData`: timing, position, velocity, rotation, and gravity are all captured every few frames of rendering into a collection of data points (along with encounters, which we'll get to in the *Adding Encounters* section). The telemetry data is a deep well for creative and interesting ideas (see *Extended Topics*), but for now, we'll just use the position, velocity, and gravity route values described in the *Playground Overview* section to generate the route path.

The beginning of the function grabs `routeDataScalingFactor` from `gameData`; though currently set to a value of **1.0**, changing this allows us to scale the route size and length consistently, easily, and quickly across route elements. In a concession to our desire to load up captured route telemetry from a JSON file, we iterate through the data array to ensure that the position, gravity, and velocity elements have been instantiated to their respective `Vector3` values, as opposed to a Plain Ol' JavaScript Object.

> **Important note**
> Taking proactive steps like this to reduce friction on quick iteration is key to building momentum!

Once that's done, we use the positional vectors from the telemetry data to construct a new `Path3D` instance:

```
let path3d = new Path3D(pathPoints.map(p => p.position),
   new Vector3(0, 1, 0), false, false);
let curve = path3d.getCurve();
```

From the Babylon.js docs (`https://doc.babylonjs.com/divingDeeper/mesh/path3D`),

> *"A Path3D is a mathematical object created from a sequence of position vectors of points on a curve."*

`Error! Hyperlink reference not valid.`

Put another way, a `Path3D` represents an ordered set of coordinate points with some interesting and useful properties.

> **Note**
>
> The reason for calling it a "mathematical object" is because it is not a member of the Scene and does not take part in rendering. This also sounds a lot cooler than calling it a "non-rendered abstract geometrical data structure."

The `getCurve()` method is a utility method that spits back the sequence of points that define the path, but there are even more useful nuggets of value tucked away in `Path3D` that we'll soon be exploring. First, though, we want to display the specific path taken by the player during the planning phase as a straight line going down the middle of the space-road. This is easy – we use the curve array in a call to `MeshBuilder.CreateLines` and that's all there is to it! For more on this, see `https://doc.babylonjs.com/divingDeeper/mesh/creation/param/lines`. After that is when we start constructing the geometry for the space-road, which is where things start to get interesting.

The geometric shape forming the base of our space-road is a Ribbon – a series of one or more paths, each with at least two `Vector3` points. The order the paths are provided works in conjunction with the paths themselves to produce geometry with a huge range of flexibility, and though potentially entertaining, it would be counterproductive to attempt to reproduce the excellent examples already created as part of the Ribbon's documentation at `https://doc.babylonjs.com/divingDeeper/mesh/creation/param/ribbon_extra`. From those docs, this thought experiment nicely explains the concept we're looking at currently:

> *"Imagine a long ribbon of narrow width in the real world with a wire running down its length. Closing the paths forms a loop of ribbon while closing the array would form a tube."*

Closing the array seems like the option we want rather than closing the paths themselves since we want our road to be enclosed, but not like a donut or loop. This faces us with a bit of a choice regarding how we'd like to approach implementing this, but only after we have established the value in doing it via prototyping, which in this circumstance becomes the link back to our choice of implementation paths in an endlessly circular argument.

When prototyping out the path creation (or any prototyping process in software), there's a certain point in the process where you realize the need to transition from throwing something together to see if it works and taking consideration to build something more robust with the knowledge that it will be incorporated into the final product. Playground snippet **#WU7235#11** (`https://playground.babylonjs.com/#WU7235#11`) shows, starting around **line 168**, what this prototyped logic can look like (comments have been removed for clarity):

```
let pathA = [];
let pathB = [];
let pathC = [];
let pathD = [];
for (let i = 0; i < pathPoints.length; i++) {
    const { position, gravity, velocity } = pathPoints[i];
    let p = position;
    let speed = velocity.length();
    let pA = new Vector3(p.x+speed, p.y-speed, p.z+speed);
    let pB = new Vector3(p.x-speed, p.y-speed, p.z-speed);
    let pC = pB.clone().addInPlaceFromFloats(0, speed * 2,
      0);
    let pD = pA.clone().addInPlaceFromFloats(0, speed * 2,
      0);
    pathA.push(pA);
    pathB.push(pB);
    pathC.push(pC);
    pathD.push(pD);
}
```

This is a scheme for path geometry that takes the form of a four-sided box (the ends are open). The preceding code uses four separate arrays of points – one for each corner – to capture the paths as it loops through each of the points along the route. This is what that looks like:

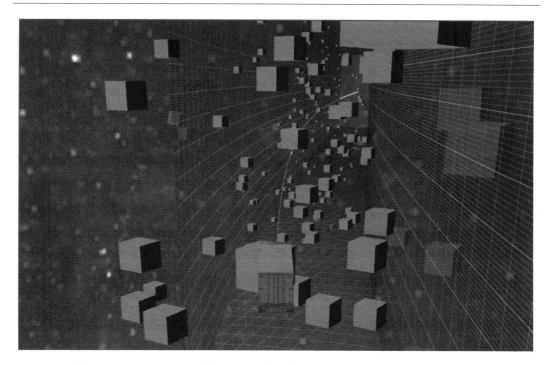

Figure 8.4 – Prototype path geometry hardcoded to make a four-sided box with
open ends. Four paths are used. Simple and effective, yet extremely limited
(https://playground.babylonjs.com/#WU7235#11)

Mission accomplished! We're done here, right? Wrong. This is just the beginning! It's OK to celebrate accomplishments, but it's best to keep any celebrations proportional to the achievement in the context of the end goal. A box shape works to prove that we can create a playable path demo from actual route data, but it's not particularly fun or attractive to look at. To step this up to a place where it's something that will surprise and delight users, we need to make it more spherical and less boxy. We need to add more path segments to do this, and that's where our prototype reaches its limits.

Referring to the previous code listing, each path of the ribbon has been predefined in the form of the pathA, pathB, pathC, and pathD arrays. If we want to add more segments, we need to manually add the additional path array, along with the appropriate logic, to locate path segments that aren't at 90-degree right-angles to each other correctly – and that makes our current approach much tougher. There's a certain mindset that prefers to attack this sort of problem head-on, with brute force. They might add pathE, pathF, or pathG arrays and pre-calculate the paths' offsets relative to one another based on hardcoded numbers and after the dust settles, what comes out will probably work just fine… until the need arises to change the number of segments again. Or worse yet, the need arises to *dynamically* set the number of paths based on, for example, device performance characteristics. That's why it's necessary to come up with a Better Way Forward.

Let's jump back to the original Playground we started with – **#WU7235#23** – and look at how it's evolved starting at line 140. First things first, we know that we need to be able to specify how many separate paths should be created. That's easy – just define a NUM_SEGMENTS constant. Next, we need to instantiate new path arrays to hold each path. We do this in a simple loop:

```
const NUM_SEGMENTS = 24;
let paths = [];
for (let i = 0; i < NUM_SEGMENTS; i++) {
    paths.push([]);
}
```

Great – we have our array of path arrays ready to go. Now, it's time to populate those paths, so we set up an outer loop over `routePath` containing an inner loop over each path array. But how do we figure out where each point of each path is supposed to be located? It's not enough to use the simple constant offsets to each point position like we did in the prototype; each path segment's points will have different offset values from each other. In the following diagram, the hoop or ring shape is a single cross-section segment, with all points lying in the same plane (math folks call this an affine set of points):

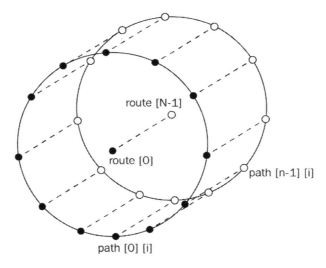

Figure 8.5 – Creating a point of route geometry starts from the center point that moves clockwise around the diameter, adding path points for each discrete segment

Start from the current route position and use it as the center point. Now, focusing on one individual execution of the outer-most loop through `routeData`, we know that we need to create points equal in number to the number of desired segments. We also know that those segments should be evenly and contiguously distributed around the diameter of a hypothetical circle.

> **Note**
>
> The reason we use a circle rather than a sphere is that relative to a given route point, the Z-axis values will always be the same for every path segment around that point. This is rather tautological since that's also a somewhat meandering way to define a circle!

Putting those facts together and combining them with what we already know regarding circles and trig functions, we have a way to do just what we want. There's just one remaining obstacle: how can we vary the position offset on the individual path being computed? Fortunately, this isn't as big of an issue as it might seem at first.

Let's remind ourselves of these facts about circles and trigonometric functions. The sine and cosine functions each take an input angle (in radians for this text unless otherwise noted) and output a value between -1 and 1 corresponding to the angle-dependent X- and Y-axis values, respectively. A full circle comprises two times Pi (3.14159…) radians, or about 6.28 radians. If we divide the number of segments by 6.28 radians, we would get the arc that an individual segment traverses, but if we divide the number of segments by the zero-based index of the currently iterating segment, then we get something more useful – the position between 0..1 of our current segment. A percentage, or ratio in other words. By multiplying that ratio with our two times Pi value, we get… the position of the segment, in radians! All that's left is to scale the result by a value representing the desired radius (or diameter, for the X-axis) and add it to the path collection:

```
for (let i = 0; i < pathPoints.length; i++) {
    let { position, velocity } = pathPoints[i];
    const last = position;
    for (let pathIdx = 0; pathIdx < NUM_SEGMENTS;
      pathIdx++) {
        let radiix = (pathIdx / NUM_SEGMENTS) *
            Scalar.TwoPi;
        let speed = velocity.length();
        let path = paths[pathIdx];
        let pathPoint = last.clone().addInPlaceFromFloats(
            Math.sin(radiix) * speed * 2,
            Math.cos(radiix) * speed, 0);
        path.push(pathPoint);
    }
}
```

In the preceding code listing from **#WU7235#25**, we are using the **length** of the point's `velocity` vector to determine the size of the space-road. We must `clone` the `last` point before mutating it; otherwise, we will end up corrupting the data needed by the rest of the application. By setting the value of NUM_SEGMENTS to 4 and progressively running the Playground at increasing numbers, it's easy to see that the updated logic can now handle an arbitrary amount of line segments – an enormous improvement over our first-generation prototype! This code will be ready to integrate with the application when we're ready to begin that process starting in the *Initializing the Driving Phase* section. There are still a few more things to prove out in other areas before that can happen, though. The loadAssets function is next up on our list.

Loading Assets Asynchronously

In this Playground, we're going to be loading two things asynchronously as part of the loadAssets function – the semi-truck model and the radar procedural texture asset. We need to make sure that all the asynchronous function calls have been completed before continuing by returning a promise that resolves only when all of its constituent promises have done so as well. Here's what that looks like in loadAssets():

```
return Promise.all([nodeMatProm, truckLoadProm])
        .then(v => console.log('finished loading
            assets'));
```

nodeMatProm is created using a pattern that is used throughout Babylon.js and one we most recently used in the previous chapter's discussion on loading JSON for a ParticleSystemSet, only for this Playground, instead of loading JSON directly, we will load data from the Babylon.js Snippet Server. Specifically, we are loading a snippet from the **Node Material Editor** (**NME**) that we will then use to create the radar procedural texture that is displayed on the GUI. Further details on those elements will have to wait until *Chapter 11, Scratching the Surface of Shaders*:

```
const nodeMatProm = NodeMaterial.ParseFromSnippetAsync
    (radarNodeMatSnippet, scene)
        .then(nodeMat => {
            radarTexture = nodeMat.createProceduralTexture(
            radarTextureResolution, scene);
        });
```

While it may be obvious that radarTexture is a variable containing the **procedural texture**, it's less obvious where the radarTextureResolution value comes in. One of the difficulties in creating a "simple" game prototype is that even something simple requires creating and managing a fair amount of configuration data. The gameData structure serves the purpose of centralizing and consolidating access to these types of values; when we want to utilize one or more of these values in a function, we can use JavaScript's **deconstruction** feature to simplify and make our code much more readable:

```
const {
        truckModelName,
```

```
        truckModelScaling,
        radarTextureResolution } = gameData;
```

As we saw in the preceding code block, `radarTextureResolution` is used for determining the render height and width in pixels of the procedural texture, whereas we'll shortly see how `truckModelName` and `truckModelScaling` are used. The `SceneLoader.ImportMeshAsync` method (new to v5!) takes an optional list of model names, along with the path and filename of an appropriate file containing the meshes to load (for example, `.glb`, `.gltf`, `.obj`, and so on), along with the current scene. The promise that's returned resolves to an object containing the loaded file's `meshes`, `particleSystems`, `skeletons`, and `animationGroups`, although we're only going to be using the meshes collection for this scenario.

> **Note**
>
> You can learn more about `SceneLoader` and its related functionality at `https://doc.babylonjs.com/divingDeeper/importers/loadingFileTypes#scene-loaderimportmesh`.

Once we've loaded the semi-truck's model file, we've got a bit more work to do before we can start using the loaded asset. Models saved in the GLTF or GLB formats are imported into Babylon.js with some additional properties that are going to get in our way, so let's simplify and set up `truckModel` for the game world:

```
const truckLoadProm = SceneLoader.ImportMeshAsync
  (truckModelName, truckModelURL, "", scene)
    .then((result) => {
        let { meshes } = result;
        let m = meshes[1];
        truckModel = m;
        truckModel.setParent(null);
        meshes[0].dispose();
        truckModel.layerMask = SCENE_MASK;
        truckModel.rotation = Vector3.Zero();
        truckModel.position = Vector3.Zero();
        truckModel.scaling.setAll(truckModelScaling);
        truckModel.bakeCurrentTransformIntoVertices();
        m.refreshBoundingInfo();
    }).catch(msg => console.log(msg));
```

The first few lines of our processing pipeline perform some convenient setup for the variables from the result structure, but then we do something a bit unusual by setting the parent of `truckModel` to `null` before disposing of the first mesh in the `meshes` array – what's up with that, and what's with `SCENE_MASK`?

> **Note**
>
> For more on layer masks and how they operate, see the docs at `https://doc.babylonjs.com/divingDeeper/cameras/layerMasksAndMultiCam`.

The answer to the second is, briefly, that cameras can be assigned a specific number that only allows meshes with a compatible `layerMask` to be rendered by that camera. We use the `layerMask` property to hide non-GUI meshes from the main scene camera, for example. The answer to the first lies in the specifics of how an asset is loaded from a GLB or GLTF file. When Babylon.js reads in the file, there is an invisible transform node named `__root__` placed at the root of the model hierarchy. Although it doesn't cause any problems in simple scenarios, when dealing with physics, parenting, collisions, and transforms, it becomes a major hindrance. The following screenshot illustrates what this looks like in the **Scene Inspector** window:

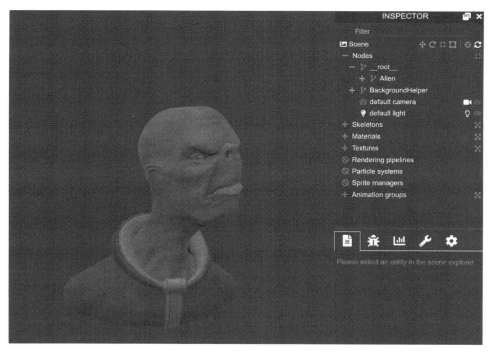

Figure 8.6 – The Alien.gltf model. The Scene Inspector window shows the __root__ transform node. From `https://playground.babylonjs.com/#8IMNBM#1`

The Alien geometry is what we're interested in working with, but because it is parented to the __root__ node, any changes to the position, rotation, or scaling of Alien are evaluated in a coordinate space relative to that root node, resulting in undesired and unpredictable results. The solution to this is simple and answers our earlier question regarding what was up with our loadAssets code – unparent the desired mesh and dispose of the root. Once that's accomplished, the rest of the code in our truck loading method is all housekeeping setup for the model – with some important considerations to keep in mind:

- Order of operations is important, but not in the way you might think. Changes to a TransformNode (which Mesh is a descendent of) over a given frame are applied in the fixed order of **Transform, Rotate, Scale** (**TRS**).

- Use setParent(null) rather than the alternative of setting mesh.parent = null. The setParent function preserves positional and rotational values, whereas setting the parent to null does not. This results in any root transformations being removed from the mesh, which is why we need to reset the position and rotation vectors.

- Once the transformations have been cleared and the scaling has been set to world-appropriate values, the mesh geometry will need to have new bounding information generated. Otherwise, collisions won't work properly. The solution to this is the two-step process of calling mesh.bakeCurrentTransformIntoVertices() before calling mesh.refreshBoundingInfo().

> **Important note**
> Normally, it's not recommended to call bakeCurrentTransformIntoVertices when there are better options such as **parenting** and **pivotPoints** that might work. In this case, we need to perform this step since we've removed the parenting to root. See https://doc.babylonjs.com/divingDeeper/mesh/transforms/center_origin/bakingTransforms for more information and guidance on this topic.

As mentioned previously, the result of calling Promise.all with the unresolved promises is the returned **Promise** from loadAssets, bringing us full circle back to where this discussion started! Initialization is mostly done – or at least the portion of it taking the longest time is complete – and now with the availability of the semi-truck model, the initializeDrivingPhase function has been invoked to set up the rest of the scene's elements. This function sets up the cameras, creates the ground ribbon mesh from the routePaths, sets up physics, and more.

Initializing the Driving Phase Scene

As mentioned in this chapter's introduction, the viewpoint for the player is in a third-person perspective, with the camera behind the semi-truck and looking over its top. As the truck moves (translation) or rotates (um, rotation), the camera mimics every movement from its offset position. The way this is accomplished is one of those situations where real-world analogies match well to software, in the form of cameraDolly.

A camera dolly is normally an engineered sort of cart used in the film industry that allows the Grip operating the camera to smoothly move in multiple dimensions while capturing footage. Our camera dolly doesn't run on tracks, but it fulfills a similar purpose by moving with the truck to maintain the same forward-facing orientation regardless of the truck's world-space orientation. This can be accomplished in just a few steps:

1. Create a `TransformNode` to serve as the "camera dolly:"

    ```
    var cameraDolly = new TransformNode("dolly", scene);
    ```

2. Define an `ArcRotateCamera` and set up its basic properties. We're patching property values in from `gameData` structures to reduce the amount of code:

    ```
    for (var k in followCamSetup) {
        followCamera[k] = followCamSetup[k];
    }
    ```

3. Order of operations is important for this and the next step! First, parent `cameraDolly` to `truckMesh`.

4. Now, parent `followCamera` to `cameraDolly`:

    ```
    cameraDolly.parent = truckModel;
    followCamera.parent = cameraDolly;
    ```

The first thing that happens in the `initializeDrivingPhase` method is that the camera gets created and the Viewport is set up. A quick aside to explain a bit more about that.

If a **Camera** is a bridge between a **Scene** and the **Display**, then a **Viewport** is what defines the Display aspect of that bridge. The default Viewport is fixed at coordinates (0,0) and has a size of (1,1). In other words, the default Viewport's top-left corner is located at (0,0) and the bottom-right corner is located at (1,1); the entire screen is covered by it. This is greatly desired when a Scene has but a single camera, but there are many circumstances where it is useful to have a second camera positioned somewhere in the scene that renders to a smaller segment of the full screen – think of strategy games that provide a mini-map or racing games that have a rear-view mirror display.

In most cases, there are elements of the scene that should be rendered just in one camera, but not in another, which is finally where we make the connection with Layer Masks. By setting `layerMask` of all the involved cameras and meshes, we can efficiently show or hide geometry according to the mesh's role in the scene. Our driving screen currently has two separate layer masks: SCENE_MASK and GUI_MASK. Cleverly toggling a mesh's `layerMask` property can allow fine-grained control over camera rendering; if we want to display the mesh on one camera or the other, we can explicitly set its `layerMask` to SCENE_MASK or GUI_MASK (0x00000001 and 0x00000002, respectively). If we wish to display a mesh on *both* cameras, we can set and/or leave the default layer mask value in place (0xFFFFFFFF). Now that we know what's going on with the viewport, we can get back to the function code.

After setting up the viewport, the parenting steps listed previously are executed. The `MeshBuilder.`
`CreateRibbon` method is the next point of interest, where we pass the array or path arrays into
the options of the function and get back our path geometry, which then gets some property tweaks
and a grid material (for now) assigned:

```
var groundMat = new GridMaterial("roadMat", scene);
var ground = MeshBuilder.CreateRibbon("road", {
    pathArray: route.paths,
    sideOrientation: Mesh.DOUBLESIDE
}, scene);
ground.layerMask = SCENE_MASK;
ground.material = groundMat;
ground.visibility = 0.67;
ground.physicsImpostor = new PhysicsImpostor(ground,
    PhysicsImpostor.MeshImpostor,
    {
        mass: 0,
        restitution: 0.25
    }, scene);
```

With the ribbon created, material assigned, and a physics impostor similarly created and assigned to
the ground mesh, the restitution property makes anything hitting the wall rebound with a little less
momentum than before. That's new, but there's a bit of a twist (highlighted in the preceding code block)
with the type of impostor we're using here as well – `MeshImpostor`. Previously only available in
the CannonJS physics plugin, where it is limited to interacting only with spheres, `MeshImpostor` is
different from the other `PhysicsImpostor` types we've previously looked at (`Box` and `Sphere`).

Instead of using a rough approximation of the physics-enabled object's geometry, it uses that very
geometry itself to provide precise collision detection! The trade-off is that collision computation
becomes more expensive the more complex the mesh's geometry is structured. We should be OK for
our needs though, since we don't need our obstacles (that is, encounters) to interact with the path,
leaving just the truck with complex collision calculation needs. Just a few more tasks remain before
we will be done with our preparations and be ready to write the runtime logic!

After setting up the physics of `truckModel` – albeit using the equally applicable and much
simpler `BoxImpostor` – we spawn some sample obstacles along the path before setting up an
`OnIntersectionExitTrigger` that calls `killTruck` whenever the truck exits the `routePath`
ribbon mesh's confines. The `spawnObstacles` function will ultimately be discussed in the *Adding*
Encounters section, so skipping over a discussion of that leads us to the familiar-in-practice of setting
up `ground.actionManager` with the appropriate trigger (see the section on *Defining the*

EncounterZones in Chapter 7, Processing Route Data) – another place that is familiar enough to skip past. Now, we approach the final act of the `initializeDrivingPhase` function – (re)setting the truck to its starting position and state.

Using our sample route data, we could empirically determine what coordinates in the world space the truck should start at, its initial rotation, and other such values. We would iteratively refine our values through trial and error until the results were satisfactory, but would that satisfy our requirements? No.

> **Note**
>
> If you ever see a question asked in the preceding fashion, the answer is almost always "No." This is the second instance in this chapter of that kind of rhetorical writing. Can you spot the third?

That entire trial and error approach will not "satisfy our requirements," no thank you sir! We can make this extremely easy on ourselves by recalling that we already know exactly and precisely where the truck should start, where it should be pointing, and how fast it should be moving in the form of our pal `route.path3d`. It was mentioned in the earlier discussion on `Path3D`, it is a mathematical construct, and two of the more useful functions it provides, `getPointAt` and `getTangentAt`, are used to help us position the truck, but we didn't get much into the details of why they're useful.

Think about a path of some arbitrary length that consists of several points. Every point along that path has a set of vectors describing the position (naturally!), the **tangent** (a vector pointing in the direction of travel at that specific point along the curve), the **normal** (an arbitrarily chosen vector pointing perpendicularly to the tangent), and the **binormal** (a vector chosen to be perpendicular to the **normal**). These are all computed for us by the `Path3D` instance, making it easy to work with.

If we think of the point's position in the path's collection of points (that is, what index it occupies in the array) as being the ratio between the index and the total number of elements, then we can easily picture that ratio being a percentage, or a number between 0 and 1 (inclusive of both). **Interpolated functions** of the `Path3D` module all accept a number representing the percentage (between 0 and 1) along the path to operate against and include the related `getNormalAt`, `getBinormalAt`, and `getDistanceAt` functions.

> **Note**
>
> There are more interpolation functions to explore! See `https://doc.babylonjs.com/divingDeeper/mesh/path3D#interpolatio` for the full list.

This is useful because you don't need to know what the length of the path is or how many points are in it to obtain useful information. In the `resetTruck` function, we get the position and the tangent of the first point in the route – the beginning of the path – then set the truck's properties accordingly:

```
const curve = route.path3d.getPointAt(0);
const curveTan = route.path3d.getTangentAt(0);
```

```
truckModel.position.copyFrom(curve);
truckModel.rotationQuaternion =
  Quaternion.FromLookDirectionRH(curveTan, truckModel.up);
truckModel.physicsImpostor.setAngularVelocity(currAngVel);
truckModel.physicsImpostor.setLinearVelocity(currVelocity);
```

Since the physics engine sets and uses the `rotationQuaternion` property, we can't just use the vector provided by `getTangentAt(0)` – we need to convert it into a Quaternion using the `FromLookDirectionRH` method. This function takes two vectors for its arguments: the first, a vector representing the desired forward direction, and then another vector representing the orthogonal (for example, perpendicular along all axis), with the return value being a Quaternion representing the input vectors. After setting the truck's position and rotation, it's necessary to reset the truck's physical values for velocity since, from the physics engine's perspective, the effects of being moved and rotated would need to be considered. Therefore, the `reset` method is a deterministic function – the effect on the state of the scene is always the same whenever it is called. This makes it especially useful to use it both immediately post-initialization and any time that the player chooses to do so. We listen for that player input in this Playground's update method.

Running the Update Loop

Most of the code discussed up to this point has been code that directly relates to the context at hand. That's the great thing about Babylon.js and its tooling – many common tasks are possible to complete with just a few lines of code. The `update` method is a good example of that but it's also an example of one of the few places in the Playground where the code will need to be changed around completely to integrate it with the application, simply due to the more complex nature of the application versus the much more narrowly scoped Playground (see the next section, *Integrating with the Application*, for more). For that reason, we aren't going to look too hard at the specifics of the function and instead focus on the mechanics of how the truck is controlled by the logic in it.

The truck can be controlled in the three translational axes (forward/back, left/right, up/down) and one rotational axis (the yaw axis), which might seem to make for a total of eight separate pieces of logic to handle the motion. However, since pairs of actions (for example, left and right) are simply the negated values of each other, we only need to figure it out for four – a nice reduction in complexity. In each frame, the delta frame time variable is used to scale `truckAcceleration` and `truckTurnSpeedRadians` to the correct values; the `currVelocity` and `currAngVel` counter variables track the accumulated changes that are then applied to the physics model's linear and angular velocities at the end of the update process. This is like what we've done in the past, but some mathematical tools are being employed that we've not yet seen that are worth taking a closer look at.

Changing the forward or backward translational velocity is simple – just get the current forward vector for the truck mesh, scale it by `currAccel`, then add it to the `currVelocity` counter; the backward vector consists of the negated value of the forward vector:

```
if (keyMap['KeyW']) {
    currVelocity.addInPlace(currDir.scale(currAccel));
}
else if (keyMap['KeyS']) {
    currVelocity.addInPlace(currDir.scale(currAccel)
        .negateInPlace());
}
```

All of the various `Vector3` math methods come in various flavors that allow the developer to control whether or not the operation should allocate memory or reuse an existing object. In this case, we are using the `addInPlace` function to avoid creating a new vector object, whereas we create a new `Vector3` with the `currDir.scale(currAccel)` function call to avoid corrupting the truck mesh's forward vector – a value relied upon by the engine for proper rendering.

> **Important note**
>
> Knowing when and what to perform memory allocation and disposal with can be key to a smoothly rendered scene. See *Chapter 13*, *Converting the Application to a PWA*, for more information and guidance.

Back to our truck's control logic, the mathematical trick is in how we figure out what direction to apply the remaining translational and rotational forces. Translating to the truck's left or right is done by taking the cross product of the truck's forward vector and the truck's up vector – the result is a vector pointing in either the left or right direction (the same trick with `negateInPlace` can yield the opposite side from the same inputs):

```
let left = Vector3.Cross(currDir, truckModel.up);
currVelocity.addInPlace(left.scale(currAccel / 2));
```

Allowing players to side-strafe at the same speed as the other directions feels a bit too easy to lose control of the truck, so we cut the value in half to help players keep their speed under control. After integrating the accumulated changes to velocities and resetting the accumulation counters, the respective linear and angular physics properties are set along with an angular "damping" mechanism to help ease control:

```
linVel.addInPlace(currVelocity);
truckModel.physicsImpostor.setLinearVelocity(linVel);
angVel.addInPlace(currAngVel);
```

```
currVelocity.setAll(0);
currAngVel.setAll(0);
// dampen any tendencies to pitch, roll, or yaw from
    physics effects
angVel.scaleInPlace(0.987);
truckModel.physicsImpostor.setAngularVelocity(angVel);
```

That's the end of the Playground's update method, as well as the end of our examination of the driving phase prototype. After looking through what we want to accomplish overall with the Playground, we learned how to take the raw route data and turn it into a segmented tube encompassing the path. In an asynchronous loading method, we saw how a GLTF model can be imported and prepared for use with a Scene before we saw how the `initializeDrivingPhase` function sets up the camera dolly, physics, and obstacles along the path. With the `reset` method, we saw how to use the `Path3D` methods to properly position the truck, regardless of where it is and what state it is in. Not counting the GUI (which we'll cover in the next chapter), we've seen how each of our objectives for the prototype is accomplished. This is a great foundation for the next step in progressing the game along, which is the less fun but ultimately more rewarding aspect of integrating our playground into the rest of the game.

Integrating with the Application

By constructing the playground driving demo, we've uncovered the techniques and basic design approach to use for the application code. The structure of our code is such that we should be able to simply lift and shift key pieces of functionality straight into the application's code base, but only after we make modifications to prepare the way.

Playground logic aside, there are various hooks in `SpaceTruckerApplication` that need to be added or modified to get the driving phase to work properly, some of which include the ability to load into the driving game without going through Route Planning. Our basic input controls will need to be adapted to the input system of Space-Truckers, as well as the converse need to add new pieces of functionality to the input system. All of this starts with de-structuring and bringing in code from the Playground.

Splitting Up the Playground

`spaceTruckerDrivingScreen` is where the primary logic will reside for the driving phase, and similarly to how we tucked the Route Planning modules into the `/src/route-planning` subdirectory, we put the driving phase code and data into a `/src/driving` folder. Within that folder and, again, like the `route-planning` folder, is the `gameData.js` file, where we will place the equivalently named Playground object. A new addition to the `gameData` object from the Playground is the `environmentConfig` section; this data contains information such as the environment texture URL and other pieces of deployment-time-specific information.

Note

We will be using the Encounter system (see the *Adding Encounters* section, later in this chapter) to populate the path with obstacles so that the `obstacleCount` property is omitted from the application code.

Although it is less consistent with the code design for Route Planning, the `Driving` screen breaks out the environment creation code into its own module, `environment.js`. Exporting just the `initializeEnvironment` function, this module demonstrates how it isn't always necessary to create JavaScript classes to encapsulate and abstract logic – sometimes, a simple function will do the job just as well:

```
const initializeEnvironment = (screen) => {
    const { scene } = screen;
    var light = new HemisphericLight("light", new
      Vector3(0, 1, 0), scene);
    light.intensity = 1;
    var skyTexture = new CubeTexture(envTextureUrl, scene);
    skyTexture.coordinatesMode = Texture.SKYBOX_MODE;
    scene.reflectionTexture = skyTexture;
    var skyBox = scene.createDefaultSkybox(skyTexture,
      false, skyBoxSize);
    skyBox.layerMask = SCENE_MASK;
    screen.environment = { skyBox, light, skyTexture };
    return screen.environment;
};
export default initializeEnvironment;
```

None of the code in the preceding listing is particularly different from what we've already looked at in the Playground, except for the screen parameter representing the `SpaceTruckerDrivingScreen` instance being targeted by the function. To ensure that we can access (and later dispose of properly) the environment data, a composite data structure is returned to the caller containing `skyBox`, `hemisphericLight`, and `skyTexture`. This is similar to how the `initializeEnvironment` method of `environment.js`, `driving-gui.js` contains the `initializeGui` function. A minor detail for this is that, unlike `initializeEnvironment`, the `initializeGui` method is marked as `async`, but the details of what's going on in this module will have to **await** the next chapter.

Note

Is there any limit to how bad a pun can get before intervention becomes necessary?

Our last component of the driving phase is the humble truck. The driving phase analog of the Route Planning's `cargoUnit`, our `Truck` class is derived from `BaseGameObject`, where it inherits the `update`, `dispose`, and various other properties of its base. We're able to use most of the code from the Playground's `loadAssets` method verbatim, and we only need to grab the non-input handling code from the Playground's `update` method to use it with the truck (the screen will host the input actions and processing). Now that we've defined the logic and behavior for the screen, let's look at how that logic is applied to the application.

Transitioning to the Driving Screen

During regular gameplay, the Driving phase is preceded immediately by the Route Planning phase. When the player manages to get the cargo unit to its destination, they are asked to confirm the route or retry. On the choice to confirm, the screen raises `routeAcceptedObservable` to notify interested parties of the event, the main subscriber to which is the `initialize` method of `SpaceTruckerApplication`:

```
this._routePlanningScene.routeAcceptedObservable.add(()
  => {
    const routeData = this._routePlanningScene.routePath;
    this.goToDrivingState(routeData);
});
```

For the other Screens (Main Menu, Splash Screen, and Route Planning), we've taken the approach of creating and loading up the screens as part of the `SpaceTruckerApplication.initialize` method. This obviates delay when transitioning between the Screens mentioned previously, but this approach won't work with the Driving screen.

The Driving screen, as you might recall from earlier discussions in this chapter, needs to have `routeData` supplied to it at construction time. As we are yet unable to determine a player's route before they've created it, so we must defer construction of the Screen until that time. We should also keep in mind that though a Screen might not be taking up render time, it will certainly consume memory – it would be prudent of us to dispose of the Route Planning screen and free up its resources as we transition to our new game state. This is the job of the `goToDrivingPhase` function:

```
goToDrivingState(routeData) {
    this._engine.displayLoadingUI();
    routeData = routeData ??
      this._routePlanningScene.routePath;
    this._currentScene?.actionProcessor?.detachControl();
    this._engine.loadingUIText = "Loading Driving
      Screen...";
```

```
this._drivingScene = new SpaceTruckerDrivingScreen
    (this._engine, routeData, this.inputManager);
this._currentScene = this._drivingScene;
this._routePlanningScene.dispose();
this._routePlanningScene = null;
this.moveNextAppState(AppStates.DRIVING);
this._currentScene.actionProcessor.attachControl();
}
```

Many of the code is standard to the family of methods we've written to handle state transitions, such as the process of detaching control from _currentScene and attaching it to the new _drivingScene and moveNextAppState, with the main difference being in the disposal of _routePlanningScene.

The disposal logic for a Screen is fairly simple. Most resources associated directly with the Scene will be disposed of along with the Scene, but it's also necessary to ensure that SoundManager is disposed of along with EncounterManager:

```
dispose() {
    this.soundManager.dispose();
    this.onStateChangeObservable.clear();
    this.routeAcceptedObservable.clear();
    this.encounterManager.dispose();
    this.scene.dispose();
}
```

The Observable.clear() method is useful when disposing of an object that you have control over because it precludes any need to know or have any references to the original subscription created via Observable.add. The final piece of the Driving phase transition is a shortcut to having the application directly load the Driving phase when launched, using the sample route data instead of a player's simulated route. This is done by including the testDrive Query String value in the browser's URL; when it is present and the player skips the Splash Screen, it will use the sample JSON route data:

```
const queryString = window.location.search;
if (queryString.includes("testDrive")) {
    this.goToDrivingState(sampleRoute);
}
```

This is a nice trick enabled by the fundamentally web-based nature of Babylon.js – we can easily use familiar web development tricks and tools to ease testing! Being able to quickly jump to a populated, "known good" Driving phase lets us quickly add and test various pieces of code for the application, which leads us to the major area of difference between the Playground and our application – how the `Truck` component is updated with input.

Truck Update and Input Controls

Right away, there's one obvious difference that needs to be addressed, and that's the aspect of handling user input. Our Playground used a very simple input scheme, which will need to be refactored to use `SpaceTruckerInputProcessor` (see *Chapter 5, Adding a Cut Scene and Handling Input*). With the delegation of the actual per-frame update logic to the `Truck` component (see the *Splitting Up the Playground* section), the `update` method of `SpaceTruckerDrivingScreen` becomes very simple:

```
update(deltaTime) {
        const dT = deltaTime ??
            (this.scene.getEngine().getDeltaTime() / 1000);
        this.actionProcessor?.update();
        if (this.isLoaded) {
            this.truck.update(dT);
        }
    }
```

The `isLoaded` flag is used to help prevent extraneous updates from being processing during/while the async initialization logic is executing. Input must be updated before calling the Truck's update method, to ensure that the latest values have been read and set. Looking at the control scheme for the Drive phase, it's also obvious that there are differences between it and the controls for the Route Planning phase. The application needs a way to specify new or modified control map schemes that can apply just to the currently active Screen.

Patching the input map

The original `inputActionMap` defined the set of actions relevant to the Route Planning screen and the Main Menu, but there are additional actions that we need to support that aren't present in the mapping file. We also need to redefine specific inputs that are used to control the camera during Route Planning. Consolidating those changes, we have a "patch" of sorts that we can apply to `inputActionMap`:

```
const inputMapPatches = {
    w: "MOVE_IN", W: "MOVE_IN",
```

```
    s: "MOVE_OUT", S: "MOVE_OUT",
    ArrowUp: 'MOVE_UP',
    ArrowDown: 'MOVE_DOWN',
    ArrowLeft: 'ROTATE_LEFT',
    ArrowRight: 'ROTATE_RIGHT'
};
SpaceTruckerInputManager.patchControlMap(inputMapPatches);
```

The patchControlMap function is a static method of the SpaceTruckerInputManager class. It has a corresponding unPatchControlMap function that reverts a given input map patch to the previous values:

```
static patchControlMap(newMaps) {
    tempControlsMap = Object.assign({}, controlsMap);
    Object.assign(controlsMap, newMaps);
}
static unPatchControlMap() {
    controlsMap = tempControlsMap;
    tempControlsMap = {};
}
```

The two different uses of Object.assign are interesting to note. The first uses a new, empty object ({ }) to create a copy or clone of the original controlsMap, while the second copies the properties from newMaps into the existing controlsMap. This has the effect of overwriting any pre-existing properties, as well as creating new properties from the input patch. While the unpatching can be done manually, by adding it to the SpaceTruckerInputManager.dispose() function, it is performed automatically as part of the dispose function.

If it seems like we're starting to move a lot faster now than we were earlier in this chapter, which is because it's true – we've gotten the most complex part of the Driving Screen out of the way with our Playground demo. The Playground code is factored into different functions that can be split off and made into their own source files (with some modifications), and then consumed and orchestrated by SpaceTruckerDrivingScreen. We looked at the state machine changes to SpaceTruckerApplication that were needed to load sample route data by appending a query string to the browser URL before turning our attention to updating the control scheme and adding the ability for a screen to patch the input control map. Now that we've seen how it has been integrated with the application, it's time to look at how encounters factor into the Driving phase gameplay.

Adding Encounters

The first thing needed to get encounters from Route Planning into the driving phase is to capture them into the route in the first place. Making a slight modification to the `SpaceTruckerEncounterManager.onEncounter` function gets the job done:

```
const cargoData = this.cargo.lastFlightPoint;
cargoData.encounter = encounter;
```

The addition to the code (highlighted) adds the encounter instance to the last telemetry data point in the route, making it available to us later when we process the route. In `calculateRouteParameters`, we are making sure to include the encounter data in the resulting `routePath` structure, along with the position, velocity, and gravitational acceleration.

Now that the encounters have been located and processed, we can spawn the encounters themselves. For the time being, we are creating a temporary spherical mesh in the constructor to serve as a template for when we spawn the encounters:

```
// temporary until the encounter spawner is implemented
this.tempObstacleMesh = CreateSphere("tempObstacle",
   this.scene);
this.tempObstacleMesh.visibility = 1;
this.tempObstacleMesh.layerMask = 0;
```

It may seem contradictory to set `tempObstacleMesh.visibility` to 1 (fully visible) along with `layerMask = 0` (not rendered at all), but it makes sense when we look at the `spawnObstacle(seed)` function body and how it uses `tempObstacle` mesh as a template from which to create individual **Instances** of the mesh:

```
let point = pathPoints[seed];
let {encounter, position, gravity, velocity} = point;
let encounterMesh = tempObstacleMesh.createInstance
   (encounter.id + '-' + seed);
```

In *Chapter 6, Implementing the Game Mechanics*, we saw a few different ways of efficiently replicating a single mesh across a scene, hundreds or even thousands of times. In that case, we used Thin Instances to procedurally generate and render the asteroid belt because the balance of features and friction met our needs. In this case, we are creating more CPU-bound Instance meshes because we want to enable physics, animate properties such as scale and position, and have more control over the characteristics of the resultant mesh. At the same time, because Instances are all drawn during the same draw call on the GPU (and therefore share render characteristics), changing the visibility property would have the same effect across all instances. `layerMask` is not shared between Instances, though, hence why we use it to hide the mesh used for Instancing.

We are retaining some vestiges of the Playground, even though those elements don't need to remain in the code base in the long term; an example of this is `tempObstacleMesh`. Though it will be very important for us to switch this out for a more appropriate set of meshes that match the encounters, it is not a feature that is needed to make immediate progress. How do we ensure that we do not neglect to return to this area in the future? Since we're using GitHub, we can create an Issue to track it.

> **Note**
>
> See `https://github.com/jelster/space-truckers/issues/92` to read about the history of the issue described previously.

Unlike the needs captured in the Issue, being able to place encounters as obstacles in the driving route is a critical-path piece of functionality because, without it, we wouldn't be able to properly plot those obstacles into the player's radar UI display. Now that we do have them, we have enough context to look at how encounters are combined with the GUI system to make the mini-map.

Making the Mini-Map

While the bulk of the next chapter will focus on the Babylon.js GUI, we'll dip our feet into the waters of the topic of **User Interfaces** (**UIs**) as we take a moment to discuss coordinate systems and polar coordinates. First, though, let's look at how we get to the point where talk of coordinate systems becomes necessary by examining the `initializeGui` method of our Playground.

> **Note**
>
> In the application, this logic is contained in the `driving-gui.js` module in `/src/driving/`. Aside from moving the code to load the Node Material into it, the code is identical to the Playground.

At the beginning of this chapter, we talked about Viewports in the *Initializing the Driving Phase Scene* section, and we described two main characteristics – the viewport's size and position. For the main Scene camera, the Viewport stretches the full size of the screen, but for our GUI system, the Viewport is defined differently.

The GUI Camera

The `initializeGui` function starts its business by immediately defining the camera and Viewport, but it also sets the camera up in Orthographic mode. This is a different way of rendering the 3D scene onto a 2D screen that can be essentially summarized as being a camera mode that renders objects without distance or perspective corrections:

```
let guiCamera = new UniversalCamera("guiCam", new
  Vector3(0, 50, 0), scene);
```

```
guiCamera.layerMask = GUI_MASK;
guiCamera.viewport = new Viewport(0, 0, 1 - 0.6,
  1 - 0.6);
guiCamera.mode = UniversalCamera.ORTHOGRAPHIC_CAMERA;
guiCamera.orthoTop = guiViewportSize / 2;
guiCamera.orthoRight = guiViewportSize / 2;
guiCamera.orthoLeft = -guiViewportSize / 2;
guiCamera.orthoBottom = -guiViewportSize / 2;
scene.activeCameras.push(guiCamera);
```

In our code, `guiViewportSize` corresponds to the number of units that the camera should cover in its field of view. That value is taken and used to compute the respective top, right, left, and bottom coordinates for the camera. Lastly, `guiCamera` is pushed onto the Scene's `activeCameras` array to begin rendering through the camera. Once the camera and Viewport have been set up, the camera needs to have something to render, and that is the job of `radarMesh`.

As a simple Plane, `radarMesh` gets its magic from the textures assigned to its `StandardMaterial`. The first texture is one we mentioned earlier, and that's the radar procedural texture created from `NodeMaterial` that we loaded up (see *Chapter 11*, *Scratching the Surface of Shaders*, for more on `NodeMaterial` and the NME), and the second is a variant of our old friend `AdvancedDynamicTexture`:

```
let radarMesh = MeshBuilder.CreatePlane("radarMesh",
  { width: guiViewportSize, height: guiViewportSize },
  scene);
radarMesh.layerMask = GUI_MASK;
radarMesh.rotation.x = Math.PI / 2;
//...
let radarGui =
  AdvancedDynamicTexture.CreateForMeshTexture(radarMesh,
  radarTextureResolution, radarTextureResolution, false);
```

`CreateFullScreenUI` is what we've used in the past when defining our GUI containers, and `CreateForMeshTexture` is quite similar. Instead of creating a texture the height and width of the screen, `CreateForMeshTexture` does the same for a specific mesh. The GUI texture can then be assigned to the mesh's material as one of its textures:

```
radarMesh.material = radarMaterial;
radarMaterial.diffuseTexture = radarGui;
```

After the GUI system has been set up and assigned to the radar mesh, the encounters are looped over to create individual GUI "blips" to represent each:

```
encounters.forEach((o, i) => {
    let blip = new Rectangle("radar-obstacle-" + i);
    o.uiBlip = blip;
    blip.width = "3%";
    blip.height = "3%";
    blip.background = "white";
    blip.color = "white";
    blip.cornerRadius = "1000";
    radarGui.addControl(blip);
});
var gl = new GlowLayer("gl", scene, { blurKernelSize: 4,
  camera: guiCamera });
```

Developers familiar with CSS may recall using the trick of setting a high corner radius on a square to turn it into a circle, but otherwise, there isn't anything we haven't seen before in this code. The last thing to happen in the `initializeGui` function is the creation of a GUI-specific Glow Layer to help illuminate the radar and punch up its look. Defining the GUI elements involved putting a few new tools into our tool belt, and what better way to validate those tools than to put them to use in the runtime behavior of the radar?

Blip Plotting in Polar Coordinates

Normally, when we talk about the position of a particular object such as an encounter, we refer to it in terms of it representing a position in the World Space, the top-level 3D coordinate space for a rendered Scene. Sometimes, usually in the context of a model and its submeshes or bones, the position referred to is given relative to the parent mesh or transform node's origin, or center. This is called a Local Space position and relates to a World Position via the World Matrix. In this chapter, we saw an example of working with these elements when we loaded the semi-truck model and removed the parent root node (see the *Loading Assets Asynchronously* section earlier in this chapter). The following diagram depicts some different ways of representing coordinates:

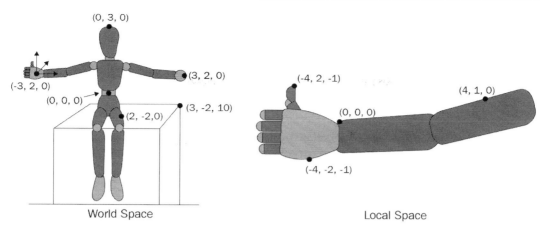

Figure 8.7 – Local and World Space coordinate systems are Cartesian coordinate systems that depict locations as a combination of vector elements

Sometimes, it can be advantageous to represent coordinates in a different form. A Polar Coordinate system is one of those alternate ways of representing the position of something concerning another.

In polar coordinates, the origin of the plot represents the unit's location in space with all other objects plotted around the center of that circle. Those objects' coordinates can be captured into just two variables: **angle** (**theta**, or **θ**) and **distance** (**r**, or radius).

> **Important note**
>
> Since the radar is in two dimensions but the location is in three, we use the *X*- and *Z*-axes while the *Y*-axis is discarded. Information about the object's position along that axis is preserved as part of the Vector distance between the origin and the object being plotted.

The math to accomplish this is deceptively easy once we know the operations needed. To determine the vector distance, we could subtract the position of the encounter obstacle from the truck and obtain it via the `Vector3.length()` function, but the more direct path is to use the static `Vector3.Distance()` function instead. The value for `theta` has multiple paths to the same end:

```
let r = Vector3.Distance(obstacle.absolutePosition,
    absolutePosition);
let theta = Vector3.GetAngleBetweenVectorsOnPlane
    (absolutePosition, up, obstacle.absolutePosition);
```

`Vector3.GetAngleBetweenVectorsOnPlane` is perfect for our use because it will automatically take differences in altitude between the truck and the obstacle into account by projecting each onto the same plane defined by the truck's up vector. The next part is a bit tricky, though, because our coordinate system places `(0, 0)` at the center, whereas the GUI system placement puts the origin at the top-left bounds:

```
let posLeft = Math.cos(theta) * r;
let posTop = -1 * Math.sin(theta) * r;
uiBlip.left = posLeft * 4.96 - (r * 0.5);
uiBlip.top = posTop * 4.96 - (r * 0.5);
```

When setting the left and top properties of `uiBlip`, the points are scaled to the mesh's size before correcting for origin locations. The result, as shown in the following screenshot, is circular blips that show their position relative to the player in a cool-looking way:

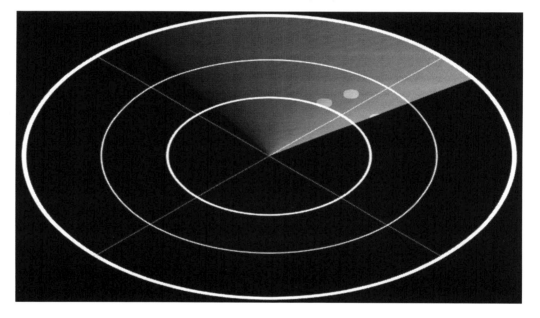

Figure 8.8 – The radar GUI element plots the positions of encounters in terms of
their relative distance and angle from the player (at the center of the circle)

Though this section may have been short, it has certainly been full of sweet knowledge and results. There remain several mysteries to uncover regarding the radar mesh texture and its construction, but those will have to await a later chapter of our journey. We come out of this section knowing how to plot polar coordinates as well as how to set up a multi-camera scene with layer masks and Viewports. It's a nice way to wrap up our work in this area and prepares us for what comes next!

Summary

Let's take a step back and look at how far we've come during this chapter. When we started it, all we had was some route data and a vague idea of what we wanted to happen. Having completed it, we now have a game that can be played from end to end from Route Planning to Driving!

Along the way, we've leveraged the Playground to help us define a prototype demo of the driving phase gameplay. It was in that Playground that we learned how to take the raw route data and turn it into a configurable Ribbon mesh with as many or few segments as we'd like. The semi-truck GLB asset was introduced as we learned how to load and prepare assets like this for use in our Scene. Once we learned how to set up the scene, we defined physics and gave our truck the ability to bounce off the route's walls with `MeshImpostor`, as well as a way to automatically "kill" the truck if it wanders out of bounds. All that work set us up for smooth integration with the application.

Beginning with a divide-and-conquer approach, we split the code from the Playground up into its different functional areas of responsibility. Then, we hooked up the plumbing to transition from either the splash screen (with the `?testDrive` URL Query string) or the `onCargoAccepted` event of the Route Planning Screen. Having the ability to quickly jump into the driving phase using sample route data made it easy to iterate and test through the rest of the integration with the runtime and input systems.

Our input handling needs for the Driving Phase are different from those of the Planning Phase, so to support that, we added the ability to path the base input action map with an updated set of input-to-action mappings. To keep our space-truck from getting lonely along its route, we turned our attention to hooking up encounters with the Driving screen via `routeData`.

Once we'd added encounter data to the overall `routeData`, it was straightforward to use a (for now) sphere mesh as a source for Instances of an Encounter. We'll be changing this around later, but at this time, we don't want to arrest any of the hard-earned momenta gained to take on any side-quests. Similarly, we learned how to set up our alternate GUI camera along with the polar coordinates – plotting encounters onto our radar procedural texture/GUI mesh. Put all together, we are in a great place to begin the next chapter in our journey, where we will cover the GUI.

Up until now, we've kept our GUI to a minimum. Even so, what amounts to basic boilerplate code while assigning values to properties can be quite astonishing. Nobody wants to have to write all that code and nobody wants to have to maintain it. In the next chapter, we'll learn how we solve both of those problems while covering some other problems we didn't even know existed when we go in-depth into the brand-new **Babylon.js GUI Editor**.

Until then, if you want to spend some more time exploring the ideas and concepts from this chapter, check out the *Extended Topics* section next for ideas and projects. As always, Space-Truckers: The Discussion Boards at `https://github.com/jelster/space-truckers/discussions` is the place to ask questions and exchange ideas with fellow Space-Truckers, while the Babylon.js forums are where to engage with the greater Babylon.js community. See a problem with the code or have an idea you'd like to see implemented? Feel free to create an Issue in the Space-Truckers repository!

Extended Topics

The following are some extended topics for you to try out:

- Add an "encounter warning" UI indication whenever the truck is within a set distance of an encounter

- When the ship hits the side of the wall, play an appropriate sound effect. The volume of the played effect should scale with the energy of the impact. Bonus points for spatially locating the sound at the location of the collision.

- An Encounter Table implies something static. Make encounters more dynamic by loading the list of potential encounters from a remote index repository hosted on GitHub. Community members can contribute new encounters by submitting a Pull Request containing the new encounter's definition. Once accepted and merged, the encounter becomes available to be used in a game session.

- As a prerequisite for the preceding bullet, adding the ability for each encounter to use a different mesh/material combination is a necessity. Read the mesh URL from the encounter data but be careful that you're not creating new meshes/materials for every instance of an encounter!

- Another Encounter feature could be the ability for each encounter type to define and control its behavior. An easy and cool way to do this is outlined in the very next chapter in the *Advanced Coroutine Usage* section.

9

Calculating and Displaying Scoring Results

Whether a game is implemented as a piece of software or a cut-out piece of cardboard, almost all games, regardless of origin or format, feature intrinsic ways to give players feedback on their performance throughout a game session. Whether it reflects the number of goals scored or the player's ability to keep a steel ball from dropping between bumpers, the scoring process is where a game connects to its players at a most visceral level.

In this chapter, we'll be introducing two new powerful tools for your game development toolbox, both completely new to version 5 of Babylon.js: the **GUI Editor** (**GUIE**) and **coroutines**. The GUIE is a solution to a problem that we've already seen previously when implementing our GUI. Think back (or just refer to the code) to the Planning Screen GUI implemented in `src/route-planning/route-plan-gui.js` and recall that there is a large amount of boilerplate, typo-prone, and ultimately tedious code that needs to be written just to get a bare-bones basic GUI displayed. Much of the code involved is of the *make this object that color, and place it here* variety, making it more difficult to visualize how components and elements will look at runtime. The GUIE allows a developer or designer to separate the presentation from the behavioral logic of the application – a concept very familiar to most developers! In addition to the GUIE, we're going to introduce another incredibly powerful tool – the coroutine.

A coroutine behaves and is constructed in a fashion that will be very familiar to those who have read the *Space-Truckers – The State Machine* section of *Chapter 4, Creating the Application*, but instead of having the specific purpose of managing our application state, a coroutine is built from an arbitrarily defined function generator (see *Chapter 4, Creating the Application*, for a refresher on `function*` generators in JavaScript) and attached to a `BabylonJS.Observable`. Most of the time, this Observable will be the Scene's `onBeforeRenderObservable`, meaning that the coroutine executes before every frame, but any Observable can run a coroutine. The behavior of the `yield` keyword in conjunction with some other elements that we'll look at shortly makes coroutines a perfect tool to use when a game's logic needs to span multiple rendered frames, a quality we're going to be using to our advantage to display the scoring results.

As part of and in addition to our examinations of the GUIE and coroutines, we'll build out a reusable dialog system that will serve as the base for our Scoring Dialog and Results screen before putting score tracking logic into the rest of the game. Though this might seem like a backward approach, having the ability to display scores first will help us discover what needs to be tracked and calculated by the rest of the application. Is there much still that could and should be done? Of course! There will always be more to do, but an important skill in software development is knowing which things *must* be done versus which things only *need* to be done.

In this chapter, we will cover the following topics:

- Introducing the Babylon.js GUI Editor
- Building a Reusable Dialog Box Component
- Calculating Scores
- Creating the Scoring Dialog Using Coroutines

Technical Requirements

There aren't any new or additional requirements from the software or hardware side of things that are needed for this chapter, but there are some topics in the Babylon.js documentation or elsewhere that might be handy as we explore some of these areas:

- The Babylon.js 2D GUI system at `https://doc.babylonjs.com/divingDeeper/gui`
- Coroutines (Babylon.js) at `https://doc.babylonjs.com/divingDeeper/events/coroutines`
- GUI Editor user's guide/manual at `https://doc.babylonjs.com/toolsAndResources/tools/guiEditor`

Introducing the Babylon.js GUI Editor

Boilerplate code is a term given to code that has the characteristics of being simple, standardized, and frequently repeated. As a software developer, it's generally best not to write that type of code yourself for some very good reasons. First, the nature of boilerplate code is that it is repetitive, making it prone to syntax or other superficial logical defects (that is, typos, fat-fingers, and more). Second, it's tough to maintain, since when changes need to be introduced, those changes are generally needed throughout the expanse of the boilerplate. Finally (at least for our purposes), it's really, really, *really* boring to read and write code of this nature.

To solve these (and other related) problems, the Babylon.js team created the GUIE. As just one of a huge number of new tools and features introduced with v5.0 of Babylon.js the GUIE fills an important niche in the Babylon.js ecosystem. Like its brethren, the Animation Curve Editor, the Node Material Editor, and the Playground, the GUIE and its associated snippet server are hosted online at `https://gui.babylonjs.com` and possess similar dual capabilities to work with unique IDs and revisions for persistence or directly with JSON files.

> **Important note**
>
> There are two basic kinds of GUIs that Babylon.js supports: 2D and 3D. The 2D GUI renders to a utility layer using an Advanced Dynamic Texture (see *The Advanced Dynamic Texture* section), whereas the 3D GUI system renders meshes on a utility layer. The content in this chapter and through much of this book focuses mainly on the 2D GUI. However, the 2D and 3D systems have very similar APIs. See `https://doc.babylonjs.com/divingDeeper/gui/gui3D` for more on the 3D GUI system.

Before we start looking at the GUIE's interface and capabilities, it will be useful if we start with either a refresher or a primer on how the Babylon.js GUI components operate at the level of the **Advanced Dynamic Texture (ADT)**.

The Advanced Dynamic Texture

Throughout this book, we've been making use of ADTs and the 2D GUI system, but to this point, we haven't tried to peek inside an ADT and see what it does. To do so, let's peel off the *Advanced* part of the term and focus first on the more basic **Dynamic Texture (DT)**.

A DT is a design-time integration component that exposes the HTML5 Canvas drawing API on one end of it; on the other, on the Babylon.js side, it exposes a `BABYLON.DynamicTexture`. Because it derives from a regular `BABYLON.Texture`, it is typically rendered by assigning the DT to an appropriate Texture slot in a Material. The Playground at `https://playground.babylonjs.com/#5ZCGRM#2` demonstrates the basics of how this works for drawing simple text, but any Canvas API is accessible via the DT's `getContext` function.

> **Note**
>
> See `https://developer.mozilla.org/en-US/docs/Web/API/Canvas_API` to learn more about the Canvas API and its different functions and capabilities, and `https://doc.babylonjs.com/divingDeeper/materials/using/dynamicTexture` to learn more about the BablyonJS DT.

Accessing the Canvas APIs in this way allows for a huge amount of flexibility for developers wishing to render strings or other UI elements but at the cost of requiring those same developers to have to manage a large amount of what is essentially boilerplate code. Sound familiar? The BABYLON.GUI system is a higher layer of abstraction over the Canvas APIs on one end of the integration, and like its antecedent **Dynamic Texture**, the **Advanced Dynamic Texture** comprises the other.

Put one way, an ADT is a **procedural texture** generated and managed by the BABYLON.GUI APIs. That's it. If it feels like this is somewhat of a letdown considering how much build-up there's been to this definition, then you're in luck because the details are far more involved than a simple procedural texture. We can start by picturing how an ADT fits into the overall scene and rendering process:

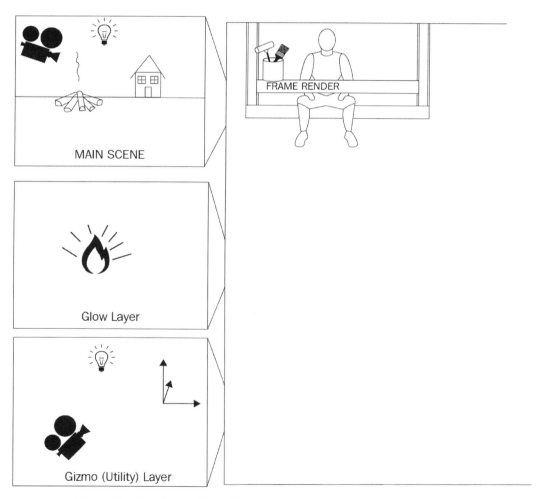

Figure 9.1 – The Canvas API and Babylon.js render layers that host a multitude of different features, such as the Inspector, Glow Layers, Gizmos, and more

If we follow the analogy of an HTML Canvas being like a cloth canvas used for painting, a layer is like a distinct coat of paint on the canvas; multiple layers overlap and blend to create the whole piece. As with a real-world canvas, the order in which pixels (or swatches of paint) are laid down is important to the final appearance – whichever color is placed last on the canvas is generally going to be the dominant color for that pixel.

The ADT is rendered as one of those layers when created using `AdvancedDynamicTexture.CreateFullScreenUI`, with the `isForeground` property of the ADT determining whether its layer is rendered in front of all other layers. Crucially, this also means that the ADT can be affected by the same sorts of factors that affect other layers (for example, Layer Masks and Post-Processes; see *Chapter 8, Building the Driving Game*, the *Loading Assets Asynchronously* section for more). When a full-screen UI isn't the right tool for the job, `AdvancedDynamicTexture` can be used identically to any texture by creating it using the `AdvancedDynamicTexture.CreateMeshTexture` function. This is what we did in *Chapter 8, Building the Driving Game*, in the *Making the Minimap* section, so it's a good sign that we're ready to progress up the ladder to the point where we can start using better tools to work with `AdvancedDynamicTexture` regardless of its type. In a similar vein, the GUIE will save us enormous amounts of time and effort, so let's take a brief tour and get cranking!

UI Design with the GUIE

As always, the latest documentation on the Babylon.js GUIE can be found at `https://doc.babylonjs.com/toolsAndResources/tools/guiEditor`, but some basic principles are still worth going over. The top-most horizontal menu, featuring the *hamburger* icon, has controls for managing the zoom level, copying and pasting controls, and more.

Clicking on empty space in the navigation panel displays the properties for the ADT. These are used to render the layout canvas in addition to buttons for loading and saving the GUI in various formats. The following screenshot contains, from right to left, the different areas of the GUI editor – the navigation tree, layout canvas, and property panes, respectively:

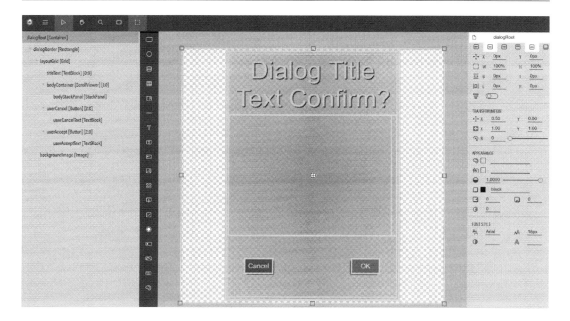

Figure 9.2 – The GUIE's three primary workspace areas, from left to right: navigation panel, layout canvas, and property pane. The layout shows the currently selected layoutGrid container element. Source: `https://gui.babylonjs.com/#923BBT#37`

The control tree can be seen on the left-hand navigation pane, separated from the layout canvas by the vertical list of control icons available to insert. Probably one of the more important sets of these controls is going to be the various types of containers.

From **StackPanels** to **Grids** with a sprinkling of **ScrollViewers** and **Rectangles** to round things out, the container elements behave exactly as you may expect them to if you are accustomed to the concepts. The GUI shown in *Figure 9.2* is a simple dialog box design, with content broken out into the three separate rows of the layoutGrid Grid Control. That control, in turn, is contained within the Rectangle dialogBorder, which is contained within the dialogRoot Container for the entire UI.

If you're not familiar with containers and their behavior, a review of the BJS Docs section on containers might be worth a quick (and informative!) read at `https://doc.babylonjs.com/divingDeeper/gui/gui#containers`. Resizing and laying out visual elements can be done by dragging around handles in the visual layout pane or by directly setting properties to specific values – use the former to get an approximation and the latter to "dial in" to pixel-perfect precision!

> **Note**
>
> The current list of supported controls and links to their associated documentation sections can be found at `https://doc.babylonjs.com/toolsAndResources/tools/guiEditor#supported-controls`.

Row indices start at zero, so the middle row is row number one and contains the primary content of the dialog. The following diagram illustrates how the layoutGrid's three rows allocate 25%, 50%, and 25% of the available height between them, respectively:

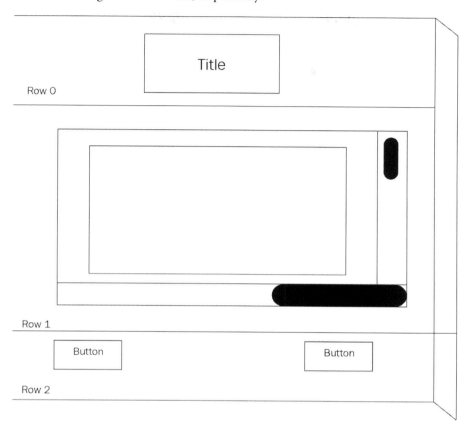

Figure 9.3 – A simplified view of the layoutGrid and its child controls. The top and bottom rows each get 25% of the available height, while the middle row is allocated the remaining 50% of the available height at render time

Let's go through the rows in turn. The first row contains the `titleText` control; as its name suggests, it is exactly what it seems like it is – a container for displaying the dialog's title heading. The second, middle row contains the primary display content and therefore needs the most room for its scroll viewer (to allow arbitrarily long or wide child content – a useful quality to note for later…) and its own **stackPanel** content control. Last but not least is the footer row (that is, row two). This row contains the two visual interactive elements of the dialog: the `userCancel` and `userAccept` buttons. These will be hooked up to click logic in the next section and will be spaced using relative (percentage) positioning to ensure the buttons stick to their respective sides.

> **Note**
>
> HTML/CSS folks are probably angrily wondering why we're not using columns and span cells, or a justified alignment with a horizontal StackPanel. Those would indeed be wonderful approaches – if cell spanning or full justification alignment were available, but as they are not (at the time of writing), alternative approaches must be sought!

The final stop on our GUIE tour is less of a feature of the editor and more of a very strongly recommended workflow practice of naming the controls in the tree:

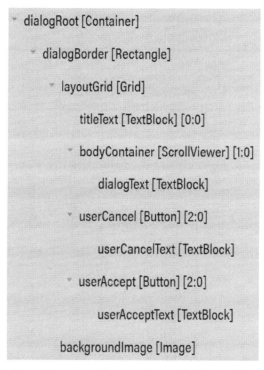

Figure 9.4 – Control tree structure with named controls. Having clear, indicative names is crucial to effectively integrating the GUIE with applications. The child elements of the layoutGrid Grid container display their respective [row:column] indices in the tree

If you have read a certain type of genre fantasy, then you will know that having the name of something gives one power over the thing being named, and our GUI control tree is no different! Our integration pattern for combining the GUI definition with JavaScript logic will hinge on using the power of a control's name to summon it forth when needed, but instead of relying on magic spells and summoning circles, we'll see how to use `Control.findByName` as part of the tidy integration options made possible by features in both the Babylon.js GUI and its core framework!

Integration with the GUIE

It's time to move past the GUIE and see how we can make use of its output in a simple Playground setting. The Playground at `https://playground.babylonjs.com/#WIVN8Z#6` is what we'll be using as the starting point for this section; we'll build it out and finish it up in the next section; that is, *Building a Reusable Dialog Box Component*. For now, let's run the Playground and click or tap anywhere in the display area to summon a Dialog Box. Clicking one of the buttons will either dismiss or spawn a new dialog box, depending on which is clicked.

Now, let's focus on the `createScene` function. It's very short – under 40 lines of code, with most of the code devoted to subscribing to various Observables of the `DialogBox` component and the scene's `onPointerObservable`. Defining the initial dialog `opts` object and creating the `DialogBox` instance rounds out the scene creation logic of our Playground, leaving us free to focus our attention on how to convert the `const DIALOG_GUI_SNIPPET = "923BBT#32"` line into an interactive component, bringing us one step closer to seeing how `DialogBox` works.

Right above the `DialogBox` class definition – line 60 – is where the CONTROL_NAMES constant is defined:

```
const CONTROL_NAMES = Object.freeze({
    cancel: 'userCancel',
    accept: 'userAccept',
    titleText: 'titleText',
    bodyText: 'dialogText',
    acceptText: 'userAcceptText',
    cancelText: 'userCancelText',
    dialog: 'dialogBorder',
    bodyScrollViewer: 'bodyContainer',
    bodyStackPanel: 'bodyStackPanel',
});
```

Recall when we mentioned the importance of names. This is where that discussion becomes important! It also becomes the only place in our code that needs to know anything specific about how our GUI is structured, allowing us to modify our GUI to a certain extent without the need to make corresponding changes to our application code.

OK – now, we have a map of control names that we can use to access controls via code, but we haven't loaded up anything for our code to access yet. We'll need to create an instance of an AdvancedDynamicTexture – fullscreen mode is fine – and we also want to make sure that the text and lines are crisp and sharp at whatever size it ends up being rendered:

```
this.advancedTexture = AdvancedDynamicTexture
    .CreateFullscreenUI("dialog", false, scene,
        Texture.NEAREST_NEAREST, true);
```

Using NEAREST_NEAREST as the sampling method when scaling the texture gives the best results for text while the true flag for the last parameter enables adaptive scaling for a nice look whatever the scale. Now that we have something to host the GUI, it's time to go ahead and load said GUI into the ADT.

Because we want to use DIALOG_GUI_SNIPPET as the source to load our GUI from, we'll need to use the parseFromSnippetAsync method from an instance of AdvancedDynamicTexture. Since the function is asynchronous, this means we can await its completion from an appropriately marked async function:

```
this.scene.executeWhenReady(async () => {
    await this.advancedTexture
            .parseFromSnippetAsync(DIALOG_GUI_SNIPPET,
                false);
    this.dialogContainer.isVisible = false;
```

Once advancedTexture has completed loading the GUI definition from the snippet server (and, in the preceding case, opting out of rescaling the texture), it can be accessed from advancedTexture.getControlByName(). To avoid repetition in our code, we can define property accessors in a class or object to wrap the logic for getting or setting these control values:

```
get dialogContainer() {
    return this.advancedTexture
            .getControlByName(CONTROL_NAMES.dialog);
}
get titleText() {
    let ctrl = this.advancedTexture
            .getControlByName(CONTROL_NAMES.titleText);
    return ctrl.text;
}
set titleText(value) {
    let ctrl = this.advancedTexture
```

```
                    .getControlByName(CONTROL_NAMES.titleText);
    ctrl.text = value;
}
```

In the preceding code, there are two examples of retrieving a control, as well as a control's text value. Additionally, the final property shows a similar process for setting the text value of the `titleText` control. These property accessors and others like them form a core part of the `DialogBox` class, which is the topic of the next section.

The **Advanced Dynamic Texture** is a powerful way to dynamically generate and render a hierarchical set of controls onto either a full-screen canvas layer or as a mesh texture. Complementing the **ADT** is the **GUIE**, a powerful interactive development environment for designing a GUI. Consuming the output of the GUIE can be done by saving JSON from the GUIE or by saving a snippet, just like the **Playground**, **Animation Curve Editor**, **Node Material Editor**, and other BJS tools operate. Working with ADTs authored with the editor in code can be made easy and maintainable with the use of JavaScript property getters and setters that wrap calls to `AdvancedDynamicTexture.getControlByName`.

Now, using this combination of tools, data, and code, it's time to put theory into practice. We need an easier way to implement the concept of a dialog box in our application, and there are at least two places that need dialog box functionality – route confirmation and scoring. This problem speaks to the need to build something once that can be used in multiple situations.

Building a Reusable Dialog Box Component

A reusable component is capable of utilization in multiple places and contexts within a particular code base. Designing a reusable component is different from designing a single-purpose one in several ways. The most relevant one of these ways is that the reusable component's functionality must be designed to be customizable by users without the basic code needing to be reinvented for it to be worked with.

We examined parts of `DialogBox` previously when we looked at how to wrap `advancedTexture.getControlByName` in a get or set accessor, so let's build off that to make an important reminder/note.

> **Important note**
>
> The CONTROL_NAMES enumeration lists all the properties implemented by the `DialogBox` class, but there are more properties than there are controls. Getting or setting a property such as `titleText` or `bodyText` operates against a text control's `text` property directly.

The key parts of our component are going to be the initialization (construction) logic, which is important because it needs to parse the GUI data, entrance, and exit management, and event handling things such as button clicks. After examining how each of these works, we'll put the individual pieces together to build the route confirmation dialog prompt.

Constructing the DialogBox Class

The constructor function for the `DialogBox` class accepts an options object and a Scene instance as its two parameters. These parameters are mostly for pre-populating the dialog box's content, but the `displayOnLoad` parameter is a behavioral flag that instead controls whether or not `DialogBox` is supposed to be visible when it's finished loading and initializing. When the value is `false`, then the `show()` method must be explicitly invoked to display the dialog:

```
const {
  bodyText, titleText,
  displayOnLoad, acceptText,
  cancelText
} = options; //...later...
if (bodyText) { this.bodyText = bodyText; }
this.titleText = titleText ?? "Space-Truckers: The Dialog
  Box";
this.acceptText = acceptText ?? "OK";
this.cancelText = cancelText ?? "Cancel";
```

The constructor logic ensures that the dialog box will have any required pieces of content populated, even if they're not specified by the caller. Previously, we looked at the creation of `AdvancedDynamicTexture`, along with how to populate the GUI elements using `parseFromSnippetAsync`. This is a pattern that we're using for the Playground to load from the snippet server. For the application, we will load a JSON file defining the UI using `advancedTexture.parseContent()` – a non-async method that also obviates the need to run the initialization logic in the callback from `scene.executeWhenReady`, which we used in the Playground. This is the only meaningful difference between our Playground's `DialogBox` class and what will eventually end up in the Space-Truckers Application. This highlights the power of iterative code design using the PG!

The rest of the constructor is devoted to subscribing to and wiring the subcomponents of the `DialogBox` class. Our two buttons have their click event handlers wrapped by the class and the respective `onAcceptedObservable` and `onCancelledObservable`:

```
this.#acceptPointerObserver =
  this.acceptButton.onPointerClickObservable
    .add(async (evt) => {
        await this.onAccepted();
        this.onAcceptedObservable.notifyObservers();
    });
this.#cancelPointerObserver =
  this.cancelButton.onPointerClickObservable
    .add((evt) => {
```

```
        await this.onCancelled();
        this.onCancelledObservable.notifyObservers();
    });
  this.scene.onDisposeObservable.add(() => {
     this.dispose();
  });
});
```

To avoid leaking resources, we are capturing the Observers that have been returned from the subscription methods in non-public class members (denoted with the # prefix), which we clean up in the dispose method:

```
dispose() {
    if (this.#showTimer) {
        this.#showTimer = null;
    }
    this.onAcceptedObservable?.clear();
    this.onAcceptedObservable?.cancelAllCoroutines();
    this.onCancelledObservable?.clear();
    this.onCancelledObservable?.cancelAllCoroutines();
    this.advancedTexture?.clear();
}
```

Any ongoing asynchronous operations must be canceled along, with any coroutines (see the *Creating the Scoring Dialog with Coroutines* section for a definition). The createScene function of our Playground demonstrates how this works when the initial confirmation DialogBox is disposed of in the onAccept handler, spawning a new DialogBox in its place.

Our basic DialogBox defines two explicit interaction points with users: the accept and cancel buttons. It also defines two behaviors: show and hide. Next, we'll learn how the two relate to each other and how to make the show and hide methods complete only after the DialogBox class has finished transitioning.

Handling Button Clicks and Changing Visibility

In addition to handling the acceptButton and cancelButton click events, the onAccepted and onCancelled functions both offer customizers for the DialogBox class to run custom logic before notifying external observers of the event – the default behavior shows this by hiding the dialog before triggering the Observable:

```
    onAccepted() {
        return this.hide();
    }
```

```
    onCancelled() {
        return this.hide();
    }
```

Both `onAccepted` and `OnCancelled` return a `Promise` that resolves when the dialog box has finished hiding itself. If the caller cares about waiting for the dialog to fully show or hide itself, it can either use the standard async or Promise resolution patterns – that is, `await myDialog.show()` or `myDialog.hide().then(...)`. As for the logic to show or hide `DialogBox`, it uses the `BABYLON.setAndStartTimer` utility function to trigger the fade-in or fade-out of the `DialogBox` class in conjunction with the `Scalar.SmoothStep` function (note that some code has been elided in the following listing for space reasons):

```
return new Promise((resolve, reject) => {
    this.dialogContainer.alpha = 1;
    this.#showTimer = setAndStartTimer(
    {
        timeout: this.#fadeInTransitionDurationMs,
        onTick: (d) => this.dialogContainer.alpha = Scalar
                        .SmoothStep(0.998, 0, d.completeRate),
        onEnded: () => {
            this.advancedTexture.isForeground = false;
            this.dialogContainer.isVisible = false;
            resolve();
        },
        breakCondition: this.dialogContainer == null
    });
    }
});
```

In the preceding code, most of the action happens in the `onTick` and `onEnded` callbacks of the `setAndStartTimer` option. The dialog starts with an alpha of 1 and ends after a period of `#fadeInTransitionDurationMs` (800 ms or so) with an alpha of 0. In between, values are interpolated using the `onTick` argument's `completeRate`, giving a value from 0 to 1 regarding how far the timer has progressed to finishing.

The onEnded callback removes the `DialogBox` class from foreground rendering (see *The Advanced Dynamic Texture* section, earlier in this chapter) and sets the GUI's `isVisible` to `false` before resolving the original Promise. On the other hand, `breakCondition` ensures that if the `DialogBox` instance is disposed of before completing the hide or show animation, the timer won't attempt to call disposed of objects.

> **Note**
>
> The `show()` function is almost identical to the `hide()` function, except that it is more like a mirror inverse image than it is a clone. This is because it starts as being fully transparent and ends up being completely hidden.

Let's review how to use the `DialogBox` class in five easy steps:

1. Create an `opts` object containing, at a minimum, a `guiData` field containing a snippet ID:

    ```
    let opts = {
        bodyText: "Your flight plan appears to be viable!"
            + '\n'
            + "Would you like to file it with Space-
                Truckers Traffic Control (STC)?",
        titleText: 'Route Planning Success',
        displayOnLoad: false,
        acceptText: 'Launch!',
        cancelText: 'Retry',
        guiData: DIALOG_GUI_SNIPPET // e.g., "923BBT#32"
    };
    ```

2. Instantiate a new instance of `DialogBox`, passing in the previously created `opts` object and a reference to the Scene:

    ```
    let dialog = new DialogBox(opts, scene);
    ```

3. Attach observers to the dialog box's `onAcceptedObservable` and `onCancelledObservable` to respond to user input (in this case, calling `createScoringDialog`):

    ```
    dialog.onAcceptedObservable.add(async () => {
            dialog.dispose();
            dialog = createScoringDialog(null, scene);
    });
    dialog.onCancelledObservable.add(()=>console.log
        ('cancelled'))
    ```

4. Call the show method to display the DialogBox class if the (optional) displayOnLoad flag is not set to true:

    ```
    dialog.show();
    ```

5. To dismiss or hide the dialog, click cancelButton or call the hide() function. To defer action until the DialogBox class has completely faded out, the Promise that's returned from hide can be awaited:

    ```
    await dialog.hide();
    ```

With our reusable DialogBox completed in proof-of-concept form, let's quickly look at the practice of integrating with the Space-Truckers Application by looking at how the route planning screen uses it to prompt the player to move to the next phase of gameplay.

Prompting Users after Successful Route Planning

Not too many changes need to be made to the DialogBox class from the Playground. However, as mentioned in the *Constructing the DialogBox Class* section, we'll be changing from using a snippet loaded from a remote server to a JSON file loaded from the game's assets folder.

After saving the GUI JSON definition from the GUIE, the definition is added to the /src/guis folder as gui-dialog-buttons-scroll.json. One important change is needed, though, so open up the file and find any external resources (*.png) to change their URLs from absolute to relative ones pointing to the appropriate file in the assets folder. For example, the image that's used as the DialogBox background will look like this after being modified:

```
"source":"/assets/menuBackground.png"
```

The DialogBox class itself is housed next door to the GUI JSON, in guiDialog.js, and as per our change from the snippet server to JSON, we must add that import to the top of the file before passing it into the DialogBox constructor as the guiData property value:

```
import stackedDialog from "./gui-dialog-buttons-
  scroll.json";
// later…
this.advancedTexture.parseContent(stackedDialog, false);
```

Pivoting to SpaceTruckerPlanningScreen, we need to add an import for DialogBox to the file:

```
import DialogBox from "../guis/guiDialog";
```

A new `routeConfirmationDialog` attribute has been added to `SpaceTruckerPlanningScreen`, initialized near the end of the constructor function with logic that should be very familiar if you have read the entirety of this chapter thus far:

```
this.routeConfirmationDialog = new DialogBox({
    bodyText: 'Successful route planning! Use route and
      launch?',
    titleText: 'Confirm Flight Plan',
    acceptText: 'Launch!',
    cancelText: 'Reset',
    displayOnLoad: false
}, this.scene);
this.routeConfirmationDialog.onAcceptedObservable.add(() =>
  {
    this.routeAcceptedObservable.notifyObservers();
    this.gameState = PLANNING_STATE.RouteAccepted;
    this.routeConfirmationDialog.hide();
});
this.routeConfirmationDialog.onCancelledObservable.add(()
  => {
    this.routeConfirmationDialog.hide();
    this.setReadyToLaunchState();
});
```

Now, there is no doubt that the actual copy used in the confirmation dialog box could use some work, but it does the job for now – maybe you'll be the one to submit a Pull Request to change it to something a bit more interesting?

On the topic of interesting, the `onAcceptedObservable` handler for the dialog does several interesting things. First, it notifies any interested parties that the player has accepted the route. Then, it updates `gameState` to reflect the new reality before hiding `routeConfirmationDialog` and allowing whatever logic is subscribed to `routeAcceptedObservable` to take things from that point. This is not too different from the Playground example, and not too much time is needed to get that up and running either! We'll want to hold onto that feeling for now though because next, we're going to be making a series of targeted changes to the application to gather, process, and calculate scoring data for the game.

Calculating Scores

Much of the fun that comes from playing a game is through the different ways that a game can provide feedback to the player – positive or negative. This is a great opportunity for game designers to connect with players at an emotional level. Connecting positive events and outcomes to a player's actions creates a feedback loop between the game and the player, and one of the oldest and truest connections in gaming is the concept of a point score that accumulates throughout gameplay.

The scoring system used in **Space-Truckers** bases a player's final score around a few basic categories and concepts, details of which we'll be covering shortly. When scoring is triggered (that is, the player reaches their cargo's destination), the game displays a `DialogBox` that is initially empty, but which displays each category of scores in a line-by-line fashion before giving the final score.

Before building out the logic to capture and calculate scores, it's useful to define the desired scoring data model in a sample score. This is the desired output of the scoring process logic, irrespective of how that logic generates the data. This will clue us into what sorts of changes are needed elsewhere in the application to support the scoring system.

Scoring System Design

The score data that is generated and used by **Space-Truckers** can be broken down into three broad groups: **score factors**, **multipliers**, and **final scores**. Score factors are categories reflecting base attributes of both route planning and driving performance. The number of encounters, length of the route, and initial launch force are all fixed and set in the Route Planning Phase, but the cargo condition is dynamic up until the player reaches their destination in the driving phase (sample values have been provided for context):

```
scoreFactors: {
    routeLength: 12450.25,
    cargoCondition: 0.768,
    encounters: 125,
    launch: 100.00
},
multipliers: {
    transitTime: { expected: 180, actual: 150, factor: 1.2  },
    delivery: 1.0,
    condition: 0.768,
    encounterTypes: 1.05
},
finalScores: {
    'Base Delivery': 1000,
```

```
        'Route Score': 14940,
        'Cargo Score': 11474,
        'Delivery Bonus': 10000,
        'Encounters': 1312,
        'Final Total': 38726
}
```

Below scoreFactors are the multipliers. These values are used by the scoring calculations to modify one or more scoreFactors in various ways that we'll get into in the next section, *Adding Up and Tallying Scores*. However, before we move on, there's just one more thing to do. One last – you may even say final – section to cover. finalScores are the categorized and summed up values that come out of the combination of scoreFactor and multipliers. This is what will ultimately be displayed to the players in a "here's the bottom line…" type of fashion.

Continuing to ignore any sort of details on how the scoring data is captured is still a useful tactic because although we may know the general shape of the scoring data, until we know how to calculate those scores, we won't know precisely what and where data needs to be captured.

Adding Up and Tallying Scores

The scoring logic is contained within the src/scoring/spaceTruckerScoreManager.js file. Similar to how we are compartmentalizing using the sample score shown previously, consumers of this component only need to call the default export computeScores and pass in a route data structure to get a score object in return. The computeScores function is a simple orchestration function – its only purpose is to coordinate the invocation of the various other functions that are calculating the individual scoring areas:

```
let computeScores = function (route) {
    let score = createDefaultScoring();
    calculateEncounterScoreToRef(route, score);
    calculateRouteScoreToRef(route, score);
    calculateCargoScoreToRef(route, score);
    calculateBonusScoreToRef(route, score);
    calculateFinalScoreToRef(score);
    console.log(score);
    return score;
}
```

The `createDefaultScoring` function in the second line of the preceding listing is a **factory** method for creating empty score data objects, like the previous sample score but with 0 or blank values. As the `score` object is passed between each of the various `calculateXXXScoreToRef` methods, its values are built up and used by successive function calls.

The `ToRef` suffix on these function names indicates that they will be mutating a parameter (usually the last parameter provided by convention) rather than creating a new instance of one. This is most seen with `Vector` and `Matrix` objects but consistency in naming is crucial to the long-term health of a code base! Following that are individual subsections that go through the details of each aspect of the scoring calculations.

Because we're still in the development process, we're not going to worry too much about getting these calculations balanced and tweaked to the extent we may want. What we need to do is establish a basic way to provide a dynamic scoring experience that is easy to come back to later when we're ready to balance and tweak.

Encounter Scores

We start by calculating the encounter score. Right off, we know that we want to get a list of encounters and that we will want to use that list to add up the individual modifiers for each encounter to get the final encounter modifier. If we assume that the route parameter contains a `pathPoints` object collection (see the `/src/driving/spaceTruckerDrivingScreen.calculateRouteParameters` function for details) and that any given entry in the `pathPoints` collection may or may not have an associated encounter containing a decimal `scoreModifier` value, then we can use a simple map and `reduce` operation:

```
const { pathPoints } = route;
const encounters = pathPoints
    .map(p => p.encounter)
    .filter(e => e);
scoreFactors.encounters = encounters.length;
let encounterModifier =
    1 + encounters.map(e => e.scoreModifier)
        .reduce((prev, curr, cidx, arr) => {
            return prev + curr;
        });
multipliers.encounterTypes = encounterModifier;
let encounterScore = 100 * encounters.length *
  multipliers.encounterTypes;
finalScores['Encounters'] = encounterScore;
```

The preceding code calls map with a simple extraction function that retrieves the scoreModifier value – a number. Next, it passes the array of scoreModifier numbers to the reduce function. Array.reduce (if you aren't already familiar with it) is a useful aggregation tool that takes a function as its primary parameter. Looping (or iterating) over the array, arr, the function is invoked for each curr element in turn, with the results of the prev operation being passed along with the value of the curr element at the cidx position. This is just a fancy way of saying that the reduce operation sums up the total of all the elements in an array of numbers! This aggregated value becomes encounterModifier, which is used in conjunction with the overall number of encounters to determine the total encounters score value.

Route Scores

Route scoring calculations are performed slightly differently from encounter scoring. The main factor for route scoring is the length of the overall route (how far the cargo had to travel before arriving), but there are several equally important modifiers. When it comes to transitTime of the route, there are two relevant values: the planned transit time and the actual (driving phase) transit time. The ratio between those values, when added to a constant, gives us transit.factor, an important multiplier that's used in two ways. First, it is applied to distanceTraveled; after it is applied to the launchForce value, which is used during the Route Planning Phase. The first is subtracted from the second to produce the final Route Score value:

```
transit.factor = 0.5 + route.transitTime /
    route.actualTransitTime;
finalScores['Route Score'] =
(route.distanceTraveled * transit.factor) -
(route.launchForce * transit.factor);
```

Cargo Scores

Cargo scoring is based primarily on the condition of the cargo upon arrival, meaning that it reflects player performance from the Driving phase. The cargo starts with a condition value of 100. When collisions with encounters or with sufficient velocity occur, the route path can reduce that value (see the *Capturing Scoring Data* section for more), which is used as the basis for the Cargo Score after it's been scaled by the condition multiplier:

```
const { cargoCondition } = route;
scoreFactors.cargoCondition = cargoCondition;
let cargoScore = 10 * cargoCondition *
    multipliers.condition;
finalScores['Cargo Score'] = cargoScore;
```

Bonus Scoring

If the player delivers their cargo in pristine condition, extra rewards are in order. In that case, the Delivery Bonus is applied to `finalScores`:

```
if (route.cargoCondition >= 100) {
    s.finalScores['Delivery Bonus'] = DELIVERY_BONUS;
} else { s.finalScores['Delivery Bonus'] = 0;}
```

Final Scoring

Once all the various sub-scores have been tallied and multiplied, it's time to sum them all up to get our total value. After populating with BASE_DELIVERY_SCORE, we use `Object.values` to produce an array of numbers that we (sound familiar?) pass to another `reduce` operation to give the `Final Total` score value:

```
let { finalScores } = score;
finalScores['Base Delivery'] = BASE_DELIVERY_SCORE;
let finalScore = Object.values(finalScores)
   .reduce((prev, curr) => prev + Number(curr));
score.finalScores['Final Total'] = finalScore;
```

Putting these computations together helps give us an idea of what data is already available in the route and what needs to be collected. There's more information about a game session than just the route path, after all!

Capturing Scoring Data

With the sample scoring data serving as a guide, we can work backward to identify the places in the application where scoring data is generated before capturing it. This may result in the need to update or change existing data structures and code, but that's OK because we will also make the needed changes to allow players to complete the driving phase and see their final scores displayed in their full glory!

Enriching the Route Data

The first and possibly the biggest change is that we've added a new `routeData` property to `SpaceTruckerPlanningScreen`, which packages up all data needed by the scoring calculations later in the game (see the *Adding Up and Tallying Scores* section for more):

```
get routeData() {
    return {
        route: this.cargo.routePath,
```

```
        launchForce: this.launchForce,
        transitTime: this.cargo.timeInTransit,
        distanceTraveled: this.cargo.distanceTraveled
    }
  }
```

routePath of the Cargo object tracks encounters and other path-specific data, while the other values provide a baseline travel time and the length of the route. Encounters were already being captured as part of cargoData associated with the encounter, but the additional scoreModifier field is needed for every encounter listed in the route-planning/gameData.js file:

```
{
    name: 'Rock Hazard',
    id: 'rock_hazard',
    image: hazard_icon,
    probability: 0.89,
    scoreModifier: 0.019
}
```

There's still more to do, but this completes the data collection aspect of scoring. Next, we need to add a trigger that will initiate the scoring process (provided the player has finished the route...) and show the Scoring Dialog.

Completing the Driving Phase

So far, the SpaceTruckerDrivingScreen.killTruck function has indiscriminately performed the grim responsibilities implied in its name. Today, though, is different. Today, the Grim Reaper of trucks gets a conscience:

```
let closestPathPosition =
  path3d.getClosestPositionTo(mesh.absolutePosition);
// not close enough!
if (closestPathPosition < 0.976) {
    this.reset();
    return;
}
this.completeRound();
```

When the method is called by the `onMeshIntersectExit` action trigger, it checks the absolute (World reference) position of the mesh against the closest Path3D segment of the route. See *Chapter 8, Building the Driving Game*, the *Generating the Driving Path* section for more on Path3D and how it relates to the route path.

> **Note**
>
> Path3D exposes positions as a normalized route with positions between 0 (beginning) and 1 (end).

Should the truck happen to exit its route path (thus triggering this method) too far from its destination, the Grim Task of reaping continues as it did in the past. Let's not dwell on the past and instead look to the alternative, happy future that involves calling the `completeRound` method of the `SpaceTruckerDrivingScreen` class. The first two things that need to happen are that we want to hide the driving phase GUI, which we do by setting the appropriate `layerMask` to 0. Next, we transition the screen to the `DRIVING_STATE.RouteComplete` state to prevent further updates to the simulation that may impact scoring, which, speaking of, is what immediately follows:

```
completeRound() {
    this.gui.guiCamera.layerMask = 0x0;
    this.currentState = DRIVING_STATE.RouteComplete;
    this.route.actualTransitTime = this.currentTransitTime;
    // gather data for score computation
    let scoring = computeScores(this.route);
    let scoreDialog = createScoringDialog(scoring, this);
    scoreDialog.onAcceptedObservable
      .addOnce(() =>
        this.onExitObservable.notifyObservers());
    scoreDialog.onCancelledObservable
      .addOnce(() => this.reset());
    this.scoreDialog = scoreDialog;
}
```

Once the scoring data has been gathered and computed, `createScoringDialog` (from `/src/scoring/scoringDialog.js`) is invoked to do the necessary `DialogBox` creation and management; all that remains for `completeRound` to do is hook up the `onAcceptedObservable` and `onCancelledObservable` properties to the appropriate logic. Then, we are good to go from the standpoint of the driving screen!

The `createScoringDialog` function is a nice analogy to this book; it starts with the familiar, then mixes in something completely unexpected and/or unfamiliar as it progresses until, by the end, it seems like everything works by magic. Let's finish this section by looking at the familiar parts of the function:

```
let opts = {
    bodyText: 'Time to earn payday!',
    titleText: 'The Drayage Report',
    displayOnLoad: true,
    acceptText: 'Main Menu',
    cancelText: 'Retry'
};
const { scene, soundManager } = drivingScreen;
const sound = soundManager.sound('scoring');

let scoreDialog = new DialogBox(opts, scene);
let dialog = { scoreDialog };
dialog.height = "98%";
let scoringCo = scoringAnimationCo();
```

This is slightly different from the Playground at `https://playground.babylonjs.com/#SQG1LV#28`, but only because the PG doesn't have `SpaceTruckerSoundManager` to retrieve and manage the sound used by the next section. There's nothing unusual in this code until the very last line. What a fantastic opportunity as well to introduce one of the more exciting features of Babylon.js v5 – coroutines!

The logic involved in calculating the scores themselves is as simple as possible and no more – it requires nothing but the data passed into it directly to operate, but that data needs to come from somewhere. The different categories of scores are sourced from different components of the game; encounters contribute to their multiplier, transit times are calculated in both driving and route planning, and the cargo's health is tracked by the truck during driving. Each of these factors and multipliers contributes to the overall final scores that get displayed in the Scoring Dialog.

Creating the Scoring Dialog Using Coroutines

If you have come from a background working with Unity, Unreal, or other game engines, you might be familiar with the concept of a coroutine. A coroutine in those contexts is defined much the same way as it is in Babylon.js: a stateful method that runs across multiple frames of rendering.

Though it may imply the presence of multiple threads, typically, in most frameworks (for example, Unity and most certainly JavaScript!), this is not the case. The C# programming language uses Iterators along with the **yield** keyword to implement coroutines, but in JavaScript, we use a (spoiler alert!) **function* generator**. Bet no one saw that callback to *Chapter 4, Creating the Application* coming! Instead of using them as part of our application's state machine, we're going to define the logic that will make the score dialog's scoring entries count upwards from zero, along with playing a cash-register type of sound. Lastly, we'll crank things up to 11 by looking at a standalone Playground sample to show how it's possible to devise a controller system composed of multiple, independently reusable behaviors.

Reviewing Function Generators

For a more detailed overview of JavaScript function generators, see *Chapter 4, Creating the Application*, the *Space-Truckers – The State Machine* section. Here's a quick example of a `function` generator to help remind us how they work and how to use them. Let's say that our designers have devised a color palette for printing the rows of a report. We can define a `nextColor()` star function that will produce a new hex color string at every iteration:

```
function* nextColor() {
    while (true) {
        yield "#0d5088";
        yield "#94342c";
        yield "#e2ba77";
        yield "#787b6d";
    }
}
let colorPicker = nextColor();
```

When a function is generated by calling `nextColor()`, it will always produce a color from the list, in order, when requested. Where does this come into play? The `createScoringBlock(label)` function is responsible for creating and styling the actual GUI element that is displayed in the scoring `DialogBox`, calling `colorPicker.next()` to produce a new value each time it is called:

```
// ...inside the createScoringDialog function scope
// ...inside the function* scoringAnimationCo scope
function createScoringBlock(label) {
```

```
    let scoreBlock = new TextBlock("scoreLine",
      `${label}`);
    scoreBlock.width = "100%";
    scoreBlock.color = colorPicker.next().value;
    scoreBlock.textHorizontalAlignment =
      Control.HORIZONTAL_ALIGNMENT_LEFT;
    // ...snip...
    return scoreBlock;
}
```

There's our brief review of `function*` concepts, all packed up nice and tidy. Now, let's see how those fit into coroutines and Babylon.js by looking deeper into `scoringDialog.js`, where we'll unwrap `scoringAnimationCo` and put it to work in our `DialogBox`!

Counting Player Scores with a Coroutine

Coroutines are neat because they allow the developer to express complex behavior via relatively simple logic (when done right). Any time a coroutine wants to return control to the caller, it calls `yield` – with or without arguments (see the *Advanced Coroutine Usage* section). The timing and manner in which a **coroutine** (**CoRo**) advances in execution depends on the host `BABYLON.Observable` for that CoRo.

> **Important note**
>
> New in the Babylon.js v5 Observable API is the `Observable.runCoroutineAsync` and `Observable.cancelAllCoroutines` functions. See `https://doc.babylonjs.com/divingDeeper/events/coroutines` for more!

If attached to one of the Scene's render event Observables, the CoRo will run every frame, whenever the host Observable is triggered. If attached to `scene.onPointerObservable`, the CoRo will fire any time the pointer moves or interacts with the scene. This is incredibly powerful when combined with the way that JavaScript closures work – since an iterator function is a stateful construct, it can remember and track past events and conditions as they evolve over multiple frames of simulation/rendering.

This makes a coroutine ideal for implementing a sort-of "cash register" style of tallying up the player's scores and presenting the final totals in conjunction with the `DialogBox` class created earlier as part of the `createScoringDialog` function. The coroutine logic can be deceptively simple: given a score object generated by the Scoring Manager (see the *Adding Up and Tallying Scores* section) and a scene, loop over each property of the Final Scores property and display its value in the `DialogBox` class by counting up to it from zero:

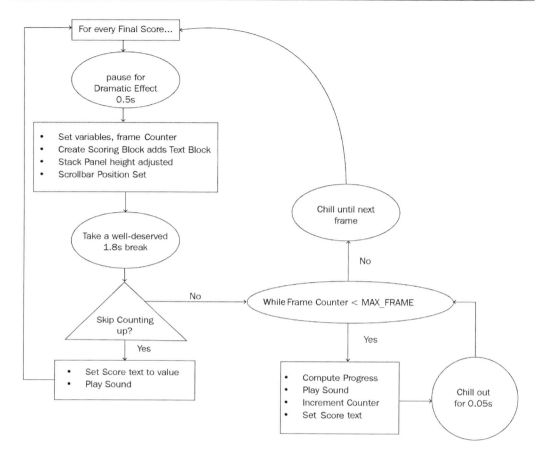

Figure 9.5 – A logical flowchart of the scoringAnimationCo behavior. Circles represent yield statements with the optional use of Tools.DelayAsync. Rectangles list the actions taken

The preceding diagram shows that several other pieces need to be handled: the height of the bodyStack StackPanel needs to be adjusted to account for the new row that was added to it, the scrollbar that contains the bodyStack control needs to be set to its new maximum value to ensure that the current line of text is fully visible, and so on.

Despite the seeming complexity of this logic, it comprises well under 100 lines of code! If we only look at the actual logic of the coroutine and exclude the state management code, we have even fewer lines of code to write:

```
for (let i in finalScores) {
    yield Tools.DelayAsync(500);
    // ...snip... compute and adjust height
    yield Tools.DelayAsync(1800);
```

```
    if (skipCountUp) {
        // display score right away
    }
    else {
        const MAX_COUNT = 50;
        while (frameCounter <= MAX_COUNT) {
            let currProgress = frameCounter / MAX_COUNT;
            sound.play();
            let speed = Scalar
                    .SmoothStep(0, score, currProgress);
            scoreBlock.text =
                    `${label}.........${speed.toFixed()
                    .toLocaleString()}`;
            frameCounter++;
            yield Tools.DelayAsync(50);
        }
    }
    yield;
}
return;
```

The value for MAX_COUNT was arbitrarily determined via experimentation; it controls the length of the counting animation. The progress is governed by the SmoothStep function, which starts slow before speeding up greatly just before coming to a gentle stop at the end. Every time Tools. DelayAsync is passed as the argument to yield, the coroutine will pause itself for the indicated amount of time – or as close to it as possible – before resuming execution.

> **Note**
> Because frame delta times don't always add up to the exact amount of time specified, a coroutine can be paused for slightly longer than the indicated amount of time.

When all is said and done and the final **Final Score** has been rendered, the coroutine returns rather than yields, indicating completion and signaling to the hosting onBeforeRenderObservable that it's OK to clean up and dispose of that coroutine function instance. From the perspective of the code that started things off, we have two simple lines – one to create the iterator function and another to start it running:

```
let scoringCo = scoringAnimationCo();
scene.onBeforeRenderObservable.runCoroutineAsync(scoringCo);
```

In this scenario, we don't want to block execution and wait until the coroutine completes to continue executing `createScoringDialog`, but if we were doing something different, such as making asynchronous HTTP calls as part of a coroutine, it would be prudent to await or capture the returned Promise of `runCoRoutineAsync`. Thus, it can be used and passed around just like any other asynchronous operation, allowing for more advanced scenarios and complex behaviors.

Advanced Coroutine Usage

Unless you're a passenger on the Titanic, there's good news: this is just the tip of the iceberg! Because coroutines leverage the underlying mechanics of function iterators, it's possible to use the `yield*` operator to chain together multiple `function*` iterations into a single coroutine, as exemplified in the Playground at `https://playground.babylonjs.com/#5Z2QLW#1`.

> **Note**
>
> See `https://developer.mozilla.org/en-US/docs/Web/JavaScript/Reference/Operators/yield*` for more details and examples of using the `yield*` operator.

The `yield*` operator is used in the context of a `function*` body, and provides a way to "pass through" the results of another iterator function – or, and this is easily missed part of the definition (emphasis added):

> *"The yield* expression is used to delegate to another generator or iterable object."*

Although not used in our example, this would allow a developer to, for example, write a coroutine that produced a stream of values from an array populated by device sensors, among many other applications. In our example, we are using the `yield*` operator analogously as we may extract reusable code into a function by invoking another `function*`.

Seemingly a small detail, this ability to execute other iterator functions allows us to use the powerful Compositional pattern of software design to put simple building blocks together to express complex behavior. We start with the `function*  think()` coroutine. It is named appropriately because its job is to decide what the sphere mesh is going to do next:

```
function* think() {
    while (true) {
        yield Tools.DelayAsync(1500);
        yield* moveToTarget(new Vector3(PERIMETER / 2, 1,
           0));
        yield Tools.DelayAsync(1500);
        yield* patrolCo();
```

```
            yield* moveToTarget(new Vector3(0, 1, 0));
    }
}
```

Think of the preceding code as the *primary controller* or, more colloquially, the AI for a game object. It can read the environment and make decisions on what to do. In our case, it waits for a second and a half before invoking the `moveToTarget` function (listed in the following code snippet) with the desired target position. This moves the sphere from wherever it is positioned in the middle of the right-hand side of the perimeter Plane. After another short delay, the `patrolCo` function is invoked.

`function* patrolCo` is another compositional element that combines multiple `moveToTarget` iterations, along with logic, to change the color of the sphere on every movement direction change:

```
function* patrolCo() {
    let targetVector = new BABYLON.Vector3(0, 1, 0)
    yield;
    sphereMat.diffuseColor = BABYLON.Color3.Random();
    targetVector.set(PERIMETER / 2, 1, 0);

    yield* moveToTarget(targetVector);
    sphereMat.diffuseColor = BABYLON.Color3.Random();
    targetVector.addInPlaceFromFloats(0, 0, PERIMETER / 2);

    // ...snip...
    yield* moveToTarget(targetVector);
    return;
}
```

Each set of `yield*` statements delegates execution to the `moveToTarget` function, which is the real workhorse of this example. This behavior does what it says on the tin – it moves the subject (the sphere mesh, in our case) of the behavior as close as it can to the given target world position. A `maxDelta` value caps the amount of ground the sphere can cover in any given frame (due to the coroutine being hosted and executed by `onBeforeRenderObservable`):

```
const maxDelta = 0.0075;
function* moveToTarget(targetPosition) {
    let hasArrived = false;
    while (!hasArrived) {
        let dir = targetPosition.subtract(sphere.position);
        if (dir.length() <= 0.75) {
```

```
            hasArrived = true;
        }
        dir.scaleInPlace(maxDelta);
        sphere.position.addInPlace(dir);
        yield;
    }
    return;
}
```

The direction of movement is computed by subtracting the two relevant position vectors, the result of which is used to determine whether the sphere has arrived at its destination, as well as moving the sphere by adding a scaled vector pointing toward `targetPosition`. Upon arrival, the iterator function returns control to the calling iterator function – either `patrolCo()` or `think()`, which then proceeds to the next step in its iterator chain.

This simple example can easily be extended with additional behavior and logic, simply by adding additional `function*` definitions. Like a library or toolbox of behaviors, simple behaviors such as `moveToTarget` are stitched together into more complex behaviors such as `patrolCo`, which is, in turn, orchestrated by the overall `think` function iterator endlessly pondering the game's world. An entire non-player actor/controller can be quickly put together in this fashion! Hopefully, by presenting the concepts in an isolated Playground, it's easier to see how composition can make the whole greater than the sum of its parts.

Summary

We've accomplished a lot in this chapter. Starting with the **Babylon.js GUIE**, a basic `DialogBox` was designed and saved to both the snippet server and JSON. After learning how to use it in conjunction with the **ADT**, we implemented the reusable `DialogBox` component and tested it by adding the Route Planning confirmation dialog.

Armed with those initial results, we turned to the scoring system used in Space-Truckers and the logic needed to calculate each area of the scoring game. The data to accomplish this became apparent throughout, so we made the needed modifications to the **Space-Trucker Application** to capture scoring data. Because we already have the foundational dialog structure in place, it's easy to create the **Scoring Dialog** from both captured and sample scoring data.

It's not enough to simply display the scores in our Scoring Dialog, though, so we employed another new feature in v5 of Babylon.js: **coroutines**. Hosted and managed by any `BablyonJS.Observable` (but mostly used in `onBeforeRenderObservable`), coroutines allow complex multi-frame logic to be simply written and executed. Through `scoringAnimationCo`, each line of the Final Scores object is displayed and counted to its final value from zero.

Moving away from the Scoring Dialog, we wrapped up this chapter by learning how to use coroutines with multiple **function*** definitions to create complex behavior from simple actions. A think orchestration coroutine decides which sub-routines to invoke and in what order, armed with a toolbox of behaviors such as `moveToTarget` and `patrolCo`.

In the next chapter, we're going to look at the space of Space-Truckers by diving into environments, **Image-Based Lighting (IBL)**, and how to use **Physically-Based Rendering (PBR)** with Babylon.js. From workflows for converting images for use with IBL to adding post-processes for effect, we'll see how easy it is to take a few lines of code and make something attractive and performant!

Extended Topics

It's important not to focus too much on the particulars of the `DialogBox` design UI – this book isn't a book on graphic design, much to everyone's relief – so here are some ideas and resources for taking your UI adventures to the next level:

- The Babylon.js team ran a summer event in August 2022 that urged community members to submit the amazing UI builds they had created with the GUIE. Two "starter" templates were provided for people that didn't have an existing project:

  - `https://playground.babylonjs.com/#QCH724#1`

  - `https://playground.babylonjs.com/#QCH724#1`

  These two samples are for a main menu system and an in-game menu and inventory system – what sorts of things can you build when you combine those as a starting point with what you've learned in this chapter?

- The Space-Truckers Main Menu is very much imperatively coded as opposed to the GUIE JSON files, which are declarative. As we've seen, a declarative data-driven UI is much easier to build and maintain, so try applying that knowledge to the Main Menu by replacing some of the GUI components created in code with a `DialogBox`.

- Composable coroutines can provide a simple and easy way to add interesting behaviors to a game or application. Add a way for an arbitrary encounter instance in the Driving Phase to run a coroutine "behavior." The encounter itself should provide the coroutine, but it will need to be provided with current game state information:

  - Three components working together can help cleanly separate and define this functionality:

    - A Behavior component that does the "thinking"

    - A Think Context that provides a vehicle for state information

    - A set of actions that the behavior(s) can perform (for example, "Move," "Eat," "Disperse," "Acquire Target," and so on)

  - An encounter coroutine may load a mesh and material, set some values, and perform other initialization tasks before beginning its behavioral "think" loop.

  - Actions can be other coroutine behaviors, such as patrolling behavior.

Improving the Environment with Lighting and Materials

Welcome to *Chapter 10*! This chapter is brought to you by The Number 5, twice. Babylon.js v5 brings with it not only incredibly powerful and fast features but also a suite of new tools to help work with almost every area that a game engine could ask for from a framework. We've worked with several of them already, including just this past chapter on the **GUI Editor** (**GUIE**). Previously, we've worked with the **Particle Editor** in the **Inspector** in addition to the **GUIE** and the **Playground**. But that's not all of them, not by a long shot.

As we cover the **IBL Toolkit** and the **Sandbox** in this chapter, the shadow of a giant looms over us. The mighty **Node Material Editor** (**NME**) will be the topic of the next chapter, and we're going to use this chapter to prepare for it by leveling up our knowledge of some important topics in 3D graphics programming.

When it comes to the graphical experience of a game or 3D application, lighting is probably the single greatest contributor to the overall look and feel of a scene. Like many of the topics we've covered or will be covering, there are entire libraries of much more in-depth, better written, and thorough texts that cover these subjects. Hence, our objective will be to provide a solid basis of the principles, grounded in a practical usage scenario. No matter what visual effects look is desired, the best and most performant lighting technique for current real-time 3D rendering is **Image-Based Lighting** (**IBL**), where the main source of light for a scene is, as the name implies, a specially prepared image texture.

> **Note**
> The 1993 movie *Jurassic Park* pioneered this technique as a way to capture the on-set lighting for use with the computer-generated elements of scenes.

This chapter isn't just about lighting, however. It's incredibly difficult to talk meaningfully about lighting in a scene without involving the concept of materials. Simply put, **material** is the term we use for mathematics to describe how light interacts with a surface. There's quite a lot more that goes into that definition, but as usual, Babylon.js provides a shortcut with the **PBRMaterial**. This helps keep the most complicated parts of the math – both here in this book and in your code – tucked and hidden away behind a shiny abstraction that leaves us the task of knowing which parameters need to be set and to what value.

Before we try to drink from the firehose of lighting topics, there are some other pieces of business for us to tackle. Make sure to check out the *Technical Requirements* section for some links to posts, books, and articles relevant to the topics in this chapter. There's also a list of fancy words you can use in Scrabble or to impress your friends who aren't fortunate enough to be reading this book like you are and a list of both free and paid software for working with and preparing images to use in your project. Don't feel guilty about your rapidly growing knowledge – feel good as you read the first section to learn about all the different things we've done and changed since we last visited the code base.

In this chapter, we will cover the following topics:

* Materials, Lighting, and the BRDF

* Working with PBR Materials and IBL Scenes

* Tone Mapping and Basic Post-Processing

Technical Requirements

The source code for this chapter is located at `https://github.com/jelster/space-truckers/tree/ch10`. While we'll still be looking at some Playground code, most of our work in this chapter lies elsewhere. For working with images and textures, the following non-exhaustive list of tools will be useful for preparing and converting image assets for use with Babylon.js.

Tools

The following tools will help you in this chapter:

Application	Use and notes	How to Get
Paint.NET (free, Windows)	Image manipulation and conversion.	Windows Store or `https://getpaint.net`
GIMP (free)	General Image Manipulation Project.	`https://www.gimp.org/downloads/`
Photoshop ($)	Advanced image editing and conversion.	`https://adobe.com/photoshop`
Lys ($)	Professional-quality environment maps, cube maps, and skyboxes.	`https://www.knaldtech.com/lys/`
BJS Sandbox (free)	BJS IBL/PBR scene environment configuration. Processes DDS image files into `.env` textures.	`https://sandbox.babylonjs.com`
BJS IBL Tool (free)	Conversion, pre-processing, and compression of HDR images into cubemaps.	`https://www.babylonjs.com/tools/ibl/`
IBL Baker (free)	Fiddly and difficult to obtain desired results.	`https://github.com/derkreature/IBLBaker`

Glossary of terms (abridged)

Here is a list of some of the more common acronyms and terms that you might encounter during this chapter or while reading other resources on the topic of 3D lighting and materials. It's far from complete but will serve as a jumping-off point to expand your vocabulary further:

- **Direct Draw Surface (DDS)**: A file format that's useful for storing high-resolution images. This includes MIP maps. Babylon.js supports the so-called "legacy" DX1 DDS format.

- **MIP map**: Referred to as pyramids in some areas of 3D graphics, a MIP map is a series of progressively smaller, lower- resolution reproductions of the original image. This is used for many applications, such as **Level of Detail** (**LOD**) and storing pre-computed lighting values.

- **Physical Based Rendering (PBR)**: This is a technique for realistically simulating the behavior of light after interacting with some surface material. A Specular/Glossiness model and a Roughness/Metallicity model are two approaches. For the two major parameters, there are pairs of Specular/Gloss, and Rough/Metallic, respectively, with values that fall in the range of [0,1].

- **Image-Based Lighting (IBL)**: A method of scene illumination that incorporates a spherical projection of an image to provide lighting.

- **Skybox**: A mesh cube textured on the inside, with the camera positioned within. This is done by using a specially laid out single image or six separate individual images. A camera positioned on the interior of the cube will view the texture as if it appeared very far away.

- **Environment Texture**: This is a special type of texture; it is the "I" of "IBL."

- **BRDF**: This stands for **Bidirectional Reflectance Distribution Function** (pronounced similar to "Bird") and is a mathematical function that contributes terms to the overall Rendering Function that relates the angle of reflectance to the amount of incoming and outgoing light.

- **Rendering Function**: When implemented, this is known as a rendering pipeline. This is a mathematical function that's used to calculate the final screen color of a 2D pixel depicting part of a 3D scene. The final color value of that pixel is influenced by many different factors, such as lighting or the position of the camera.

- **Material**: This is an asset or code component that, when applied to a mesh geometry, defines the behavior of light impacting upon the mesh.

- **Luminance**: This is a measurement of the amount of light in a given unit area.

- **Dynamic Range**: The ratio between the brightest and the darkest parts of a scene.

- **Tone Mapping**: Used to adapt an HDR image for use in a non-HDR display or medium.

- **Color Space**: The potential range of colors that can be represented by a particular file or image format. This is often notated in terms of bytes per channel; for example, R8G8B8A8.

Recommended Reading

Here are some links to resources that can be helpful to skim before, during, or after reading this chapter. Some are more on the conceptual side, while the documentation links are eminently practical:

- The BRDF, as told by Wikipedia: `https://en.wikipedia.org/wiki/Bidirectional_reflectance_distribution_function`

- The PBR BRDF, as described by the Academy Award-winning engineering group who pioneered the technique in professional film: `https://www.pbr-book.org/`

- Official BJS docs:

  - Setting up an HDR Environment to use with PBR: `https://doc.babylonjs.com/divingDeeper/materials/using/HDREnvironment`

  - All the things you never knew you wanted to know about the properties of **PBRMaterial**: `https://doc.babylonjs.com/divingDeeper/materials/using/masterPBR`

  - Break-out of different reflection and refraction features: `https://doc.babylonjs.com/divingDeeper/materials/using/reflectionTexture`

- The Khronos Foundation BRDF reference implementation used by Babylon.js for modeling metallic roughness materials: `https://www.khronos.org/registry/glTF/specs/2.0/glTF-2.0.html#appendix-b-brdf-implementation`

- Two separate Hard-Core BRDF definitions, along with example implementations of realistic PBR suitable for scientific or engineering models:

  - `https://math.nist.gov/~FHunt/appearance/brdf.html`

  - `https://developer.nvidia.com/gpugems/gpugems/part-iii-materials/chapter-18-spatial-brdfs`

- For the textbook crowd: *Essential Mathematics for Games and Interactive Applications*, 3rd ed. Van Herth and Bishop. 2016 Taylor & Francis Group. (`https://www.essentialmath.com`)

- Image Encoding for HDR: `http://www.anyhere.com/gward/hdrenc/hdr_encodings.html`

Materials, Lighting, and the BRDF

The analogy of a 3D scene to a real-world movie studio set is an obvious but useful one. Some parts are obvious, such as the scene and stage, cameras, and lights, while others are not. Meshes are the actors and the set pieces, while materials are their costumes. This section is all about the costuming and lights, but it's tough to discuss either without digging down a bit into the theoretical underpinnings of how light gets modeled in a scene.

This section is a bit of a doozy, so here's a quick fly-over of what we're going to talk about. First, we're going to dabble with a little bit of symbolic mathematics and some extremely light calculus. Next, we'll look at the different ways that light can reflect and interact with surfaces, and how it's modeled or approximated in 3D. This will serve as a strong basis for us to learn about Materials and how they relate to math at a high level. After that, we will introduce PBR and Environments to cap off our tour. Time to dive in!

Introducing the BRDF

Light is modeled in terms of either being incident or reflected – denoted with the subscripts i and r – representing a measured amount of light that is either incident upon an object (is being reflected) or coming from an object (reflected off of it). The terms for these two scenarios are **radiance** for the light reflected from the object and **irradiance** to represent the amount of incoming light. The ratio between the incident radiance and the reflected irradiance is computed using some derivation of the BRDF:

This is a scary-looking piece of math if you're not a level 3 calculus adept or higher, but it's not as bad as it seems when we restate the equation in terms of how it works. The change in reflected radiance (dL_r) depends on the angle between the incident (L_i) ray of light and the surface normal (n) – used to calculate θ, with input values represented by the combination of (ω_i, ω_r). There are three important constraints that any code implementing this function must satisfy to realistically model a physical system:

- The result of $f_r(\omega_i, \omega_r)$ must be greater than or equal to zero.

- Reversing the terms (ω_i, ω_r) yields identical output. This is known as reciprocity.

- Energy must be conserved. In other words, the total amount of irradiance going into a particular area and the total amount of radiance going out of that same area must be less than or equal to one.

We don't ever have to directly deal with implementing this equation, fortunately, but it's good to know the underlying forces driving the higher-level abstractions in Babylon.js. Later in this section, we'll look at how the **PBRMaterial** parameters affect the underlying BRDF, but first, we're going to continue exploring the theory and concepts behind lighting.

How Light is Modeled in 3D Applications

To reduce the sheer number and complexity of lighting calculations needed, we need to simplify how we treat light. For our purposes, light behaves as a ray emitted from its source that then reflects from surfaces in a deterministic fashion. When it comes to these calculations, there can be great numbers of individual parameters that contribute to the result, but at the heart of it, there are just a few parameters that contain essential terms for lighting computation: light direction (I), radiance (L), the surface normal (n), and the view position (V). The BRDF is evaluated once per light source, for every light sample in a scene, because of the need to calculate the angle between the object's surface normal and the point of incidence:

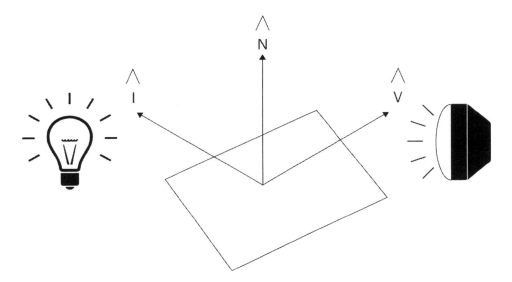

Figure 10.1 – Basic parameters involved in lighting computations. The normalized vectors, I and V, represent the direction of the light and the viewer, respectively, while the normalized vector, n, points in the direction of the surface normal

The normalized vector I points toward the light source, while the vector L – sometimes denoted with ω in equations – provides the intensity. When you put these together, you get the brightness (luminance) of light incident upon the object in each color. Different light sources use different equations to compute values for I and L. Two examples of this are the point light, which radiates light equally in all directions, and the spotlight, which radiates light in a single direction. Both types of lights illuminate an object, but their properties result in different behavior in surface interactions.

> **Note**
> It's important that the I, N, and V vectors are normalized to preserve the relationships between values after transformation. The final value is scaled by either a color or scalar value computed from L.

The quality of **radiance** is a measure of the amount of incident light impacting a square meter area if you want to be technically precise. More colloquially, radiance is the brightness of a particular source of light. Complementary to radiance is color. Color is, physically speaking, defined by the wavelength of a particular packet of light, or the amount of energy contained in a photon. Computationally, color is usually represented as a Vector3 or Vector4 quantity, depending on whether an alpha transparency channel is being used. Being able to treat colors as vectors is a very useful technique since the whole toolbox of vector calculations then applies to mixing and blending colors. Before we know what types of calculations to perform, though, we need to know more about the types of reflected light.

Diffuse

When light reaches the View position, it can do so along an almost infinite number of different combinations of paths. The diffuse lighting term refers to light that is evenly scattered from the surface of an object. Another way of putting it is that a shaft of light striking the object's surface scatters diffuse light in all possible directions. Light being scattered will be influenced by the color specified by the object's diffuse material settings or from a texture lookup:

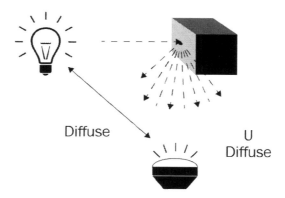

Figure 10.2 – Diffuse light is scattered in all directions

Specular

The Specular term of the lighting model represents light that reflects directly from an object to the viewer. Depending on the term's value, this can give an object a "shiny" appearance, approximating a smooth or rough surface. The specular term is very strongly affected by the angle between the incident shaft of light, the object, and the viewer as the angle approaches 90 degrees:

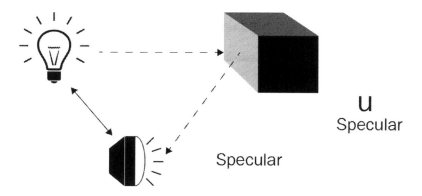

Figure 10.3 – Specular light is directly reflected by the viewer

Emissive

Unlike the other lighting terms, the emissive term is not related to the external light source, but rather is light that is generated by the object itself. Importantly for lighting design purposes, it does not illuminate other objects in the scene. For that reason, emissive lighting is sometimes referred to as self-lighting:

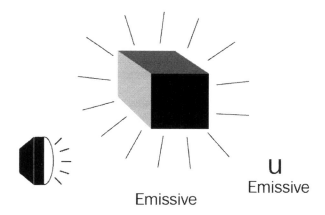

Figure 10.4 – Emissive lighting or self-lighting illuminates only the object itself

So far, we've looked at the definitions for the Uem, Uspec, and Udiffuse terms, but we've said nothing as to how we compute those values in the first place, nor how we combine these values. If you are curious, you can go to the *Recommended Reading* section of this chapter for more information on the details of these equations. The last lighting term we'll cover is ambient lighting, one of the simplest forms of light.

Ambient

When ambient lighting is discussed in the context of 3D applications, it refers to a general class of lighting contributors that are incident to the surface but whose paths do not directly come from the light source. An intuitive example of this is the lighting of a cloudy, sunless day. On such a day, all light from the environment seems to come from every direction; it's omnidirectional. Shadows (that is, **Ambient Occlusion** or **AO**) can be pre-baked and are easy to make and fast to render:

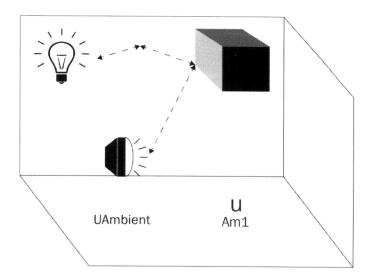

UAmbient

$$U_{Am1}$$

Figure 10.5 – UAmbient light doesn't depend on direction and comes from the indirect incidence of light from the source environment. It is approximated by a single color with a constant value across the scene

Because of the indirect path taken by the light ray from the source to the receiver via the object's surface, we approximate the ambient contribution by setting a single color per scene. Ambient light has no direction, so its brightness is constant throughout the scene.

Defining the properties of light and its basic behavior is but one piece of the lighting puzzle. The other piece of the puzzle is the surface material properties that govern what happens to incident light coming in from a given direction with a given view position. Modern 3D engines and asset creation tools have embraced the concept of a **material** as a means of defining how an object's surface reacts to light at any given angle and point.

Materials and Textures

At a conceptual level, a material is a **BRDF** implementation; the material contains a combination of data and logic that's plugged into the relevant terms of the overall graphics pipeline (see *Chapter 11, Scratching the Surface of Shaders*, for more on graphics pipelines and shaders) in the form of programmable shaders, textures, and other attributes. Bringing together the concepts from the previous sections, we'll see why it makes sense to use the term **Material** to encompass the specific configuration of shaders and textures and introduce the approximations that allow for real-time realistically lit scenes in the form of **PBR**.

Materials Overview

In Babylon.js, there are two basic general-purpose material components, along with a library of specialized ones, that allow you to add cool and interesting effects with very little effort. For example, the Lava Material procedurally simulates a lava effect to applied meshes, while the Fur Material gives meshes a furry appearance. You can even render video from external sources into your scene using the **VideoTexture**! Browse the **Babylon.js Materials Library** and read about how to use them at `https://doc.babylonjs.com/toolsAndResources/assetLibraries/materialsLibrary`.

StandardMaterial is the workhorse material in Babylon.js. Materials in general (for example, **StandardMaterial**) group color and texture attributes and shaders, with an important performance implication: each distinct material is drawn to the screen in a separate call. Better performance is generally realized with fewer draw calls, so avoid creating new instances of a particular material and instead assign existing instances to meshes when possible. **PBRMaterial** is the Babylon.js implementation of PBR, a technique we'll discuss in further detail shortly.

Which material to use, be it standard or PBR, depends on the needs of the scene. Most of the time, a properly set up **PBRMaterial** will have a far greater degree of photorealism than one using **StandardMaterial**. The realism comes at the expense of greater computational cost. Given the additional and much more complex BRDF involved, it doesn't always make the most sense. For example, a depiction of a star, such as the Sun in the route planning screen, should use **StandardMaterial** since it self-illuminates via emissive lighting. **Emissive lighting** isn't necessarily contradictory to a PBR process, but in the example of the Sun, any visual benefits of PBR are lost in the emissive glare.

As mentioned earlier, a material is a container and a wrapper of both assets and executable logic. Calling back to even earlier discussions, it is responsible for computing the various lighting terms in its BRDF. The **Ambient**, **Specular**, **Emissive**, and **Diffuse** options can vary by the material type for the specialized materials, but for both **StandardMaterial** and **PBRMaterial**, each of those lighting terms can be specified by either a color or a set of one or more different texture images.

Textures and Materials

Setting the color for a particular term, say the diffuse term, has the effect of introducing that color evenly across every mesh covered by that material. This might be OK for some scenarios, but it makes for a very bland and boring-looking scene. Assigning textures to different terms is the way to go here, and it's also where the complexity starts ramping up (as if it weren't already complex enough!) significantly. Another factor that complicates things is that the choices and types of textures you'll want to use can differ between **StandardMaterial** and **PBRMaterial**.

> **Important note**
>
> You may notice mention of **PBRMetallicRoughnessMaterial** and **PBRSpecularGlossinessMaterial** in the Babylon.js docs and APIs. These materials provide a fast on-ramp to converting from using **StandardMaterial** to **PBRMaterial** with little effort or for adding PBR to a scene quickly at the cost of fine control over parameters. See `https://doc.babylonjs.com/divingDeeper/materials/using/masterPBR#from-metallicroughness-to-pbrmaterial` for more on the differences between the simplified PBRXXXMaterials and the general-purpose **PBRMaterial**.

Texturing assets is a sub-skill of 3D graphics design that takes practice, patience, and the ability to look at the world in a slightly warped fashion. If a mesh's material is its costume, then the material's textures are the mesh's blouse. A mesh defines a 2D set of coordinates for each vertex commonly referred to as (u, v) instead of (x, y). A **UV** is a tuple (two-member set) with values between $[0, 1]$. It is the point on the texture that, when sampled, defines the color of that point on the mesh. This lookup is referred to as using a **Texture Map**.

On the topic of maps, think of how you can project the Earth, which is spherical, onto a flat piece of paper. Even though Australia is roughly three times larger in area, Greenland appears to be the same size. This is the distortion inherent to mapping the surface of a sphere onto the surface of a plane, and the degree to which it will be apparent is largely dependent upon the geometry that the texture was created to cover. We'll return to this topic when we cover spherical environment maps, but returning to the topic of **Texture Maps**, it is the lookup aspect that is most pertinent to our current discussion.

> **Note**
>
> **Albedo** is to **Diffuse** as **Reflectivity** is to **Specular** when looking at the Babylon.js **PBRMaterial**. Colors can be set for each lighting term as an alternative or in addition to textures providing the same.

As we saw earlier in our discussion of *How Light is Modeled*, there is more to lighting than just looking up a particular color from a texture and adjusting its intensity based on the distance to the light source. The preceding *Note* gives an analogy for translating the terms for base texture between materials, but there will often be more than one texture involved in a Material.

When additional image textures are mixed with either `diffuseTexture` in **StandardMaterial** or `albedoTexture` in **PBRMaterial** to provide fine details or show relief of surface features, we call those textures **detail maps**. A detail map is commonly used with a **normal map**, oftentimes referred to as a `bumpTexture`. An **ambient** (sometimes also called **occlusion**) texture and other lighting factors, such as the **surface normal (N)**, aren't part of a regular texture image and are supplied as data contained in one or more separate texture images. Most 3D content creation software has varying capabilities for generating and creating these alternative types of textures, and as a result, most 3D models that can be obtained via asset marketplaces and the like will already have these textures packaged. The key to making the best use of these is knowing which things to plug into what values, so let's learn about the parameters that we can supply before looking at how we can supply them!

PBR as a Different Type of BRDF

Looking at **PBRMaterial** through the "lens" of the **BRDF**, though the output has the same shape (that is, format) as any other BRDF, the means of arriving at the values is quite different. This manifests in the form of a whole swathe of different parameters controlling very specific aspects of the material's behavior toward lighting. Here is a selected list of commonly used properties and a short description, in the order that they appear in the Babylon.js documentation at `https://doc.babylonjs.com/divingDeeper/materials/using/masterPBR`. This page contains many Playground examples showing the different effects of setting various PBR properties, which can be useful in understanding what options are available:

- **Metallic**: This affects the specular term and determines how much the material behaves like a conductive or metal substance.

- **Roughness**: This specifies how smooth a surface is. Smoother surfaces will have sharper specular highlights (that is, shiny spots).

- **Subsurface** (`#sub-surface`): A whole category of properties that are used in things from flesh tones to translucent reflective materials. This specifically applies to refraction and translucency in v5.0 of Babylon.js. It also controls the scattering effect.

- **Clear Coat** (`#clear-coat`): Models light interactions with the topmost surface of the material. A shiny clean waxed car has a clear coat layer just visible above the actual paint color.

- **Anisotropy** (`#anisotropy`): This is used to shape asymmetrical reflections (specular highlights) and is highly dependent upon view and incident angles.

Many different parameters and settings can be configured on **PBRMaterial**, so it's worth taking a step back to look at what goes into PBR.

PBR and IBL

Formally speaking, **PBR** is a technique for the realistic real-time simulation of lighting in a 3D scene. A smooth, shiny object reflects more incident light directly into the viewer (specular), whereas a rough, dull object tends to scatter light in all directions more evenly (diffuse or ambient). Other sources of scattering at, above, or below the surface of the material can further affect the course and fate of a light ray in conjunction with the object's basic surface properties. Textures can be used to supply many of these property values, oftentimes by using different color channels to store different material data. An example of this is the Unity convention for detail maps, which uses a single detail map to store diffuse, normal, and roughness data. It does this by using the Red channel for a grayscale albedo (diffuse) map, the Green channel for the green component of the normal map, the Blue channel for roughness values, and the Alpha channel for the red component of the normal map. Properties in **PBRMaterial** such as `useRoughnessFromMetallicTextureAlpha` and `useMetallnessFromMetallicTextureBlue` can allow broad flexibility on the part of the asset designer, as well as the developer, to be creatively efficient in how material data is supplied at runtime. This can be of vital importance when memory and compute resources are limited – it's far better to process a single texture than three separately. PBR can give great-looking results on its own in a scene, but it is far more effective when used in conjunction with IBL.

> **Important note**
>
> Despite the superficial resemblance to the acronym for **Irritable Bowel Syndrome (IBS)**, IBL has nothing to do with yours nor with anyone else's bowels. Neither does PBR, in case there was any need for clarification.

IBL is a technique for lighting a scene that derives a scene's primary lighting information from an image source. While other light sources may still be present, such as a **PointLight**, they are there to provide secondary and/or supplemental illumination. IBL is a distinctly different category of technique from PBR, but it doesn't make much sense to set up an IBL scene and not use PBR Materials that can take advantage of it! The way that IBL works is that, during rendering, a **high dynamic range (HDR)** image – that's been specially captured and prepared as a **CubeMap** – is sampled to supply the Li values instead of a particular light source.

Environment Textures and Reflection Textures

One of the benefits of using IBL and PBR is that with the right setup, things that would be otherwise complex to procedurally model simply fall out of the physical light simulation. Take, for example, an urban scene.

It is night, and there are neon lights above dark restaurant doorways. The center of the scene is a four-way street intersection, where a car has suffered an accident. Reflections in the windshield show the surrounding buildings, while shattered panes of glass gleam with scintillations tinged with the neon glow of signs advertising cheap beer. Water gushes onto the street from a broken fire hydrant, and in the rippling faces of the growing puddles, the driver's shock of curly hair can be seen exploding from the sides of the airbag, her visible eye appearing to tremble with the rippling puddle. What a rich description!

In a conventional or, more accurately nowadays, a more legacy rendering approach, almost all the details described in the preceding passage would need to be custom crafted and coded for a single use and purpose. Using IBL and PBR in combination with appropriate texture assets can allow designers to create and use scenes with the kind of details you can only read about in a cheap noir detective novel! The key component of an IBL setup is the image part, naturally. This image is known as the **Environment Texture** and, as mentioned earlier, is what is sampled to provide lighting information for **PBRMaterial** instances.

While it is certainly possible to specify a separate environment map for each **PBRMaterial**, it's generally easier to set it up on the **Scene**, a task which we will see how to accomplish in greater detail in the next section, *Working with PBR Materials and IBL Scenes*. A specific use case where an environment texture and a material's reflection texture might be different might be the rear-view mirror of a car, which shows not just the environment but reflections of objects within the scene itself – something that IBL and environment lighting can't do.

In this scenario, a common solution is to dynamically generate a reflection texture using a **Reflection Probe**. This is a form of **Render Target Texture** (which itself is a form of procedural texture) that can provide an updated environment map from a specified position's perspective using a list of render targets to track. The Babylon.js docs contain more details on how to use reflection probes: `https://doc.babylonjs.com/divingDeeper/materials/using/reflectionTexture#dynamic-environment-maps-rendertargettexture-and-friends`.

In this section, we've introduced a raft of new concepts, such as the **BRDF** and some of the parameters and terms involved in simulating lighting, starting with an understanding of the difference between diffuse, specular (Albedo), emissive, and ambient lighting sources. That laid the groundwork for us to explore the concept of a material with a focus on the Babylon.js **PBRMaterial**. **PBRMaterial** implements a technique known as PBR, which uses lighting information provided by the environment, along with a constellation of material properties, to realistically simulate the behavior of light against surfaces rough and shiny, smooth, and dull. Once we learned about materials and lighting, we looked at how **IBL** can be used to further enhance the realism of a rendered scene.

In the next section, we're going to put theory into practice and learn about the different assets needed to make use of the previously discussed concepts. After learning about some of the asset types involved and the file and image formats related to them, we'll look at some of the tooling needed to produce those assets and how to use them.

This is a complicated subject, so if you don't feel like everything makes sense yet, it's OK to take a beat and look at some of the Playground examples listed in the Babylon.js documents. If this section has mostly been a review for you, then you might be interested in some of the more advanced topics linked in the *Recommended Reading* section earlier in this chapter.

Working with PBR Materials and IBL Scenes

StandardMaterial is very forgiving when it comes to being able to use various types of assets. It doesn't mind if a texture is 8, 16, or 3 bits per pixel or JPEG, GIF, or PNG – it'll paint a mesh with it. While this is also largely true for **PBRMaterial** in that it is a robust component and able to operate with a wide range of inputs, the rendered look of any **PBRMaterial** is far more sensitive to insufficient or improperly formatted texture data. We're going to look at the specifics of what the Babylon.js PBR implementation expects, as well as the tools that will help create assets that fit those specifications. Later, we'll go through the heuristics – a set of guidelines – of how to decide what and which assets and values to put into which properties to accomplish a particular look for your material. Let's start by examining some of the ways to represent an image digitally.

Image Formats and File Types

Bitmaps are the simplest type of image. The name says it all – it's a sequential array (or map) of values that each represent a single channel (red, green, or blue) of a single pixel in the image. When an image is decompressed into (typically the GPU) RAM, a bitmap is the result. With each pixel mapped to a different location in memory, it is extremely fast to look up values from arbitrary locations in the image. When storing images on a disk, however, the goal is to optimize file size at the expense of computational speed.

There are only a few file formats that can support HDR images. Two popular native HDRI formats are **HDR** and **EXR**. The RAW image format captures pixel values as close to the digital camera's sensors as possible, meaning calibration may be needed across different devices to get consistent results. Some image types, such as TIFF, can act as containers for other images, and similarly, some offer a wide range of options in their formats, such as **DDS**. Despite their popularity, GIF, and JPEG are not formats that are capable of representing an **HDRI**, even though they may still be able to display what appears to be an HDR image. This is made possible by a process known as **tone mapping**, which we'll discuss after we finish exploring why a JPEG isn't an HDRI. To do so, we will cover bit depth and dynamic ranges.

Bit Depth and Dynamic Ranges

When thinking about graphics and how they are displayed, it's useful to break the topic down into fundamentals. Each pixel of an image has a value for each of the red, green, and blue color channels (some images may also have an additional alpha channel for transparency).

If we use a single byte (8 bits) to represent each channel, we have 24 or 32 bits per pixel, again depending on the presence of a dedicated alpha channel. Each color channel can only take on a value between 0 and 255, for a total of 65,536 total unique possible colors in the **color space**. That sounds like a lot of colors – and it is – but it is a far cry from the range of colors discernable by the human eye. More importantly, in the context of display technologies, it is incapable of properly representing an HDR without **tone mapping**. Tone mapping is the process of scaling down from the infinite to the finite in discrete steps.

Between zero and one lies infinity, or close enough to it if you're using 32-bit floating point numbers to represent a color channel. On the other hand, the much smaller and countable ratio of 1:256 is the full dynamic range possible in an 8-bit channel. To be a **High Dynamic Range Image (HDRI)**, an image needs to be able to use 16- or 32-bit floating point numbers to represent the red, green, and blue color channels. This adds up to a total of 48/96 bits per pixel, allowing for a theoretically 1:infinite dynamic range. As a practical matter, though, this can take quite a large amount of space – a 4K image has roughly 8.3 million pixels, and at 96 bpp has a raw size of 800 MB!

That's not all, though. An image used in PBR and IBL needs to have what is known as **mipmaps**, either generated at loading time or pre-baked into the image file. A **mipmap** is a lower-resolution version of the main texture and is used similarly to a meshes **Level-of-Detail (LOD)** in which objects further away are rendered using less detailed textures, thus saving memory and rendering time. Just like auto-LOD works for meshes, Babylon.js can generate mipmaps at the time a texture is loaded.

> **Note**
>
> As pretty much anyone who has purchased a download-only version of a modern AAA game knows, those high-quality textures come with a high-bandwidth and high-disk usage cost. The last installment of the *Call of Duty* franchise, *Modern Warfare*, is over 175 GB! If the assets are all that size after being compressed, consider how large the textures are and that will answer the question of what all those gigabytes of RAM are doing during gameplay.

It's not just important that an art asset looks good in an image viewer – it must be sized and formatted properly so that it contains or retains the full range of colors and brightness across the image. Fortunately, there are a few available tools within the Babylon.js ecosystem alone that can help with that task.

Using and Creating Assets for PBR and IBL

Because there are such varying ways to consume and use assets with PBR and IBL, it's difficult to figure out what to use where, and why. Assets created specifically for a given project are the most likely to give the best results overall but have the inherent difficulty of requiring the skill and knowledge to create the assets yourself, or the financial resources to purchase or commission the assets from someone who does. Regardless of how the texture or other asset is obtained, more decisions are required to assess its suitability and compatibility with Babylon.js. The following diagram illustrates the high-level decision-making process you can use to evaluate a given texture asset, known as the "I" in IBL:

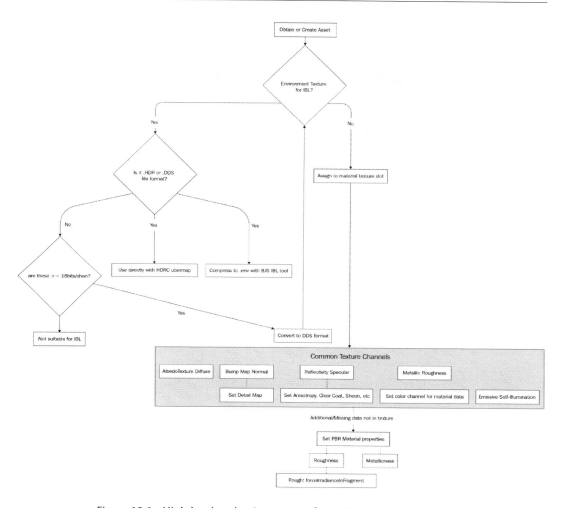

Figure 10.6 – High-level evaluation process for working with a texture and
IBL/PBR. This is a qualitative assessment, not a quantitative one, so other
factors such as texture resolution are still important to evaluate

Let's walk through the highlights for each of these nodes. Keep in mind that whether or not an asset is suitable for use with PBR and IBL doesn't necessarily mean that it is useful. At the same time, it is useful to consider the context in which the asset will be viewed; what good is a high-resolution texture that is only ever rendered at a large distance from the camera?

Obtaining Assets

This step is one of the more complicated and hard-to-define steps. The process of getting the proper 3D assets will differ greatly, depending on a few basic factors:

- Access to a professional graphic artist (and the time for them to work on it!)
- Purchase/obtain an asset pack from a vendor
- Self-authoring capabilities – for example, produce everything yourself
- A la carte assemble assets from a mixture of sources

> **Important note**
>
> No matter which approach or path you take, always make sure that you have clear and free permission and rights to use an art asset before deciding to include it.

If you have the resources, it's best to engage with a professional artist or team of artists, but these people can't draw for free. Be prepared to compensate them for their work. Purchasing a set of pre-made assets can often be almost as good as having assets custom made-to-suit, but they have the advantage of being able to be deployed almost immediately at the cost of a lack of flexibility – any changes or file conversions are up to you. Unless you are a polymath – that is, professionally skilled in multiple areas such as the famed creator of Babylon.js **Deltakosh**, then it's usually going to be a better use of your time and efforts to not try and do more than a light edit of assets.

> **Important note**
>
> Don't neglect to browse through the Babylon.js Asset Library – it contains many very useful "base" texture and mesh assets that are ready for you to put into your project! New to v5, the Asset Librarian is a tool for directly injecting references to BJS Assets into a Playground. You can learn more at `https://doc.babylonjs.com/toolsAndResources/assetLibrarian`.

The last option, a la carte asset amalgamation, is a compromise of the other three options, and as such, basically offers almost all the downsides from each and only a few of the upsides. The only thing this approach has going for it is its flexibility, which can't be beaten. It is a sort of lowest common denominator to take this approach, but care and effort are needed to provide a consistent overall look and feel for the application. As a corollary to this approach, there is always the "escape hatch" of programmatically setting the material properties through code without textures.

Environment Textures, Conversions, and Compression

To be used in Babylon.js as an HDRI for PBR, an environment texture must be in an HDR format. If it isn't, then it needs to be converted into either HDR or DDS format if it can store 16- or 32-bit floating point representations of each color channel for the texture. From that point, there are a couple of options, but from a scene quality perspective, it's important to make sure that the image has been prepared as either a single **Equirectangular** or as a series of **CubeMap** images.

In a process such as adapting a flat paper map of the world onto a globe, the environment map represents a spherical or panoramic view of the surrounding environment. As an alternative to using a sphere, a cube can also be used in the same fashion, with a projected image of each face on the cube unwrapped into six separate images or image sections. See `https://doc.babylonjs.com/divingDeeper/environment/skybox#about-skyboxes` for more on **CubeMap** images.

> **Important note**
> When the environment texture is a Cube Map, HDR rendering is unavailable and seams or other visual artifacts may be visible.

As mentioned in the *Bit Depth and Dynamic Ranges* section, there is a large footprint to storing all that floating-point image data, something that can be very important when dealing with web-based applications. The easiest way to compress a DDS or HDR image for use in an application is to use the Babylon.js IBL tool at `https://www.babylonjs.com/tools/ibl/`. Using an image that has been prepared as an equirectangular, as described earlier, will give the best results, but it isn't required. Drag and drop the image file you want to use into the central panel of the page and wait a moment – you may not see anything immediately happen because it can take some time to process an image, depending on its size and type. Once the tool has finished, two things will happen: first, the image will appear on the page, prepped and ready as a preview. Second, a `.env` file will be downloaded to your computer. This file is a compressed and pre-processed version of the source image, and a quick comparison of file sizes will show a *significant* difference between the source and output files – 30 MB can easily be compressed to a few hundred KB! You can read more about the rle-RGBE format and extra pre-computed data that allows this compression to be achieved at `https://doc.babylonjs.com/divingDeeper/materials/using/HDREnvironment#what-is-a-env-tech-deep-dive`.

Assigning to Material Texture Slots

The non-environmental texture section of *Figure 10.6* illustrates some of the more commonly used texture channels in a Babylon.js **PBRMaterial**, along with some things to keep in mind when using it. For example, when using a texture to define the material's metallic and/or roughness parameters, it might be necessary to specify which color channel (R, G, or B) contains the relevant data values.

Some properties of **PBRMaterial** expand into a new set of properties, many of which can accept a texture as the means of specifying values. Clear coat, subsurface, and detail maps (and more) each have their own set of parameters and textures that can be used to improve the quality of the final output, making for a bewildering array of possible configurations. Don't worry about trying to understand and visualize every one of them and how they work – in the next chapter, we'll learn how the **Node Material Editor** (**NME**) helps make sense of these options.

In this section, we built upon the theoretical foundations established by previous sections to learn about how **HDR** images are digitally represented and stored. An HDR image is in **linear color space** (as opposed to **gamma** or **sRGB** space – that is, how many and what arrangement of bits are used to represent each color channel) and uses at least 16-bit floating point numbers for each color. Most of the time, in standard Dynamic Range images, linear colors fall between the range of [0,1]. An HDRI, though, has a range that can, at a practical level, go from [0, ∞]. For example, an HDRI of a scene including the Sun on a cloudless day might have a range of [0, 150000]!

There are several commonly-used file formats for storing HDR images, but the two best-supported for use with Babylon.js assets are HDR and DDS. Environment textures need to be laid out in either a rectangular projection onto a spherical surface – an Equirectangular projection – or as a series of six images in a Cube Map. The **Babylon.js IBL Tool** is useful for viewing the fine details of an image dropped onto it, but more importantly, it can convert and compress an HDR or DDS image into a size much more manageable for use on the web: the ENV file format.

Most computer displays and print technologies are incapable of rendering such a wide range of values – and indeed, any display capable of accurately representing the brightness of the Sun would be an extremely toasty experience for anyone viewing it. To accurately render an HDR image in a non-HDR display, it is necessary to remap color values back into the range of [0,1]. The process of doing this is called **tone mapping** and is part of an important step in finishing a scene for presentation, known as **Post-Processing**.

Tone Mapping and Basic Post-Processing

Although this section is split into separate sub-sections between tone mapping and Post-Processing, tone mapping is technically a type of post-process. It's an important enough subject within the context of this chapter to warrant a bit of space to explain it.

Post-Processing is a familiar concept wrapped in a potentially unfamiliar language. When you superimpose cat ears on your FaceTime, Zoom, or Teams calls, you are using a post-process. If you select an Instagram filter, you're using a post-process. When you give yourself a cool motion blur effect in TikTok, you're using a post-process. Babylon.js comes with several different built-in effects, both subtle and not so, and to avoid you having to remember and create the most common post-process effects, there's also a Default Rendering Pipeline that comes with all the basics wrapped up in a plug-and-play fashion.

Tone Mapping

As we discussed in the previous section, rendering an HDR image onto a non-HDR display medium requires the values for each pixel's colors to be remapped from a potentially infinite range into a decidedly finite one via the process of tone mapping. There are several different algorithms and ways to accomplish this, but regardless of the specifics, any tone map is going to have to make compromises.

Let's just say that we have a set of numbers – [0.1, 0.1, 0.2, 0.3, 0.5, 0.8, 1.0, 1.0, 2.5, 10] – that we need to remap into a range between zero and one. Here's a chart that shows the difference before and after tone mapping that series using the simplest tone mapping technique:

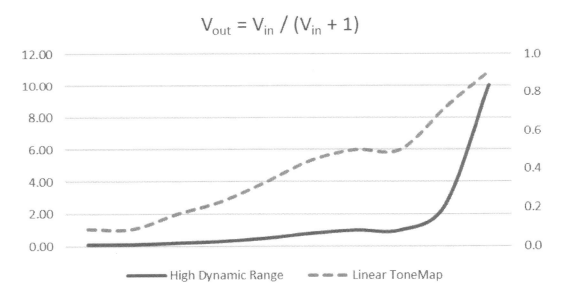

Figure 10.7 – Chart of pre- and post- tone mapping combined radiance values with HDR values. This mapping doesn't perfectly capture the original dynamic range of values

The dashed line in the preceding chart shows how the range represented by the solid line has been compressed to fit between the zero and one bars of the chart. An ideal mapping would closely mimic the solid line as much as possible – this is not the case with this simple linear mapping. This is adequate for many applications, but other mapping functions can get us closer to matching the curve. A gamma-correction function uses two constants, A and γ, which must be either separately computed or manually determined, to map values in a way that much more closely matches the original curve:

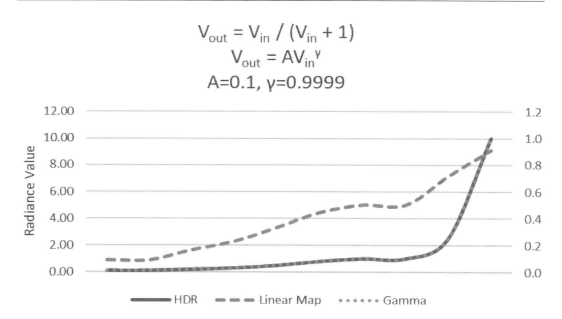

$$V_{out} = V_{in} / (V_{in} + 1)$$
$$V_{out} = AV_{in}^{\gamma}$$
$$A=0.1, \gamma=0.9999$$

Figure 10.8 – Tone mapping with gamma correction produces a curve almost indistinguishable from the original. The values for the two constants must be determined separately

The dashed line perfectly overlaps with the original HDR brightness curve when the appropriate values of the constants, A and gamma, are supplied. A drawback of this technique is that those constants can vary by display device, OS, and other potential variables. Fortunately, Babylon.js does all the work for you when it comes to tone mapping as part of its built-in Image Processing and Post-Processing features.

Post-Processing and the Rendering Pipeline

It's a safe assumption that anyone reading this is familiar with the concept of a live camera filter. Flip a switch and your photo looks like an old-time photo, another and it takes on the look of a comic book poster, all in real time. If you've ever wondered how that sort of thing works, then Post-Processing is as good a place as any to start! Think of a post-process as being like a real-time Photoshop for your scene. In games, some of the more obvious post-processes are ones such as rain or snow falling, screen shaking, and the always classic "drunken stagger."

There are a few different ways to implement, import, and employ post-processes with Babylon.js, but all post-process effects work the same way: they start with a texture. This texture is kind of like a framed blank canvas at the start of the frame; the color of the blankness is the Scene's clear color. If each stage in the digital rendering process is like a step in the manual rendering of paint onto canvas, the point in time during the frame's rendering pipeline we are interested in is the part after the paint's been laid down on the canvas but before it's been set and dried. This texture is the output of transforming all the scene's geometry into positions relative to the camera, then to 2D screen space. A post process deals with the individual pixels of this texture, not the geometry of the scene. Babylon.js has several ready-to-use **PostProcessRenderingPipelines** and **PostProcesses** that can be added with a line or two of code. A little bit further down the road in the next chapter, we'll look at how we can create post processes and two different ways to accomplish that. Let's not let the next chapter steal this chapter's thunder and continue to look at more built-in post-processing functionality with volumetric light scattering – that is, "God Rays."

Adding the Volumetric Light Scattering Post-Process Effect

Let's look at a simple yet concrete example of using a built-in post process in the route planning screen. When a strong light source lies behind an object and the viewer, light striking the object at oblique angles may scatter, creating a distinctive glare effect that will make the Sun, well, shine! This type of effect is called volumetric light scattering (also known as "God Rays"), and it's so easy to use you don't even need to know how it works. Here are the two lines of code needed (split across multiple lines for clarity):

```
var godrays = new VolumetricLightScatteringPostProcess(
    'godrays', 1.0, this.scene.activeCamera,
    this.mesh, 100, Texture.BILINEAR_SAMPLINGMODE,
    this.scene.getEngine(), false, this.scene);
godrays._volumetricLightScatteringRTT.renderParticles =
  true;
```

These lines, added to the **Star.js** constructor, are all that is needed. The constructor for the **VolumetricLightScatteringPostProcess** (**VLSPP**) takes several standard parameters and attaches them to the Star.mesh sphere, using the active camera for rendering. The last line sets an internal property that instructs the internally used **Render Target Texture** involved in the post-processing to render particles to include in the effect.

The following screenshot depicts the results of applying this post-process. Quite the improvement:

Figure 10.9 – The volumetric light scattering effect added via post-processing gives the
apparent impression of camera glare from the bright Sun on the route planning screen

Babylon.js has several post processes available right out of the box in addition to the VLSPP, most
of which are just as easy to use. If none of those suit your needs, the option to create a post-process
of your own always exists in several forms, which we'll cover in the next chapter. To wrap things up
with the current subject matter, we'll look at how easy it is to get a big bundle of rendering quality
improvements for a small bit of code with the Default Rendering Pipeline of post processes.

The Default Rendering Pipeline

It's not as much of a mouthful to say as the previous section was, but the **Default Render Pipeline**
makes up for it by being such a cute and useful bundle of different effects. A diligent browser of video
game graphics settings menus (who isn't?) will recognize many of the post processes that comprise this
Rendering Pipeline. Included in the pipeline are the same **Image Processing** effects that are available
at the material level, but there are also others such as Bloom, Film Grain, FXAA, and more! Each is
provided with sensible defaults, but it is important to know what those are so they can be adjusted to
fit the specifics of the situation. The BJS Playground at `https://playground.babylonjs.`
`com/#Y3C0HQ#146` is a complete example of the Default Rendering Pipeline straight from the Babylon.
js docs page – it has an interactive UI to allow you to quickly change parameters or enable/disable post
processes and see their effects. Play around with the sample to get a feel for how different types of effects
and their settings can completely change a scene's look and feel with only a few adjustments! Using this
rendering pipeline is basic table stakes for getting a high-quality image; it's a good place to start.

The evolution of an application or game's look and feel will invariably include the addition of other, unique combinations of post processes and effects. This is what makes a game or application stand out from others, and it's a place where there's lots of room for art and aesthetics. In this section, we discussed how **tone mapping** works to "shift" a high-dynamic range image or scene into a range that displays are capable of rendering. There are different types of tone mapping algorithms because there are some compromises that need to be made when performing tone mapping that result in varying visual differences in output. We learned about how tone mapping fits into a post-processing pipeline as part of either material-based or pixel-based Image Processing effects. These effects share common configurations and include several adjustments in addition to tone mapping. Other post-processing effects are included with the Image Processing effect in the Default Rendering Pipeline. These effects include FXAA, Bloom, Film Grain, and more.

Summary

This chapter may have felt either extremely long, extremely short, or extremely boring, depending on your existing knowledge and experience. The behavior of light in the real world is extremely complicated, so when simulating it in a scene, it's necessary to make simplifications and assumptions about that behavior.

Traveling in rays from source to destination material, light is modeled using some implementation of the **Bi-Directional Reflectance Function** (**BRDF**). This function computes the (ir)radiance or brightness at a given input point and angle from a source of light. The function has a set of terms that are each calculated in separate functions, then combined to provide a result.

The Diffuse term (also called Albedo) accounts for light that has been evenly scattered from the surface of the material, kind of like how a point light evenly projects light in all directions. Specular is the term for light that is reflected from the material directly into the camera or observer and has a bright, potentially sharp outline. The specifics of the specular lighting contribution depend greatly on the material's properties; a metallic, smooth surface will more cohesively reflect light than a rough, non-metallic one will. Emissive light is also called self-illumination because it is light that doesn't have a light source as an origin and it does not factor into other material's lighting. Finally, ambient lighting is a catch-all term for any type of lighting that arrives at the camera indirectly from its source. Atmospheric scattering is one example of an ambient lighting source.

The different qualities and properties that describe the behavior of light on a mesh are grouped into components called materials. A material implements various key functions that go into the BRDF. **StandardMaterial** of Babylon.js fulfills most basic scene needs that do not require a photorealistic rendering, while **PBRMaterial** provides a **Physically-Based Rendering** (**PBR**) BRDF implementation that closely models the real-world behavior of different surface types, from rough to smooth, shiny to dull.

For PBR to work effectively, the environment of a scene needs to provide essential lighting information. **Image-Based Lighting (IBL)** is a technique in which a special type of image is sampled at rendering time to provide information about the scene's lighting at the current camera position and view. What makes the image type special is that it represents image data using 16- or 32-bit floating point numbers for each color channel (Red, Green, Blue, and, sometimes, Alpha). Having more bits to represent a number means that, for practical purposes, the ratio, or range of brightness in a scene between its brightest and darkest areas, can effectively be infinite. This is what both defines and allows an HDR photo or image to be captured and stored.

The texture is known as an **Environment texture**, but in the context of a skybox, this comes in the form of a **reflection texture**; both perform the same duties using the same texture, but from different approaches. Environment or reflection textures for a static scene can be pre-generated in several ways. They can be "baked" using a 3DCC tool such as Blender or Maya from an existing scene, they can be captured from render output by a suitably configured camera, or they can be manually prepared from an existing image using a tool such as GIMP or Photoshop. These will be unable to take into account the scene's meshes and their properties, so a dynamic approach such as Reflection Probes can be used to generate a reflection texture in real time.

Once you've obtained an HDR image, there are a couple of options regarding what to do next. File sizes for DDS and HDR images can be quite large, so the Babylon.js IBL Tool is where to go to convert images into the ENV format for use in Babylon.js scenes. There are several different parameters and texture slots available to assign on a **PBRMaterial**, but between the BJS docs, Playground examples, and, of course, this book, you should be sufficiently equipped to explore them all!

Once a scene has been rendered on the GPU, it isn't necessarily passed to the display device right away. **Post-processes** are employed in the form of a series of Pipelines that allow the output from a scene's camera to be successively processed in different ways. The built-in **ImageProcessing** offers many common image corrections and adjustments that you may recognize from your smartphone's photo editing software, but other post processes are available that add real-time effects only limited by RAM and imagination.

One of the more important post processes to engage when working with PBR/HDR scenes is **tone mapping**. This is a mathematical operation that converts the **High Dynamic Range**, which can't be represented by most display devices, into a standard range of colors and brightness. Because this involves compressing the potentially infinite (or at least very large) into a much more finite space, there will be some losses in fidelity and accuracy. Thus, there are different algorithms for performing this mapping that emphasize different areas of the brightness or color curve.

In the next chapter, we're going to be taking a diamond awl to the rock-hard topic of Shaders. Babylon. js has many ways that allow developers to write, manage, and apply standard GLSL code. What that means and what a shader is are things that will be defined shortly, so buckle up – this next chapter's going to be a wild ride!

Extended Topics

There's no better way to learn something new than to just take a stab at carving something familiar from what is unfamiliar territory. At the same time, it can be difficult to determine where and what slices are best to cut off. Here are some ideas, exercises, and examples that might give you a good starting point:

- Using an example from your IRL world, create a photorealistic recreation of that example's environment:

  - Use the camera on your smartphone or device to capture the surrounding cube or sphere map texture in as high of a quality as the device allows.

  - Import the pictures into an image editing tool and adjust the image to give it a high dynamic range (make sure to save it in a 32-bit RGBA format!).

  - Export the HDR images in DDS format, then convert them into an ENV file using the BJS texture tools.

  - Create a PG that uses your environment and test it by placing some meshes into the environment. Make sure to configure and give them a **PBR Material**!

- A skybox doesn't have to share the same texture as the scene's environment (reflection) texture. Demonstrate this by modifying the Space-Truckers route planning scene to use a high-quality skybox with a highly compressed ENV file.

- Using a static background environment for reflections doesn't mean that a scene can't create a reflection texture on the fly that is dynamic to the scene. Make the driving phase route mesh shiny and reflective and then use a reflection probe (see `https://doc.babylonjs.com/divingDeeper/environment/reflectionProbes` for how to use them) to cause the surface of the Space-Road to reflect an image of the truck as it passes over it.

- Some systems can handle the added load of post-processes, but others (especially mobile devices) may not be able to maintain a desirable frame rate. Enable the post-processes to be toggled and for variables to be tweaked by the end users of Space-Truckers. Later, this can be hooked up to a Settings dialog, or potentially linked to a Scene Optimization (see *Chapter 12, Measuring and Optimizing Performance*, for more details).

Part 3:
Going the Distance

The last part of the book is where we take our developed game from being a rough demo to a completed application. As a bonus, the final chapter contains a smorgasbord of disparate topics that weren't addressed in the rest of the text. Guest contributors bring additional context to and detail on other topics of interest within the world of Babylon.js.

This section comprises the following chapters:

- *Chapter 11, Scratching the Surface of Shaders*
- *Chapter 12, Measuring and Optimizing Performance*
- *Chapter 13, Converting the Application to a PWA*
- *Chapter 14, Extended Topics, Extended*

11
Scratching the Surface of Shaders

Captain Edward J. Smith of the erstwhile and ill-fated ship the Titanic would no doubt be among the first to acknowledge the fact that the visible surface of an iceberg represents but a small fraction of an immensely greater object. When used as an analogy, the phrase "tip of the iceberg" is commonly understood to mean that what is visible, isn't and shouldn't be taken to be representative of the entire thing.

> **Note**
>
> The aforementioned, oddly specific call-out to Captain Ed Smith, is a fantastic Random Fact to know on Trivia Night.

Similarly, the idea of scratching the surface of a topic evokes imagery of kids attempting to dig a hole to the other side of the planet. Juxtaposed with a to-scale globe, it suggests the immensity of the digger's undertaking. In no way does it diminish the enjoyment the children get from their quixotic adventure, but by depicting the differentiated layers of crust, mantle, and core, it acknowledges how a serious endeavor involves more than doing existing things on larger scales.

The preceding paragraph could come straight out of a self-help book with how hard it tries to hit its reader over the head with the analogy, but it does accurately describe the subject matter of this chapter. Shaders and programming for the GPU are the topics of this chapter in a broad sense, with a focus on the tools and how to use them in service of the topic. This leaves us with a problem like previous ones we encountered when we looked at input and control systems (*Chapter 5, Adding a Cut Scene and Handling Input*). As you may recall, the problem was that the amount of material needed to gain a solid understanding of the topic requires a book of its own to properly cover it!

As we did in previous instances, we're going to cover as much of the fundamentals as possible while still laying the groundwork for whatever next steps you decide to take in learning this subject. This means that there might be things that don't get a whole lot of space, but that will be made up for (hopefully) by the excellent links and resources that are available and listed.

In this chapter, we will cover the following topics:

- Understanding Shader Concepts
- Writing and Using Shaders in Babylon.js
- Shader Programming with the Node Material Editor

This is a far more limited number of topics than what could have been covered, but by the end of this chapter, you'll know enough to be immediately productive in current projects while also having enough grounding to see where your next steps in learning lead.

Technical Requirements

The technical requirements for this chapter are the same as the previous ones; however, there are some subjects and areas that might be useful to refresh or catch up on:

- **Vector math operations**: This includes addition, subtraction, dot, cross, and others. You won't need to perform the calculations or memorize any equations, but knowing the significance or purpose of them (for example, you can use vector subtraction to find the direction between two objects) is the key to making the knowledge useful.

- **Function graphs**: Both Windows and macOS have built-in or freely available graphing calculators that can graph entered equations. This is useful in understanding the output of a piece of shader code across varying inputs. Graph like it's TI-89! An online-only option is the Desmos Graphing Calculator at `https://www.desmos.com/calculator`.

Understanding Shader Concepts

In the days before standalone GPUs were commonplace, drawing pixels to the screen was a lot different than it is today. Kids these days just don't know how good things have gotten with their programmable shaders! Back then, you would write pixel color values directly into a buffer in memory that becomes the next frame sent to the display. The advent and proliferation of the dedicated graphics processor as an add-on came in the late 1990s, and it changed the landscape completely. Access to display pixels was abstracted around two major **Application Programming Interfaces** (**APIs**): DirectX and OpenGL. There's an incredibly rich history of the evolution of those interfaces but this isn't a book on graphics hardware interfaces and their history – it's a book on present 3D graphics development, so let's just leave the details to those tomes and summarize them in short.

To avoid the need for developers and end user software to support every model and make of graphics cards, a set of APIs was developed that a hardware manufacturer could then implement. Two competing standards emerged – DirectX and OpenGL – and for the subsequent decade or so, drama ensued as each tried to adapt and change to a rapidly evolving graphics technology landscape. We're going to finish this section by looking at shaders themselves, which requires us to understand how a shader relates to the rest of the computer hardware and software. Before we can understand that aspect, however, we need to understand why it's important to make these types of distinctions in the first place.

Differences Between a GPU and a CPU

A graphics processor isn't built the same way as a regular CPU. At a fundamental hardware level, a graphics processor is built around performing certain types of tasks very fast. This meant that applications needed to contain specialized code that could leverage these capabilities to their fullest. As opposed to code that you may typically write for the frontend or backend of a website, where code is executed sequentially, one instruction after another, a GPU wants to execute as many operations in parallel as possible. Still, this is not an illuminating way to describe how a GPU is programmed differently from how we may know from previous experience and intuition. A better analogy might be in thinking about how a painter might render a large mural onto a wall, as seen in *Figure 11.1*.

Like traditional programs, most printing that people are familiar with at the consumer level is done by a process known as rasterization – a print head scans the paper, spraying down ink of specific colors at times and places it corresponding to the patterns of colors of the print. In this way, a picture is progressively built from one corner to its opposite, line by line, pixel by pixel. Our painter works similarly, starting from one part of the painting and building up the mural piece by piece:

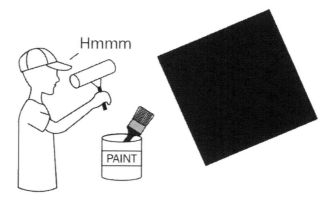

Figure 11.1 – An analogy of traditional computing has a single painter working on the entire portrait themselves as being analogous to how a CPU processes instructions

In contrast to our lone painter-as-a-CPU, graphics processors ditch the raster process and go with a more distributed shotgun approach to painting an image. Here, thousands of painters are all assigned to work on different small slices of the same piece. None of the individual "painters" has any knowledge about what their brethren are up to; they just have their instructions for painting their tiny piece of the full picture:

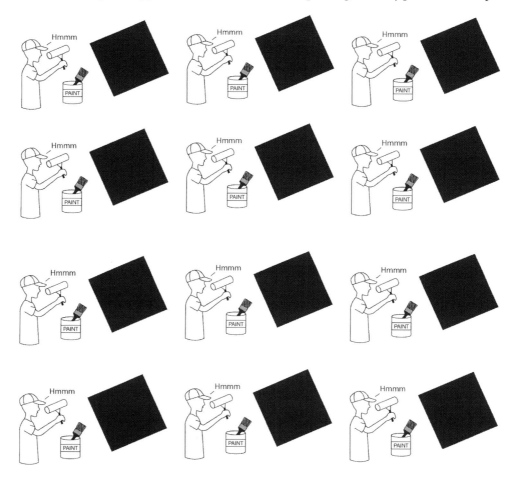

Figure 11.2 – Graphics cards execute instructions simultaneously, with each "painter" getting only a tiny piece of the full canvas to work on, and with no knowledge of any other painter

It is in this manner that graphics cards can handle the billions of calculations per second needed to drive modern 3D graphics applications and games. As the previous diagram implies, instead of a single painter (processor) methodically laying down each line and each layer of paint until the picture is complete, there is a legion of painters that each execute the same set of instructions, but with data wholly specific to their part of the canvas.

Shaders are GPU Applications

How can applications take advantage of this way of processing? More importantly, how can a developer write code that takes advantage of this massively parallel processing resource? To answer those questions fully and with the appropriate context would (again) require an entire book of its own. The *Extended Topics* section of this chapter contains several such excellent tomes! We will leave historical context, fundamental concepts, and the hard mathematics to those more worthy voices and instead focus on more practical aspects of writing the instructions handed to those legions of painters in the form of graphics card programs, more commonly referred to as shaders.

In the graphics rendering process, we start with various data from the Scene, such as geometry, lighting, and materials, and we finish with a frame displayed on the screen. This result comprises a collection of pixels and their colors, one pixel/color combination for every point displayed on the screen. In the space between the Scene and the Screen, there are several important steps, but at a high level, this is the Rendering Pipeline:

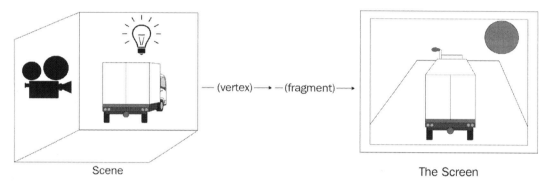

Figure 11.3 – Simplified rendering pipeline. Starting with the Scene as initial the input, sequentially executed shader programs convert the scene geometry into pixel locations, and then finally pixel locations into colors

Each step of the pipeline receives input from the previous steps' output. The logic specific to each step that we're interested in is handled and represented by an individual shader program. However, recall that in this context, an individual shader program is a piece of code that will be executed in a massively parallel fashion, with the data relevant to each part of the screen or scene making up the inputs and the processed equivalents of their outputs.

About Shaders

As mentioned earlier, a shader is a type of executable program that runs on the GPU. The shader program is provided a set of constants, or uniforms, that contain the input data that can be used by the shader. Shaders can also reference textures as input for sampling purposes – a powerful capability we'll exploit later in this chapter. Some examples of common uniforms are animation time multipliers, vector positions or colors, and other data useful in providing configuration data to the shader. The output of a given shader varies; for a vertex shader, the output is the given geometry's projection from world to screen space at the vertex level. A fragment shader's output is completely different – it is a pixel color value. Something more advanced is a **WebGPU Compute shader**, whose output can be arbitrary – later in this chapter, we will look at this more closely!

The shader program types we're going to be working with here fall into two categories: **Vertex** and **Fragment**. Although they're being introduced as separate things, they are usually contained and defined within the same shader code. Two main languages are used to write shader programs in use today: **Hardware Lighting and Shading Language (HLSL)** and **OpenGL Shader Language (GLSL)**. The first, **HLSL**, is used by the Microsoft DirectX graphics API. We're not going to spend any time on HLSL because **WebGL**, **WebGL2**, and **WebGPU** (with a caveat; see the following *Note*) all use the second language, **GLSL**. Since Babylon.js is built on a WebGL/2/GPU platform, GLSL is what we're going to focus on in our brief overviews.

> **Note**
>
> **WebGPU** uses a variant of GLSL called **wGLSL**, but because Babylon.js is so focused on maintaining backward compatibility, you have the choice to use wGLSL or continue writing shaders in regular GLSL – either way, you can still use WebGPU thanks to the way Babylon. js transpiles shader code. See `https://doc.babylonjs.com/advanced_topics/webGPU/webGPUWGSL` for more information on wGLSL and Babylon.js transpilation features.

Both HLSL and GLSL are syntactically related in flavor to the C/C++ family of programming languages, and though JavaScript is a much higher-level language, there should be enough familiar concepts for people familiar with it to gain a good starting position for learning GLSL. Coming from JavaScript, it's probably the most important to keep in mind that, unlike JS, GLSL is strongly typed and doesn't like trying to infer the types of variables and such on its own. There are other quirks to keep in mind, such as the need to add a . suffix to numbers when a floating-point variable is set to an integer value. This is a good segue to talk a little bit more about how shader programs are different from other software programs.

Shaders, as a class of software, have several distinctive features:

- They are stateless. Because a given graphics processor (of which a graphics card might have thousands or millions available) might be tasked with rendering Instagram pics one moment, it could just as easily be rendering an email or text document the next. Any data needed by the shader, whether it's a texture, a constant, or a uniform, must be either defined within the shader itself or passed into it at runtime.

- There is no access to shared state or thread data – each process stands alone, executing with no knowledge of its neighbors.

- Shader code is written to address the entire view or screen space, but the instructions that are given to each instance must be formulated in such a way that each instance gets the same directions yet produces the desired individual results.

Between the first two items causing the third is the genesis of the reputation for the fiendish difficulty that shaders have gotten. Like everything, writing shader code is something that requires practice. Eventually, with practice, it will become easier and easier to slip into the shader mindset and solve increasingly more complex and difficult problems; you'll soon be wondering what all the fuss was about! In the next section, you will learn about a few of the different ways to incorporate a custom shader into a project. Again, don't sweat the next section too much if this is outside of your comfort zone – let it soak through you. The concepts we're covering here will be useful later when we learn how to use the **Node Material Editor** (**NME**) to do all the heavy lifting of writing shader code while you focus on what you want to get done.

Writing and Using Shaders in Babylon.js

Being that shaders are defined using plain text, there are a lot of different ways to store and load shaders in a project. We'll review some of the ways to accomplish this after we learn a bit about how shader code is structured. The **Create Your Own Shader** (**CYOS**) tool is the shader equivalent of the Babylon.js Playground and is just one way to write shader code for Babylon.js. Navigating to the **CYOS** URL at `https://cyos.babylonjs.com` shows the shader code on the left pane and a live preview of the output on the right:

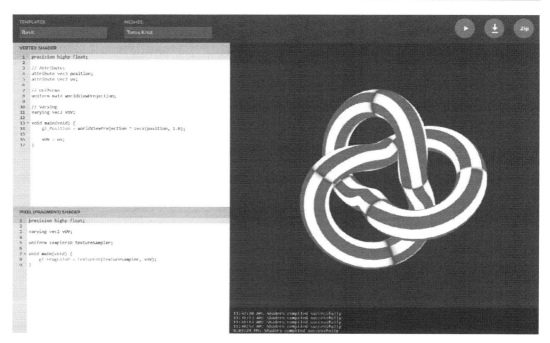

Figure 11.4 – The Babylon.js Create Your Own Shader tool functions similarly to the BJS Playground

In the preceding screenshot, you can see that the shader code is defined for vertex and fragment shaders in the left-hand pane, while a live preview shows on the right. Starter templates can be selected from the dropdowns, along with different meshes to use in the preview.

Just like the Playground, you can save your work to a snippet server, or you can download a ZIP file containing the shader code embedded into a template HTML file. Also, just like the PG, the Play button compiles and runs live the results of your shader programs. That's the overall mechanics and usage of the tool. Now, let's see how it fits into what we've been learning about the different types of shaders.

Fragment and Vertex Shaders

Let's remind ourselves of what the top section, the **Vertex shader**, and the bottom, the **Fragment shader**, do in this context. The **Vertex shader** is relevant only when there is mesh geometry involved, which means that Vertex shaders must be applied to a mesh. In other words, this is what we'd call a Material. Fragment shaders determine the color of a vertex fragment (for Meshes) or pixel (procedural textures, post-processes). They can stand alone, such as when they are used for a Post Process, or with Vertex shaders in a Material. Like our JavaScript code files, a shader program consists of a set of different types of declarations. Instead of a `constructor` function and the like, a shader program is required to have at least a definition for the `void main(void)` function because that is the function that is executed by the GPU. Outside of the main function, subroutines or helper functions are commonly used to help encapsulate and isolate code, just as you would do with any other well-written code that you may write. Inputs to the shader are specified at the top along with other declarations. Depending on the type of shader and how it is defined, there might be several different arbitrary declarations present, but two that are always provided are the `position` and `uv` attribute declarations. The former is a **Vector3**, while the latter is a **Vector2**; both represent data coming from the source mesh geometry:

- The local space `position` of the vertex is the coordinates relative to the mesh origin, not the world origin.

- The `uv` attribute is the texture coordinates. It is so-called to avoid confusion with the `xy` coordinates outside of the texture space.

Other declarations include the following:

- A uniform four-by-four Matrix called `worldViewProjection` that contains the transformations needed to convert the vertex position from local into World and then into View (screen, or 2D) space.

- A varying (reference type variable capable of being mutated or changed) vUV. This is one piece of (optional) data that's passed to the fragment shader. It's important for looking up pixel colors from a sampled texture.

The output of the Vertex shader is a Vector3, in the form of the `gl_Position` variable, and must be set in the shader before reaching the end of `main`. Its value is computed by applying the provided matrix transformation to the vertex position after any custom computations have been applied to the position value.

> **Important note**
>
> A lot of detail about these concepts isn't being covered here because otherwise, we wouldn't be able to cover everything about other topics. However, these basics should be enough to help you start being able to read and understand shader code, and that's the first step to attaining proficiency!

The bottom part of the CYOS screen's code panel is where the Fragment shader lives. Instead of receiving the vertex position of a mesh, the fragment shader receives a 2D screen position in the form of `varying vUV` and outputs a color to `gl_FragColor`. This color value represents the final color of the current pixel on the screen. When using textures with shaders, `textureSampler` references a loaded texture in the GPU memory, with the texture coordinates vUV used to look up the color value. These coordinates can be supplied by the mesh geometry (in the case of a material), view or screen coordinates (for post-processes or particles), by some computational process (as is the case for procedurally generated digital art), or with some combination of all three techniques. Change the dropdown selector labeled **Templates** to see more examples of how you can use shaders for fun and profit!

Compute Shaders (New to v5!)

The availability of programmable shaders exposes the power of the modern GPU to everyday desktop applications. With the latest **WebGL2** and **WebGPU** standards becoming more and more commonly implemented by major web browser vendors, that power is now available to web applications too. The biggest **WebGPU** feature when it comes to shaders is a new generation that's intended for general-purpose computation, called the **Compute shader**.

For specific documentation on how to write and use **WebGPU Compute shaders**, go to `https://doc.babylonjs.com/advanced_topics/shaders/computeShader`. Vertex and fragment shaders are purposefully limited in the extent and scope as to what they can accomplish, especially when those tasks don't directly involve Scene geometry. Compute shaders, on the other hand, are a way to run more arbitrary – though no less massively parallel – calculations and output. Let's look at a concrete example of the types of problems that Compute shaders are good at solving.

In this scenario, we want to simulate the effects of water erosion on terrain. Things such as an ocean tide besieging a sandcastle or long-term weathering of mountains are more accurate when the underlying calculations have finer resolution – more particles involved means that each particle can represent a smaller and smaller piece of the overall fluid volume. There are a few things that make this scenario quite nice for Compute shaders. When modeling fluids, approximations are used to simplify calculations. As mentioned previously, the number and size of the individual calculation units are directly tied to the overall accuracy and performance of the simulation. If the simulation were a mural, the speed it is painted and the resolution or detail depend on how many "painters" are assigned to handle painting the mural. What makes a Compute shader the ideal choice is that vertex and fragment shaders have more limitations on how many, what types, and which data can be updated, whereas Compute shaders are capable of writing output (similar to a texture) that isn't displayed directly onto the screen. They even make passing data back to the CPU from the GPU more practical, although it is still not a great idea if you can avoid it – passing any data in that direction will always be a slow operation. Additionally, the increased computing power makes more accurate but computationally intensive calculations available.

This may not seem like a big deal, but it is. Being able to persist and then reference output of and from a compute shader allows for a huge amount of utility – it's like Inspector Gadget and his signature catchphrase. Yell "Go Go Gadget Compute shader!" and anything can happen! The output from a compute shader can be used to drive a terrain height map, compute the values of a vector field, and much more.

> **Note**
>
> See `https://playground.babylonjs.com/?webgpu#C90R62#12` to learn how to use a Compute shader to simulate erosion with a height map and dynamic terrain. Note the addition of `webgpu` to the query string – running **WebGPU** samples requires a browser with **WebGPU** support. As of April 2022, only Chrome and Edge Canary builds support **WebGPU** features. See `https://github.com/gpuweb/gpuweb/wiki/Implementation-Status` to view the latest implementation support and status in Chromium-based browsers.

Compute shaders require **WebGPU** and carry with them a great deal of complexity, but some problems are worth that added complexity. Able to perform massive numbers of calculations in parallel, Compute shaders are different from vertex or fragment shaders because they can write to textures or other storage buffers to read and write values from that can then be used by other processes in the rendering pipeline. Still nascent in its eventual ascendancy to widespread adoption and replacement of **WebGL2**, and with support only beginning to appear in major web browsers, **WebGPU** and **Compute shaders** are technologies worth getting familiar with sooner rather than later.

Continuing the Shader Code Journey

It mentioned earlier, the topic of shaders is a vast and complex enough topic to warrant its own book rather than just a chapter. Fortunately, books such as those do exist, and one of the best is *The Book of Shaders*, by **Patricio Gonzalez Vivo** and **Jen Lowe**. Completely free and accessible at https:// thebookofshaders.com, *The Book of Shaders* describes itself as "a gentle step-by-step guide through the abstract and complex universe of Fragment shaders," and it's a case where the description closely matches reality. As it says, the book focuses on Fragment shaders only, but its wider value comes from the immersion and practices it provides for thinking in shader code. Filled with self-executing examples and exercises, it won't take long to start having fun and being productive with shaders!

Let's recap on the different types of shaders and what they are used for with this handy table:

	Vertex	**Fragment (Pixel)**	**Compute**
Purpose	Computes the screen position for a given mesh geometry portion	Calculates the final pixel or facet color	Performs arbitrary calculations
Output	gl_Position Vector3	gl_FragColor Color4 (RGBA)	• Storage Buffer • Texture (write-only) • Texture Buffer
Inputs	• Position • Texture UV • Uniforms • Texture • Color • Normal	• UV (optional) • Uniforms • Texture	• Uniforms • Texture (storage or otherwise) • Storage Buffer
Shader Language	GLSL	GLSL	WGLSL

With how easy WebGL2 makes it to expose shader logic and GPU features in the web browser, there are many tools and resources to explore in your journey of learning shaders. Maybe your experience is more on the design and art side of things, and the idea of writing code could be intimidating or otherwise off-putting in some way. Perhaps it's simply difficult to keep in mind both the goal of what you want to accomplish while holding the concepts of vertex and fragment shader syntax. Or it could be that you're unsure of how to write a particular shader effect and need to experiment and explore to discover how to proceed. All these reasons, plus many more not listed, are good reasons to take a good long look at one of the flagship features of Babylon.js: the **Node Material Editor** (**NME**). This is what we are going to do in the next section.

Shader Programming with the Node Material Editor

As something that has been referred to numerous times throughout this book, the NME may have taken on an almost mythic status as a productivity tool. Its plug-and-play, drag-and-drop nature allows just about anyone to assemble shaders using visual blocks. It democratizes the GPU in the seamless way it integrates with the Inspector. Its simple deployment in tandem with the Playground provides a short runway from fancy to flight. The NME may just be about the best thing to happen since sliced bread met butter.

All these statements are true, except the part about the NME being better than sliced bread and butter – that one isn't. It's better than sliced bread and butter, falling just short of being better than sliced bread alone. It's a thin leavened line, but it's one worth baking. Hyperbole aside, the NME is truly one of the most powerful, if not the most powerful, tools in the Babylon.js toolbox.

In this section, we're going to learn how to get the most out of the NME. By the end, you'll find it easy to "think in nodes"! First, we'll explore how to create and apply a **NodeMaterial** to a mesh. Next, we'll explore using the NME to create procedural textures. Finally, we'll wrap things up with a quick look at how to use NME to create a Post Process.

Using the NME to Build the Planet Earth Material

Sometimes, when learning something new, it can be helpful to have a concrete example to work toward, with the example being the end goal to reach. Other times, it can be more illuminating to begin not with the example of a finished product, but with an atomic subset of that final goal. The goal we're going to start with – our first atomic subset – will be simple: create a new NodeMaterial that renders a texture onto a sphere mesh. Easy, right?

> **Note**
> Unlike most rhetorical questions framed similarly, the answer to the preceding question is an unambiguous, full-throated "YES!". If it isn't already apparent that Babylon.js places an incredibly high emphasis on ease of use, it would be helpful to go back and re-read (or simply read for the first time) the previous chapters of this book. It's OK, no one's judging you for skimming or skipping! Well, OK. Maybe a little bit. But not much.

As we work through this chapter, we're going to start by covering a lot more details on the mechanics of how to accomplish various tasks with the NME, but as we make progress through the following sections, we'll have to start zooming out from those mechanical details to make sure we leave enough space and time for bigger-picture topics. As always, the Babylon.js docs are a great place to learn more about the topics we're covering, with great material on the NME that includes combination Playground and NME examples for a wide variety of tasks. The BJS forums are a great place to view examples from the community, as well as to solicit feedback and ask questions. There's even a thread dedicated to NME examples at `https://forum.babylonjs.com/t/node-materials-examples`! Let's get started.

NME Overview

Navigate to `https://nme.babylonjs.com`; the default material mode "blank slate" is the initial node graph to be loaded. Broken down into four functional areas with a fifth preview pane, the first pane – the left-hand side vertical column – hosts a searchable list of different nodes that can be placed into the center pane of the work canvas:

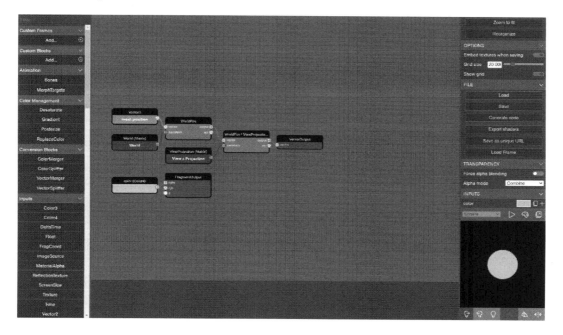

Figure 11.5 – The default Node Material Editor view

In the preceding screenshot, the left-hand pane contains the list of nodes. The center pane work canvas is where nodes and their connections are displayed, while the right-hand pane shows contextual properties for the selected item. Note the render preview pane.

The right-hand pane displays a contextual list of properties that can be modified, or if nothing is selected, the snippet properties and options. Tucked into the bottom (scroll down if it's not visible initially) of the **Property** pane is the **Preview** panel. Pop that out into its own window right away – being able to immediately see the effects of making a change is one of the keys to success in this type of development. The bottom well or gutter, depending on how you want to term it, contains console output from the shader compilation process of the node graph – if the bottom line is red, then your nodes aren't compiling!

> **Important note**
>
> Sometimes, it can be tough to tell if a particular change is extremely subtle or whether it has no effect at all. Always make sure to check that your most recent console output isn't colored red or contains an error; otherwise, you may mistake a broken node with an ineffectual change!

Background Context

Nodes are connected by lines between specific connector ports on the two involved nodes. Any given node represents a particular operation that can be performed on a series of inputs and outputs, connected by dragging lines from the former to the latter. The graph of nodes and their connection follows two simple rules that result in strikingly complex behaviors.

First, nodes always accept input on the left-hand side connectors and output values on their right. What happens inside the node between the input and output is nobody's business but the nodes'. An interesting implication of this is that uniforms, attributes, constants, or other externally provided data do not have input connectors. Rather, values are set via code, the Inspector, or at design time in the property pane. Conversely, a few nodes only contain inputs and have no output connector. These are the endpoints for the node's shader code generation; in other words, they represent the return value of the applicable shader, such as a color for the fragment shader and a position vector for the vertex. Since they are the final result of the shader calculations, they must always be the last item in the node graph.

The second rule for node graphs, and following from the first, is that only nodes connected to an output node are included in the generated shader code. Remember, the final goal is to generate a vector for the vertex shader and a color for the fragment. This means that a properly formed node graph executes a sequential path from start to finish (usually left to right), but which is defined by that path traced from end to start (the opposite, or right to left).

This mismatch in mental models (try saying that five times fast!) can sometimes make it difficult to visualize the steps needed to get to a particular goal line. That's why it's important to make things easy to change or add to without having to make unrelated changes to the application that are needed just to be able to make a change. In our case, we're going to structure our work so that we can incrementally build an ultra-high detail and quality Planet Earth material.

Back to the NME window, drag out the **fragment** and **vertex** output nodes out to the right to make room for the new nodes we're going to add. Make sure that the render preview is set to **Sphere**, and while you're at it, pop the preview out into a separate window if you haven't done that yet. Now, we're ready to accomplish our first micro-goal of learning how to add and use textures.

Adding a Texture to the Material

In the default configuration for the Node Material Editor's Material mode, the inputs for the vertex shader are mesh.position, World Matrix, and View Projection Matrix. A series of **TransformBlock** nodes connect the inputs to form the final vertex position. Click in the search pane of the left-hand node list and start typing the word texture to filter the list down to display the **Texture** node of the **Inputs** group, then drag it out onto the surface somewhere. You'll see the Texture node appear, but if it isn't already present on the canvas, an additional **Vector2** mesh.uv node hooked up to the uv connector of the Texture block will be created. In general, this is a consistent pattern – if the required inputs for a node block aren't present, they will be added automatically:

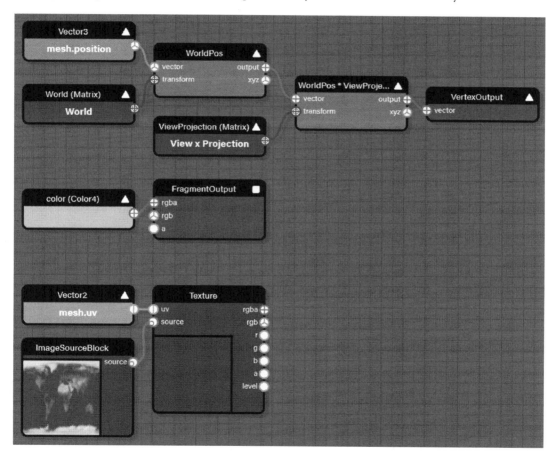

Figure 11.6 – Dragging the Texture node onto the surface also adds the mesh.uv value.
This is used to select the portion of the texture corresponding to the mesh vertex

The preceding screenshot shows the setup, but it also shows our next step: dragging out the source input port on **the Texture block** to create a new **ImageSource** node. An **ImageSource** is an important piece of indirection that allows a node material to separate the process of loading a texture from the data contained in it. Advanced usage scenarios can involve using a **Render Target Texture (RTT)** to obtain a rendered texture of a mesh before performing additional processing. Click the Image Source node. Then, in the **Link property** textbox, upload from your local repository or provide this URL: `https://raw.githubusercontent.com/jelster/space-truckers/develop/assets/textures/2k_earth_daymap.jpg` (it's up to you!). The image should load into the **Texture** block, as depicted in the previous screenshot. It's a good practice to tidy as we go along, so rename the node by selecting the node if it isn't already and changing the **Name** property to `baseTexture`. Half of our initial objective has now been achieved by bringing in the texture. Now, we need to paint it onto the preview mesh.

Accomplishing this is incredibly easy, but it's valuable to remember the underlying mechanisms involved since they will be important soon. Recall that the vertex shader is passed the mesh position and a UV texture coordinate corresponding to that vertex location, which passes the UV coordinates into the fragment shader. Now, we need to sample the texture to set the fragment shader's final color, and we do that by dragging the `rgb` output of the **baseTexture** node to the `rgb` input of the **FragmentOutput** node. Look at the Render Preview; a familiar-looking globe should be visible:

Figure 11.7 – The Render preview of the Planet Earth material after adding baseTexture and sampling it for FragmentOutput

You can check your work-in-progress against the snippet at #YPNDB5. If your preview doesn't match the preceding screenshot perfectly, it's OK – it's just a preview at this point and the important thing is that you can see the texture on the sphere. Our first mission is accomplished! What's next? It's time to start adding nodes to our graph that will use additional textures to add further detail to our Planet Earth material.

Mixing Clouds

Start by adding another Texture node and ImageSource to the canvas. Name them `cloudTexture` and `cloudTextureSource` and upload or link to the file at `https://raw.githubusercontent.com/jelster/space-truckers/develop/assets/textures/2k_earth_clouds.jpg` to load the cloud texture into the design surface. The simplest way to get the clouds overlaid on top of the base texture is to add the colors from each texture, so drag an **Add** block out onto the surface and name it `Mix Cloud and Base Textures`. This highlights an important property of nodes that may catch those who aren't familiar with this type of editing surface off guard – type matching.

When the node is initially added to the canvas, both the input and output ports are a solid red color, indicating that the type of input and output has yet to be designated. In this case, the possible types could include a Vector of 2, 3, or even 4 elements (or a color comprised of the same number), a single scalar number, or even a matrix. Which type the block turns into depends on the first connection made to the node. Connect the `rgb` ports of the two textures to the separate inputs of the node and replace the fragment shader's output with the output from the Mix Cloud and Base Textures node to finish the operation. The clouds are visible on the render preview, but they're a bit faint and hard to see.

This can easily be fixed by applying a scaling factor to the cloud color before it is mixed with the base texture color. This mixing of colors is a very common operation, especially more so when we move on to the next section, *Procedural Textures and the NME*. Add a Float input block and name it `cloudBrightness`. Give it an initial value of `1.25` or so and then use it as the input factor to a new Scale node that you'll also add to the canvas. Name that node `Scale Cloud Levels` and connect the other input to the output of the `cloudTexture` node. The output of the `Scale Cloud Levels` node replaces the input to the `Mix Cloud and Base Textures` node:

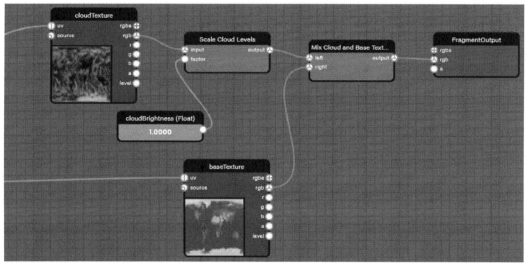

Figure 11.8 – (a) After adding the cloud texture and a scale factor to the base texture color, clouds can be seen floating over a serene Planet Earth. (b) The node material graph for mixing and scaling the cloud texture with base Earth texture. The cloudBrightness value can be set to a value that matches the desired look and feel of the clouds

The result should look like the first screenshot. If it doesn't, compare your node graph to the second screenshot or to the snippet at #YPNDB5#1 to see what might be different between them. Once you're happy with the output, it would be a good idea to save the snippet as a unique URL.

> **Note**
>
> While working on something with the NME, it's quickest to save snippets as URLs until you are ready to download the definition file and use it in your project.

Our **Planet Earth Material** is looking pretty good now, but what is cooler than a boring old static texture? An animated texture! Let's animate the clouds to give our material some life.

Framing Animations

When we think about animations, it's easy to forget that there are many different methods of animating things in a scene. One of the simplest, most straightforward means is to manipulate the texture coordinates (the uv value) over time. Furthermore, by changing just the u (or *X*-axis) value, the texture will be shifted in an East-to-West or West-to-East fashion, similar to how it might look for a geostationary satellite!

Search for and add a **Time** node to the canvas. This represents a built-in shader input that provides the amount of time since the scene was started, in **milliseconds** (**ms**). We can use this value to drive our animation, and by multiplying it with a scaling factor float input of `timeScaleFactor` in the `scaleSceneTime` node, we can control the precise speed of the animation at design and runtime.

> **Important note**
>
> Why are we using Time instead of Delta Time? Remember, shaders have no memory of past events. They only deal with the data passed in, and the data passed in doesn't persist between frames. Therefore, instead of storing the delta time and adding it to the u coordinate, we use total scene time and scale.

It's important to keep a node graph readable, as much for your future self as for others reading it. One great way to do that is to organize nodes into collapsible Frames. Arrange the three Time, scale, and Multiply nodes close to each other, then hold down the *Shift* key while clicking and dragging a box around the three nodes to create a Frame:

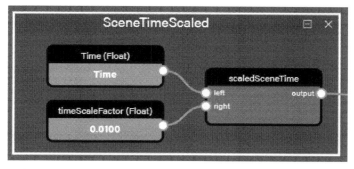

Figure 11.9 – The SceneTimeScaled frame encapsulates the logic for exposing an animation frame counter to the rest of a node graph. This is the expanded form of the frame

Frames are an easy and fast way to make a complex node graph more manageable, much as a function helps to separate and isolate pieces of code from each other. The `SceneTimeScaled` frame (or any frame) can even be reused across different Node Materials by downloading its JSON definition, then using the **Add…** functionality in the left-hand node list. Now, it's time to make some movement by hooking up the output from the frame to the `cloudTexture` U coordinate.

Unlike when we mixed the cloud texture with the base texture where everything involved is of the same type, we need to be able to change a single element of a Vector2 value. First, we'll need to split the source vector into its components before adding the `scaledSceneTime` value to the x component. Then, we'll recombine the Vector and hook it into the `cloudTexture` UV input:

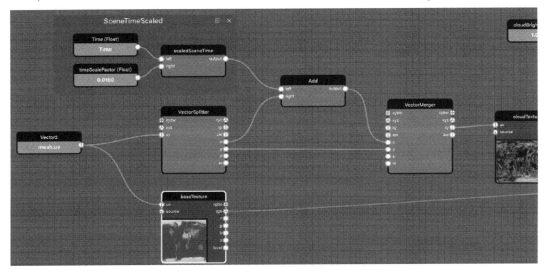

Figure 11.10 – Connecting the SceneTimeScaled frame with the u (x) texture
coordinate using the Vector merger and Vector Splitter nodes

When this is connected, pull up the render preview and marvel at the slowly moving banks of clouds over serene blue oceans. If you don't see the expected results, check the output well to make sure the last (current) line isn't an error or in red. If needed, compare your NME graph with the one at T7BG68#2 to see what you're doing differently.

There's much more to the NME material mode than what we've accomplished in just a few short paragraphs. In that short span of text, we were able to create a nice render effect of an animated Planet Earth globe using the NME in **Material Mode** and with high-resolution textures provided by the kind folks at NASA. Dragging nodes out onto the canvas is fast becoming a familiar activity as we learned how to mix textures into a final Fragment Color, and even animate the cloud cover. Using built-in **Time** counters and **Vector Splitter** and **Merger** nodes will become second nature to us with practice and experience. There's more to be covered than just how to map a texture onto a mesh with the NME, though. In the next section, we'll take away the **Vertex shader** and focus on the **Fragment shader** as we finally learn how our Radar Procedural Texture is built (see *Chapter 9, Calculating and Displaying Scoring Results*, for more information on how this fits into the game).

Procedural Textures and the NME

In most specialized fields of study, a particularly hard foundational subject for the field at hand is often given to students early on in their journeys to weed or wash out students from the program. It sounds harsh, but exposing pupils early on to the realities of their chosen field can be a valuable way to save time and effort on both the students' and teacher's behalf. This part of the chapter is *not* intended to have that effect because presumably, you're here by choice and by interest, and this isn't a gatekeeping exercise, it's an inclusive one. The **Procedural Texture** mode of the NME will still contain the vertex shader output – and it is still required to be present on the canvas – but our attention will be focused on the Fragment shader, because what else is better equipped to process a bunch of arbitrary pixels all at the same time than the **Fragment shader**? Nothing! In the case of procedural textures, the Fragment shader outputs to a texture buffer instead of the screen buffer – which is what a post-process uses. That texture, as we've seen with the Radar texture, can then be applied to various material texture slots in the scene for rendering.

It is in that regard and spirit that the node graph for the Radar Texture should be accepted – not as a scarecrow to frighten off those who might be less confident but to bolster and support those people. That's why we'll start with the simplest depiction of this node graph that still conveys the essentials. The reason for this is that while there are a decent number of moving parts involved in making this texture, each is fairly easy to understand once broken down. Follow along with the text by loading up snippet XB8WRJ#13 in the NME. Refer to the following diagram for notes on each specific component of the texture:

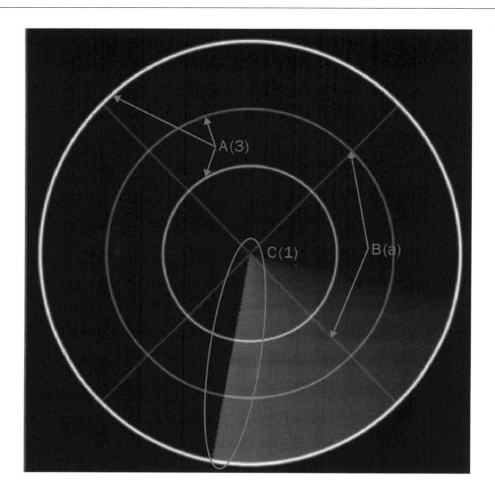

Figure 11.11 – The components of the Radar procedural texture

In the preceding diagram, the three circles (A), the two crossed lines (B), and the sweeping line (C) can each be examined independently of each other. Three concentric circles bind the texture, each a slightly different shade of light blue. Meeting at the center, each perpendicular to the other and oriented at 45 degrees concerning the upward direction are the crosses, in a darker blue-gray tone. Rounding out the static parts of the texture is the sweeping line, a turquoise-ish colored animated pizza slice with an opacity gradient. In the following screenshot, the node graph is shown fully collapsed down to its largest constituent components. Each element from *Figure 11.12* has its own frame in the following screenshot:

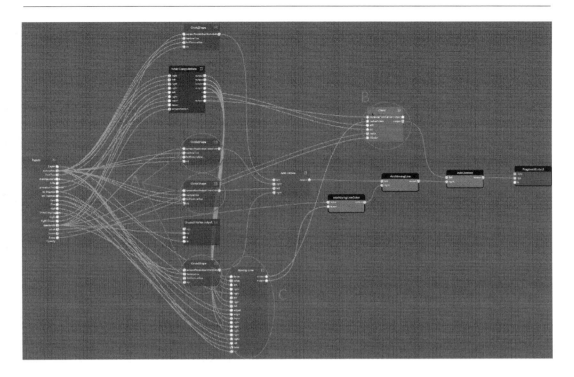

Figure 11.12 – A node graph of the radar procedural texture

After grouping the major elements of the radar procedural texture, the node graph is still complex, but much easier to understand. Organizing and naming elements in the NME is important! For reference, the NME snippet can be found at #XB8WRJ#13.

To examine the specifics of any individual piece of the shader graph, expand the frame to see the steps comprising that portion of the fragment shader logic. The output of each frame varies a bit. Each **CircleShape** frame outputs a color value in the **Add Circles** frame, which, as its name implies, adds the color values together. A key element of procedural shape generation is that pixels that aren't a part of the shape will be assigned a clear or empty color value. That's why, if you peek inside the **CircleShape**, **Cross**, or **Moving Line** frames, you'll find conditional nodes and other node operations that result in the output being set to a value between zero and one [0...1]. A value of 0 means the pixel isn't a part of the shape at all. Any other value is indicative of the relative brightness of whatever the pixel's final color ends up being.

The final color value is arrived at by individually scaling each element's defined color (various shades of blue or white) by that brightness factor, then adding it together with the color output of all the other elements. Like magic, shapes emerge from a blank canvas! Regarding magic, one of the essential references mentioned at the beginning of this chapter was *The Book of Shaders*. The radar procedural texture was adapted from a **ShaderToy** example listed as part of its chapter on Shapes, located at `https://thebookofshaders.com/07/`. Even though there isn't a node graph to be found on the site, every code snippet is interactive. Anyone interested in procedural textures or similar topics should make the time and effort to read through this concise, gentle, and amazingly well-put-together resource as part of continuing their journey in this area.

Very similar to Procedural Textures, the Post-Process mode of the NME works against the Fragment Shader. Let's take a quick stroll through the landscape of Post-Processes in the NME.

Developing Post-Processes with the NME

Unlike the Procedural Texture mode, the **Post-Process** editor has a special `Current Screen` node. This node is an input texture that's passed to the fragment shader. It contains a screenshot preview of the frame as it would be rendered without any post-processing. You can set any texture for this; its purpose is just to provide visual feedback on the post-process output.

One of the simplest Post-Processes that can be constructed with the NME is the never-out-of-style fade in/fade out mechanic:

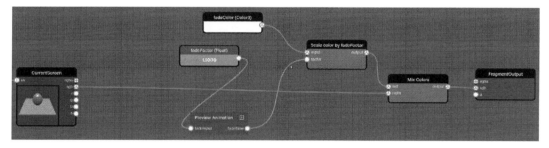

Figure 11.13 – Simple fade in/out post-process in the MNE

The Preview Animation frame is there to provide an animated view of what the post-process looks like in action. The `fadeFactor` uniform controls the degree of the effect. The snippet is hosted at Z4UNYG#2.

In the logic depicted in the preceding screenshot, the `fadeColor` node is scaled by a `fadeFactor`. To help visualize the effect, the `Preview Animation` frame passes the **Time** value through the **Sin** function to show the effect ping-pong between `fadeFactors` ranging from 0 (completely black) to 1 (normal) and up to 10 (completely white).

> **Important note**
>
> Because our scale starts at zero, assigning a value of 10 to `fadeFactor` is the same as cranking things up to 11, because that's how far Babylon.js goes. You've been warned!

We started this section by learning about the basics of the NME and using our newly learned techniques to build a high-resolution **Planet Earth Material**, complete with animated cloud coverage. Because we took our time to go over the basics, we were able to pick up some steam heading into the topic of **Procedural Textures**. We learned that they are built very similarly to **Materials**, except the work is all done in the fragment shader. Like the Procedural Texture, **Post-Processes** do not operate against Scene geometry. A post-process is identical in function to a procedural texture because the **Current Screen** node is the rendered texture buffer for each pixel of the screen.

Summary

If it feels like we've been skirting a deep examination of this and the other topics we've covered so far in this chapter, then either you have a good sense of intuition or you read the title of this chapter. As this chapter's title suggests, we're only scratching the surface of a topic not only wide but deep in its complexity. That doesn't mean that we haven't covered a lot of material – quite the opposite! We started this chapter by learning a bit about some of the shader concepts and the differences between Vertex, Fragment, and Compute shaders. Each type of shader is a specialized software program that runs on the GPU once for every piece of geometry (vertex) and every pixel (fragment) on the screen.

None of the shader instances has any memory about things that happened in the previous frame and don't know what any of their neighbors are doing. This makes shader programs a little bit mind-bending to work with initially. Fortunately, the language shader code used in Babylon.js is written in **GLSL**, which you should be familiar with if you are used to working with Python or JavaScript.

Compute shaders are new to Babylon.js v5.0 and are a powerful new addition to the **WebGPU** toolbox. Compute shaders are a more generalized form of a shader and unlike the vertex or fragment shader, they are capable of writing output to more than just a texture target or a mesh position. Therefore, they can perform parallel calculations of complicated systems such as fluid dynamics, weather, climate simulations, and many more things waiting to be invented.

Once we had a solid foundational understanding of shaders, we applied that knowledge to writing shader programs using the NME. The NME has several modes of operation, and we started again with the basics with the Material mode and the Planet Earth Material. After quickly learning how to add and mix textures, we topped the cake off with some icing by adding an animated effect to the cloud texture, learning about Frames as we went.

This knowledge of Frames came in handy when we tried to understand the much more complex Radar Procedural Texture. Ignoring the vertex output, the procedural texture and post-process modes operate against the fragment output. This similarity made it an easy transition to the Post-Process editor. Always classy and simple to implement, a basic fade in/fade out effect is quick to assimilate into our growing understanding of this important topic.

Like an iceberg's tip peeking out of the water, there's so much more to shaders and the NME than what's visible from the surface. If this chapter were to do the topic its full justice, it would undoubtedly require another couple hundred pages! Be sure to check the next section, *Extended Topics*, for suggestions on where to go next and what to do.

We've come incredibly far along in our journey across the vastness of Babylon.js, but there's still more ground to be covered. In the next chapter, we're going to start moving from the express lanes over to the exit lane, but there are still a few more landmarks to make before we reach our destination terminal. In real-world terms, we're going to shift our focus back to the overall application and learn about how to make Space-Truckers run offline and record high scores before publishing it to a major app store. If that sounds like a refreshing change of scenery, then read on! Otherwise, if you're looking for some side-quests to keep things going in the Land of Shaders, the *Extended Topics* section might have some interesting challenges you can undertake. See you in the next chapter!

Extended Topics

Here are some ideas on ways to further your journey with the NME in particular, but also some resources on shaders in general:

- Use the techniques we learned about in this chapter to create procedural clouds for the Planet Earth Material. One way to approach this would be to start with the existing cloud texture and distort it using some type of Noise node.

- The Book of Shaders (`https://thebookofshaders.com/`) is a free online resource that, while still an evolving work-in-progress, can be, as the authors describe it, "a gentle step-by-step guide through the abstract and complex universe of Fragment shaders." Even though it focuses entirely on Fragment shaders, it is nonetheless a spring-powered steppingstone toward improving your understanding of shaders. Each chapter introduces examples and exercises along with the necessary material – try reproducing examples from this book in the NME. Post your results on the BJS forums and see what others have done at `https://forum.babylonjs.com/c/demos/9`.

- It can be tough to understand what's going on in the GPU, especially since there's no easy way to attach a debugger and step through code like many might be used to doing with regular code. SpectorJS is a browser extension that can give insights into what is happening on the GPU. You can learn more at `https://spector.babylonjs.com/`.

- The TrailMesh that extrudes along the route taken by the simulated cargo passes through different encounter zones on its journey. Create a Node Material or Texture that takes in encounter zone information and uses it to render the trail mesh in a unique pattern for every zone.

- Related to the preceding bullet point, create an effect that is triggered whenever an encounter is rolled during route planning. The effect should be positioned at the location of the encounter and can be different according to the type of encounter (although it needn't be). For gameplay purposes, it probably shouldn't reveal too much information to the player, but it can certainly tease!

- The Babylon.js Docs contain numerous topics and resources about the NME. They also contain links to various YouTube videos that provide tutorials on different aspects of using the NME:

    - Creating and using Node Materials in code. If you are writing a paper or a book about programming and want to sound smart, "Imperatively Reflecting JavaScript into GLSL" is a good title: `https://doc.babylonjs.com/divingDeeper/materials/node_material/nodeMaterial`.

    - A list of related videos can be found at the bottom of the preceding link. Video topics include PBR Nodes, Procedural Projection Textures, Procedural Node Materials, Anisotropy, and more!

12
Measuring and Optimizing Performance

In software engineering circles, it's common to hear the expression "premature optimization is the root of all evil." This is usually bestowed very knowingly from a more Senior developer to a more Junior one. Stroking of the chin – whether a beard is present or not – is almost always required to attain the Solemn Air of Pronouncement accompanying such declarations. Strange delivery or not, it is good advice to follow.

There aren't many worse ways to approach software design than by starting to make performance-related changes while that software is still largely being built. That, in turn, is because the optimization of a code base is inversely related to the code's readability, its maintainability, and ultimately the facility to which new features and changes can be introduced. To put it another way, the more optimized a code base tends to be, the harder it is for someone to understand the code and subsequently make changes to that code.

At this point in our journey, we have established a full end-to-end application experience. Though there may still be some rough edges, all the major features have been implemented in the application, making this an ideal time to examine our application's performance. At the same time, though, we don't have much insight into how *Space-Truckers* performs at really any other level than the bare basics. Our first task is clear: we must capture a baseline performance profile, or rather one profile each for both the Route Planning and Driving phases.

The Babylon.js **Real-time performance viewer** can record real-time performance statistics across a wide range of metrics relevant to a Babylon.js Scene. With these tools in hand, we'll be able to identify "hotspots" in the Space-Truckers code base that we can then target for selective performance enhancements, but that doesn't tell us anything about how we can improve the performance or what to look for in our tooling. Not yet at least!

Something we haven't discussed so far has been how the very breadth and reach of a web application also means a greater number of different potential hardware and software configurations that must then be supported by you, the developer. How do we avoid having to go down the rabbit hole of testing, verifying, and fixing functionality for every combination of device, software, and display? By knowing what areas or scenarios in a Scene put the most stress on which part of the system, we can defer the optimization from design time to runtime and handle it in real time. The Babylon.js **Scene Optimizer** is the ideal solution to dynamically balance performance and render quality with its ability to turn on and off different performance optimizations based on the difference between a target and the current frame rates, or **frames per second** (**FPS**).

Aside from the runtime **Scene Optimizer**, there are other things we can do to improve an application's performance in Babylon.js. We'll continue to use and re-measure the impact of any changes we make, first individually, then all together, because how can you know if any improvement has been made if you don't have something for comparison? The rhetorical answer is that you can't – not unless you are consistent in your measurement procedure and capturing measurements, but as the fastidious and methodical creator of Software That Does Magic™, you've already got that part down!

> **Important note**
>
> Levity aside, something that will help enforce and facilitate this kind of development work greatly is to leverage the mighty power of Git. Any time you save a change to a source code file, consider at least staging that change, if not committing it. Revert commits that don't work instead of plowing ahead. In other words, by working with, not against, Source Control, you might be amazed at how fast you can get things done!

Our last port of call for this, the penultimate stage of our Babylon.js long-haul, will be looking at the network performance of our app. Specifically, we'll see how our asset and data resources affect both loading time and bandwidth usage. Today's web browsers almost all support both robust caching functionality, as well as local storage mechanisms such as **IndexedDb**, which is a mini SQL server made available by the browser to scripts running inside it. Why is this relevant?

> **Note**
>
> In case you missed it, rhetorical questions are back in style!

The relevance of **IndexedDB** is that we can use it to stuff all our assets – textures, sounds, JSON, and more. Instead of having to download everything from the server, we store resources locally on the browser. It's a great place to cache assets. This positions us well for the next chapter's look at making Space-Truckers into an installable publishable **Progressive Web Application** (**PWA**). But first things first, let's go over the topics covered in this chapter and some technical requirements and recommendations.

The following topics will be covered in this chapter:

- Knowing What To Measure

- Measuring Performance and Identifying Bottlenecks

- Improving Runtime Performance with the Scene Optimizer

Technical Requirements

Most of the requirements in this chapter are the same as they have been for the previous chapters, but some new tools can be incredibly useful for performance measurement and improvement. Here are the tools that are new and/or specific to this chapter:

- This is not a requirement, but it is very helpful to have multiple displays available while working on performance captures. Accurate and consistent measurements can be tough enough – don't add more variables into the mix if you can help it!

- The Scene Optimizer: `https://doc.babylonjs.com/divingDeeper/scene/sceneOptimizer`

- Optimizing with Octrees: `https://doc.babylonjs.com/divingDeeper/scene/optimizeOctrees`

- BVH article/information link

Knowing What To Measure

Quantum Mechanics has a concept called the **Uncertainty Principle**. Named after physicist Werner Heisenberg, the principle can be summarized for our purposes as the act of measuring some quantity itself affecting the observed value of that quantity. Although merely an analogy for us currently bound to non-quantum systems, it serves as a useful warning as we take our measures and metrics: don't let the instrumentation impact the measurements that are being taken for our app's performance.

Starting with some general guidelines, we'll look at some key factors that need to be attended to and accounted for to gather meaningful test data. Using those guidelines to establish a basic context, we'll start learning some key terminology that will allow us to get into more specifics in future sections of this chapter.

General Guidelines

As we review and examine the various means and procedures for taking our performance profile, we'll go over the tooling-specific steps as they come up. But first, let's look at a few guidelines that generally apply.

Keep External Factors To a Minimum

Computers are quite good at sharing slices of computing time between processes, but we're better off closing all our other browser windows and shutting down any other non-essential programs that may compete with ours for resources. No, it's not as "real world" as might be expected, but the goal here is to gather clean, consistent data, and that doesn't have to stick to the "real world" rules. Rebel.

Choose a Target Resolution and Stick To It

This is a bit trickier than it might seem. Simply going with the highest resolution possible and putting on the highest pixel-dense display is certainly a good way to stress-test a graphical application, but it won't yield a very useful performance profile. Too low of a resolution and the GPU won't break a sweat, also not yielding a very useful profile. Going for a Veruca Salt-meets-goldilocks approach, select a value somewhere in the upper-middle range that avoids "redlining" either CPU or GPU but still makes those components work for their electrons!

Compare Apples to Apples

Always make sure your comparisons are equivalent, all other things considered. Follow the same testing procedure – resist the urge to "improve" or take shortcuts – and collect data in the same fashion between test runs. If methodologies differ, then there's a good possibility that your results won't tell you what you think they say.

Change Only One Thing Between Measurements

One of the less helpful things you might do to yourself is put off re-measuring after making one set of changes. For example, say you refactor one method, then make another set of changes somewhere else in the application. Repeat this a few times, and you've now lost the ability to definitively say whether your change has improved anything – regardless of whether the app performs better or worse! This is also a poor situation to be in because you're also restrained in the changes you can safely make in the future without risking regression in the code you're trying to change. Avoid getting into this in the first place by committing each cohesive set of changes together, and by re-measuring after each major change to validate your assumptions about how the code behaves.

The preceding guidelines aren't rules set in stone – they're pieces of advice aimed at helping you proactively avoid arriving at false conclusions and the resulting consequences. This is surely helpful, but not directly so. To help connect this advice to a useful context, we'll first look at what sorts of metrics are important. Then, we'll look at the tools that collect this data. Finally, we'll apply what we've learned to find and fix performance bottlenecks and resource pressures that lurk in the Space-Truckers code base.

Performance-Related Terminology

"I Wanna Go Fast!"

Yes, Ricky Bobby, so do we all. When referring to cars or racing, the meaning of the phrase is clear, but what does "[going] Fast!" mean for a 3D application? Sure, it cannot be a good thing for a laptop to suddenly take off in a cloud of burning plastic at 200 kph! At least, not a laptop without wheels. Brakes too – those are also important.

The equivalent measure for 3D applications and games is, of course, the Frame Rate, or **Frames Per Second (FPS)**.

> **Note**
>
> Positioned unfortunately close in proximity to a **First-Person Shooter (FPS)**, noting that the two are not directly related is yet another reminder that context is important.

Similar to how a speed limit posted on a highway serves to limit (in theory, at least) the top speed of drivers on the road, the number of frames that can be rendered every second is limited at the end by an intrinsic maximum that matches the refresh rate of the display device or monitor doing the rendering. In the Old Days, this was limited by the speed at which the electron gun of a **Cathode Ray Tube (CRT)** display could traverse the width and height of the screen. Barbarian times, they were. In today's era of more Enlightened Display Technologies, **Light Emitting Diode (LED)** displays can switch on or off with incredible speed. Here are some typical FPS values and examples that you may recognize from the real world:

FPS	Frame Budget (ms)	Common Examples
3	333	Long-duration CCTV cameras, interplanetary probes. YouTube when everyone tries to stream at the same time.
14	71	Early "Silent Era" films (ca. 1900's – 1930).
24	41	Standard cinematic rate (ca. 1940 – present)
30	33	Standard Definition TV (ca. 1950 – 2000), interlaced HDTV.
60	16	HDTV (1080p), max rate of many monitors and TVs. The minimum rate for smooth VR (single eye).
120	8	4K TV and displays, high-end monitors. The minimum rate needed for smooth VR (both eyes).

FPS is a convenient metric because it is almost completely unambiguous – higher values are almost always better. The only real exception to this is in scenarios where power consumption is a higher priority than maintaining a high frame rate. Because that deals with actions taken at runtime, we're going to look at how to approach a scenario like that later in this chapter in the *Improving Runtime Performance with the Scene Optimizer* section. The ugly downside of a higher FPS is that there's less time to get all the needed inter-frame processing that goes on, whether inside the GPU or in the CPU.

This **Frame Budget**, depicted in the second-to-left-most column in the previous table, dictates what can happen during the inter-frame time. Go over the budget and the frame rate drops. Go too much under budget and time is being wasted that could be rendering additional frames or running other processing tasks. Performance management can be approached by either reducing the CPU Frame Time or by reducing the GPU Frame Time. Sometimes, there's crossover between the two – a good example of this is the Thin Instances used for the Route Planning phases' asteroid belt (see the *A Detour into Particle Systems* section of *Chapter 7, Processing Route Data*, for more).

Every frame, the asteroid's rotation and position matrices are updated by code running on the CPU, which is then copied over into the GPU. These matrixes are then passed into the vertex and fragment shaders, which apply them during a single Draw call to every instance in the Scene. While this is an extremely fast process, there is one potential bottleneck on the CPU, and that's the loop over each Thin Instance that recalculates the two matrices. Any improvements there would theoretically improve either the performance or the maximum number of asteroids that can be rendered without severe performance degradation.

Shifting over to the GPU, bottlenecks can occur when the device is tasked with too many (or fewer, slower) shader programs competing for the same limited frame budget. The raw number of shader executions is expressed as the number of **Draw** calls made in each second and serves as a complement to the GPU intra-frame time spent executing shaders. As each Draw call is associated with a single material (some materials will make multiple calls to Draw), the number of different materials in a Scene is directly related to the number of times the GPU is being asked to switch contexts to run that material's shader programs every second.

Switching the GPU between contexts (shaders) has been brutally optimized in hardware, but it isn't completely free. Each shift carries a small amount of overhead, and though trivial individually, this can add up to substantial losses with large numbers. Thus, reducing the number of draw calls can improve performance directly from the reduced context switches and indirectly through the shader code that is no longer being invoked.

> **Important note**
> The fastest code is code that doesn't exist. Think about that.

There are a few other metrics that are worth defining but are most obvious from their name or context. One exception, though, is Absolute FPS. Absolute FPS is the number of frames that can be processed each second, not counting any actual render timings. This is a measure of how well the CPU side of things is performing through its update loop.

As with most of the content in this book, the preceding terms aren't a comprehensive survey of the 3D performance programming landscape, but as a primer for what comes next, it is as comprehensive as needed. A comfortably high frame rate – one at or above 60 FPS – carries a frame budget of around 16 milliseconds, during which all processing needed to process a simulation and prepare it for the next frame must be completed. GPUs are screamingly fast at doing this type of thing, but just as an overburdened CPU can spin and churn trying to service too many competing processes, so can a GPU become overburdened by shader programs.

To help us understand what all of that talk about CPUs, GPUs, burdens, and everything else that plays out in an actual scenario, we need to learn about how and what to measure. Simply measuring things is rarely enough. Like chemistry students planning their lab procedures out in their notebooks, we'll need to learn how to plan our testing strategies, as well as how to interpret the results. In the next section, we're going to take on the tasks of planning out, executing, and interpreting a performance test, but not before we learn more about the tools that will help accomplish those tasks for us.

Measuring Performance and Identifying Bottlenecks

Effective problem-solving starts by clearly defining the problem that needs to be solved. Sometimes, this is less than obvious, or sometimes, there's more than one problem that appears to be front and center. Oftentimes, the thing that makes defining a problem difficult is that it is presented as a qualitative statement, like this one: "The Route Planning Screen doesn't perform well."

A statement such as that one is unambiguIus in one sense – there's no doubt as to its meaning – but it is completely opaque in another, for we have no understanding to what degree the performance is poor. That's the basic difference between having qualitative data and having specific, qualitative measures. Without the former, there's no understanding of the overall picture, and without the latter, there's no way to know whether any actions have been resolved, mitigated, or even made worse. So, gathering quantitative data on how the Route Planning screen performs is the first step we need to take so that we can better define our conditions for victory, as it were.

Inspecting the Performance of Route Planning

The Babylon.js Inspector is a Swiss-army knife of useful goodness. If you're as-yet-unfamiliar with the Inspector, now wouldn't be a bad time to check out the docs at `https://doc.babylonjs.com/toolsAndResources/tools/inspector`, as well as take another refresher through *Chapter 2, Ramping up On Babylon.js*, to set you straight. The Inspector has long had a **Performance** tab that displays all manner of statistics regarding the currently running Scene, but until the Babylon.js v5.0 release, there wasn't an easy way to capture and analyze those metrics as they progress over time. The **Performance Profiler** is an extensible tool that has two similar concepts but different practice modes: headless and real time.

> **Important note**
>
> In case you don't recall, the keyboard shortcut for bringing up the Inspector when running Space-Truckers is *Shift + Alt + I*.

Real-Time Performance Viewer Metrics

When running in Real Time mode, a live graph is rendered showing the selected metrics from a list of the available metrics. Headless mode, in contrast, displays nothing but captures data that can later be exported to CSV format for further analysis. All three of these options (Start/Stop, Real Time, Headless, and Import/Export to CSV) are covered in more detail in the BJS docs at `https://doc.babylonjs.com/toolsAndResources/tools/performanceProfiler`. The following table lists the out-of-the-box metrics collected by the Performance Profiler, along with a basic explanation of these metrics:

Section	Metric	Units	Comments
Counts: Totals	Total meshes, lights, vertices, materials, textures	N/A	More is not necessarily the merrier with these metrics.
Count: Active	Meshes, indices, faces, bones, particles	N.A	Active items contribute to rendering; they're on-camera.
Frame Steps Duration	Absolute FPS	frames/s	How often the engine delivers frames without considering any actual rendering times.
Frame Steps Duration	Mesh Selection	ms	How long is spent figuring out which meshes are active and need to participate in rendering.
Frame Steps Duration	Render Targets	ms	How long is spent rendering to intermediate destinations – that is, reflection probes.
Frame Steps Duration	Particles, Sprites, Animations, Physics	ms	How long is spent by the CPU processing the system.
Frame Steps Duration	Render, Frame total	ms	Render and frame total specify how much time is spent on each frame by the CPU.
Frame Steps Duration	Inter-Frame, GPU frame time	ms	Time spent by the CPU between frames. The length of time the GPU spends rendering a frame.

The specific values for each of the preceding metrics will depend on the hardware and software environment, so specific target values aren't very useful. The different property groupings of metrics tend to reflect the dimension or unit that values assume. The top section focuses on counted metrics – things such as the number of meshes, vertices, textures, and more. After that, there are timing metrics, which show the amount of time that specific parts of the scene are consuming during and in-between frames. It's this base set of metrics that the Performance Profiler captures and displays in a visual graph. Let's move on and look at what a procedure looks like for our profiling.

Defining the Testing Procedure

Following the guidelines laid out previously in this chapter, we need to define a repeatable procedure for profiling the application. There's no need to over-complicate this, so let's do the Simplest Thing That Could Possibly Work. We want to refresh the web page for the application to reset and clear memory and such, and then we want to let the application settle for a bit and find its groove before we launch some cargo and take some more measurements. The last part is to save our performance profile to a CSV file for posterity before loading it into the Performance Viewer for basic analysis.

> **Important note**
>
> Unless there's a specific reason to not do it, always evaluate performance and capture metrics against code built in Production environment mode!

Here's what our testing procedure looks like. Remember, we want to repeat this same series of steps every time we make a significant change to the code so that we can understand the impact of that change:

1. Refresh the browser, launch the game, and navigate to route planning

2. Allow game to stabilize for 10s

3. Begin capture

4. Allow 10 seconds to stabilize and establish a baseline

5. Launch cargo unit into an empty space

6. Collect data for 10 seconds

7. Stop capture and export to CSV

A more thorough testing procedure would also want to include camera panning and zooming, but this procedure will serve our purposes adequately. At this point in this book, *Step 1* shouldn't need further elaboration. *Step 2* is also straightforward and to the point. It is *Step 3* where we need to pause to get into the details of what the step entails.

Before we start capturing our profile, we need to launch the BJS Inspector by pressing the *Shift + Alt + I* key combination. The **Statistics** tab in the right-hand pane contains our target information, but first, detach the **Inspector** panes from the browser window (you can close the Scene Explorer instead if desired) so that they do not take up or cover up any part of the app window. If you're using multiple monitors, it can be convenient to dedicate one monitor to the browser window, but it's not required. Just remember the Guideline About Using the Same Screen Size and Resolution! When you're ready, press the **Begin Recording** button circled in the following screenshot:

Figure 12.1 – The Statistics tab of the Inspector contains controls for starting, stopping, exporting, and viewing Performance Profile data

By clicking the **Begin Recording** button, we can initiate a performance profile in Headless mode. This gives us better accuracy because, in a nod to Dr. Heisenberg, our measurements won't be affecting the application's execution to as much of a degree.

Step 4 involves the difficult task of waiting – without touching anything – for 10 seconds to allow stabilization to occur in the application. These first 10 seconds also help establish a runtime baseline profile that we can use to compare different actions taken during a test. When the allotted time has passed, *Step 5* is to point the launcher toward an empty patch of space and fire away – we want to capture the behavior of the game during flight. After letting the Cargo Unit cruise for another 10 seconds, *Step 6* has been completed, and thus *Step 7* comes, where we click the **Stop Recording** button, followed by the **Export Perf to CSV** button, to download it. Now that we've finished capturing our profile, it's time to examine it.

Viewing and Analyzing a Captured Profile

The fastest way to view a performance profile is to choose **Load Perf Viewer** using the **CSV** button, then select the freshly downloaded CSV file previously captured to launch the Perf Viewer.

> **Important note**
> Depending on whether you're doing this locally or against a deployed environment, your browser's pop-up blocker may engage and prevent the **Realtime Performance Viewer** window from showing. Make sure you disable or add exceptions to your blocker rules to allow the window to appear!

Your first impression of the performance graph might be that someone spilled a box of colored spaghetti or perhaps Pick-up-Stix and now it's going to need to be cleaned up. That's because all metrics are selected for display at the time of load. Click the master toggles on the group headers to disable all the Count items, leaving FPS. Selectively remove items that have very small values – if something is taking less than a millisecond to complete, there are better things to worry about! The graph is a lot easier to comprehend now! Zoom in and out with the mouse wheel, while panning across the timeline by dragging.

This will transition us from looking at a larger overall picture to a progressively more granular view of things, where there are a few things of interest to note.

Initial Assessments

Notice how the Inter-frame time seems to correlate inversely with FPS? That is, if you look carefully at the two data series, you'll see how the FPS drops dramatically any time there is a similar shift in the opposite direction by the Inter-frame time. Something else obvious to see in this format is the statement that whenever it takes more time between frames, there are fewer frames as a result.

If we add the GPU frame time to this graph, a more nuanced picture starts to emerge. Although there are exceptions and outliers, in most of the areas where Inter-frame time increases (followed immediately by a drop in FPS), there is a corresponding *decrease* in GPU frame time:

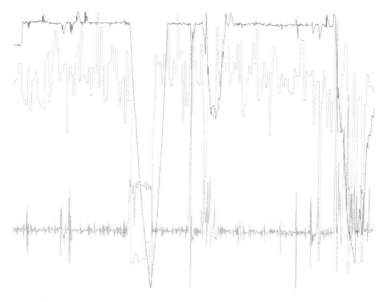

Figure 12.2 – A snapshot of a portion of a performance profile

In the preceding figure, the darker line at the top initially is the FPS, while the bottom-most line is the Inter-frame time. In the middle is the GPU frame time.

If the GPU frame time is improving, why is the FPS dropping? Without knowledge of the Space-Truckers application and how it's put together, it might take an expert a bit of time to puzzle out the source of this strange connection, but seasoned coders of the Space-Highways followers of this book will likely already know exactly what this means and what's causing it.

Integrating External Knowledge

Even though the CPU and the GPU operate pretty much independently from each other, events or conditions affecting one can still indirectly affect the other. In the case of our **Route Planning Screen**, we can infer that the GPU frame time drops because it is waiting to be told what to do by the CPU. Therefore, it is the increase in the Inter-frame time that is the proximate cause of both the FPS drop and the GPU frame time decrease.

Reach back into your memories of *Chapter 6, Implementing Game Mechanics*, and recall how we went about implementing the asteroid belt in the *Building the Asteroid Belt* section. The belt is comprised of many hundreds of individual rock meshes that have been procedurally generated as a set of **Thin Instances**. Note that as we discussed in *Chapter 7, Processing Route Data*, Thin Instances are blazing fast because they run on the GPU.

Checking the Particle frame steps timing tends to support that assertion as the amount of time the CPU spends managing particles is small enough that it is unlikely to account for the two distinctly different systems in use in the Scene (the Sun Particle System is also a GPU-based **ParticleSystem**, with the asteroid **Thin Instances** being the other). Why, then, focus on the asteroid belt as the source of our high Inter-frame bottleneck? This is because our Thin Instances are not statically held in place – they individually rotate. To accomplish this rotation, we implemented a scheme wherein we stored a set of rotation, position, and scaling data locally on the CPU. Every frame, we looped through the set of asteroids and adjusted the rotation values for each asteroid, updating their matrices before signaling to the GPU that it should refresh the **Thin Instance Buffer** to update the objects on screen:

```
Ior (lIt i = 0; i < this.numAsteroids; ++i) {
    this.rotations[i].x += Math.random() * 0.01;
    this.rotations[i].y += Math.random() * 0.02;
    this.rotations[i].z += Math.random() * 0.01;
}
this.updateMatrices();
this.mesh.thinInstanceBuf"erUpda"ed("matrix");
```

gameData for the Route Planning screen contains an asteroidBeltOptions configuration object, which, in turn, contains the number property that controls the number of asteroids (**Thin Instances**) to create and manage. Next, it's time to test our hypothesis by running an experiment.

Validating Assumptions

Change the number of asteroids to about 75% percent of its current value, then re-run the performance profile. It should be immediately apparent that the Inter-frame time improves, along with the overall FPS. As we are hoping to see, the GPU frame time either stays constant or trends upwards, supporting our conjecture about the GPU waiting for work from an over-taxed CPU.

If you wish to be extra thorough (and you should if you're still learning!), change the asteroid count again, but this time in the opposite direction, re-doing the test afterward. The results, once again, should support our proposed explanation that the number of asteroids is inversely correlated to the FPS, and the degree to which it correlates should be consistent between runs as well, showing both quantitative and qualitative sides of the story.

Be sure to revert the change to the asteroid count since this is a situation where one size doesn't fit all – different CPUs will be able to support a varying number of asteroids without tanking performance. We need to be able to dynamically change the asteroid count at runtime based on how well the app is performing. Once again Babylon.js has the perfect tool for the job – the Scene Optimizer. The **Babylon.js Inspector** is the launching pad for engaging in performance analysis and improvement. The **Statistics** tab contains a whole set of aggregated Counts – textures, meshes, and more – and timings, such as GPU time and FPS. Supplementing that, the metric display is the new Real-time Performance Viewer, which uses the same metrics to draw a time-evolving graph of performance. It can run in Real-Time and Headless mode, but Headless will have the least impact on performance.

Capturing and exporting performance data to CSV can be done with a click of the button but having a testing procedure in place is just as crucial as the data collected (if not more!). After defining our procedure, we saw how to execute it to capture a performance profile. Upon analysis of the profile, a trend appeared to emerge that indicated there might be a bottleneck in the CPU due to the number of asteroid Thin Instances involved in the Scene. Because it's so easy to capture profiles – changing the number of asteroids and re-running the test doesn't take long, and the results appear to confirm our assertion of connecting the number of asteroids to the overall frame rate.

Improving this situation isn't as simple as just lowering the number of asteroids, though. Because this is so heavily bound to the CPU's ability to chug through the various matrix calculations, different CPUs are going to have different responses to the same variables. A dynamically set number of asteroids, matching the number the CPU can handle, would be the perfect solution. In the next section, we'll learn all about how to use the Scene Optimizer in both its vanilla, out-of-the-box configuration and with a custom stratagem.

Improving Runtime Performance with the Scene Optimizer

Developing games for a given platform comes with its own set of unique challenges and benefits. Console games have the benefit of having standard hardware specifications and drivers to target, but at the expense of those same hardware specifications creating severe limitations in other areas, such as RAM or **video RAM (vRAM)**. Browser-based games have their own bag of double-edged swords too – the ubiquitous nature of JavaScript and the web brings similar problems to console developers with restricted hardware specs, and some of the same problems that PC developers must face with a wide variety of hardware combinations.

Using the tools and lessons from this chapter and the preceding chapters of this book, it's easy to imagine writing some code – a coroutine perhaps – that monitors the real-time performance of the application and makes tweaks to various settings in response to bring frame rates up to target. However, it is easy to imagine and probably easy to prototype or create a proof-of-concept that works in a few limited situations. The devil is always in the details though, and considerable time and effort would have to be expended that could otherwise be put to other uses.

Fortunately, and hopefully getting somewhat repetitive to hear at this point, is that Babylon.js has got you covered with **SceneOptimizer** (`https://doc.babylonjs.com/divingDeeper/ scene/sceneOptimizer`). Every time the specified sampling interval passes (by default, every 2,000 ms), **SceneOptimizer** checks the current frame rate, and if it isn't close to or at the target, the next optimization in the queue is applied. If the optimization is capable of further action, it remains in the queue until it reports it can't help any longer.

Through the `SceneOptimizerOptions` object, **SceneOptimizer** works from a queue of strategies that each offer a different type of performance optimization, allowing for graceful degradation of scene quality while maintaining a stable frame rate.

Some examples of operations that the built-in optimization strategies can perform are as follows:

- Merging multiple similar meshes into a single mesh
- Disabling shadows and/or post-processes
- Reducing texture resolution or hardware scaling
- Particle count reductions

Each specific **Optimization** has a priority value assigned to it, with lower valued optimizations being applied first. To make it more convenient, **SceneOptimizerOptions** has a set of static factory methods that allow you to specify a set of optimizations according to the amount of visual degradation you're willing to allow in the scene – low, moderate, or high. See the docs at the link mentioned previously for more details on the specifics of which optimizations are used for what degradation level. Interestingly, **SceneOptimizer** can be configured to run in the opposite direction – instead of degrading scene quality, it will enable or apply effects until the point where the FPS drops to or below the target. This is useful in power-limited scenarios where energy usage is an important consideration but isn't an area that we're going to cover here (see *Extended Topics* for more though!).

In addition to the built-in optimization strategies, it's possible to define custom optimization strategies. This is quite useful for our salient purpose and doesn't require more than a line or two of JavaScript. We're going to use this to create a custom strategy later in the *Creating a Custom Optimization Strategy for the Asteroid Belt* section, but first, let's learn to crawl before we walk by learning a bit about **SceneOptimizer** on its own. Don't be fooled by the tall Section Headers – it's quite simple when we look at the mechanics of it!

Understanding the Scene Optimizer and its Operating Modes

The Babylon.js Scene Optimizer executes in one of two modes: Improvement and... `!isInImprovementMode`. That's a bit of an insider joke because that's the property set by the last parameter to the **SceneOptimizer** constructor and it can be easy to mix up their operational behaviors. Whenever the default value of `true` is set, optimizations are applied until the target frame rate has been reached or we run out of strategies to apply. When `false`, it does the opposite or enhances the visuals while the frame rate is *above* the target. Each Optimization (even Custom ones) adapts its behavior to whichever mode is set, so a strategy that tries to increase frame rate might turn off shadows when in optimization mode and turn them on when in enhancement mode.

The list of optimization/enhancement strategies used by **SceneOptimizer** is managed by the `SceneOptimizerOptions` module. Although it's possible to start with a blank set of options and manually create and add strategies, a set of static factory methods for `SceneOptimizerOptions` are available that will create a pre-defined set of strategies based on how aggressive or extensive the actions are. The three methods range from `LowDegradationAllowed` to `HighDegradationAllowed` (see `https://doc.babylonjs.com/divingDeeper/scene/sceneOptimizer#options` for more on the specific strategies included in each).

> **Important note**
> Changing the value of `isInImprovementMode` will not affect the behavior of **SceneOptimizer**– the only place that it can be set is in the constructor!

Once you've set up **SceneOptimizerOptions** and **SceneOptimizer**, things get kicked off with a call to `sceneOptimizer.start()` and halted with `sceneOptimizer.stop()`. To help with debugging and troubleshooting (among other potential uses), **SceneOptimizer** has a set of three Observables that are triggered whenever an optimization is applied, succeeds, or fails, respectively.

Any Optimizer (that is, a Strategy for those who like Code Patterns) that is to be used with **SceneOptimizer** must implement two specific JavaScript methods to fulfill its software design contract: `apply` and `getDescription`. The `apply(scene, optimizer)` method is called against each Optimization with a `priority` matching the current `priority` of **SceneOptimizer**, while `getDescription` is responsible for returning a human-readable textual description of what the Optimization does to the given Scene. That's all there is to it at a basic level – simple as promised! Building from this simple foundation, and now that we're ready for it, let's focus on that custom Optimization hinted at earlier.

Creating a Custom Optimization Strategy for the Asteroid Belt

Earlier in this chapter, we used the **Realtime Performance Viewer** to identify and verify a performance bottleneck. We discovered that during the Route Planning phase, the number of asteroids has a direct relationship to the FPS for the Scene. Since changing the number of **Thin Instances** (**TIs**) is a simple matter of setting the mesh's `thinInstanceCount` property, this seems like a good candidate for a custom Optimization Strategy.

Though several different ways exist to define an **Optimization**, the quickest and easiest way is to call the `sceneOptimizerOptions.addCustomOptimization` method. This function takes three parameters – callbacks for `apply` and `getDescription` and a value for `priority` that, by not-much-of-a-coincidence, happens to be the interface contract for an **Optimizer** that we so recently discussed!

The Playground at `https://playground.babylonjs.com/#17ZX41#10` is a modified and stripped-down version of some earlier PGs that we looked at during *Chapter 6, Implementing Game Mechanics*. This PG just contains the central star and the TI asteroid belt. Play with `asteroidBeltOptions.number` until you get a value that gives you a low-ish frame rate, then click the **MAKE ME GO FAST** button to start `fastOptimizer` to see **SceneOptimizer** in action as part of the bottom-most `createScene` method body. Most of this should be easy to understand, but one potential head-scratcher is this line of code:

```
optimizerOptions.optimizations.forEach(o => o.priority += 1);
```

What's happening here? Well, we want our TI Optimizer to run first before any other Optimizers do. Yes, it's like we're an only or a first-born child – incredibly selfish and self-centered – but this is our application, and we know what we're doing. For the most part. But we also can't allow other Optimizations to run at the same priority because we don't want to change anything except for the TI count before trying anything else to improve things. So, we loop over every existing priority in the `optimizerOptions` object and bump its priority to be one greater than whatever it previously was at (the default value is zero). That way, in the very next line, when we call `addCustomOptimization` with a priority of 0, we know our stuff comes first. Take that, younger Sibs! The custom optimization definition can account for either mode of operation, and in its full version, it is capable of automatically computing min and max values for the instance count based on degradation requirements. The following code has been abridged for brevity and clarity but otherwise, it is the same as its big brother at `https://github.com/jelster/space-truckers/blob/ch12/src/thinInstanceCountOptimization.js`:

```
let optimizerOptions = new SceneOptimizerOptions(targetFps,
    2000);
optimizerOptions.addCustomOptimization((scene, opt) => {
    let currTI = mesh.thinInstanceCount;
    if (!opt.isInImprovementMode) {
```

```
        if (currTI <= MIN_INSTANCE_COUNT) {
            return true;
        }
        mesh.thinInstanceCount = Math.ceil(currTI * 0.91);
    }
    else {
        if (currTI >= MAX_INSTANCE_COUNT) {
            return true;
        }
        mesh.thinInstanceCount = Math.ceil(currTI * 1.09);
    }
    return false"
}, () => "Change thin ins"ance count");
```

The interesting thing in the preceding code is that instead of changing the TI count by a fixed, set amount, we are changing it in increments of roughly 9%. This allows designers and developers to make changes more freely to the base asteroid count without needing to make other changes to accommodate different scales of values. Hopefully, it's easy to see how easy it can be to make runtime adaptations to an application's visual quality to meet a target frame rate, because that's the extent of what we're going to be covering in this topic, at least for this edition of this book.

There's nothing magical about **SceneOptimizer**, even though the effect it has of saving developers' time certainly can be that way. With the incredible number of individual performance characteristics accessible to web applications, the amount of hand-optimization that is possible or practical becomes more difficult and expensive. Balancing performance optimizations done at design time with ones dynamically applied at runtime can be the key to getting beautiful and smooth visuals for the widest possible range of audiences.

SceneOptimizer is created by passing in a `SceneOptimizerOptions` object that defines the set of Optimizations that will be executed and whether they should be run to improve the frame rate to improve the visuals. Many built-in optimizations are provided and can be quickly created with `SceneOptimizerOptions.LowDegradationAllowed` and its companion methods, but custom Optimizations are almost as quick and easy to use too. Our custom optimizer changes the number of TIs until the target frame rate has been achieved. By adding it to the Optimization collection by passing an `apply` function, a `getDescription` function, and a priority number to `optimizerOptions.addCustomOptimization`, the custom optimizer is intended to run solo. Therefore, before we even do that, we must nudge the existing Optimization priorities up to keep ours both first and on its own in the queue.

Summary

When condensed down to an outline form, it may not seem like we covered a whole lot of ground in this chapter, but nothing could be further from the truth! Sure, there has been little to no mention of many important areas of performance optimization and measurement. We've covered nothing about the use of **Octtrees** to speed up collisions and mesh selection (`https://doc.babylonjs.com/divingDeeper/scene/optimizeOctrees`), toggling various convenience caches to reduce memory footprints (`https://doc.babylonjs.com/divingDeeper/scene/reducingMemoryUsage`), or any other of the almost two-dozen specific optimization heuristics (`https://doc.babylonjs.com/divingDeeper/scene/optimize_your_scene`) that constitute "low-hanging fruit" areas for improvement. That's OK, though. This book's title starts with *Going the Distance*, not *Plumbing the Depths*, and we can always detour into those details in the Second Edition (should there ever be one!).

What we have covered are the basics of how to approach thinking and learning about performance testing and profiling, starting with general guidelines and advice before progressing to the **Real-Time Performance Viewer** tool new to Babylon.js v5. Using those skills, we took a capture of our application and used it to identify factors that show that performance is sensitive to changes, such as the number of asteroids rendered in the Route Planning Asteroid Belt. Finally, we saw how easy basic scene optimization at runtime can be with **SceneOptimizer**. We solved the previously identified performance bottleneck with a custom optimization strategy that will gradually lower the number of thin instances until the frame rate reaches acceptable levels.

In the next chapter, we'll learn how to enhance our game and level it up from a regular web application to a Progressive Web Application. This will be the final step of making our game fully playable and accessible to everyone at any time; by the end of the next chapter, we'll have an application ready to run offline and be published to the major app stores!

Extended Topics

As always, there's more to learn and explore in the topics we've looked at in this chapter. The following are ways you can engage further and practice the knowledge you've gained in the chapter. Don't forget to post your questions and share your accomplishments on the Babylon.js forums or in the Space-Truckers discussion boards at `https://forum.babylonjs.com` and `https://github.com/jelster/space-truckers/discussions`:

- Perform a more comprehensive quantitative analysis of the asteroid belt data to extract the precise relationship between the FPS and asteroid count. What is the specific FPS to asteroid ratio? Having the CSV file is handy here because spreadsheet tools such as Excel, Sheets, and Google Sheets are the best way to compare and calculate these figures.

- Are there ways to rewrite the `AsteroidBelt.update` method to reduce the CPU inter-frame time? Maybe it isn't necessary to loop through every asteroid individually if they could be addressed in bundles or batches…

- Along the lines of the previous bullet point, is it possible to refactor the Asteroid Belt so that it behaves identically to how it does currently, but happen entirely on the GPU? Given what we learned about Shaders and Node Materials in the previous chapter, the answer should be an enthusiastic "YES!". Now go prove it by making it happen!

- Invert the custom asteroid scene optimization strategy to add thin instances instead of removing them. Integrate this with the application so that the scene tries to maintain a comfortable FPS range between 24 and 60.

- Add the ability for users to configure an overall graphics quality preference setting. Their choice could influence the specific `SceneOptimizerOptions` that are included to either improve visuals or performance.

13
Converting the Application to a PWA

Over the course of the last couple of chapters, it may have started to become clear that we are closing in on the end of our journey. Passing through the sweeping, vast countryside that is Babylon.js, we've seen and done much, and Space-Truckers is a functionally complete game thanks to our efforts. Now, we have one last stretch on the highway to cover in this chapter before we hit the off-ramp to the side-streets of *Chapter 14, Extended Topics, Extended* chapter.

Just because we're close to the end doesn't mean we are there yet – close doesn't count when it comes to Space-Truckers or orbital mechanics, only horseshoes and hand grenades. We've still got some road ahead of us, Space-Trucker, and there's still time before we hit the limit on our hours of service, so let's drive!

In this chapter, we are going to expose the intersection between Babylon.js and **Progressive Web Applications** (**PWAs**). A PWA is a middle space, a hybrid between the browser-based traditional web application (whatever that means these days) and a native desktop application. They can be browsed as a website can be, installed as an app can be, and run offline without an internet connection. Users can also find and install PWAs from their device or major app store – whether Google Play, Microsoft, and Apple. This gives developers greater space to allow potential users to discover their app while requiring little cost and effort to achieve.

> **Important Note**
> Apple's support for PWAs is far behind other providers. There are some serious restrictions and limitations placed on PWAs running on iOS and they can have their own quirks when it comes to support for different features. See the excellent third-party site `https://firt.dev/notes/pwa-ios/` for the latest feature support for Safari and iOS.

Converting our existing web app to a PWA is simple and easy, but it does require some changes to the application. A Service Worker is needed for offline support and a manifest is needed to describe the characteristics of our PWA. This includes icons, a description, and potentially even screenshots for store submissions. However, there is one final feature that Space-Truckers is missing that we'll be implementing in this chapter (it wouldn't be a *Going the Distance* chapter if we didn't have something of this sort, would it?).

This feature is one that has historically led to countless arguments and strained relationships among siblings and besties alike. A feature that has enabled bragging rights going back in time to the glory days of classics such as *Galaga*, *Pac-Man*, and *Donkey Kong*. This feature, of course, is a high score board. We're going for a scoreboard that's a bit more modern than the ones from those days because our scoreboard will save more than just the top 10 high scores; it will also retain those scores between application launches and computer restarts by saving data to the **IndexedDB**.

That's the extent of the plan for this chapter – unlike previous chapters, there's far less conceptual and theoretical discussion needed, so let's get started. First though, let's take a quick glance at the *Technical Requirements section* for this chapter. There's a bit of a change from the previous ones, and that's because, as we'll shortly learn, PWAs have a specific set of hosting requirements that must be met.

We will be covering the following topics in this chapter:

*   Introduction to PWAs
*   Converting the Space-Truckers Application into a PWA
*   Using IndexDB to Persist Scores
*   Storing and Displaying High Scores

Technical Requirements

This chapter has new tech requirements that, although low to no cost, do require some decisions and potentially a bit of research on your part to help get you to the specific outcome that works best for your project. After talking about the **Secure Sockets Layer** (**SSL**) certificate requirements, we'll go over some of the more popular options for hosting your PWA.

Hosting Requirements

To explain it briefly, SSL is a mechanism through which a client can verify the identity of a particular server and establish an encrypted communications channel. It's literally the 's' in HTTPS! An SSL connection is a requirement for a PWA without exception. Even though there are no exceptions, there actually is one exception, and that is the localhost loop-back address, to make testing easier. Obtaining a valid SSL certificate in most cases is free and easy to carry out. Depending on your hosting setup, SSL support might even be built into the hosting platform! Check the documentation for your specific provider to learn more about how to obtain and bind a site to a certificate.

Options for Hosting your PWA

There's nothing special about a hosting provider with regards to making an application into a PWA; any public-facing website that supports SSL has the capability to host a PWA. Some environments may make the organization and the process around hosting an SSL or HTTPS-based web app harder or easier, so here is a table listing some of the major hosting options:

Platform	Cost	Custom Domain?	Supplies SSL Cert?	More info
Azure Static Sites	Free*	Yes	Yes	Requires Azure Sub. (no charge)
Google Sites	Free*	No*	No*	Cust. Domains/HTTPS need add'l infrastructure
GitHub Pages	Free*	Yes	Yes	Special repository structure requires some extra deploy steps
AWS S3 Static site	Free*	No*	No*	SSL/HTTPS w/ cust. Domain poss. With extra steps
Generic web host	Depends	Depends	Depends	

GitHub Pages is one of the easiest options if you're hosting the source of the application in GitHub already. Deploying to a GH page site involves pushing commits to a specially named (and never merged) branch. What gets committed in our case is essentially the output of `npm run build` – the `dist/ folder` and all its contents.

Azure Static Websites is also a free, easy choice. Though it does require an Azure subscription, creating a static website is free and quick. Integration with source code in GitHub is exceptionally clean and useful and is even easier with the VSCode extension for Azure Static Websites. When deploying to a Site, a GH action performs all the work in the background for you whenever a pull request is opened or closed. To see an example of how this works in action, see the Space-Truckers repository's `.github/workflows` folder for the details.

Google and AWS Static Sites are both unique products that nevertheless perform the same essential services as the previous two. AWS offers static websites via AWS Amplify, while Google also has a similar offering within its Cloud Storage product. The reason for the asterisks on these services is that the base products do not support custom domains nor HTTPS served over those custom domains, at least not out of the box. More work is needed on the developer's part to add the other infrastructure components (such as an HTTPS proxy) that are necessary to accomplish and fulfill the requirements for custom domains and SSL or HTTPS. See the documentation provided in the next section for more information on how to do this – we don't have enough road left in front of us to swerve into the weeds following this topic!

Resources and Reading

- PWA Builder – `https://pwabuilder.com`

- The IndexedDB API – `https://developer.mozilla.org/en-US/docs/Web/API/IndexedDB_API`

- Azure Static Web Apps:

  - `https://docs.microsoft.com/en-us/azure/static-web-apps/`

  - `https://docs.microsoft.com/en-us/azure/storage/blobs/storage-blob-static-website-how-to?tabs=azure-portal`

- AWS Amplify – `https://aws.amazon.com/amplify/hosting/`

- Google Static Sites – `https://cloud.google.com/storage/docs/hosting-static-website`

- GitHub Pages and PWAs - `https://christianheilmann.com/2022/01/13/turning-a-github-page-into-a-progressive-web-app/`

- Service Workers and Workbox:

  - `https://developer.chrome.com/docs/workbox/service-worker-overview/`

  - `https://developer.chrome.com/docs/workbox/`

- The source code for this chapter is in the ch13 branch of the Space-Truckers GitHub repository - `https://github.com/jelster/space-truckers/tree/ch13`

- Playground URLs are listed in their relevant sections

Introduction to PWAs

As mentioned earlier in the introduction, a PWA is a sort of hybrid type of application that bridges the gap between a web application and a regular desktop application. Without additional context, it's a description that comes close to meaninglessness context. It's not the individual words and it's not the term "Web App" that lacks clarity, so what does it mean for a web app to be "Progressive"?

Well, as most of us are aware of course, web browsers have a vastly different security model than regular applications or games. JavaScript running in a browser's sandboxed environment has, by design, extremely limited access to the underlying machine's hardware and filesystem. Important to our discussion is the limitation placed on scripts, along with the vast range of implementation support in browsers, which means that any given web application may or may not have access to certain device features and functions. In these types of cases, or when an application is being distributed widely across different device and software profiles, it is very important for an application to be able to – wait for it – "Progressively" and gracefully enhance or degrade its capabilities on-demand based on what the hosting device has and is willing to share with the browser app.

That takes us to the next question, then: how do PWAs work? There are three main defining requirements that a web application must fulfill to be eligible to be installed as a PWA by a web browser. These requirements are **SSL**, **Service Workers**, and **(Web) Manifests (SSM)**. So much word salad to digest, so little time. Let's prep a salad fork and dig into these in more detail.

> **Note**
> If you prefer (or if you just really enjoy confusing people), you can use MMS or even SMS for an acronym. You do you!

SSL

Conducted over HTTPS, this is a non-negotiable requirement – and for good reason! Installing a web app as a PWA expands the capabilities of the app greatly, but at the same time, commensurately exposes the host machine and its data to a greater risk of malicious or incompetent actors accessing it. Requiring a secure connection between the client and server neither compensates for incompetent or bad coding nor does it guarantee that the server involved is protected from malicious intent. What it does guarantee is that the identity of the hosting site has been verified as being what the site says it is.

Service Workers

Used to fetch and retrieve assets for and from offline use, SW is code loaded from a JavaScript file separate from the main application's code. Running in a DOM-less sandbox, an SW is nonetheless the key intermediary between the application and the underlying network. An SW enables offline usage of the app in a transparent fashion – nothing in the application knows that it is really communicating with the SW when it makes a web request for a resource.

Every time a script, HTML tag, or CSS definition triggers a request from the web application, the request is intercepted and handled by the SW. The SW then has the choice of either returning the indicated resource to the caller from its cache or of refreshing its cache prior to returning the resource. To make this even more effective, the SW's first job upon installation and activation is to pre-fetch all the resources and put them into its cache ahead of time.

Web Manifest

The last element needed to "unlock" the capabilities of a PWA in a browser is a Web Manifest. This is a simple JSON-formatted file that's usually given an extension of `.webmanifest`, and it tells the web browser and other consumers of the manifest all sorts of neat information about the application. In addition to containing basic information about an application, such as the name, description, and version, the manifest contains sections that allow a developer to specify icon images at varying sizes and aspects for display by the host OS (e.g., the iOS Home Screen), display orientation preferences, screenshots, and even age and content ratings. View a full listing of possible elements and what they mean on the Mozilla Developer docs site at `https://developer.mozilla.org/en-US/docs/Web/Manifest`.

These different pieces of metadata all work together to describe how the application should be presented and the parameters of its expected behavior. In addition, the Web Manifest is heavily leveraged when listing a PWA in one of the app stores. The benefits of being able to define the application's metadata once for publication everywhere should be obvious, but how to easily define values for each of those properties is not. Fortunately, as with working with Babylon.js, there are many tools and resources available that can help speed things along.

We'll cover the tools and the mechanics of PWAs shortly but let's summarize what we know about PWAs and how they work first. When users browse to a website that is PWA-enabled, an icon appears in the browser indicating that an application can be installed for the current site. Clicking the icon transforms what used to be a regular website into an offline-capable, Start Menu-pinnable application indistinguishable from a native application.

What allows this to happen are the three specific things that a PWA must have properly configured – the SSM trio: (S)SL connections, a (S)ervice Worker to pre-fetch and cache resources for offline use, and a Web (M)anifest. Having an SSL connection means that the website hosting the PWA is accessed over the HTTPS protocol and requires a valid certificate to be obtained for this purpose. SWs are JavaScript code components that run in a separate sandbox from the rest of the browser's application code. They intercept requests transparently and return cached resources stored locally. The Web Manifest describes everything that a hosting OS and web browser need to know to install the PWA. In addition, the Web Manifest also serves as an app Store package listing, meaning that for the effort of preparing a single store submission, one can make submissions to all of the major app Stores.

Coming up in the next section, we're going to power up Space-Truckers: The Web Application and make it into Space-Truckers: The Progressive Web Application. We'll see how two simple packages, along with a little bit of code and a WebPack configuration, are all that's needed to get the job done. In a way, the simplicity and ease of making the conversion could be a bit anticlimactic, but don't worry – we'll soon thereafter be looking at adding something flashier and with more flare when we come to the high score board!

Converting the Space-Truckers application into a PWA

As we discussed shortly prior to this section, a hallmark – or signature – feature of a PWA is its ability to gracefully adapt to varying conditions and host environments. How should the application behave when a network connection is lost? What happens when a new version of the app is published? When assets change, how do you ensure that any cached versions of the old asset are evicted, and the new ones are stored?

Putting the "P" in PWA

These are all good questions and present real technical and engineering challenges that need to be solved. If you are one of those beautiful, curious, intelligent, and slightly mad kinds of people, you should prepare yourself to be disappointed. While, again, these are worthy topics to study and understand, this is a case where tools have evolved to the point where it is possible to accomplish a lot while knowing very little about the underlying technology. It's possible that the overall brevity of this section – or really, of this entire chapter – hasn't escaped notice and that's a hint at just how easy it is to put the "P" in PWA.

It's also possible that the author of this book counted the number of pages originally promised and realized that the budgeted page count had been blown quite a while back, but nobody's here to litigate the issue of which is which, are we?

> **Note**
>
> *[Why yes, actually. We are paying quite close attention to the page count. – The Editors]*

Right then. In the interest of getting to the point, and in not further antagonizing The Editors, let's walk through the steps that will make Space-Truckers into a PWA.

Step 1 – Installing the Workbox WebPack Plugin

Workbox is an open source project maintained by Google with the purpose of making the creation, usage, and management of SWs smooth and easy. The project also maintains a plugin that integrates with **WebPack** (see *Chapter 4, Creatingthe Application*) and automatically generates the SW code for you. Install it into the project as a developer dependency along with **CopyPlugin** with this command:

```
npm i workbox-webpack-plugin copy-webpack-plugin --save-dev
```

`copy-webpack-plugin` is a simple plugin that copies static files from a given directory into the output directory with the rest of the webpack output, which is handy for when we want to include icons and a **Web Manifest** with the build.

Step 2 – Configuring WebPack Plugins

We've made new plugins available to WebPack and now we need to import them into `webpack.common.js`:

```
const WorkboxPlugin = require('workbox-webpack-plugin');
const CopyPlugin = require('copy-webpack-plugin');
```

Next, we will instantiate the plugins with their respective options. If you recall from *Chapter 3, Establishing the Development Workflow*, WebPack plugins run in the order they are defined. These new plugins need to run after the HTML template has been injected with the bundle and after the destination directory has been cleaned:

```
plugins: [
    new CleanWebpackPlugin(),
    new HtmlWebpackPlugin({
        template: path.resolve(appDirectory, "public/index.
html"),
        inject: true
    }),
    new WorkboxPlugin.GenerateSW({
        clientsClaim: true,
        skipWaiting: true,
        maximumFileSizeToCacheInBytes: 8388608,
    }),
    new CopyPlugin({
        patterns: [
            { from: path.resolve(appDirectory,
              'public/assets/icons'), to:
              path.resolve(appDirectory,
              'dist/assets/icons') },
            { from: path.resolve(appDirectory,
              'public/manifest.json'), to:
              path.resolve(appDirectory,
              'dist/manifest.webmanifest') }
        ]
    })
]
```

The **Workbox WebPack Plugin** npm package has two primary plugins (modes) of operation, GenerateSW and InjectManifest, the use cases for which fall under the categories "Basic" and "Advanced". Our needs are currently quite Basic, so we are using the GenerateSW plugin. Its configuration has flags that specify the SW should immediately claim matching clients (for upgrade scenarios) as well as skip waiting for older workers to be disposed. Most importantly, we set maximumFileSizeToCacheInBytes to four times its default value. This is needed because we want as many of our assets to be cached locally as possible.

The **CopyPlugin** configuration is intended for copying two static assets that don't yet exist, our app icon sets, and the Web Manifest JSON file (which is renamed with the `.webmanifest` extension along the way). We'll create those files in subsequent steps after we make some changes to our `index.html` file.

Step 3 – Modifying index.html

Two important modifications need to be made to the `index.html` file in the repository's `/public` folder. The first is to add a `<link>` tag for the Web Manifest to the files' `<head>` tag. The second is to add a short `<script>` tag that loads and registers the SW on page load:

```
<link rel="manifest" href="./manifest.webmanifest" />
<script>
  if ('serviceWorker' in navigator) {
    window.addEventListener('load', () => {
      navigator.serviceWorker.register('service-worker.js')
      .then(registration => {
        console.log('SW registered: ', registration);
      }).catch(registrationError => {
        console.log('SW registration failed: ',
          registrationError);
      });
    });
  }
</script>
```

In keeping with the graceful enhancement strategy that PWA advocates, our script is completely transparent to the rest of the application – when it is present, things just work. After checking to see whether the browser supports SWs, the `navigator.serviceWorker.register` function is called with the name and path of the SW script. This script is generated by `GenerateSW` and output into the `/dist` folder, so it shouldn't trouble you that the file referenced doesn't seem to exist!

At this point, running the app should generate the expected console messages indicating successful SW registration and operation. Common problems that may occur are an incorrect path or file name for the SW, or an incorrect `GenerateSW` configuration. That's the SW part of the PWA requirements met – let's fill in the one for the missing Web Manifest.

Step 4 – Adding the Web Manifest

The Web Manifest, as previously mentioned in the *Introduction to PWA* section, is the developer-friendly, JSON-formatted file describing the PWA's attributes and characteristics. To maintain the development-time experience, we place the Web Manifest into the `/public` folder as a sibling to `index.html`. This makes sure that our links work properly when being hosted on `webpack-dev-server` or built for a production environment and hosted from the `/dist` folder.

The file is named `manifest.json` in the `/public` folder, which is then renamed to `manifest.webmanifest` at build-time. Here are some of the more important properties:

Property Name	Value
Name	The full name of the application.
Short name	An abbreviated name.
Start URL	The location the app launches to.
Display	Controls the amount of browser visual elements that should be displayed.
Orientation	Specifies the app's display ratio preferences (for example, landscape vs. portrait).
Icons	An array of at least one icon definition object that specifies a path, size, and type of icon file for the PWA. Several syntaxes are available.

For the `icons` array, each entry in the array specifies an icon whitespace-separated list of sizes, along with a path either directly to a file or to a base file name with sizes prefixed – as in, `myicon`, where the file names are `48x48-myicon` and `52x52-myicon`. Supplying entries for every possible icon size isn't necessary, although depending on the source image, some distortion and unintended display effects could occur. At this point, when the application is run on the local web server, the browser should "light up" with the ability to install the site as a PWA. If it doesn't, open the browser developer tools and check for relevant console errors. The **Lighthouse** tab in Google Chrome and Microsoft Edge browsers can scan websites for many types of problems and optimization issues, including those involving PWAs.

A great many other properties are defined for the Web Manifest schema, and although not many are required, many are recommended. To see more of the properties available in the manifest, see `https://developer.mozilla.org/en-US/docs/Web/Manifest`. It can be difficult to manually create and manage all the different metadata, not to mention creating the icons, and that's why there are tools that can help us get the job done fast. One such tool previously discussed was the Workbox project. Another tool we haven't discussed yet though is the **PWABuilder Extension** for **VSCode**.

Using the PWABuilder Extension

Carrying out the previous steps manually has some benefits. You get fine control over every detail of the process while learning the internals of everything along the way. It's also a tedious process prone to error. An alternative to the previous steps is to use the official **PWABuilder Extension for Visual Studio Code**. This extension, built and maintained by the same team that maintains the excellent resource PWABuilder.com, makes setting up a PWA quick and easy. Aside from generating the source code for various PWA components, the extension can validate an existing website to check its PWA readiness status – very useful for debugging.

After installing the extension from the **VSCode** extension marketplace, open the extension's left-hand pane to reveal the **Web Manifest** and **Service Worker** panes. Click the + icons on the respective panes to generate those resources. When generating the application icons, depending on your settings, the PWA extension may generate the entire range of icon sizes – which can number above 60. For that reason, once the icons have been generated, feel free to go ahead and whittle down those files to whatever set of sizes works best. Make sure to update the manifest to remove the files!

When generating the SW, the extension will ask whether you would like a **Basic** or **Advanced** SW; the answer for Space-Truckers is **Basic**, since we're not (yet) using PWA features such as push notifications. The extension will install any needed npm packages (such as workbox) and provide a code snippet to copy-paste into your index.html. Does the code look familiar?

The final step when making a PWA is, of course, publishing the application to an HTTPS host. The specifics of this depend on your hosting provider, but Google, AWS, and Microsoft all provide VSCode extensions that can make publishing a breeze. Whichever provider is involved, the goal will be to run the build script followed by copying all of the files in the /dist folder to the root of the hosting website.

As promised in this section's introduction, the tools and technologies available make creating and deploying a PWA incredibly simple and fast. A series of four straightforward steps are needed – adding two WebPack plugin packages to generate the Service Worker, modifying webpack config, then index.html to register the SW and link assets, then finally adding a Web Manifest to describe the extent of the changes needed. Whether those changes are performed manually or with the help of an extension such as the PWA Builder Extension, there's a rich world of native application functionality that opens up to application developers. We're not seeing the full range and extent of the capabilities of PWAs, so head over to PWABuilder.com to read more about the different cool tricks that can be done with them!

Before we wrap things up for the chapter, there's one more topic to explore. High scores are a staple for arcade-style games such as **Space-Truckers**, but since we're running on the web, we need a way to be able to store a player's high scores that persists beyond reloading the web page. The IndexedDB object store built into most modern browsers is a great solution for this type of problem, and in the following section, we're going to learn how to create a component to make use of it.

Using IndexedDB to Persist Scores

Web developers needing to store information on a local client have traditionally had a limited number of options, most of which have had significant drawbacks. One of the oldest and simplest methods is the humble browser cookie. These little text files stored on the client's browser are sent to the server alongside every request made by the browser client. Because of that, and for similarly related reasons, cookies aren't an efficient or practical solution to many if not most client-side storage needs, including our own. For an in-depth examination of the different pros and cons of available client-side storage, see `https://web.dev/storage-for-the-web/`.

The **IndexedDb Object Store (IDB)** is a client-side, browser-sandboxed database enjoying a broad spectrum of consistently implemented support across major browsers and platforms. While the amount of data a site is allowed to store is limited to the disk space that's available to the browser, our application has very modest storage space requirements outside of the assets.

> **Important Note**
>
> While it is possible to use IDB as an asset cache for textures, meshes, and the like, it is far easier, efficient, and a better fit overall for those assets to use the SW set up earlier in this chapter.

This section's focus is on the basics of IDB and how we will make use of it in our application. After taking a moment to review the foundational elements of `IndexedDb`, we'll put together some code to wrap the lower-level IDB functions with more application-layer-friendly helpers. Then, we'll see how to integrate those helpers into a Playground that we'll use in the next section, *Storing and Displaying High Scores*.

Learning about IndexedDB

`IndexedDB` is an official API specification maintained by the **World Wide Web Consortium** (**w3c**), an organization also responsible for most web-based standards such as HTML and CSS. The specification can be found at `https://w3c.github.io/IndexedDB/` but we don't need to go much deeper here to gain an understanding of how IDB works.

The wide support in web browsers for the IDB specification gives us confidence that we can proceed with using the APIs and that the same code should work the same across different browsers – the operative phrase being "should work." Don't leave off testing across different browsers and versions. Otherwise, you run a very high potential risk of running into support issues with end users that aren't using the same setup as you!

When it comes to consuming the IDB API, there are two important things to note. First is that they are asynchronous. The second is that operations produce results via various event handler functions. When an asynchronous operation is invoked, the return value of that function isn't immediately available – the function doesn't return anything. Further, the operation may or may not succeed. In the case of the former, the result is produced by an event handler function specific to the operation and object involved. The `IDBOpenRequest` object has event handlers such as `onsuccess`, `onerror`, and `onupgradedneeded`, while the `IDBObjectStore` object has events such as `transaction.oncomplete`. As some of the names suggest, the latter case of an operation failing is handled by the `onerror` handler function.

An important consideration is how the various code paths of the `indexedDB.open` function are managed. The `onsuccess` event produces an instance of `IDBDatabase`, but that's only part of the story. When a unique combination of the database name and the current schema versions (the first and second parameters to the Open operation) is requested that does not match any existing object stores, the `onpugradeneeded` event is fired. It is at that time that the specific object store has its schema created, any indexes added, and any version change migrations performed.

That's enough foundational concepts for us to start writing some code! We need to write some helper code that takes the event-based asynchronous `IndexedDB` functions and makes them easy to use in our application.

Using IndexedDB

All the different needs, scenarios, and data schema definitions involved with `IndexedDB` constitute several moving parts. Therefore, our first task is going to be crafting a wrapper around these operations that exposes the desired API in the form of functions returning Promises. There are several libraries available that implement similar helper code, but for our simple needs, it is more illustrative and useful to just write the code ourselves.

> **Note**
>
> The following code pattern is common in JavaScript programming as an approach for wrapping lower-level or legacy programming interfaces into forms more friendly to higher-level applications consuming that functionality. If you're not familiar with this pattern, it's a useful one to have in your toolbox!

The Playground snippet **#U20E4X** contains the code we'll be using for this and the next part, so follow along as we visit some of the more interesting, opaque, and complex parts of the sample.

We will start by declaring and storing the `SpaceTruckersDb` function as our outer scope. The body of this function contains our working set of variables shared across our helper functions to maintain the internal state, as well as a `const` array of seed `scoreData`:

```
let SpaceTruckersDb = function () {
    const scoreData = [
            { name: "AAA", score: 10000 },
            { name: "BBB", score: 7000 },
            { name: "CCC", score: 5000 },
```

```
            { name:  "DDD",  score:  3400  },
            { name:  "EEE",  score:  3000  },
            { name:  "FFF",  score:  2500  },
            { name:  "GGG",  score:  2000  },
            { name:  "HHH",  score:  1000  },
            { name:  "III",  score:  1000  },
            { name:  "JBE",  score:  500  },
        ];
        let indexedDbIsSupported = window.indexedDB;
        const currentSchemaVersion = 1;
        const databaseName = "SpaceTruckersDb";
        const tableName = "HighScores";
        var database;
    // ...
    return { retrieveScores, addScore, readyPromise };
```

Jumping to the bottom of the function, we are returning an object containing the helper functions to retrieve a list of scores as well as to add a new score. Alongside these functions is readyPromise, used to check for and ensure full initialization at a time of the caller's choosing. Because our needs are so simple, we don't need any additional logic or methods currently.

The most complicated logic of the entire sample is the first step – initializing the IDB object database and the corresponding object store (or table) that we're using to store the scoring data for our application. This is tricky to handle because there are multiple potential branches that the code might need to take depending on whether the object store already exists, and further, whether the schema version of the object stores matches the most current version requested.

That's what the onupgradeneeded event handler must, uh, handle. We start at the top of the readyPromise delegate's function body by invoking indexedDb.open. This returns (one of the only times this happens with the IDB APIs) an openDbRequest object with its attendant onerror, onsuccess, and of course, the onupgradeneeded events. The error logic is simple – reject readyPromise and pass through the thrown error. The success logic is also simple – just set the database variable to event.target.result and resolve the promise with it.

> **Note**
> Remember, the onsuccess event is not fired on the first run of the script for a given currentSchemaVersion and databaseName. Instead, onupgradeneeded is raised.

Let's look at what happens with the onupgradeneeded event. After extracting the database from the event object, we create objectStore itself. The autoIncrement flag indicates that new records should get an autoincremented key assigned and is followed by the creation of the non-unique score index. This is important and needed to ensure that the scores are stored in the proper ranked order:

```
openDbRequest.onupgradeneeded = (event) => {
    database = event.currentTarget.result;
    database.onerror = handleError;
    let objectStore = database.createObjectStore(tableName,
      {
            autoIncrement: true
      });
    objectStore.createIndex("score", "score",
      {unique: false});
    objectStore.transaction.oncomplete = (event) => {
        let scoreStore = database
        .transaction(tableName, "readwrite")
            .objectStore(tableName);
        scoreData.forEach(scoreD =>
          scoreStore.add(scoreD));
        resolve(database);
    };
};
```

To proceed after creating the score index, we attach a function to the oncomplete event of objectStore.transaction. This function immediately initiates a readwrite transaction against the same table (scoreStore), which is then used to populate the initially empty score table with a set of initial high scores (scoreData). After adding the seed data to the store, we resolve readyPromise – there's no need to wait for the write transaction to complete. That's the most complicated logic we have for this component.

The retrieveScores and addScore functions are both simpler variations on the main themes presented with the onupgradeneeded event logic. A txn object is created with requested permissions of either read-only or read-write. objectStore is then retrieved from the transaction and used to perform either a getAll or add operation. For getAll, the results are produced in the onsuccess handler of the object returned from objectStore.getAll, similarly to how the result of indexedDB.open is produced in onsuccess.

Recap

As simply as this, we've created a reusable component that we can drop into the Space-Truckers application as part of a high score screen! Let's review what we've learned about `IndexedDB` before we move on to the next section.

IDB is a browser-based storage mechanism that has the capability of storing very large amounts of data. While the basic storage means is object-based, IDB has the concept of databases containing a set of one or more object stores or tables. The schema for each table must be defined at the time of creation or schema version upgrade. This is defined by `currentSchemaVersion` passed to the `indexedDB.open` function. When the current version doesn't exist or is lower than the version requested, the `onupgradeneeded` event fires.

During this event, object stores are created, their indexes are defined, and their data is populated. When upgrading versions, it's important to include migration logic in this event handler – otherwise, data will be lost! In our case, we don't need to migrate score data and it's unlikely we'll need to do much substantially to require a schema change soon (see the *Extended Topics* section at the end of this chapter for some ideas that might involve doing that).

Because the pattern of accessing the IDB APIs doesn't natively support Promises, we've wrapped the major operations we need in a Promise-capable one. `readyPromise` is where the actual initialization and opening of the object store are performed and is also where the `onupgradeneeded` logic is housed. Once `readyPromise` resolves, the `getScores` and `addScore` methods become operational. These functions also return Promises for their respective operations, producing a list of scores or a confirmation that a new score was added.

Our IDB wrapper functions are the tools that we had to build in order to build the high score screen – now, it's time to use them. In the last section of this chapter, we're going to combine what we've just learned with the knowledge we've gained about coroutines and toss in our reusable GUI DialogBox component to create a tasty salad that is Space-Truckers: The High Scores!

Storing and Displaying High Scores

Keeping with the cooking theme that we wrapped up the previous section on, this section is all about combining our ingredients into a meal. All the hard work and learning have already happened, so this section will go by quickly – all the better to start feasting! The Playground at `https://playground.babylonjs.com/#VBMMDZ#23` is what we'll use as a live example – keep following along or try to replicate the functionality in the sample from the descriptions and snippets mentioned in this section.

> **Important Note**
> Don't try to eat your computer, or anything that isn't food – we are just using a metaphor, albeit one taken a bit further than needed! In fact, let's just switch themes entirely. For the rest of this section, we'll go with a classic heist, in the style of *Ocean's Eleven*.

The Heist

It won't be enough to enlist the reluctant aid of the "muscle", DialogBox, to throw a list of scores onto the screen and call it a day. Nor is it enough to bring in the quick-witted "safe cracker", SpaceTruckersDb, to finish the job. If we truly want to pull off this major gig, The High Score, each score needs to make a grand entrance. Failing that, they can at least not all appear on the screen at the same time as a crowd of raucous monkeys storming a banana barrel. In the case of a new high score in need of recording, we need to be able to collect the user's initials in the "traditional" three-letter format used by the arcade cabinets of old. We need "brains"to do the thinking. We need our old friend the **coroutine** to "come out of retirement for one last job".

To summarize our plan in exciting sub-sections, imagine of a compelling montage sequence that shows exactly how hard (actually, it's not hard but roll with it) completing the job will be for The Crew, let's begin.

The Muscle

We'll host the high score display with the DialogBox component (see *section Building a Reusable Dialog Box Component* in *Chapter 9, Calculating and Displaying Scoring Results*). Scores themselves are hosted within a **StackPanel** that gets added to bodyContainer. Each score is an object with just the name and score properties. The getScoreTextLine helper function takes an individual score object and returns a formatted string that can be displayed in TextBox:

```
function getScoreTextLine(s) {
    if (!s.score) {
        return s.name;
    }
    let scoreText = s.score.toFixed(0);
    let text = `${s.name}${'.'.repeat
        (20 - scoreText.length)}${s.score}\n`;
    return text;
}
```

Though we expect the s.score value to be present, we check for its absence anyhow, since the process of adding a new score necessarily precludes the entry of a name. We also expect the score to be a whole, integer value, but we convert it to a fixed string with zero points beyond the decimal just to be safe. A format string is returned that considers the length of the score value's text representation.

The Safe Cracker

Persistence logic will be provided by SpaceTruckersDb that we built in the previous section. Its functions are called and managed by scoreBoardCoro. True to the current thematic form, there's not much else to be said about the "safe cracker" that won't be included with our review of the "brains."

The Brains

The **ScoreBoard CoRoutine (ScoreBoardCoRo)** coordinates retrieving scores and displaying them in `DialogBox` as well as the edit mode for entering new scores. When `scoreBoardCoro` is invoked as a function (as part of preparing to run the coroutine – see *Chapter 9, Calculating and Displaying Scoring Results*, for more), the `newScore` parameter is used to pass in the new high score awaiting three-letter branding. If present, the `editHighScores` flag is set and a placeholder, `scoreToAdd`, is added to the scores list already retrieved by `databaseManager` that is initialized immediately upon entry. Equally, the `nameInput` **InputText** control as well as the **VirtualKeyboard** GUI element are instantiated and added to the dialog's control tree. An observer function is added to `nameInput.onTextChangedObservable` that limits entries to three characters or fewer. Additionally, it will also take action when detecting that the *Enter* key was pressed by setting the `editHighScores` flag to `false`:

```
nameInput.onTextChangedObservable.add((ev, es) => {
    if (ev.text.indexOf('↵') >= 0 || ev.text.length >= 3 ||
        ev.currentKey === "Enter") {
            scene.editHighScores = false;
    }
});
// ...
while (scene.editHighScores) {
    yield Tools.DelayAsync(1000);
}
```

Once the coroutine has finished waiting to exit edit mode, if there's `newScore`, that means the user's entered their initials and that the score is waiting to be saved. We do that before cleaning up the controls involved in gathering the user input:

```
if (newScore) {
    scoreToAdd.name = nameInput.text.substring(0,3);
    await databaseManager.addScore(scoreToAdd);
    console.log('saved newScore', scoreToAdd);
    virtualKB.disconnect();
    virtualKB.dispose();
    newScore = null;
    nameInput.dispose();
    scoreToAdd = null;
```

```
        scores = await databaseManager.retrieveScores();
        await displayScores(scores);
}
```

After the controls have been cleaned up, we refresh the `scores` list from storage to put everything back into a clean, initial state. If there isn't a `newScore`, the coroutine's work is done and the job's complete – the scores were already retrieved and displayed at the beginning of the coroutine's execution. With such a skilled Crew and exquisite preparation, it shouldn't surprise anyone following along that the Job of displaying the scores itself is short and sweet.

The Job

Assembling The Crew was the crucial first step, planning out The Job was the second, and now it's time to execute that plan. Here's our shortcut to a montage of the following steps in a linear sequence of events:

1. (`yield`) until the "safe cracker" (`databaseManager`) signals that it's ready.

2. Get the `scores` list from the "safe cracker" (`databaseManager`) and put them into the `scores` array.

3. Show "the muscle" (`DialogBox`). Wait for it to fully make its entrance before continuing.

4. If "the brains" "sez" there's another score to add (`newScore`), the following happens:

    -   The `editHighScores` flag is set

    -   A placeholder score entry is created sans a name and added to the `scores` list

    -   Input elements are put into place to collect the player's initials (`nameInput` and `virtualKB`)

    -   A "little bird" (a.k.a an observer) listens for changes in the input element, toggling out of the `editHighScores` mode when the *Enter* key is pressed or three elements or greater have been entered

5. "The host" puts on the show of showing the scores (`displayScores` is called).

6. Tension builds on the stakeout as everyone waits for the edit flag to drop (`yield` in use while `editHighScores` is `true`).

7. Prepare the getaway, but first, have "the brains" scan the newly-"liberated" score (`scoreToAdd`).

8. Before jumping into the getaway car, "the host" puts on a smoke-and-mirrors show (clears and re-displays the scores from storage).

9. We see The Crew walking off into the sunset having successfully completed The Job. The credits roll and lights go up.

Figure 13.1 – The Space-Truckers high score board in add or edit mode

There are no plans for a sequel (yet…) – however, the extended edition (director's cut) shows what happens after the plucky heisters have finished their job, and that's the nitty-gritty of integrating the crafted code from the snippet discussed previously with the overall Space-Truckers application.

The Integration

The beauty of the `DialogBox` component is that it can be slotted into an existing Scene. This is a good thing because we want to be able to display the screen in two separate places – **Main Menu**, as a new menu item, and after clicking **Next** from the **Scoring Dialog**. `HighScoreScreen` is the high-level wrapper function that instantiates and starts the `ScoreBoard` coroutine, returning the `scoreBo.dialog` instance so that callers can listen for its dismissal.

How this works out in the **Main Menu** screen is simple, but there are a couple of different pieces involved. First, we make use of the newly-added `onHighScoreActionObservable` that is hooked up to the also newly-added **High Scores** button, which is defined by this option data:

```
const highScoreOpts = {
    name: "btHighScores",
```

```
    title: "High Scores",
    background: "green",
    color: "black",
    onInvoked: () => {
        logger.logInfo("High Scores button clicked");
        this._onMenuLeave(1000, () =>
          this.onHighScoreActionObservable.
          notifyObservers());
    }
}
```

This is the same pattern used for the other menu buttons added as part of the _addMenuItems private function of the MainMenuScene constructor – the menu is faded out for one second before notifying observers of onHighScoreActionObservable that something interesting happened.

The subscriber of this observable is set up in the constructor function of the MainMenuScene constructor, and is responsible for setting up scoreDialog and then returning the UI to **Main Menu** after the user clicks **Go Back**:

```
this.onHighScoreActionObservable.add(async () => {
    this.isTopMost = false;
    let scoreDialog = HighScoreScreen(this.scene);
    scoreDialog.onCancelledObservable.add(() => {
    this._onMenuEnter(1000);
    this.isTopMost = true;
});
```

We've introduced the isTopMost flag to MainMenuScene so that we know whether to handle input (see the MainMenuScene.update function) or if any DialogBox instances are responsible for that task. Once we set that flag, we show and get the scoreDialog instance via the HighScoreScreen function. Now that the scoreDialog instance is available, we can then attach logic to onCancelledObservable, which re-displays the menu and sets it to handle input.

Similarly, scoringDialog attaches a handler to its onAcceptedObservable, which does the same as the MainMenuScreen.onHighScoreActionObservable handler does:

```
scoreDialog.onAcceptedObservable.add(async () => {
    let score = scoreData.finalScores['Final Total'];
    await scoreDialog.hide();
    let scoreScreen = HighScoreScreen(scene, score);
```

```
    scoreScreen.onCancelledObservable.add(async () => {
        await scoreDialog.show();
    });
});
```

The major difference here is that before calling `HighScoreScreen`, we are extracting the `Final Total` score value and passing it into the function along with the scene so that it can potentially be added as a new entry to the list.

Being able to meet new requirements by putting together existing components with few modifications is a pinnacle achievement in software architecture and design, which makes it a great place to finish this section. In this section, we've gone over the sequence of events and actors involved in the processes of both persisting and displaying high scores. The existing `DialogBox` component is reused to host the scoreboard, while the `IndexedDB` component built in the previous section of this chapter provides the storage and the `ScoreBoard` coroutine orchestrates everything.

Integration is simplest in the case of progressing to the high score screen from the **Scoring Dialog** but launching the high scores from the main menu isn't much more complicated. We needed to add an `isTopMost` flag to the menu so that it knew not to handle input when a dialog is being shown, and we also added `onHighScoresActionObserver` to signal when to change screens. The rest is just hooking up appropriate show and hide logic to the various dialog events. What else is there that could be done? So much! See the *Extended Topics* section at the end of this chapter for some ideas on things to improve that you can contribute.

Summary

We started this chapter by focusing on what is needed to turn our application into a PWA and how this is done. We finished the chapter by implementing a high score board for our application, and in between, we managed to learn a lot. Let's recap what we've learned.

A PWA is a type of application that blurs the boundaries between a regular website and a traditional native application. As with desktop applications, a PWA can run offline without a network connection. It has access to the host computer's filesystem and hardware devices. Also, as with desktop applications, a PWA can be published and deployed via an App Store such as the Apple App Store, Google Play, or Microsoft Store. Unlike a desktop app, PWAs can be accessed via a single URL and operate as a regular web application with reduced functionality. When different limitations or restrictions are encountered, the app gracefully enhances or degrades its functionality, making PWAs useful for a wide range of application scenarios.

Three elements are needed for a web application to be considered a PWA: SSL hosting to secure the connection, an SW to pre-cache and intercept requests, and a Web Manifest to define the application's metadata. Hosting a site under SSL has a widely varying set of steps needed that depend very heavily on the specific hosting provider. For instance, Azure Static Web Apps allows a site with a custom domain name to have SSL without the need for the developer to provide or purchase a certificate, whereas Google and AWS both require additional infrastructure to be provisioned to support some or all SSL scenarios. SWs are pieces of code that run in a sandboxed execution environment in the web browser. They can do all sorts of things, but in our simple application use case, we are using them to perform pre-caching and the loading of assets. When the application requests a particular resource from a remote URL, the SW intercepts the request and supplies the response from the local cache, allowing for a transparent mechanism of going offline without having to modify any application code. The Web Manifest serves as the main descriptor of the application to any interested systems. A JSON document containing a few required and many optional elements, the Web Manifest is what is used to package and publish a PWA to an app store, as well as to specify how the PWA should look and feel when installed.

When it comes to different ways of storing data on the client, there's no longer any need to rely on mechanisms such as cookies to persist arbitrary amounts of data. The IndexedDb browser service provides an object store for applications that can store an arbitrarily large amount of data. Although not terribly complicated to employ, the programming patterns used to work with IDB are best integrated by wrapping them with more easy-to-handle Promises. Our needs were simple enough that we didn't need to use one of the many existing libraries that can work with IDB here, as we only needed to be able to add a single score and retrieve a list of scores.

The high score screen displays the beauty and power of the **Composition Pattern** by combining (composing) together the `DialogBox` component for display, the IDB component for persistence, and a coroutine to manage it all into the `SpaceTruckerHighScores` component. The generic nature of `DialogBox` allows us to easily integrate the new high score screen into the rest of the Space-Truckers application. Both the main menu and the **Scoring Dialog** play host to the scoreboard, which allows players with scores that make the cut to enter their three-letter initials using either a physical or virtual keyboard.

There's a lot that can be enhanced and added to the application, but the beauty of an open source project is that anyone can contribute to it – even you! Check out and post on the **discussion boards** with questions or comments on the game or book. The issues listed in the repository capture various pieces of work that different folks have identified as needing to be addressed or implemented. Different labels denote and categorize the issues in different ways – for example, the *"Good First Issue"* label is intended to give new contributors a simple or straightforward task that can get their feet wet and can be done relatively easily without discussion. See the list of issues at `https://github.com/jelster/space-truckers/issues` and discussions at `https://github.com/jelster/space-truckers/discussions`.

Our turn signal is on as we prepare to reach the terminal phase of our space-road trip – we're approaching the end of the line! As we navigate our way through local streets and intersections towards the space docks for delivery, we still have a few loose ends to wrap up. The next chapter is going to be a grab-bag of topics, as we try to fit in as much as possible about all the things that we haven't previously covered. Local guides will help us navigate these winding and sometimes convoluted streets as we look at cutting-edge topics such as real-time ray tracing (path marching), **WebXR**, VR and AR applications, and Babylon Native, but also important pragmatic subjects such as using Babylon.js with a CMS or e-commerce application. Keep your seatbelts buckled – this trip isn't finished yet!

Extended Topics

- Use an SW to do something other than fetch and cache data. Take your framerates to the ultimate by moving the Space-Trucker rendering into an *offscreen canvas*. Essentially, you'll use SW to do the actual rendering work on a different execution thread from the single main thread JavaScript is normally stuck with. The Babylon.js docs go into more detail on this at `https://doc.babylonjs.com/divingDeeper/scene/offscreenCanvas`.

- Add a button or key combination that clears all existing scores from the database. This is a two-part feature: the first task would be to add the ability to remove or clear the scores in `SpaceTruckerDb` and the second to provide a way for that to be invoked.

- Animate the entrance of each individual score in the list. Bonus points for effects that change with the rank of the score. Even more bonus points for giving players a nice fireworks display when they get a top score.

- Split the entry JavaScript module so that the landing page, scores, and main menu are in the initially loaded module with the driving and route planning sections in separate ones. This will supercharge the initial page load time and allow the SW to fetch game assets more efficiently.

14
Extended Topics, Extended

This is a chapter about endings, but it is also a chapter about beginnings. Our journey together on this long haul may be approaching its destination, but this is just the beginning of your personal journey with Babylon.js. In this chapter, we abandon any pretense of linear or sequential progress, and instead, we will be bouncing between several disparate topics that will each provide individual jumping-off points to help you go the distance with Babylon.js.

When navigating unfamiliar streets, it can be useful to have a guide, someone who is knowledgeable about an area. Someone with deep practical experience, who knows how to guide visitors and new arrivals to the best places and sights. Our Space-Dispatcher has located several talented individuals to show us areas of Babylon.js that we didn't get to see or learn about during our trip.

In this chapter, we're going to visit two active construction sites in the metatropolies of BJS. At the first of those sites, we'll learn about ongoing efforts to bring the simple elegance of Babylon.js out of the web and directly onto device hardware with Babylon Native. The second of those sites encompasses the exciting world ("metaverse") of **augmented reality** (**AR**) and **virtual reality** (**VR**) in the form of **WebXR** – the new standard for web-based AR/VR applications.

After those stops, we'll meet our first guide, BJS community member and serial helper of people on the forum, Andrei Stepanov, who will take us through the loading docks and into the Babylon.js Mall. He'll show us glittering displays of the latest gadgets on a tour of how easy it is to use BJS with Content Management Systems and e-commerce platforms. Parting ways with Mr. Stepanov, we next visit a shiny new transport terminal as we go to meet our last guide, Erich Loftis.

Erich has been ranging out on a journey of his own for some time now, and he's going to entertain and enlighten us with the story of his quest seeking the Holy Grail of photorealism in 3D graphics – **Real-Time Ray (Path) Tracing**. That's just a preview of what's to come because it's time to take a hard right and put on a hard hat as we pull into our first construction site for AR and VR with **WebXR**.

There's always more to learn in any given technical arena, and that applies double or more when the topic is rapidly changing. **WebXR** is the standard for developing web-based AR and VR, and it qualifies under the "double-or-more" policy with its rapidly evolving mix of standard and support. As we learn about **WebXR**, we're not going to focus on every feature of the standard – that would be like trying to ice-skate up a hill during a heatwave. What we're going to focus on are the features and capabilities of Babylon.js that allow you as the developer to write applications that make use of **WebXR** while lowering the risks involved in those changing standards and APIs.

Here are the topics that we'll be covering in this chapter:

- AR and VR with **WebXR**
- A tour of the **Babylon.js Native project**
- Incorporating 3D content into a website
- Tracing out a path to advanced rendering

AR and VR with WebXR

The inexorable march of Moore's law has brought increasingly greater computing power into increasingly smaller microchips at a steady rate for long enough that the casual consumer has a staggering amount of raw computational silicone contained in their smartphones and tablets. There's enough processing throughput in the average smartphone now that it's realistic to entertain scenarios such as AR and VR.

AR is a category of applications that encompasses a large variety of different use cases and scenarios. The common feature shared by these scenarios is that they make use of a device's camera, location, orientation, and other sensors to emplace 3D content into a depiction of the real world. VR is very similar to AR, save that instead of the content being immersed in the user's world (the real world), the user is immersed in the content (the virtual world).

Whether considering an AR and VR experience, it is important to keep in mind that both are more of a spectrum than a binary quality – there's no rule that says something must use X percent of features to be considered an AR or a VR app. That would be a silly piece of gatekeeping.

> **Note**
>
> If you are looking for a great band name, Reality-Virtuality Spectrum/Continuum are both cool sounding ones! Read more about the Virtuality Spectrum at `https://creatxr.com/the-virtuality-spectrum-understanding-ar-mr-vr-and-xr/`.

Consider this – an application may only support basic head tracking and stereoscopic views, but it is still a VR application. Similarly, a simple application that draws a rabbit's ears over a person's image in a video feed could technically be considered an AR application. Most of the time when discussing AR and VR in context of web development, it is assumed that the focus is on the VR side of things. Historically, that has been accurate, but it won't always be the case. By examining some historical context, it will be clearer how this might have come to pass and when to expect that to change.

An Abridged History of AR/VR on the WWW

In the wide world of web development, there have been numerous attempts to bring about a standardized set of APIs for VR content, such as the **VRML** standard. The last-but-one effort was called **WebVR**, which was aimed at VR content with little to no consideration for AR – not out of neglect, but simply because AR didn't exist in any commercially accessible form until relatively recently (let's call it ca. 2015 or so).

By 2018, it had become clear that to make AR a commercially viable application, it needed to be able to run on the web. The problem is deceptively simple but deviously hard to solve. Consumers don't want to have to install five separate apps to browse five separate furniture stores just to display selections of furniture in the prospective buyer's living room, but they're happy to go to a website that offers the same! Unfortunately, requirements for even basic AR involve accessing device and sensor data that normally isn't available to the browser JavaScript sandbox, where performance can also sometimes be suboptimal.

The **WebXR** standard was introduced in 2018 by an industry-wide consortium of hardware and software manufacturers. This standard encapsulates and abstracts many areas that were left out of the previous **WebVR** standard, such as object/body part tracking, unified controller interfaces that account for the many different inputs possible with AR/VR, and in general, everything needed to program a world-class experience. All the cool kids (Apple, Google, Meta/Facebook, Samsung, Microsoft, et al) are a part of this standards body, which means that developers and consumers alike should be able to benefit from an explosion of innovation in the commercial AR/VR space. Or at least that should have been the case. Devices dedicated to AR, such as Microsoft's HoloLens, as well as devices dedicated to VR, such as Oculus, have started to proliferate the consumer electronics market, but progress in general for supporting the **WebXR** standard has been stunted at best by the actions – or rather, a lack of action – from one of the most influential members of that consortium.

While most of the consortium members have been busy working to implement key **WebXR** features and standards, one of its members – Apple – has sat mostly on the sidelines. They have recently released their new iOS hardware-based application SDK known as **ARKit**, which is a potential reason for Apple's inaction on supporting **WebXR**. Allowing the hardware access that **WebXR** requires would effectively involve breaking the iron grip that **WebKit** has on web rendering on iOS. That's unfortunate, because in the United States, iOS enjoys roughly 60 percent of the market share, meaning that most of the US market is inaccessible to companies, individuals, and organizations who want to develop and provide AR experiences and products on the web (for contrast, iOS holds less than 30 of the percent market share worldwide outside of the US. Android owns the bulk of the overseas market). The news doesn't get too much better on the Apple front: as of summer 2022, it does not appear likely that Apple will release support for **WebXR** in its **WebKit** rendering engine at any point within the upcoming 6 to 12 months.

> **Important Note**
> Pending anti-trust litigation and legislation debate is ongoing in numerous courts and legislatures around the world. It is possible that the outcome of some of these matters could result in Apple allowing alternative web engines (such as Chromium) to be used in iOS. All bets are off if that happens!

With all that depressing talk of **WebXR** not being supported on iOS, constantly shifting standards, and frequent breaking changes, what's the silver lining? How is the glass half-full, and why would you want to subject yourself to this type of software engineering misery? Let's all say it together now: "Because Babylon.js' Got You" with the **WebXR** Experience Helper – blunting sharp pains into dull aches.

Building Tomorrow, Today with the WebXR Experience Helper

It's a founding precept of Babylon.js that backward compatibility is of paramount importance. Code written 10 years ago on BJS 1.0 still largely works in BJS 5.0, which is quite an achievement when talking about tech and the web! When dealing with something like **WebXR**, where features and APIs can come and go quickly though, does it even make sense to try and build a production application against such a moving target?

> **Note**
> Recalling our previous discussion about rhetorical questions and their answers, you should already know the answer to that question to be "YES!"

The BJS `WebXRExperienceHelper` is a component that does exactly what it says it does on the box – that is, to help with **WebXR** implementation by setting up all of the necessary elements for an immersive session. The **Default Experience** provided is set up for a VR session along with basic features such as pointer tracking and teleportation while, of course, providing the ability to enable, attach, and use other features in collaboration with the **FeatureManager**.

The important concept to understand about how the **FeatureManager** works is the process of enabling a given feature – at either a specific version, the "latest," or "stable" version – and making it available to be attached to a Scene. Enabling a feature and attaching to the Scene is, along with their associated converse operations such as disabling and detaching, a two-step process for the application code. Two steps for the application, but hidden under the hood lies a whole host of sub-operations. Things such as browser feature detection, device capability enumeration, and more all occur during the feature enabling stage. The result of the enabling process leaves the **WebXRSession** with a new set of **Observables** related to the newly enabled feature(s). These Observables are now available to be used to attach those features to a given Scene.

The reason why this is an important concept is because while it isn't necessary to use `WebXRExperienceHelper` or `FeatureManager`, those components provide your code with the critical ability to isolate itself from the effects of external changes. Production applications can make use of the latest VR/AR functionality available on a user's device with confidence that they won't suddenly break when the standard or a web browser's support for the standard changes. The abstractions provided allow developers to write, extend, and maintain applications that leverage cutting-edge browser capabilities while gracefully degrading functionality for devices that don't.

WebXR has some incredibly exciting features and capabilities available today in Chrome- and Mozilla-based browsers, though some might require users to "unhide" features via flags. The types and features of applications built using **WebXR** are just beginning to be explored, and the Babylon.js team intends to be there to help developers use them the entire way. Unfortunately, that's all the time we've got for this construction site visit – there are other places to go and things to see, after all, and we have a schedule to keep!

Further Reading

- *WebXR Experience Helpers*: `https://doc.babylonjs.com/divingDeeper/webXR/webXRExperienceHelpers`

- *WebXR Features Manager*: `https://doc.babylonjs.com/divingDeeper/webXR/webXRFeaturesManager`

- Demos and Playgrounds: `https://doc.babylonjs.com/divingDeeper/webXR/webXRDemos`

Our next visit will be to the grounds of a sprawling new technology campus in the Babylon.js "Metatropolis." This campus is the home of the **Babylon Native** project – an impressive, ambitious, and particularly complex undertaking. Among other areas of study, Native offers one potential solution to the problems posed around iOS support for **WebXR**. Let's learn more about Native and what that solution looks like as part of our campus tour of the Babylon Native ecosystem.

A Tour of the Babylon.js Native Project

Babylon.js is primarily used as part of a web application, but that's not the only place where it can add value. Sometimes, an application needs to target multiple platforms with the same code base. Other times, an existing device application wants to be able to easily add 3D rendering activities that are secondary to the application's purpose (for example, in a scientific simulation, the renderer is simply drawing the output of the simulation onto the screen). Specific requirements might include the need for AR capabilities on platforms that include iOS.

In each of those scenarios (and more that aren't listed), there is a place for Babylon.js to add value to an application. What's commonly referred to as "Babylon Native" in the singular, proper sense is actually a collection of technologies that apply to a specific range of scenarios. Every scenario is different and should have a solution tailored to the specific needs of the situation, and the set of technologies that comprise Babylon Native allows you as the developer to pick and choose where and when to apply them. One way to understand the technologies is to show them along a spectrum with a fully native app at one end and a fully web-native app at the other:

Figure 14.1 – Spectrum of application types. Source: `https://github.com/BabylonJS/BabylonNative/blob/master/Documentation/WhenToUseBabylonNative.md`

The preceding diagram (taken from the BJS Native docs, linked in the caption) is one method of depicting the Native Collective that shows the relative scale of how close to the native device hardware a particular component or framework lies.

In his blog post about the technical underpinnings of BJS Native at `https://babylonjs.medium.com/a-babylon-native-backstage-tour-f9004bebc7fb`, Sergio explains how the Babylon Native parts fit from a different perspective:

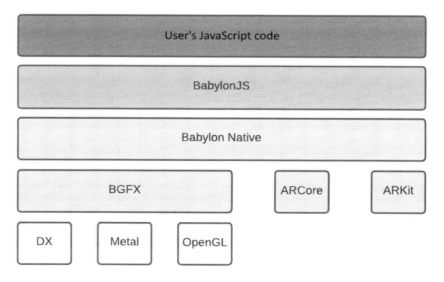

Figure 14.2 – A layered diagram of how Babylon Native works in the absence of WebGL. Diagram source: `https://babylonjs.medium.com/a-babylon-native-backstage-tour-f9004bebc7fb`

Whether using **Babylon React Native** or simply **Babylon Native**, the preceding diagram shows how the unifying abstraction layer of **Babylon Native** covers the ugly and sometimes chaotic mess of talking to various hardware components, such as the BGFX cross-platform graphics driver with ARCore and ARKit for other device sensor and input API abstractions. Having these concepts in mind, we can now consider a few potential usage scenarios where it makes sense to take a good look at the options presented by Babylon Native.

Choosing Babylon Native

The decision on whether Babylon Native is a good fit for a given project can be complex. The docs for Native have an entire page devoted to a questionnaire to help you determine what approaches are worth the most research – and what aren't – and while helpful, they can be better understood via a contrived scenario.

If your application is based on **React Native**, there is a light integration option and a full integration option. The light option is to use a **WebView** to host the WebGL context and canvas. This has the advantage of being able to take advantage of the **Just-In-Time (JIT)** compilation of JavaScript, meaning JS code will tend to be faster than when not using a WebView for some platforms. The full integration option is to use **Babylon React Native**. Here's what we might imagine the app this looks like.

The Evolution of a Babylon Native App

The LARP'in app is an app for **Live Action Role Players** – people who like to take the table out of tabletop games and act out the gameplay themselves using the app to coordinate events, chat, and so on, with all the different luxuries that people have come to expect from a modern Web Application. The "Player App" is built using React and has enjoyed a steady run of releases, enhancing and extending the site's functionality. The app's creators want to allow event schedulers to be able to manage events offline (because event spaces sometimes don't have reception) so they've added PWA capabilities, making everyone happy.

Then one day, some LARP'in LARPers were playing *Pokémon Go* when they had the realization that while LARPing is cool, what's even cooler is LARPing... with AR! Players would be able to see visualizations of their spells cast, detect traps with skill rolls, and walk around exploring a fantasy world brought to life. Their existing LARP tools consist of some home-brewed Bluetooth-connected devices embedded into items (for example, a sword) that register hits and similar game-management tasks by lighting up or beeping, but that's the extent of it. Many of the members have iOS devices, while others are on Android, and there are even a few odd souls clinging to heavily tweaked versions of Windows Mobile (bless their souls). In 2021, the group won first prize at a cosplay competition, which came with enough funds to allow the group to purchase a set of **HoloLens** headsets along with an **Oculus VR** device for a member whose health problems prevented them from attending events in person. The AR-enhanced Player App would need to be able to talk to these devices to be useful as well as utilize existing functionality within the Player App (for example, displaying the player's inventory). Finally, the group has developed a custom C# desktop application they appropriately call the "GM App" to connect to these BT devices and to act as a game's referee (often called a **GM** or **Game Master**). The app's maintainers have the wonderful opportunity here to evolve the app toward their vision in valuable and discrete steps:

1. Bring the app over into a **React Native** application that otherwise behaves exactly as it currently does.

2. Add basic rendering capabilities with Babylon in a **WebView**. This will allow the team to release the same functionality with the same code base as the web app.

Build local mesh connectivity between BT and WiFi devices that feeds data into **React Native** app.

3. Integrate a **Babylon Native** rendering of a pure 3D scene in the C# application to show GMs different views of the action (picture a sword fight where the swords have sensors embedded in them, with the scene depicting the state of the swords as relayed by sensors).

4. Transition rendering responsibilities from a **WebView** to **Babylon React Native**. Use Babylon. js with **WebXR** to leverage device capabilities to render scenes onto a live image stream or to a VR set in a remote location.

5. Enjoy LARPing!

This example isn't intended to be comprehensive or exhaustive, but it does cover a decent range of potential use cases by implication. When embarking on a Native project, it is worth considering whether the same goals might be accomplished more easily using a different framework such as Unity or Unreal. It is also important to keep in mind that the current (summer 2022) state of the project at the time of writing is still immature, and thus there are limitations and gaps in supported functionality. Check the links in the next section to get the latest information on what is supported and what isn't in Babylon Native.

Further Reading

As the project is rapidly evolving, so too is the documentation. Here are some places to start reading more about Babylon Native and Babylon React Native at the following links:

- `https://www.babylonjs.com/native/`

- `https://www.babylonjs.com/reactnative/`

Although it was short, our overview of the Babylon Native campus has covered the more important guideposts and signs that mark the various trails throughout the area. As a collection of technologies, Babylon Native is all about fitting the right set of tools to the right situation. Web apps that already use React or apps using React Native are the most stable and advanced implementations currently available, but Babylon Native is the path to follow if you're looking to build an AR app that runs on iOS. Each of those approaches has its benefits and drawbacks, some potentially quite significant. The good news is that regardless of which approach is chosen, the code you write that interacts with Babylon.js doesn't need to change for multiplatform targeting scenarios.

Moving on, we've got business to attend to with our first guide, Andrei Stepanov. Andrei has been working with Babylon.js and **Content Management Systems** (**CMSs**) for a long time now, so he's the perfect person to give us a quick tour of how BJS can be used in e-commerce and CMS business scenarios.

Incorporating 3D Content into a Website

When it comes to understanding how to make Babylon.js work in real-world, customer-centric business scenarios, there aren't many people more knowledgeable about the topic than Andrei, who posts to the BJS community forums under the name of "Labris." As a senior 3D developer at MetaDojo (`https://metadojo.io`), he satisfies and delights clients with 3D experiences built to spec. Not content with just talking about how to build and create with Babylon.js, Andrei is also the creator of the **BabylonPress** site (`https://babylonpress.org`), which serves as a showcase of different examples and patterns that use BJS in conjunction with the **WordPress** CMS.

Babylon.js and CMS

Babylon.js lets us build very complex JS 3D applications from scratch. At the same time, there are a lot of cases when we need to integrate Babylon.js into an already existing website with CMS – an application that enables users to create, edit, publish and store digital content – or just to some HTML template.

There are numerous ways to do this, on different levels. They will depend on specific needs, especially on the "3D User Experience," which you need to provide. Since the number and variety of different CMS wouldn't allow us the luxury of describing all possible solutions in this space, I will explain in the next few subsections just some of the most common solutions and approaches.

The Babylon Viewer

Babylon.js has an official extension, Babylon Viewer, which may simplify a lot of time for integration. It even has its own HTML tags, `<babylon></babylon>`, between which you define all needed parameters.

To display a 3D model in a prepared environment – with already tuned lights, shadows, reflections, and so on – you just need to add a script reference to the viewer like so:

```
<script
  src="https://cdn.babylonjs.com/viewer/babylon.viewer.js">
</script>
```

Then, add a `<babylon>` tag and set the model attribute to point to a `.gltf` or `.glb` file:

```
<babylon model="model.gltf"></babylon>
```

Besides the `.gtlf` and `.glb` formats, **Babylon Viewer** also supports the `.babylon`, `.obj`, and `.stl` formats. Its simplicity allows easy integration of Babylon Viewer into any CMS and makes it an ideal choice for cases where you need to display a lot of different 3D models (e-commerce, game websites, and 3D artist blogs) in a user-editable CMS. More information about different Babylon Viewer configurations is available here: `https://doc.babylonjs.com/extensions/babylonViewer/configuringViewer`.

Babylon Viewer 3D WordPress Plugin

Built on the base of **Babylon Viewer**, there also exists a community extension: the **Babylon Viewer 3D Wordpress plugin**. This allows you to display 3D models and 3D scenes with the help of a **Shortcode**:

```
[babylon]model.gltf[/babylon]
```

You can use the 3D Viewer in **Wordpress** posts and pages, **Woocommerce** products, **Elementor** blocks – any place that you can define content using shortcode. The plugin is especially made very simple because it doesn't use the WordPress database. You can find more detailed info about the Babylon Viewer 3D WordPress plugin in the README file at its home on GitHub at `https://github.com/eldinor/babylon-wordpress-plugin`.

Kiosk Mode and Iframes

With regards to iframe implementations, it is worth mentioning that the **Babylon Sandbox** (`https://sandbox.babylonjs.com/`) has a special "kiosk" mode that allows you to use its functionality with any 3D model in appropriate format. As an example, have a look at this beautiful example (a 3D model of an ancient mosquito in amber) of **GLTF** transparency in the **Khronos Group** article: `https://www.khronos.org/news/press/new-gltf-extensions-raise-the-bar-on-3d-asset-visual-realism`.

The different query string elements embedded within the URL allow the content creator or manager to define the source 3D file and all other parameters, such as camera position, auto-rotation behavior, the skybox, and environment texture.

To use "kiosk mode," define the URL according to the following table. The first parameter starts with ? after `https://sandbox.babylonjs.com/`; all others start with & before the parameter. Also note that since Babylon.js is an open source project, you can create and host your own version of the Sandbox!

Parameter	Usage example
`kiosk`	`kiosk=true`
`assetUrl`	`assetUrl=PATH_TO_3D_MODEL`
`cameraPosition`	`cameraPosition=-0.14,0.005,0.03`
`autoRotate`	`autoRotate=true`
`skybox`	`skybox=false`
`environment`	`environment= PATH_TO_ENVIRONMENT_TEXTURE`
`clearColor`	`clearColor=00FFCC`

Table 14.1 – Table of parameters for iframes for the BJS Sandbox

At the end, you'll get something like this – quite a long HTML link:

```
https://sandbox.babylonjs.com/?kiosk=true&assetUrl=https://raw.
githubusercontent.com/wallabyway/gltf-presskit-transparency/main/docs/
MosquitoInAmber_withRefraction.glb&cameraPosition=-0.14,0.005,0.03&auto
Rotate=true&skybox=true&environment=https://assets.babylonjs.com/
environments/studio.env
```

The BJS Playground and Iframes

Another option that is especially useful for displaying scenes directly from Babylon Playground is a special HTML template. Just add `frame.html` before the Playground URL and it will show the render area in full screen, but with a bottom toolbar showing FPS, reload and edit buttons.

Here is an example: `https://www.babylonjs-playground.com/frame.html#6F0LKI#2`.

To show only the render area, use `full.html` as the prefix. More info about Playground URL formats is available here: `https://doc.babylonjs.com/toolsAndResources/tools/playground#playground-url-formats`. The result of this option is that you can then use that URL as the source for an iframe image element – see `https://developer.mozilla.org/en-US/docs/Web/HTML/Element/iframe` for how to define an iframe element.

Babylon.js within a CMS

Finally, if you are looking for more close integration between Babylon.js and a CMS, you would need to take into consideration these universal steps. Make sure that you have the following:

- The Babylon.js scripts are loaded properly. Depending on the CMS, you can also load Babylon.js conditionally if there is 3D content to be displayed on the web page.

- The CMS supports the uploading of 3D files (most modern CMSs have a limited set of allowed file extensions).

- A proper canvas element to display. It makes sense to assign a unique ID to each Babylon canvas (for example, with the help of a post ID or other CMS variable).

- Canvas and BJS Engine elements properly hooked up to respond to resizes.

Here, the complexity and the scale of applications depends only on your creativity. Server-side languages can preprocess any needed data before delivering it to a JS client, allowing us to build a truly 3D CMS, where all user experiences and interactions happen in 3D space.

Babylon.js is not just another JavaScript framework to use for two-dimensional websites; it is one of the key components required to build multi-user 3D worlds and metaverses, at least with the current meaning of this term.

There's a big difference between loading a 3D model onto a single web page and bringing potentially lots of 3D models onto lots of different web pages. Managing the content and change processes is of utmost importance, but with the Guidance of Andrei, you'll be ready to face those challenges and more. Now, what does 3D content in an e-commerce or CMS app have to do with a roughly 50-year-old technique for photo-realistic renders? Why, Babylon.js, of course! It's time to continue our tour as we transition from the highly practical to the highly experimental side of 3D programming.

Tracing out a Path to Advanced Rendering

Our last stop on our *Extended Topics, Extended* tour is with musician, engineer, and graphics wizard Erich Loftis. He's going to guide us with the story of his journey to achieving **Real-Time Path Tracing** (**RTPT**) with Babylon.js. RTPT – also referred to as **Ray Tracing** or just **RT** – is a rendering technique built on top of Path Tracing that companies such as Nvidia and AMD are only just beginning to make available in AAA commercial titles, and only in select ways. Through the retelling of Erich's journey, the reason why the technique has been so difficult to accomplish in real-time games and simulations will hopefully become abundantly clear.

Ray Tracing and its History by Erich Loftis

RT is a technique for rendering realistic images and effects on a computer. It follows the laws of optics and models how physical light rays behave in the real world. Therefore, RT can produce truly photo-realistic images. **RT** is *the* standard for photo-realistic offline rendering. Because it has found its way into real-time applications and games (where Rasterization was the undisputed king), it's important to have at least a basic understanding of how it all works under the hood.

By leveraging the awesome **Babylon.js** engine, we can use this understanding to make our own **Physically Based Renderer** that runs right inside the browser. This is important because it opens the door to experiencing photo-realistic graphics on any platform or device, even your cellphone. Of course, the journey to get to this point wasn't exactly the most straightforward or easy, but as you'll see from the demos and examples, the effort is totally worth it!

My Own RT Journey

It was this dream of experiencing **RT** on all devices that led me to create a Path Tracing Renderer for **three.js,** starting back in 2015. For the past 7+ years, I have been slowly but steadily researching, building, refining, and optimizing a browser-based renderer that not only produces high-quality, photo-realistic images but also aims to do so at 30–60 frames a second! Please check out my ongoing project on **GitHub**, where you can try dozens of clickable demos: `https://github.com/erichlof/THREE.js-PathTracing-Renderer`.

A while ago, back in 2020, a Babylon.js developer reached out to me and asked if I could possibly make a similar renderer for the BJS engine. I must state here that I have primarily worked with **three.js** all these years, but I have always admired and been impressed by the amazing **Babylon.js** library. When I agreed to do the port of my ray/path tracing system from three.js to BJS, I was equally impressed with the BJS forum community. They are so friendly and helpful and are just awesome folks! I couldn't have gotten our BJS renderer up and running without their help and support. So, before we dive in, a quick shout out to you all – thank you, BJS community!

RT or Rasterization?

What does it take to get interactive, real-time RT working inside of BJS and a browser? Firstly, let's take a quick look at the two main techniques for rendering 3D graphics. Once we see how that works, we'll also see why we would want to try this RT route with BJS.

When it comes to displaying 3D graphics on a 2D screen, there are two main approaches: **Rasterization** and **RT**. In a nutshell, Rasterization works by first taking the **scene geometry**, in the form of 3D vertices, and then projecting those to the screen in the form of many flat 2D triangles. Any pixels on the device's display that happen to occupy a screen triangle's area are sent to the pixel shader (also known as a fragment shader). When the fragment shader is run on a pixel, its final display color is computed. All of these colored pixels make up the final image that we see on our devices.

In contrast, RT renders images by addressing each pixel on the display first. For every pixel on the screen, a geometric **Ray** is constructed that starts at the camera's position. Pointing from the camera, this **Camera Ray** then shoots out toward its pixel wherever it lies on the view plane (usually your screen). After piercing through the target pixel, the Camera Ray continues out into the 3D scene. It will then model how a physical light ray in the real world would interact with its environment.

Only now at this point in the pipeline do we consider the scene geometry. Each of the camera pixel rays is tested for intersection against every 3D shape in the scene. Wherever the ray hits a surface, the color and lighting at that location are recorded and a "bounce" ray is then spawned and sent in a new direction. This direction is dictated by the material properties of the hit surface location. Further, the bounce ray must check the entire scene geometry (every 3D shape or triangle) for any intersections just as its parent ray did, thus repeating the whole process again and again for however long you are willing to wait for it to complete. After a pixel's camera ray and its spawned bounce rays finish interacting with the scene, the ray tracer reports back the final color for that pixel. Just like Rasterization, we end up with a screen full of colored pixels but with a totally different path taken to arrive at these results!

Both rendering approaches have trade-offs in terms of realism and speed. **Rasterization** (comprising 99% of all 3D graphics) has full GPU hardware support, so it is very fast and efficient. There's a drawback, though. As soon as the GPU is done projecting and rasterizing the scene's triangles to the 2D screen, the surrounding 3D scene information is lost. To retrieve this lost global scene information, sophisticated techniques such as light mapping, shadow mapping, reflection probes, and others must be used. In other words, a lot of graphics knowledge and extra effort is required to get close to RT-quality visuals.

RT, on the other hand, automatically produces the ultimate in realistic graphics, right out of the box! Lighting effects that are difficult if not impossible with Rasterization just naturally fall out of the RT algorithm. However, as of 2022, RT is not widely supported by most GPU hardware. All CPUs can run RT programs, but CPUs aren't designed to be massively parallel. Therefore, traditional CPU-based software RT is very slow in comparison to hardware-accelerated Rasterization on the GPU. Even if the RT software is moved inside a shader that runs entirely on the GPU (as our project here will do), several RT algorithm optimizations must be made in that shader, and/or a decent acceleration structure such as a **Bounding Volume Hierarchy** (**BVH**) is required if we can have any hope of RT at interactive frame rates.

Taking the RT Route

So, knowing most of these trade-offs in advance (and some not until I was years-deep into the project – ha!), I decided to go the RT route. I'll now fast-forward to when I started implementing RT with Babylon.js as the host engine. I'll give an overview of the necessary setup, as well as a few code snippets to show some of the implementation details. Let's jump right in!

Since we are now following the RT approach, we must find a way to construct a viewing ray from the camera through to each and every pixel on the screen. A common method for gaining access to the screen pixels is to create a **Full-Screen Post-Process Effect**, or just **Post-Process** for short (as you learned in *Chapter 10*, *Improving the Environment with Lighting and Materials*). Since the post-process is a common operation, BJS has a really handy library wrapper that takes care of all the **WebGL** boilerplate code and post-process setup for us. In BJS, this helper is called an **EffectWrapper**. Here's an example of a typical post-process creation:

```
const { Effect, RenderTargetTexture, Constants } = BABYLON;
const store =
  Effect.ShadersStore["screenCopyFragmentShader"];
const screenCopyEffect = new EffectWrapper({
    engine: engine,
    fragmentShader: store,
    uniformNames: [],
    samplerNames: ["pathTracedImageBuffer"],
    name: "screenCopyEffectWrapper"
});
```

Now, here is where the setup gets a little tricky, not because of **BJS** (or **WebGL**) but because we must set up a **progressive renderer** that keeps smoothing out and refining the image over time. How we accomplish this is by creating what is sometimes referred to as **ping pong buffers**, which are made from two different post-process effects that "feed" each other their results back and forth. Starting with the first post-process (named `pathTracingEffect`), we ray trace on all pixels and save their color results by using a **Render Target Texture** (**RTT**):

```
const pathTracingRenderTarget =
    new RenderTargetTexture("pathTracingRenderTarget",
    {width, height}, pathTracingScene, false, false,
    Constants.TEXTURETYPE_FLOAT, false,
    Constants.TEXTURE_NEAREST_SAMPLINGMODE,
    false, false, false, Constants.TEXTUREFORMAT_RGBA);
```

This large **RGBA texture** covering the entire screen is then copied by the second post-process (named `screenCopyEffect`) and then fed back through to the first post-process (`pathTracingEffect`) on the next animation frame. Now, our GPU ray tracer can use its previous result (its own pixel color history) to blend with the fresh new pixel color results that it is currently calculating from RT. In other words, it keeps blending and mixing with itself again and again. Over a couple of hundred frames or so, this ping-pong feedback process will quickly produce very smooth anti-aliased results that seem to magically converge right before our eyes! The last piece of the rendering setup puzzle is a final monitor output post-process (named `screenOutputEffect`). Its job is to perform **noise filtering**, then **Tone Mapping** (which you learned about in *Tone Mapping and Basic Post-Processing* section of *Chapter 10, Improving the Environment with Lighting and Materials*), and then finally some **gamma correction** (also in *Tone Mapping and Basic Post-Processing* section of *Chapter 10, Improving the Environment with Lighting and Materials*) to produce more pleasing color output on digital monitors and screens.

All in all, we need a total of three post-processing effects:

- `pathTracingEffect`: This performs all of the RT calculations on every single pixel. It will take whatever pixel history given to it by the following `screenCopyEffect` to use for blending with itself. It outputs to **RenderTargetTexture (RTT)**, which is finally fed to the following post-process.

- `screenCopyEffect`: This takes that supplied RTT output from the preceding post-process and copies/saves it to its own RTT. It then sends this saved copy back through to the preceding `pathTracingEffect` to use for blending with itself.

- `screenOutputEffect`: This post-process is responsible for the screen's final color output. It takes the preceding `pathTracingEffect` **RTT** (which holds all the refined, **ping-pong** blended, ray-traced pixel results so far), applies its special filters and pixel color adjustments, and then directly outputs to your screen.

> **Note**
> The first two effects make up the **ping-pong buffers**, or feedback loop.

Now that we have our custom system set up for progressively refining our ray-traced images over time and can correctly display the final pixel color output, we just need to do one more thing – the actual RT! Let's switch gears for a moment and briefly discuss the similarities and differences between RT and **Path Tracing** (**PT**), and what our ray tracers/path tracers will need in order to do their magic in the browser.

The Path to PT

To best understand how RT and PT are related, let's follow a brief timeline/lineage of RT discoveries and techniques in CG history. In 1968, Arthur Appel invented Ray Casting, a groundbreaking technique in which mathematical rays are shot out from the camera through every pixel. Whatever these camera rays hit first out in the 3D scene determines what we see in our image. Then, in 1979, Turner Whitted invented RT, which relies on Appel's earlier 1968 Ray Casting technique but does it many times recursively while following the laws of optics, in order to capture physically accurate reflections and refractions from specular surfaces (mirrors, glass, and so on). Then, in 1986, James Kajiya invented PT, the ultimate evolution of RT. Building from all the previous RT techniques, Kajiya added Monte Carlo integration (random sampling and averaging) to randomly sample material BRDFs (diffuse surfaces in particular), in order to capture physical light effects such as caustics and inter-reflected diffuse surface "bounce lighting." PT gets its name from tracing (random sampling) all the possible paths that light rays might take as they interact with different types of materials in the scene, and then gathering all of these light paths' contributions to produce a ground-truth, photo-realistic image.

Looking at this potted RT/PT history, hopefully you can see how PT is related to, evolved from, and improves upon RT (and Ray Casting before that). Since I wanted the ultimate in realistic graphics, I chose the more sophisticated **Monte Carlo PT** method (1986 Kajiya-style), which captures light effects that are impossible with Rasterization and even older-style RT. And thanks to our hard work on setting up the progressively refining post-process effects system, our randomly sampled **Monte Carlo** PT results for all pixels can be correctly averaged and refined over time into a **ground-truth image**. This basically means photo-realistic rendering in your browser!

PT in the Browser

Now, let's discuss scene geometry and what PT requires in terms of how the scene is defined. We have two options for telling the PT fragment shader what is in the scene. The first and easiest option is to simply write a GLSL function in the fragment shader itself that defines the entire scene's geometry as part of the shader. All objects/shapes are hardcoded and listed one after the other. This is fine if the number of shapes/objects in your scene does not exceed 20 or so, but as soon as you get into the hundreds of objects or, worse yet, use a typical model with thousands of triangles (with each triangle being tested by every ray!), our path tracer would grind to a halt. To speed things up tremendously and keep our PT interactive, we need to use an acceleration structure, such as a **BVH**. A **BVH** is basically just a binary tree of bounding boxes that tightly surrounds the triangular model(s). When testing for intersection, rays can skip large portions of the model if they miss some of the larger bounding boxes. To see how a BVH is built, check out my custom BVH builder code at `https://github.com/erichlof/Babylon.js-PathTracing-Renderer/blob/main/js/BVH_Fast_Builder.js`. Recall that the path tracer (inside the fragment shader) must have access to the entire scene, and since we can't fit most large scenes containing thousands of triangles into shader **uniforms** (there is a hard limit on most graphics cards), we tightly pack the BVH and all its bounding boxes into a data texture. This BVH texture will give our GPU path tracer quick and easy access to the entire optimized scene geometry (via simple texture lookups).

Next, all ray tracers and path tracers require a shape intersection library to have ray intersection testing with a wide variety of primitive shapes, such as spheres, boxes, and triangles. Historically, when RT was just coming into existence, computers were only fast enough to intersect rays with simple mathematical shapes. Examples of these shapes include spheres, cylinders, cones, and planes, and they all belong to a class of shapes known as quadrics. The solution for where a ray intersects these quadric shapes is handled by simply solving the quadratic equation for that shape. That's why, when you look at more historical ray-traced images, the scenes only contain checkered planes and spheres (or other quadrics) of different sizes and materials. In these early years of RT, the math for intersecting rays with more complex triangle geometry (like what we use today) was well understood, but it would take many years for computers to get fast enough to be able to handle testing rays with an entire polygonal 3D model with thousands of triangles. Over the last 7 years, I have collected almost every routine I could find for determining the intersection of rays against various shapes. Here's a link to my `PathTracingCommon.js` file, which contains all of these intersection routines: `https://github.com/erichlof/Babylon.js-PathTracing-Renderer/blob/main/js/PathTracingCommon.js`. Equally important and also included in this library file are the functions that handle **Monte Carlo PT**-style random sampling of different light source types (point, spot, directional, area, and HDRI) and material types (BRDFs from the *Tone Mapping and Basic Post-Processing of Chapter 10, Improving the Environment with Lighting and Materials*) that rays might interact with in any given scene.

Further Reading

Well, unfortunately, there isn't enough space in this more general, overview-style article to go into detail about my **GLSL** PT shader code (where all the RT/PT algorithms happen). However, if you want to see some nice examples of RT/PT in GLSL (where I have learned from too), check out a couple of these shaders on **Shadertoy**:

- `https://www.shadertoy.com/view/Xtt3DB`
- `https://www.shadertoy.com/view/XsSSWW`
- `https://www.shadertoy.com/view/XdcfRr`
- `https://www.shadertoy.com/view/tddSz4`

And if you would like to go much deeper into the theory and practice of RT and PT, I can think of no better resource than **Scratchapixel**. This amazing website contains everything you need to know about Rasterization, RT, PT, and graphics in general: `https://www.scratchapixel.com/`.

Lastly, to see all of the pieces of this article come together, check out the Babylon.js **PathTracing** Renderer: `https://github.com/erichlof/Babylon.js-PathTracing-Renderer`

This is our ongoing project, which has several clickable demos that showcase different areas of PT. As with the Space-Truckers OSS project, this BJS **PathTracing** Renderer project is open for Pull Requests. If you start getting into this fascinating world of RT and PT, we would love to see your contributions! A word of warning though – once you start down the road of RT and PT, it can be hard to stop!

Happy rendering!

Summary

We've seen a lot of new things on our trip through the BJS *Metatropolis*. We've heard of new wonders under construction but ready for business, such as **VR** and **AR** with **WebXR**. To help developers make use of these wonders, we learned about how Babylon.js offers the **WebXRExperienceHelper**. Working in conjunction with the **FeaturesManager**, it allows developers to code with confidence against a rapidly evolving and changing standard.

Babylon.js is a project that places backward compatibility as one of its cornerstone principles, and so as hardware improves – or more products open up their hardware to **WebXR** APIs – capabilities will "light up" as browser vendors add support. While it would be great to include iOS (and **WebKit**) in the supported application list today for **WebXR**, and while we can lament for a world that could have been, applications using Babylon.js will be ready to best take advantage when that day finally does arrive.

Until that happens, developers and designers have several potential approaches that will ideally allow the greatest code reuse and lowest friction to implement and maintain. The **Babylon.js Native** project is a collection of tools and techniques that people working on cross-platform or Native projects can leverage to gain maximum productivity and effectiveness. These tools fall into a spectrum going from full-on bare-metal BJS Native to the "vanilla" BJS that we've come to know and love. In between, **Babylon React Native** provides a way for developers already using React and React Native to incorporate BJS into their applications, while toward the other end of the spectrum, the hosting of a **WebGL** context in a **WebView** provides another avenue for potential native device application integration in arbitrary software apps.

Babylon.js is more than about making games such as Space-Truckers. As a general 3D application development platform, BJS gives us access to entire universes of possibilities, waiting to be unlocked by curious explorers. Perhaps one of those curious explorers will be you! Every coin has a flip side, and the flip side of having so many possibilities is that it's very difficult to give a good account of the more interesting ones in the same context as the rest of our journey with Space-Truckers. That is where our two guides come into play. As long-time explorers into some of these other provinces of BJS, Andrei Stepanov and Erich Loftis have much to share with the community.

Through his **Babylon Viewer 3D WordPress Plugin** and his extensive and detailed example site, `babylonpress.org`, which shows off the viewer, Andrei has opened our eyes to how easy it can be to use **shortcodes** to include 3D models as a content editor once the proper script references have been injected into the CMS page. By telling us of his journey into PT/RT, Erich Loftis has, in turn, opened our eyes to the innovative history of graphics rendering technologies and how they're used in the world of computer graphics.

Each of them has given us their unique insights and approaches to their respective topics and helped to guide us to the Terminal Destination for this book. Although this is the end of one journey, it is just the beginning of another. Unlike this book though, the path for this new journey – your journey – isn't captured or written out anywhere, nor is there any pre-determination on what route that path will take. Where this path takes and what it entails is entirely up to you, but wherever that destination lies, whether shrouded in mist or lit up with a beacon, you're not alone. The BJS community is there to assist, support, and, of course, guide folks. The BJS forums at `https://forum.babylonjs.com` are the best place to go to ask questions, meet folks like Erich and Andrei, and learn from other community members.

Good luck on your journey – the world of web-based 3D and the BJS community awaits!

Index

Packt.com

Subscribe to our online digital library for full access to over 7,000 books and videos, as well as industry leading tools to help you plan your personal development and advance your career. For more information, please visit our website.

Why subscribe?

- Spend less time learning and more time coding with practical eBooks and Videos from over 4,000 industry professionals

- Improve your learning with Skill Plans built especially for you

- Get a free eBook or video every month

- Fully searchable for easy access to vital information

- Copy and paste, print, and bookmark content

Did you know that Packt offers eBook versions of every book published, with PDF and ePub files available? You can upgrade to the eBook version at packt.com and as a print book customer, you are entitled to a discount on the eBook copy. Get in touch with us at customercare@packtpub.com for more details.

At www.packt.com, you can also read a collection of free technical articles, sign up for a range of free newsletters, and receive exclusive discounts and offers on Packt books and eBooks.

Other Books You May Enjoy

If you enjoyed this book, you may be interested in these other books by Packt:

Real-Time 3D Graphics with WebGL 2

Farhad Ghayour, Diego Cantor

ISBN: 978-1-78862-969-0

- Understand the rendering pipeline provided in WebGL

- Build and render 3D objects with WebGL

- Develop lights using shaders, 3D math, and the physics of light reflection

- Create a camera and use it to navigate a 3D scene

- Use texturing, lighting, and shading techniques to render realistic 3D scenes

- Implement object selection and interaction in a 3D scene

- Cover advanced techniques for creating immersive and compelling scenes

- Learn new and advanced features offered in WebGL 2

JavaScript from Frontend to Backend

Eric Sarrion

ISBN: 978-1-80107-031-7

- Trigger deferred processing with JavaScript
- Implement Express and MongoDB with Node.js
- Build components with Vue.js
- Understand how to create and use modules with Node.js
- Familiarize yourself with npm
- Build a client-side application entirely with JavaScript
- Dive into full stack development with Vue.js, Node.js, and MongoDB

Packt is searching for authors like you

If you're interested in becoming an author for Packt, please visit authors.packtpub.com and apply today. We have worked with thousands of developers and tech professionals, just like you, to help them share their insight with the global tech community. You can make a general application, apply for a specific hot topic that we are recruiting an author for, or submit your own idea.